PROPHET HARRIS,
THE 'BLACK ELIJAH' OF WEST AFRICA

STUDIES OF RELIGION IN AFRICA

SUPPLEMENTS TO THE JOURNAL OF RELIGION IN AFRICA

EDITED BY

ADRIAN HASTINGS (University of Leeds)
MARC R. SPINDLER (University of Leiden)

X

"Jesus Christ must reign;
I am His prophet"

Portrait of Prophet Harris, from photo taken at Grand Bassam,
November 1914, at the height of his mission in Côte d'Ivoire.

PROPHET HARRIS,
THE 'BLACK ELIJAH' OF WEST AFRICA

BY

DAVID A. SHANK

ABRIDGED BY

JOCELYN MURRAY

E.J. BRILL

LEIDEN · NEW YORK · KÖLN

1994

Acknowledgement is made to Wilbert Shenk and Alice Roth of the Mennonite Board of Missions.

The paper in this book meets the guidelines for permanence and durability of the Committee on Production Guidelines for Book Longevity of the Council on Library Resources.

Library of Congress Cataloging-in-Publication Data

Shank, David A.
    Prophet Harris, the "Black Elijah" of West Africa / by David A. Shank ; abridged by Jocelyn Murray.
        p. cm. — (Studies of religion in Africa, ISSN 0169–9814 ; 10)
    Includes bibliographical references and index.
    ISBN 9004099808 (alk. paper)
    1. Harris, William Wade. 2. Evangelists—Côte d'Ivoire—
—Biography. 3. Christianity and other religions. 4. Côte d'Ivoire—
—Church history. I. Murray, Jocelyn, 1929– . II. Title.
III. Series: Studies on religion in Africa ; 10.
BV3785.H348S43   1994
269'.2'092—dc20   94-26022
[B]   CIP

Die Deutsche Bibliothek - CIP-Einheitsaufnahme

Studies of religion in Africa : supplements to the Journal of religion in Africa. - Leiden ; New York ; Köln : Brill.
    Früher Schriftenreihe
    Früher u.d.T.: Studies on religion in Africa
    NE: Journal of religion in Africa / Supplements
    10. Shank, David A.: Prophet Harris. 1994

Shank, David A.:
Prophet Harris : the "Black Elijah" of West Africa / by David A. Shank. Abridged by Jocelyn Murray. – Leiden ;
New York ; Köln : Brill, 1994
    (Studies of religion in Africa ; 10)
    ISBN 90-04-09980-8

ISSN 0169-9814
ISBN 90 04 09980 8

PRINTED IN THE NETHERLANDS

Dedicated to the Memory of

HELEN VALENTINE

and

MARY PIOKA

Courageous Singers of Faith
In Mission with Prophet Harris,
1913-1915

and

JOHN "JONAS" AHUI (ca 1894-1992)
Supreme Spiritual Head of the Harrist Church

*"Djafadon", bravest of Gnambo's warriors in his age-group,
in his eventful December 1928 meeting with Prophet Harris,
was transformed into an humble lamb of peace,
and was faithful unto death.*

CONTENTS

EDITOR'S PREFACE

William Wade Harris was, all in all, the most interesting African prophet of the twentieth century. He has long been recognised as quite extraordinary in the effect of his preaching on a whole series of peoples along the west African coast. Gordon Haliburton's well-researched account of his career and its achievement has provided a reliable guide to an extraordinary story and it has been supplemented by Sheila Walker's more recent study of the Harrist church. What need is there for another major book on the Prophet Harris, some might ask. The answer is clear. David Shank has explored the thought of Harris with great originality in a way that may not be possible for any other of the prophets and goes far beyond anything published hitherto. The available materials proved unexpectedly rich. Harris was better educated than most of the prophets and the transition from his earlier career through the experience of rebellion and prison provides a coherent and intriguing backdrop for his prophetic evangelism with its range of symbols, commandments and predictions. Dr Shank has given us not just a rewriting of history but also the sensitive reconstruction of a complex theology: an African theology, most certainly, but no less a genuinely biblical theology; the personal theology of Harris but, no less, a popular theology whose appeal was convincing for thousands. The phenomenal success of his brief evangelistic crusades will always retain a quality of mystery but with the help of Dr Shank we can now, far better than hitherto, enter into the mind of the man who in the early colonial period best distanced Christianity from colonialism and best rewrote it to make of mass conversion not only an idea but a reality.

Professor Adrian Hastings
University of Leeds, July 1994

PREFACE

The confrontation between expanding Western politico-economic systems and primal societies during the past five hundred years has witnessed the emergence world-wide of the so-called "prophets". They have flowered among the Indians of Latin America, the Xhosa of Southern Africa, the Maori of New Zealand, the Melanesians, the tribal people of India, and the Indians of North America. This well-nigh universal phenomenon had provided social scientists with an interesting field of enquiry, starting already with the theories of Max Weber.

The scholarly understanding of the "prophet" as a product of a clash between cultures has too often left unexplored the deeply religious nature of the prophetic event as a confrontation between Western Christianity and primal religious expressions. From within this latter perspective the "prophets" are seen as a byproduct of the Christian missionary movement—an organised programme of human transformation, as well as an innovative appropriation of Christianity from within the traditional context.

When the full story of the creation of a Christian people in Africa will be told by Africans, the chapter on their prophets will be an important one. If they have been variously interpreted it is partly because of the great diversity among them; but it is also a result of inadequate perceptions due to deep religious and cultural divides which have characterized the confrontation. In South Africa, the 19th and early 20th century prophets were usually perceived to be anti-White and anti-missionary. However, in the second and third decades of the 20th century an important prophetic wave appeared in West and Central Africa: Garrick Braide in Lower Nigeria, Wadé Harris from Liberia, Samson Oppong in the Gold Coast, Babalola and Oshitelu among the Yoruba, Simon Kimbangu in the Lower Congo. Here they did not appear essentially as opponents of the White Western missions but indeed rather as authentic African efforts to take their own people a de-westernized, African-appropriated Christian message in contrast to that of institutional missions. But they were held at a distance both by missionary suspicion and opposition as well as colonial repression.

In the long list of African prophets, from Dona Beatrice in the 18th century Portuguese Kongo to the early 19th century Tsikana among the Xhosa, to Alice Lenshina in post-colonial Zambia, two names seem to stand out above the others: those of Harris and Kimbangu. The latter after his death gave birth to the largest of the African-initiated churches, while Harris during his lifetime triggered the largest of Africa's Christian-oriented mass movements, leading to the Christianization of the Lower Ivory Coast and the western Gold Coast, and of the founding of the Harrist Church of West Africa. The mission of Harris, whose fame had grown through Western missionaries' reaping where he had sown, came more clearly into perspective with the historical studies of Dr. Gordon Haliburton in the 1960s and the anthropological studies of Dr. Sheila Walker in the 1970s. Yet the prophet's thought and the pre-prophetic life that produced it remained considerably shrouded in mystery. And rightly so. The documentation concerning the man seemed to be so limited, and that which survived within the various populations he touched had—like all oral tradition—necessarily sustained the effects of re-interpretation in the light of later events.

A new attempt to understand Harris's life and thought has become possible when there was access to three of the thin notebooks in which the missionary, Pierre Benoît, recorded his face-to-face conversations with the prophet September 24th to 27th, 1926, thirty-one months before Harris's death. From these conversations, Benoît had synthesised a report of his visit, and had brought back a "testament" signed by Harris and local witnesses. Not all of the notes got into the report and some of them could not be adequately interpreted, given lack of information about the prophet's earlier life and career. But beyond that, access was had also to another "testament" dictated for Chief Akadja Nanghui of the Ivorian village of Petit Bassam, and which his son young John Ahui had brought back from his visit to Harris between December 9–15, 1928, just four months prior to the latter's death; further, Ahui himself had been consecrated by Harris to again take up the prophetic mission. These two major sources, plus numerous additional primary sources, previously unknown, have happily permitted a clearer description of the prophet's thought and spirit, in the light of a now better-known half-century of pre-prophetic life and experience. All of this has been unravelled through tools coming out of historical, ethnological, missiological, sociological, anthropological and religious studies unavailable to Harris's own contemporaries.

All of those protagonists, whether Catholic or Protestant, missionary or trader, fellow literate Africans—lawyer or pastor, colonial administrator or traditional people—all were like the several blind men in the traditional Indian parable of the visit to the elephant, and where each "saw" a tree trunk, a rope, a wall, a hose, a fan, a horn . . . Much of this diversity of understanding of the prophet has continued into the present, and has been spelled out in my historiographical and bibliographical essay in *Journal of Religion in Africa*, XIV, 2, 1983.

These factors have dictated the present effort which has been dedicated to trying to understand the prophet Harris on his own terms. He called himself "the prophet"; what did he understand by that? He used symbolic language very effectively; what did he intend to communicate with it? To his baptized followers he was obviously having an amazing impact; what did he himself perceive that he was doing and why? He proclaimed Christ to fellow Africans; what did that mean for him? These are the kinds of questions that have remained constantly in the forefront of the research and writing of this volume. Part One describes the historic mission from 1910 to 1929. Chapters II to IV present Harris's pre-prophetic life in its traditional and modernizing context from c.1860 to 1910. These permit a better understanding of the trance-visitation which transformed his existence; with chapter V they constitute Part Two: The making of the prophet. Chapters VI to XII make up Part Three and delineate the prophetic thought patterns and spiritual dynamics which were embodied in his actions and mission. A final Post-Scriptum suggests briefly a way of situating his ministry in a broader context. And the whole gives deeper insight into the ways in which Christianity has found roots on the African content, where never before in history have so many people moved so rapidly into the Christian stream.

The research and writing of the original three volumes were done between 1976 and 1979 under the influence of Dr. Harold W. Turner, the guidance into the world of western missions by Professor Andrew Walls, and the critical counsel of Dr. Adrian Hastings, then all at the Department of Religious Studies of the University of Aberdeen, Scotland. It has been supported and sponsored by the Mennonite Board of Missions through its then Vice-President for Overseas Missions, Dr. Wilbert R. Shenk. It could not have been done without the constant collaboration of my best friend and spouse, Wilma Hollopeter Shank, who lived out the project with me on three continents. The eight hundred pages of original text have been most carefully and judiciously abridged by Dr. Jocelyn Murray of London, who has also provided the indexing. I am deeply grateful for their most important participation in this volume.

In addition I must recognise the important contributions of many others. His Eminence John Ahui, Spiritual Head of the Harrist Church, and his son Paul Ahui gave access to the final testament from Harris. Harris's three grandchildren, Robert Neal, Rose Horace and Betty Smith granted me an open, spontaneous interview that is unforgettable; the same was true of his nephew neighbour John Gyude Howe of Spring Hill, and Edward Brooks and Edwin Hodge of Harper, both of whom were contemporaries of the prophet. Robert Arnaut of *Radiotélévision Française* provided the important recording of Ahui's story of his meeting with Harris. Dr. Gordon Haliburton and Dr. René Bureau generously shared field notes from their work in the 1960s and 1970s. Ambassador Ernest Amos-Djoro of Abidjan authorized consultation of his unpublished *mémoire* done at the Sorbonne in 1956. Rev. E. Bolling Robertson of Cuttington College led us to valuable Liberian contacts. Translation from Glebo was done by George Constance of Radio Liberia, through the courtesy of Mrs. Nora Siede Johnson of the Liberian Ministry of Information. Rev. Dr. Sylvester Renner of Freetown shared memories of Harris's Sierra Leone visit in a most important interview.

Numerous people have sought and found important documents related to the research: Sylvia Horst, David Wenger, Maribeth Shank, Crissie Buckwalter, James and Jeanette Krabill, Mlle. J. Léonard, Dr. P.N. Davies, Dr. Marlin Miller, Dr. B. Warner, Elizabeth Wenger, Rt. Rev. George Browne. Former missionaries to the Ivory Coast have contributed by giving documents or details from their experience and memories: Rev. W.J. Platt, Rev. E. de Billy, Madame Renée Benoît-Meffre, Rev. J.R. Pritchard, Rev. Thomas Fenton, Rev. Daniel Richard, and Rev. Gordon Timyan.

The research service of Joyce L. White provided many of the sources in the Episcopal Church Historical Society's archives in Austin, Texas. Abbé J. Ablé obtained very useful documents from the Archiepiscopal archives at Abidjan. The most important single document, the Benoît Notes, was provided by the very persevering efforts of Mrs. Ellis, then at the Methodist Missionary Society's archives in London. The Methodist Episcopal Church archives at Lake Junaluska, N.C., provided insight into the life of John Lowrie. Archivist Nöel Douau of *Societa' delle Missioni Africane* at Rome, and Dr. Svend Holsoe of the Liberian

Studies Institute of Philadelphia merit special mention for their help. Dr. V. Nelle Bellamy, archivist of the Episcopal Church, has authorized the reproduction of original documents from the extensive Liberian collection in Austin, Texas. Special mention must also be made of the unique collection of materials available in 1976–1979 at the university of Aberdeen, Dr. Turner's Centre for the Study of New Religous Movements, now at Selly Oak Colleges, Birmingham, and Professor Wall's Centre for the Study of Christianity in the Non-Western World, now at New College, University of Edinburgh. The National Archives of the Ivory Coast, Senegal, France, and Liberia and the U.S. Library of Congress have all provided significant resources, as have many other libraries too numerous to mention. The gracious work and effort of many librarians and archivists is here gratefully acknowledged; without them the volume would have been impossible.

Scholars other than those already mentioned have either provided results of their own work or freely discussed with me the project: Professor Henri Desroche, Dr. Simon-Pierre Ekanza, Rev. Sister Rachel Hosmer, Dr. Werner Korte, Pastor B. Legbedji, Dr. C. Zamba Liberty, Dr. Jean Séguy, Bishop Bengt Sundkler, Dr. Sheila Walker, Dr. Jane Martin, Professor Marc Augé. None are responsible for weaknesses in understanding or interpretation that may be found in this volume.

Finally, continued contacts with the Harrist people from 1979 to 1989 have made me particularly sensitive to the importance of the thought of Harris to the ongoing life of this religious community. Important notes and contributions to this study have come from Superior Preacher Pita Loba, Dr. Bruno Claver, Schoolmaster Preacher Modeste Beugré, and President Félix Tchotche-Mel.

I can only hope that the present volume adequately justifies the contributions of many, and that it will in some measure contribute to a greater understanding of Christianity in Africa.

David A. Shank
Sturgis, Michigan, June 1994

ABBREVIATIONS

ACS	American Colonization Society (Archives, Washington D.C.)
BMPEC	Board of Missions of the Protestant Episcopal Church
BN	Benoît Notes: Methodist Missionary Society Archives, London.
BR	Benoît Report: MMS Archives, London
CHS	Church Historical Society: Archives, Austin, Texas
EBFM	Episcopal Board of Foreign Mission
ECHS	Episcopal Church Historical Society
FNA	French National Archives, Paris
HN	Haliburton Notes. Interact Research Centre, Selly Oak Colleges, Birmingham
ICN	Ivory Coast National Archives, Abidjan, Côte d'Ivoire
MMS	Methodist Missionary Society, Archives, London
MSMEC	Missionary Society of the Methodist Episcopal Church
PH	*The Prophet Harris*. Gordon Haliburton (1971)
RBN	René Bureau Notes, Interact Research Centre, Selly Oak Colleges, Birmingham.
SMA	Société de Missions Africaines; Archives, Rome.
USN	United States Navy: Archives, Washington D.C.

MAPS

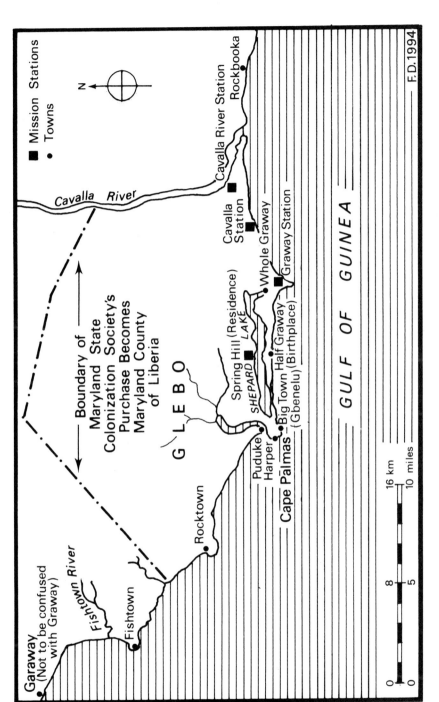

Villages of Harris's Birth and Later Residence, and Their Situation in Glebo Territory (ca 1860).

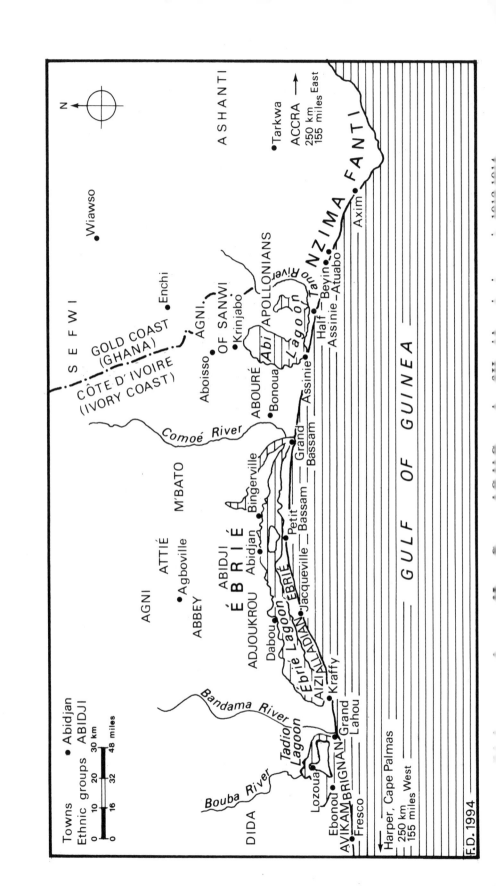

PART ONE

THE HISTORICAL MISSION OF THE PROPHET HARRIS

CHAPTER ONE

THE PROPHETIC MISSION OF WILLIAM WADÉ HARRIS[1]

On Sunday 27 July 1913[2] three African Christians from Eastern Liberia, the region about Cape Palmas, started a journey on foot towards the Ivory Coast, the French colony some ten to fifteen miles away. They were going in response to the commission of Jesus Christ: "Go and teach all nations, baptising them in the name of the Father, and of the Son, and of the Holy Ghost . . ." (Matthew 28:19).[3] They were backed by no church or missionary society, and the leader of the group was the only man, William Wadé Harris. He was a fifty-three year old widower and father of six children left behind, the youngest of whom was only eleven years old.[4]

Harris, an Episcopalian schoolteacher and catechist since 1892, had also from 1899 been the interpreter for the Maryland County authorities,[5] but had been dismissed from both jobs in late 1908 and early 1909 because he was thought to be involved in anti-government political activities. In February 1909 he supported an apparent anti-Republican *coup d'état* calling for a British protectorate. Accused of twice replacing the Liberian flag with the Union Jack, near the town of Harper, following a British- inspired military insurrection in Monrovia, he was arrested and tried for treason 11–14 May 1909. He was condemned to two years' imprisonment and fined $500, but released on parole to a local Episcopalian minister. Nevertheless he continued

---

[1] "Mission" is here used with the sense of the root-meaning of the word, viz., to send. W.W. Harris had an unusual sense of being "sent by God". The mission is a resumé of what he did and accomplished with his collaborators under the impulsion of that consciousness. In the main, we have followed in this chapter the historical work of Gordon M. Haliburton, *The Prophet Harris* (London: Longman 1971). Where new material is added or new interpretations are contributed, notes will give the documentary justification. If there is no footnote, it can be assumed that the material is from Haliburton.
[2] Cf. *Gold Coast Leader* 13, (623), 18 July 1914. An article dated Axim, June 20th, gives this date.
[3] Cf. *Benoît Notes (BN)* and *Benoît Report (BR)*: *BN* I, 29. (In the Methodist Mission Archives [M.M.A.], London).
[4] Cf. *BN* I, 7.
[5] Cf. Mr. Clarck, *BN*, II, 24.

his anti-Liberian activities, for which he was again imprisoned during the Glebo War of 1910.[6] While in prison, he had a trance-visitation from the Angel Gabriel, who called him to be a prophet, to preach a gospel of repentance, to destroy "fetish" worship, and to baptize those who obeyed. He preached in Liberia for three years, after being released from prison in 1910. (His wife had died in 1910).[7] Then in 1913 he set off east with two women companions.

These two women, Helen Valentine[8] and Mary Pioka, assisted Harris with their singing and used net-covered calabashes as rhythmic shakers to accompany the songs. The younger woman, Helen Valentine, was a widow from a westernised Christian Glebo family. Mary Pioka was an older woman of a traditional background, from Sinoe.[9] She had only begun to wear Western dress after she had become a follower of Harris.

They all wore white, the women in Western-type dresses and Harris in a cassock-type robe. They wore white turbans and simple pectoral crosses. Harris carried a cross-topped staff in his right hand and a Bible in the other. Barefoot, they set out to travel along the coastline of the adjacent French colony.

In the next eighteen months they travelled, in fact, as far east as Axim in the Gold Coast, more than 500 kilometres, before returning to the French colony. Travelling west with a third singer, they were arrested by the French authorities in late December 1914, and expelled in late January 1915. During their mission it is estimated that more than 100,000 people from more than a dozen ethnic groups in the Ivory Coast had been baptised, and thousands more in the Gold Coast. As many as 200,000 people may have abandoned the visible signs of their traditional religious practices.

Before 1913 Christian penetration into the Ivory Coast had been limited. Roman Catholics had worked briefly in the Assinie area from 1687–1704, around the French fort and mission. These were abandoned after attacks from Dutch garrisons located along the Gold Coast. There was again a French garrison from 1843–1871, but without any visible missionary significance. At the end of the 19th century Methodist

---

[6] This differs from Haliburton. The details, and references, are to be found in chapter IV.
[7] Cf. Mrs Neal in *BN* I, 2. She told Benoît that her mother died in June 1910 following Harris's trance-visitation earlier that year.
[8] Cf. Mrs Johnson in *BN* III, 25–31.
[9] Cf. Harris in *BN*, II, 13.

Christians from Sierra Leone and the Gold Coast had a limited impact. From 1896 groups were beginning to meet for worship at Grand Bassam, Grand Lahou,[10] Aboisso and Assinie, but they had limited influence, as a foreign elite. In 1895 the Protestant governor, Binger, invited in the Roman Catholic *Société des Missions de Lyon* to aid in the colony's civilising programmes. By 1913 it had established eight main stations with twenty-six missionaries—priests, brothers and sisters. Extending from Aboisso and Assinie in the east to Jacqueville in the west the mission in 1913 had about 3,000 members including Europeans. Progress in evangelisation had been slow; an increase of interest had however become apparent in March 1913.[11]

From 1910 to 1913, under Lieutenant-Governor Gabriel Angoulvant, a policy of "pacification" had been going on, under which the various ethnic groups were forcibly disarmed and their chiefs interned. These chiefs were the religious as well as the political leaders. Following the destruction and regrouping of scattered villages a poll tax was imposed and forced labour levied. How this affected the new openness to Roman Catholic mission is open to debate; it was a precondition and probably an aid to Harris's mission, at least in the Ivory Coast. But the success in the Gold Coast, itself a kind of condition to the Ivory Coast triumph, cannot be explained in this way.

The pattern of evangelism by the prophetic family—for by 1926 Harris referred to the two women as wives[12]—was generally as follows. They would enter a village playing their calabash rattles and singing, dressed in white, and would go to the chief of the village to explain their intent. Harris would then preach to the whole village, usually through an interpreter. He would invite them to abandon their "idols" and "fetishes", and worship the one true God who had brought salvation through his Son Jesus Christ. To those who destroyed their "fetishes" and were baptized, he promised deliverance from a future judgement of fire and a time of peace, concord, brotherhood and well-being which was to come with the impending return of Jesus Christ to establish his kingdom. He taught the Ten Commandments of the Old Testament and the "Our Father" which Christ taught his disciples. He instructed

---

[10] Cf. E. de Billy, *En Côte d'Ivoire: Mission Protestante d'A.O.F.*. Paris: Société des Missions Evangéliques [1931], x; also H.G. Martin, "The work of the Ivory Coast Wesleyan Mission", June 2 1916, 2. (M.M.S. Archives: West Africa).

[11] Letter from Jules Moury to Father Superior General, 16 March 1913. S.M.A. Archives: 12/80402:10.680/1913.

[12] Cf. Harris in *BN*, II, 13.

them about keeping the Sunday for worship, not work, and encouraged
them to pray in their own tongues, to praise God with their own
music, changing the words. He often chose leaders, sometimes naming
"twelve apostles", who were to supervise the building of "chapels"
from local materials. Sometimes they were told to await white men
who would come with the Bible to teach them more. If there were
missions in the area the people were told to go to those churches,
whether Catholic[13] or Protestant.

If this pattern appears too simple it is because it does not describe
the overt opposition from the traditional religious leaders, who often
confronted Harris in a contest of spiritual power. Often it was the
prophet's triumph in the contest which led to the mass destruction
of religious objects, followed by Harris's baptism to prevent their return.
Threats and promises, curses and blessings, often fulfilled themselves
in self-authenticating events, in judgements of folly or woe, or in
blessings of healing and well-being. The prophet's reputation went
before him, often with exaggerated stories of his power.

Travelling east, the party must have spent time in Tabou, for later
Harris was to state that they came from Tabou.[14] A certain Beugré,
who spoke English,[15] was their interpreter among the local people
as they moved from village to village till they came to San Pedro.
There, Harris told Benoît in 1926, he was imprisoned.[16] It seems that
the indigenous authorities had him imprisoned by the colonial authorities, as a result of which a curse was put on the town till it should
repent.[17] When the administrator heard of his preaching mission, Harris
was released and the group went on east to Sassandra,[18] where there
seems to have been a significant response.[19] It is from Fresco, further
east, that we have the best early description of Harris's preaching.

[13] This was publicly contested by the French Methodist missionary Paul Wood
in *Temps* (Paris), 19 September 1931 (Cf. Ernest Amos-Djoro, *Les mouvements marginaux
du protestantisme africain: les Harristes en Côte d'Ivoire*. Paris: E.P.H.E. 1956, 127.
[14] Cf. Haliburton Notes (*HN*), "anonymous old man" at Axim.
[15] Cf. J. Boulnois, *Gnon-Sua, Dieu des Guérés*. Paris: L. Fournier 1933, 108.
[16] *BN* I, 26.
[17] Conversation with Dr. Bruno Claver, Cocody, Abidjan, 20 May 1979. Reported
by old men of San Pedro to Harrist youth at their 1978 seminar at San Pedro.
[18] Cf. Marc Simon, *Souvenirs de Brousse*, 1905–1918. Paris: Nouvelles Editions Latines
1965, 171. Also W.J. Platt in his *Report of the French West Africa District*, 1924, mentions
messengers coming from Sassandra requesting catechists which the Methodists were
not able to furnish. M.M.S. Archives.
[19] Cf. J. Decorvet, *Matins de Dieu*, Nogent-sur-Marne: Mission Biblique 1977 (2nd
ed.), 51.

An English merchant, eleven years later, stated:

> Folks . . . were sunk in debased superstition . . . and fetich-worship, and
> had been so for years. In three days this prophet-fellow—I heard him
> preach myself—changed all that. Their fetiches were burnt, and what
> was an ordinary African coast village, steeped in superstition, became
> nominally a Christian town.[20]

From Fresco they went on to the Avikam village of Ebonou, where
rumours of opposition to them had preceded them.[21] Nevertheless,
there was a large response to Harris's preaching, and converts included
his local interpreter, Jacques Boga Sako, and a number of Methodist
foreign clerks were stimulated to evangelise. Harris asked them to
carry on his work, and went over the lagoon to an island Dida village,
Lozoua, where he had been invited. Two healings preceded preaching
and widespread burning of "fetishes", and he then went on to preach
in outlying villages. But his ministry was cut short by his arrest, and
he was transported bound to Grand Lahou, 35 kilometres east. Again
it seems to have been the local religious leaders who "arranged" his
arrest, and he was briefly jailed. His release came through the
intervention of another local leader, Ackah Lambert, who later became
a Methodist preacher. While in Grand Lahou he was able to do some
street preaching, and his release was rumoured to have been miraculous.

The French administrator at Grand Lahou reported at the end
of 1913:

> The village of Lauzoua has carried the greater part of its fetishes to
> the prophet who has burned them: some children received baptism from
> his hands and the construction of a hut to serve as a church was begun
> under his direction.[22]

So some aspects of his impacts were documented.

In early October Harris and his assistants had been travelling for
some ten weeks, covering about 160 kilometres. They had seen
substantial results around Sassandra, in Fresco, Ebonou and Lozoua
and its outlying villages. Methodist clerks were in some places carrying
on the work. Although twice briefly arrested, Harris had defeated

---

[20] Cited in W.J. Platt, *An African Prophet*, London: S.C.M. Press 1934, 34.
[21] *Cf. HN.* See Sako.
[22] Political Report, Cercle de Lahou: 4th Trimester 1914 (National Archives, Ivory Coast).

the local religious leaders. The French administration were puzzled about the man and his message.

Their next stop after leaving Grand Lahou was a village called Kraffy, in the next *Cercle*. Here they stayed for several weeks, and it was remembered as a time of triumph.[23] Thousands of people from the various lagoon groups came for baptism, and it is said that only lack of food forced them to leave. Again, he came into conflict with the traditional priests, and conquered. He was questioned about his talk of a coming great spirit. "Are you the great spirit of whom they speak?" "No," Harris replied. "I am a man coming in the name of God, and I am going to baptize you in the name of the Father, Son, and Holy Ghost, and you will be a people of God".[24]

In late December the missionary trio continued eastwards, passing from village to village. The response to their ministry sometimes came only after their departure. Those who had heard might go west to Ebonou, where the clerks were baptizing in the place of Harris. Reaction to them was essentially the same as the reaction to the message Harris himself preached.

At Jacqueville they encountered for the first time a Roman Catholic mission, for this was that church's most western station at that time. A missionary, Moly, reported the visit.

> One Sunday, I saw him at Jacqueville where he attended the parish mass with all his wives, accompanied by almost all of the population. It is useless to say that the church was much too small. Also at the end of the mass, he came to see me accompanied by the elders of the village, in order to decide to construct a more spacious church.[25]

Father Moly complained about the "cloud of other prophets" who exploited the people after Harris had left, but not all were exploiters. A certain "Sam" and "Papa Penny" in fact continued Harris's work in a newly organized Methodist Church.[26] Whether Harris himself had intended a separate institution is not clear; he seems to have

---

[23] *Cf.* de Billy, *op. cit.*, 14–19.

[24] *Cf.* Haliburton, *op. cit.*, 66.

[25] *Cf.* L. Moly, "Les Aladians" *sic* in *Echo*, December 1922, 179. There is some possibility that Father Moly referred to the return visit, but oral traditions seem to confirm the contrary.

[26] A photograph of "Papa Penny" is to be found in F.D. Walker, *The Story of the Ivory Coast*, London: Cargate Press 1926, opposite p. 29. De Billy, *op.cit.*, also wrote highly of Penny's work, and published a later photo of him, entitled "Commerçant Fanti, prédicateur laïque en Côte d'Ivoire" (18).

been intent only on providing care for his followers from the people available, whether Catholic or Protestant.

The development at Audouin illustrates this point. Harris himself never went there, but authorized the Sierra Leonean Methodist Goodman to baptize. This he did among the Ebrié who saw him as having the same power as Harris.

Harris himself, with his disciples, continued east along the coast, stopping for nights in fishing villages en route to Grand Bassam. They stayed a night at Petit Bassam, where the English-speaking people offered them hospitality.

Grand Bassam was the leading shipping centre of the Ivory Coast at that time. There was a large population of foreigners whose presence may have interested Harris. He stayed first with a Liberian washerwoman, Mrs. Johnson, who came from Cape Palmas and had been a school friend of Helen Valentine. Later he set up a more permanent home from which he conducted a preaching ministry in the town and villages. He denounced Sunday labour and witnessed the burning of a boat in the harbour when his warnings were disregarded.

After only seven days the prophet was ordered out of the country by the French commandant at Grand Bassam. He is said to have warned the commandant and a policeman who arrested him with some brutality that they would both die,[27] and this in fact happened. Father Hartz, missionary at Grand Bassam, reported that the administrator, named Cécaldi, died eight days after Harris's departure, on January 15.[28] Such stories preceded Harris as he went on east to the Gold Coast, and gave substance to his reputation.

Harris left Grand Bassam early in January, and in mid-June reached the most eastward point of his journey, at Axim. There is little evidence to account for the five months it took him to travel a distance of only ninety to one hundred miles. He could have reached the border of the Ivory Coast in about ten days. But despite the ruling from Grand Bassam, he seems to have stayed in the easternmost *Cercle d'Assinie* long enough to preach and again to be threatened with prison if he did not leave the country. Indeed he is said to have had "a great success at Assinie."[29]

---

[27] *Cf.* Mrs. Johnson in *BN* III, 25 (Conversation with Mrs. Johnson, October 1926).
[28] *Cf.* Hartz diary, August 1914, recorded by G. van Bulck, s.j. in "Le Prophète Harris vu par Lui-même", *Devant les sectes Non-Chrétiennes*. Louvain: XXXème Semaine de Missiologie, [1961], 120–124
[29] Wm. Akah Wajah, from Alangouanou, in *HN*.

> So I went with my three singers to Appolonia.[sic] I was sent by God
> too. After three months I turn back to the Ivory Coast.[30]

It seems that the orders from Grand Bassam were not enough to
expel him, and that he stayed in the Ivory Coast till the end of April,
spending May, June and July en route to and around Axim.

By May it seems that the prophetic family was going from village
to village in the Gold Coast among the Nzima people of Apollonia,
whom missionaries saw as closed to the Gospel. There were Methodist
and some Roman Catholic congregations at several settlements, notably
at Half Assinie. The Axim circuit of the Methodist Church extended
into the Ivory Coast, and it had been reported that "the spiritual
state of the society is not very satisfactory".[31] The Roman Catholic
missionary at Half Assinie had six stations under his care, but no
baptised Catholics.[32]

Now that he was in the Gold Coast colony, under the "Union
Jack", Harris could communicate in English without an interpreter.
But in a number of ways there were difficulties, especially with Father
Fischer at Half Assinie, who cursed the prophet. There Harris was
blamed for the church falling down.[33] The rumour also reached Axim
that Harris had cursed Fischer blind. When the priest appeared in
Axim with perfect sight, Harris's reputation suffered. And in the Half
Assinie period, although he stayed with a Methodist, the African
Methodist catechist, A.P. Organ, warned his congregation that Harris
was of the devil.

From Half Assinie they moved on to Atuabo where they stayed
for two weeks before going on to Essiama and thence to Axim. In
this area the *Gold Coast Leader* spoke of him as "Professor Harris" while
reporting his claim to be a prophet. In Axim the group reported their
greatest successes, but also problems arose which may have been caused
by that very success. One observer many years later claimed that
the success distorted the prophet's self-image.[34] It seems also that his

---

[30] *BN*, I, 29.
[31] *Gold Coast Annual*, 1913, 24, cited in F.L. Bartels, *The Roots of Ghana Methodism*,
Cambridge: C.U.P., 1965, 174.
[32] *Cf.* R[év] Père Wellinger, "Merveilleux succès de l'apostolat chez les Apolloniens"
in *Les Missions Catholiques, 2713, 10 June 1921*, 174.
[33] *BN*, I, 29.
[34] *Cf.* J.P. Ephson, Axim, in *HN*, August 1964: "He had such success in Axim
that he began to think he was super-human. The very day he arrived in Axim he
was asked to revive a woman on point of death, and as a result became famous."

shift of understanding of marriage took place at Axim.[35] He took on additional women disciples while at Axim; later he was to state that there he had six women as wives.[36] It was at Axim that he was said to have considered—but abandoned—the starting of his own church. Later chapters will consider these issues. Here we can only report that it was at Axim and around it that there was the most unusual response to his ministry of "fetish" destruction, baptism and "spirit" healing.

In his time at Axim Harris visited several outlying villages, and crowds flocked to see him. The local Methodist leaders were at first totally opposed to him, but a change in leadership brought the African Rev. Ernest Bruce, whose initial attitude of hostility[37] changed to one of collaboration. Harris's relationship with the Roman Catholic missionary, Father Stauffer, was marred by the prophet's connection with Casely Hayford, the British-trained barrister and African politician, who was said to have received baptism from him. Stauffer only grudgingly agreed to even speak to the prophet.[38]

It was from Axim that a number of Harris's most spectacular signs were reported. They included another burning of a boat when his teaching against Sunday work was disregarded; the death of a woman who committed adultery after being baptized; and the healing of two women, one dying, one possessed by spirits. A nearby village was said to have had seven-eighths of its inhabitants converted after throwing away their fetishes.

Western observers, both government officials and missionaries, later wrote of the differences they saw after Harris's ministry. The District Commissioner commented:

> Appolonia before Harris (sic) visit was steeped in fetishism and the towns and villages were in a most unsanitary condition All this has now been changed, places of worship and schools are to be found in every village and the villages and towns are being remodelled on sanitary lines.[39]

It is Ephson also who suggested that the title "professor" was used for people who do conjuring tricks.

[35] *Cf.* Father Stauffer, notes made in a diary, c.1926. General Archives, S.M.A. Rome: 3A4.

[36] *BN* II, 13.

[37] *Gold Coast Leader* 13 (621), 4 July 1914, 2.

[38] Stauffer, diary 1926.

[39] Cited by Haliburton, *op. cit.*, 90; ("Accra Conf. 830/407/D, Commissioner, Western Province [John Maxwell] to District Commissioner, Sefwi, 6 April 1915; also in his covering letter of 29 May 1916 to Quarterly Report for Axim District").

In April 1915 he said to a visitor, Rev. W. Goudie of the Methodist
Missionary Society's London office:

> [. . .] that he had never in his life seen such a change as had taken
> place in a certain locality. He had always considered the people there
> to be incurably fetish-ridden. A year ago their village had been low
> and mean and filthy and their people miserable. He had just returned
> from another visit and had found the whole place transformed.[40]

A Methodist missionary, the Rev. Charles Armstrong, had written
in similar terms when he visited less than a week after Harris left:

> Hundreds of people are seeking admission to the church. They want
> to serve the living God and learn more of Christ their Saviour. They
> crowd in at our services, weekdays and Sundays, and attend Sunday
> School where they are learning the creed etc.. This is now the *normal*
> state of affairs and has been for three months. Whole villages have given
> up fetich and are asking for the gospel, chiefs are offering land for
> buildings and everywhere there is an awakening that we have prayed
> for, but scarcely expected, perhaps.[41]

Mr. Goudie was able to report to the Society in person that it was
all true . . . and more.

Meanwhile Harris with a party of three women, now called his
wives, was retracing his steps to the Ivory Coast. "I had to go . . .
God asked me to do so."[42] A woman named Grace Thannie, a former
"fetish priestess", had joined the two from Liberia. As he passed again
through Half Assinie many people from the Ivory Coast came there
to be baptized. News of his mission around Axim had gone before
him. In Half Assinie he met a Methodist agent, John Swatson from
Aboisso,[43] who followed him and later became his fellow-worker. In
early September they were urged to go on to Assinie in the Ivory
Coast to baptize there, and a steam launch was sent to fetch them.[44]

From Assinie they worked their way back to Grand Bassam, where

---

[40] *Methodist Recorder* 6 May 1915, 5.
[41] Letter from Armstrong to Griffin, 2 August 1914 (M.M.A.).
[42] *BN*, II, 9.
[43] When Benoît asked Harris about his commissioning of others, the latter
commented, "Minor prophets—Rev. Swanson at Big Assinie I appointed as preacher,
I brought him to Bingerville before the governor, and the governor gave him a
paper to carry his work." *BN*, II, 8.
[44] *Gold Coast Leader* 13 (663), 26 September 1914.

Harris's reputation was still high, and where throngs came to him asking for baptism—"God water"—on their heads.

Meanwhile, in Europe, war had broken out on 4 August 1914. The Lieutenant Governor, Angoulvant, had just returned from Europe, and had to enquire into the deeds of a man whose presence caused such excitement. Harris was interviewed by him at Bingerville in late September. The governor's impression was favourable,[45] and this was confirmed by the acting Roman Catholic provincial, Father Hartz. The three women were questioned and searched by Catholic sisters who could find nothing against them.[46] Father Hartz could not present any evidence that Harris would do harm in the colony, but he saw him as a threat to the Catholic mission, which had lost many personnel because of the war. Almost a dozen missionaries were mobilized as volunteers, and others were later conscripted. Thus the advent of Harris came at a bad time for the Catholic mission. Harris continued his ministry in Bingerville and in the surrounding villages, and met with a good response among the warlike Ebrié.

The governor's enquiry had established that Harris did not accept money, but only food, lodging and laundry services. Angoulvant had, however, to send a full report to the highest administrator in French West Africa, William Ponty, in Dakar (Senegal). Ponty was suspicious of Harris's motives and suggested his removal from the colony to Liberia.[47] Harris meanwhile continued westward, contacting again those he had earlier influenced. His movement was still receiving support from Lt. Gov. Angoulvant, into October. In the same month the Catholic missionaries agreed to have nothing to do with Harris, but to exploit the results of his work.[48] At Abidjan the Commandant, Simon, was disturbed by the growth of the movement, and decided on his own to have Harris sent back to Liberia.[49] By this time the movement seemed to have an autonomy of its own, independent of Harris himself, his singers, his assistants, and of the missions.

---

[45] *Cf.* letter from Angoulvant to administrators of the different *cercles*, 24 September 1914.

[46] In R. Bureau Notes (*RBN*), from Harrist oral tradition, from 1966.

[47] Ponty to Angoulvant, 24 October 1914.

[48] J. Gorju, in "Un prophète à la Côte d'Ivoire", *Echo*, 14 (4) 1915, 111: "In a meeting held in the last days of October, it was decided to profit in the largest possible measure from this extraordinary movement [. . .] but to avoid all appearances— even of *entente*—of any compromise with the famous prophet, while following with care the development of his action."

[49] *Cf.* Simon, *op. cit.*, 174f.

The war had affected the economic situation in the colony, and
many of the immigrant clerks, from Ghana and Sierra Leone, had
lost their jobs. Some of these clerks assumed leadership of the large
numbers of people seeking religious guidance, and in numerous cases
exploited them. In addition the young men educated in the British
colonies showed an increasingly anti-French, anti-colonial and anti-
Catholic attitude, calling for abolition of poll taxes, and of forced
labour. The French military draft of "volunteers" intensified popular
opposition.

In late October the commandant at Abidjan was seriously concerned
about some of Harris's so-called "apostles", less scrupulous than the
prophet himself. Similar reports came from other quarters to the
governor, and in mid-December he sent orders to have Harris
repatriated. Harris had already gone as far west as Lahou, but had
again turned east, probably intending to return to the Gold Coast.
The party was arrested near Lahou, imprisoned in Abidjan, and from
there sent by boat to Grand Bassam. They were roughly treated while
in prison, stripped of their clothes and beaten. Liberian friends in
the city took care of them, bringing them clothes and tending their
wounds. They seem to have been held for about a month, until a
ship came which could return them to Liberia. It appears that they
were back in Cape Palmas by the end of January. It is also recorded
that Helen Valentine had been so badly treated that she died several
weeks after her return to Monrovia.

There are conflicting reports about this episode; the one dated May
1915 and shown to the Methodist missionaries in 1926 being, it would
appear, a cover-up of the brutal treatment the party received.[51] Indeed,
one administrator, Paul Marty, reported in 1922 that Harris had been
"invited to return to his country and live there quietly. . ."[52] But Harris's
own word and that of his friend in Grand Bassam must be taken
against that of the administration. It is possible that subordinate officials
were involved in concealing his brutal treatment from the governor,

[50] See Angoulvant, letter dated 16 December 1914.
[51] F.D. Walker, *op. cit.*, 20f. In a footnote, Walker gives the origin of the story:
"In February 1926, in company with Mr. Platt and Mr. Paul Wood, I had the good
fortune to meet this administrator. We took a motor journey of many miles together,
and I succeeded in getting from his own lips the details of the incident." The story
has had a long life; the administrator had placed it in good hands.
[52] *Cf.* Paul Marty, *Etudes sur l'Islam en Côte d'Ivoire.* Paris: Leroux 1922, 18.

who had protected Harris from men like Simon.[53] Father Gorju's account appears to confirm Harris's own statements:

> The Prophet himself, having most unluckily reappeared in these unfavourable circumstances, saw himself seized without any consideration, conscientiously beaten, and finally expelled from the colony.[54]

In seventeen months Harris's mission had left its indelible stamp upon the lives of some 200,000 people, and created a new kind of faith and unity across colonial borders and tribal barriers. It also represented to the colonial authorities a potential political reality which was outside their control. These people had also destroyed the material symbols of their traditional practices and now, looking back, were faced with a vacuum.

Catholic and Protestant missionaries were ambivalent about the happenings arising from his mission. Catholics saw Harris's work as part of a "Protestant plot", and were pleased by his expulsion, and also by a government order which gave them a number of Harrist chapels.[55] Protestant missionaries were scarcely yet working in the Ivory Coast; one, Martin, had arrived only in late 1914 and had never met Harris. After some hesitation they decided to follow through with the "harvest". But they were restricted in their movements by the colonial government. Both Methodists and Baptists from the Gold Coast were so limited. Fear of British influence played a part in this, and the French administration used the issue of language rather than

---

[53] *Cf.* Political Report for Ivory Coast. 4th Trimester 1914, 15 January 1915 (FNA:200 Mi 1675, 2614) Angoulvant to Ponty, which Ponty later cites verbatim in his 10 March Political Report for French West Africa to the Minister of Colonies: "Without denying the fine work of this religious personality, I feel duty-bound, by measure of prudence, to invite him to cease his travels, as a result of the appearance in several regions of imitators, improvised pastors recruited among the clerks who have broken with their trading centres, often for reasons of financial accounts. This measure, which I generalised, was dictated by the concern for the maintenance of tranquility among the populations of the colony, with the aim of hindering the birth and circulation of false rumours which might trouble the spirits." (Translation by Shank).

[54] J. Gorju, "Un prophète à la Côte d'Ivoire", *Les Missions Catholiques*, 4 June 1915, 268. In footnote 49 of this article, Father Gorju gives another version of the story: "[le prophète] se vit appréhender sans respect, arracher son bâton sacré, remplacer sa belle robe blanche par un vulgaire pagne plutôt défraîchi et finalement, expulser de la colonie."

[55] *Cf.* Gorju, *op. cit.* 1915, 268. Father Gorju wrote that already before Harris' expulsion, "by an ironical upset, an official order put our missionaries in possession of the greater part of the chapels constructed in the villages by the help of the preachers."

religion to legally exclude English-speaking missionaries, who were also Protestants. Only in 1924 were the Wesleyan Methodists, under Rev. William J. Platt, able to enter the Ivory Coast from Dahomey. Platt had learned of the Harrist churches in 1923, and "discovered" them when he was jubilantly received by them in April 1924.

Sixteen months later the British Wesleyans were responsible for at least 160 chapels with more than 32,000 people on their church registers.

In 1926 the Liberian Methodist Episcopal bishop reported to Frank Walker of the Methodist Mission that Harris was still alive and still doing a little preaching. Mr. Platt sent a missionary, Pierre Benoît, to meet the prophet in Cape Palmas. The hope was that Harris would give the Methodists the "right of succession" to his work, for despite their missionaries, schools, teaching and organisation, they had never been able to unify the Harrist people. Benoît brought back a "testament of Harris" which convinced many to become full members of the Methodist Church, accepting monogamy, rebaptism, Methodist structures, class tickets and external financial control.

In 1927 an Adjoukrou delegation was reportedly sent by the troubled local chiefs to Harris to ask advice. Harris was said to have insisted that all his converts should join the Methodists.[56] In December 1928 a further delegation was sent from Petit Bassam by an Ebrié chief, Akadja. This group came back with support from Harris for their protests against the Methodist practices. Harris was said to have repented of the authority he gave to Benoît through his "testament".[57] The youngest member of the delegation, John Ahui, was the son of Chief Akadja. He received a commission from Harris to "start over"; with the prophet's prayer and blessing, his cross, Bible and a dictated letter to his father, Ahui was to become the future leader of the Harrist Church, having begun an active ministry around 1936.[58] After 1946

---

[56] Pastor E. de Billy was told this at the time of a visit to the Ivory Coast in 1973. "Le pasteur Laurent Lasm m'a dit avoir appris que vers 1927 ou 1928 une délégation de notables de la tribu des Adjoukrous autour de Dabou, avait été envoyée secrètement par les chefs hostiles à la Mission Protestante Méthodiste, jusqu'à Cap Palmas, pour demander au prophète Harris ce qu'il pensait de la Mission Protestante Méthodiste. Harris leur aurait dit que tous ses convertis devaient la rejoindre... L'affaire est restée secrète, les chefs hostiles à la Mission n'ayant voulu avouer leur erreur." Letter from de Billy to Shank, 8 December 1977.

[57] John Ahui reported that when their delegation visited Harris in 1928. He was walking around almost beside himself, carrying a weighty stone tied with a black cloth to his back. This was said to be in repentance for his having been too trusting of the Methodist work at the time of Benoît's visit.

[58] The story is told by Ahui in Paul William Ahui, *Le Prophète William Wade Harris*,

the movement grew rapidly and was formally organised in 1955. In 1961 its statutes were published in the *Journal Officiel de la Côte d'Ivoire*. The influence of the Ebrié healer, Albert Atcho, and the movement towards nationalism were contributing influences in this growth, although Ahui's leadership during this period was not unanimously recognised.

Roman Catholic mission work in the Ivory Coast was supported and strategically exploited by the colonial authorities. So when the Government set about repressing the Harrist churches and preventing the so-called "minor prophets" from preaching, it handed some of the chapels over to the Roman Catholic authorities. However, for a brief time even Catholic activities were restricted, but this did not continue long, for their work acted as a check on Protestant expansion.[59] Nevertheless, it was obvious that the Catholic missions had also profited from the mission of Harris; they expanded their outposts, and their chapels were packed.

Monseigneur Moury, the Apostolic Vicar for the colony, admitted as much in his 1914 annual report:

> Space is lacking for exposing here the external means which the Divine Providence has used for the accomplishment of his merciful designs. I must thus limit myself to exposing the effects [which are seen in] a whole people who, having destroyed its fetishes, invades our churches en masse, requesting holy baptism.[60]

When Father Joseph Gorju returned after an absence in France, he was surprised that it was now necessary to build a large church at Bingerville. In 1915 Mgr Moury reported that the movement was maintaining itself, and in 1917 it was reported that the Grand Lahou station had a church due completely to local initiative. By 1923 the Catholic population was 13,020 with 10,360 catechumens.

The five-year report of 1925 gave credit where credit was due.

---

son *Message d'Humilité et de Progrès*. Abidjan: Les Nouvelles Editions Africaines 1988, 209ff.

[59] *Cf.* letter from A.O.F. Governor Merlin to the Minister of Colonies; copy in S.M.A. Archives, 10.607; 12/804,02, 1921. Also letter from Paul Marty to J. Gorju from Dakar. 10 March 1921: "From being quasi-suspect, the Missions [Roman Catholic] have become friends and auxiliaries. Read the enclosed document [copy of letter from Governor Merlin]. The salvation comes from a point on the horizon from which it could not be expected: the Protestants. The order now is 'Open struggle against all Protestant missions which are invading the Sudan and Guinea.' All of a sudden our utility is recognized." (S.M.A. 10.721; 12/804,02, 1921).

[60] S.M.A. 12/804,07; 28761, 1914 (Shank translation).

Providence used, in order to operate the salvation of the Ivory Coast, or at least to begin it, a quite extraordinary instrument: a Wesleyan negro who came from Liberia. This man, a visionary endued with a truly remarkable magic power, was able with the superstitious terror which he was able to arouse in several months to constrain the coastal population to abandon their fetishes. The prophet (as he called himself), after the fetishes were destroyed, invited his listeners to join whatever community there was.[61]

But this official Catholic understanding of what had taken place does not really help us to understand what were the dynamics of the man himself. This will be examined in the chapters which follow.

Three churches—Wesleyan, Roman Catholic and Harrist—were watered by the same source, but only the Harrist Church was wholly due to the mission of the prophet. Other prophet movements were to grow to fill the vacuum caused by the total break with the material symbols of traditional religion. In the late 1920s, Aké-ism was a threat to Methodism around Dabou. In the 30s, Bébé (Bégbé) Grah appeared in Sassandra and later in Alladian territory, followed by his successor, "Papa Nouveau". In the 1940s came Marie Lalou and the Déïma movement; parallel to it was the Adaï-ist movement among the Dida. We have mentioned the healing ministry of Atcho at Bregbo; more recent is the movement begun by Josué Edjro. These are only the more important of many so-called "prophet" movements.[62]

As a consequence of Harris's mission, Protestant missions, other than the Methodists, began work in the Ivory Coast, but only from the late 1920s. French Baptists came to Sassandra in 1928, and later went further to the north.[63] Through this *Mission Biblique* has arisen

---

[61] S.M.A. 12/804,07; 1401, 72, 1925 (Shank translation). Among the Attié at Memni, e.g., there were 83 baptisms reported from 1896–1906; 214 baptisms in 1916, 374 in 1926; by 1955 there were 14,349 in two parishes. Cited in Laurent Yapi, *Le communitarisme attié—ouverture sur une théologie du corps mystique*. Rome: Pont. Universitas Urbania, theol. thesis 1965, 27; no mention whatever is made of Harris' impact. A more recent Roman Catholic appreciation as to be found in *La Nouvelle* (Abidjan) Nos. 21–25, 1992–93 by "F.T" [Fr. Trichet]: "Harris vu par les missionnaires."

[62] Despite its obvious inadequacies, the only published study of the phenomenon is B. Holas, *Le séparatisme religieux en Afrique noire*. Paris: P.U.F. 1965. A much better analysis is found in the unpublished work by R. Bureau and J.P. Lehmann, *Le Prophète, pouvoir et guérison en Côte d'Ivoire*, (1975.) For the Déïma movement, see J. Girard, *Déïma—Prophètes paysans de l'environnement noir*. Grenoble: Presses Universitaires de Grenoble 1974 (2 vols). For Atcho, cf. Colette Piault (ed.), *Prophétisme et thérapeutique. Albert Atcho et la communauté de Bregbo*. Paris: Hermann 1975. For Déïma, see p. 43 of thesis, footnote 62.

[63] The story is told in J. Decorvet, *op. cit. Cf.* also J. Blocher, "Mission Biblique en Côte d'Ivoire", 355ff. in René Blanc, Jaques Blocher, Etienne Kruger, *Histoire*

the Union of Evangelical Churches of the S.W. Ivory Coast. The American-based Christian and Missionary Alliance about the same time responded to the news of Harris's mission and began work;[64] somewhat later the Seventh Day Adventists came and built on Harris's impact. The Harris breakthrough also inspired the beginning of the work of the Worldwide Evangelization Crusade from the early 1930s. Indeed, all of these bodies took advantage of the pioneer work of Harris, with its after-effects.

William Wadé Harris had been a political prisoner before he became a prophet. What were the political implications of his mission? He has been perceived in different ways by Ivorian politicians and historians. The first President, Félix Houphouet-Boigny, paid public tribute to his political influence; the diplomat, Amos-Djoro, saw him as a pedagogue-preacher-nationalist who tried to turn the peoples' nationalism into religious channels.[65] Ekanza, an Ivorian historian, saw his influence as messianic—and, therefore, latently political.[66] Harris himself encouraged respect and obedience to the colonial government; on the other hand he denounced the colonial authorities when he perceived them to be disobeying the law of God. The French authorities initially saw Harris as an aid to their goal of development, handicapped as they were by ethnic and linguistic diversity and the power of traditional religions. They saw as stumbling blocks the fears caused by traditional customs such as the "sasswood trials", the "questioning of the corpse", and the "fetish-doctor's" sacral control of society. But the creation of a new socio-religious unity was ultimately seen to pose a threat to the authorities, especially when this unity did not make a distinction between the religious and the political.

In the Gold Coast the Roman Catholic Church made a rapid expansion in the wake of the Harris mission. In Apollonia there were already in 1920 5,240 members and 15,400 catechumens where there had been no baptized Catholics in 1914. From four stations and two secondary schools then there were in 1920 twenty-six principal and thirty-six secondary stations. Although there was a two-year

---

des Missions Protestantes. Flavion: Editions Le Phare 1970.

[64] This is summarized in R.S. Roseberry, *The Niger Vision.* Harrisburg: Christian Publications, 1934, and also his *Black magic: the challenge of an open door.* Chicago: Worldwide Prayer and Missionary Union 1935, 10–12.

[65] *Cf.* Amos-Djoro, *op. cit.,* 198.

[66] Simon-Pierre Ekanza, "Le messianisme en Côte d'Ivoire au début du siècle, une tentative de réponse nationaliste à l'état de situation coloniale." *Annales de l'université d'Abidjan* S. I, T.III, 1975, Histoire, pp. 55–71.

20 CHAPTER ONE

catechumenate before baptism was (re)administered, the movement continued. Father Fischer spoke of it as "a divine fire lit by the grace of the divine Master"; but in his report of 1921 he seems unaware of the cause of this "fire".[67] Half-Assinie was the birth place of the first President of Ghana, Kwame Nkrumah, a man of messianic pretensions, who was about five years old when Harris passed through.[68] The Gold Coast Methodists were unable to retain the momentum brought by Harris's mission, but a Harris-inspired "Church of the Twelve Apostles" grew out of it. Leadership came from the converted "fetish-priestess" who followed Harris as a singer, Madame Harris Grace Thannie.[69]

In Liberia, scene of his earliest preaching, Harris was regarded with some awe by the traditional populations. His companion on his journey, Mary Pioka, bore him a son around 1916.[70] She was probably with him at Grand Cess in 1916, when he was interviewed by Father Harrington. He travelled and preached and baptised up and down the coast of Liberia, perhaps not always with the spectacular results seen elsewhere. Yet Father Harrington's report of 1916 acknowledges his important contribution at Grand Cess.[71] Benoît notes in 1926 that at his visit Harris spoke of having recently baptised over 500 people.[72] A former Methodist superintendent at Cape Palmas, Dr. Price, recorded a mass movement up and down the country before 1917.[73] It seems

---

[67] Cf. Wellinger, op. cit.

[68] This has been admirably analysed from a religious perspective by Jean Paul Eschlimann, Messianisme de N'krumah. Paris: Institut Catholique de Paris 1970 (unpublished).

[69] Cited in Haliburton, op. cit., 149. His reference: "Cape Coast C733. Petition from Madam Grace Thannie of Christen, Axim, 17 January 1950." A recent brief description of practice in the movement is found in Paul Breidenbach, "Ritual interrogation and the communication of belief in a West African religious movement", Journal of Religion in Africa, 9 (2), 1977, 95–108. More detailed description and analysis is to be found in his doctoral dissertation, Sunsum Eduma: the spiritual work. Forms of symbolic action and communication in a Ghanaian healing movement. Northwestern University, Chicago, 1973.

[70] BN, II, 13, and BR I, 7.

[71] See Rev. Peter Harrington, S.M.A., "An interview with the 'Black Prophet'". The African Missionary 18 (March-April 1917, 13–16.

[72] BR, I, 21.

[73] Cf. F.A. Price, Liberian odyssey. New York: Pageant Press 1954, 141–145 in chapter 8, "A decade of memorable events." The style of his ministry in Liberia was similar to what we know from the Ivory Coast period. "He used to walk from town to town with a stick in his hand carrying his bag on his back. The stick had on the top a cross of red cloth. He was not tall, a stout man, not too slim. The people called him the prophet Elijah." See Werner Korte, "A note on independent churches

to have begun in 1915, the year of Harris's return. This was a time of crisis in Liberia; the World War continued and there was conflict between the Krus and the Liberian authorities. Such movements are not infrequent in times of crisis, but their nature is determined by a further factor, and in this case it seems to have been the charismatic prophet. In Liberia the movement took the form of a movement towards the churches, in which the masses came to have "holy water" poured on their heads, as in Grand Bassam, Ivory Coast. The Methodist Episcopal Church seems to have benefitted most from the movement.[74] Yet Father Ogé of the Catholic Mission reported in 1920 that Harris had been a boon to their work wbich was "going ahead by leaps and bounds" as a result of Harris's impact in Liberia.[75]

Harris attempted at least eight times to return to the Ivory Coast;[76] less than six months before his death this thought was still in his mind.[77] Three times he went to Sierra Leone and preached there (in 1917, 1919, and 1921) and apparently with some success. In Freetown he preached outside and inside the churches,[78] seeking to awaken the very formal Sierra Leonean Christians, and not with the aim of founding a new body. He left a legacy of private prayer meetings, and also (in 1917) went upcountry and preached at Hangha.

On his last mission to Sierra Leone, in 1921, he was accused of using hypnotism after two well-educated young women disappeared with him. One of these may have been Letitia William of Freetown who came to Harper with Harris and became his wife. She was said

in Liberia", *Liberian Studies Journal* 4 (1), 1971–72, 85f. Also, "He forbade Sunday work, prophesied coming natural phenomena and the deaths of certain men, preached against tribal medicines [. . .] He healed the sick, delivered women from infertility. He is said to have condemned polygamy." Werner Korte, "Religiose Dissidenten, Propheten und Kulturgründungen im südöstlichen Liberia im 19– und 20 Jahrhundert," *Sociologus* 26 (1), 1976, 10.

[74] See *Liberian Conference Bluebook* of 1916. This was also confirmed by experiences in the Pentecostal Mission. See *Sowing and Reaping in Liberia*. Springfield MO: Foreign Missions Department, General Council of Assemblies of God [c. 1940] n.a.

[75] E.M. Hogan, *Catholic Missions and Liberia*. Cork: Cork University Press 1981, 103.

[76] *BR* I, 18.

[77] See Harris message in Chapter XI. It is also cited incorrectly in Sheila Walker, *Christianity African Style. The Harrist Church of the Ivory Coast*. University of Chicago, Ph.D. dissertation 1976, 157–160. Also Ernest Amos-Djoro, *Prophétisme et Nationalisme Africain. Les Harristes en Côte d'Ivoire*. Paris: Ecole Pratique des Hautes Etudes, Sciences Religieuses, 1956, 225–228. It is found correctly in Paul William Ahui, *op. cit.*, footnote 58 above.

[78] Conversation with Rev. Dr. Sylvester Renner, assistant minister of the United Brethren Church of Freetown in 1917. Renner was born in 1896.

to have come from a very wealthy family, and to have given up that wealth to follow Harris.[79] She bore him, in 1925, a short lived son.[80]

Mary Pioka, his wife-disciple, was said to be still living in 1926, but no longer with the prophet. Walter B. Williams, a Methodist missionary in Liberia, saw him with his two wives as late as 1927. Harris's open approval of polygamy was there seen as a threat to missionary endeavour; and also as rebellion against God, and as the cause of a paralytic stroke which he suffered in 1925. In 1926 Benoît erroneously saw his broken speech and trembling body as due to lack of education, simplicity and age. Williams also claimed that Harris spoke of his wish to have fourteen women disciples.

In 1926 it was reported that the Episcopal bishop of Liberia described Harris as one who was "now quite mad, and [who] used to come and bellow under his window".[81] At the beginning of his ministry his own wife thought he was mad. Then, and at the end of his life, only the non-westernized people took him seriously. Such were the 1928 delegation from Petit Bassam, in the Ivory Coast, who took back to their chief what seems to have been the last message from the prophet.[82]

Cared for by his daughter, Mrs. Grace Neal of Harper, the prophet died in extreme poverty at the age of sixty-nine, reportedly on 23 April 1929.[83] His funeral was apparently taken by the Episcopal priest of Spring Hill, and he was buried in the village cemetery close to his old home. In April 1978 there was at his grave a crude hand-made marker which said:

> In loving mem
> ory of PROPHA
> Wade Harris Born
> Died in the year
> 1928 June 15

---

[79] Conversation of April 13, 1978 with Harris' grandchildren, Robert Neal, Mrs. Betty Smith (Neal), and Mrs. Rose Horace (Neal), at Painesville, Liberia.

[80] *BN*, II, 13.

[81] Correspondence, Thompson to Platt, 3 January 1927. M.M.S. Archives, French West Africa.

[82] See Harris message in Chapter XI; *cf.* 77 above.

[83] The Harris death notice was written in a notebook now in possession of Paul W. Ahui of Abidjan. See Appendix 4, p. 323 in op.cit., footnote 58 above. The message is thought to have been written by a Liberian visitor to Ahui's father, the chief of Petit Bassam. It gives the date of death as April 23, 1929. This is the only known document attesting to the date of his death.

Erected by one
Abraham Kwang
in the year 1968

Locally it was said that the man who made the tombstone came from Ghana to pay respect to the prophet who had raised his mother from the dead. His guess at the date of Harris's death is not unlike that of many others. Indeed, over the years a body of "oral tradition" has grown up about him, and just how much of this is guessing or adulation will also be the subject of the chapters which follow.

PART TWO

THE MAKING OF THE PROPHET

CHAPTER TWO

THE ROOTS OF THE PROPHET HARRIS

Introduction

For the Cape Palmas region of the Guinea coast of West Africa, the quarter of a century that preceded the birth of the prophet Harris was a period of significant transition for the traditional Glebo people who had occupied the area around the cape for several centuries. This was due to the arrival of light-skinned Blacks from America who came as immigrant colonists, starting in 1834, and the mostly White missionaries who started arriving on Christmas Day of that same year.

At that time, the Glebo part of the Kru family numbered around 25,000 and were living in six districts of well-established villages along a forty-mile coastline from Fishtown to Cavalla in the east. Life in the extended family was patrilineal, exogamous and polygamous, with village life perceived—by a missionary—to be the "purest of democracies." Yet dissensions between clans and particularly between the two moieties—Kudemowe and Nyomowe—often led to violent and open conflict, as in 1843 and 1860 and in the terrible slaughter of 1864. An agricultural and fishing people who lived off their rice and fish, the Glebo men in their youth typically hired out to European ships as porters—kruboys—bringing back their Western trinkets as well as their newly-acquired pidgin-English.

But the confrontation with the West became more intense at Cape Palmas with the colony of returned Blacks, sent by the Maryland Colonisation Society, which represented a population of nearly 500 by 1840, approaching 1,000 by the time of Wadé's birth. Encroaching more and more upon Glebo land, they had created the independent State of Maryland in 1854, modelling it in every possible way after the American patterns of civilization and freedom they had appropriated in the New World. This, coupled with their sense of superiority and complete disdain for the local "aboriginal heathen", led to armed conflict in 1856 between local Nyomowe and the settlers, allied with the Kudomowe in the "First Grebo War". Indeed, the colonists had learned to use and exploit one moiety against the other in their own interests. But after that war, when they were saved only by the intervention of Liberian troops from Monrovia and a U.S. battleship, they realized that they could no longer remain an independent state and became an integral part of the Republic of Liberia, with access—if need be—to help in defence against Glebo attacks.

It was the American missionaries—Congregationalist, Episcopalian, Methodist—who were in their own way to become the only bridge across the deep divide between traditional Glebo and the colonists, by bringing the former into the sphere of "civilization" and Christianity through schools and preaching. These missions were among the very earliest 19th century efforts in West Africa, and they organised themselves on "stations" quite independently of the colonists and the traditional peoples. But they usually took on the defence of the Glebo people, for whom they had left home and family. At the same time, they often deplored the cultural and religious model which the Americanized Blacks demonstrated, feeling that their Glebo Christian converts were often both more Christian and more "civilized". Thus they were politically orientated to the Glebo with little confidence in the fledgling state—and later county—of Maryland in Liberia. That attitude would, however, lead to further conflicts, and especially after 1885, when for the first time a Liberian became bishop of the Episcopalian Church and decided to support the Liberian Republic with a policy of Americanization and integration of the Glebo and other people. But we are already ahead of the life story of Harris.

A. Childhood at Glogbale, Cape Palmas, ca 1860–1873
"Heathenism"

Wadé (later Harris) was born into a "heathen" family in the Nyomowe Glebo village of Glogbale,[1] known as Half Graway. It was situated on the narrow coastal strip between the ocean and the lagoon-like inner lake, and separated the two oldest Nyomowe settlements, Gbenelu (Bigtown) to the west and Bleje (Whole Graway)[2] to the east. It was

---

[1] Glogbale included several more-or-less permanent camps which were part of a whole; there are local indications that Harris came from one of the smaller ones.
[2] The names "Whole-" or "Half-" indicate an original settlement and an outlying dependent village. The names are used in different ways and are not always clear. Glogbale is the "native village" of Half Graway; the mission station of Spring Hill on the other side of Lake Shepard is also called Half Graway. The latter is the "Christian village" and can be the centre of reference.

probably then much as it was seen some sixty years later, a collection of about forty round huts scattered at the foot of cocoa trees.[3] Looking south from the village one saw the sky and sea, which supplied fish and also employment in the great ships which sometimes passed.[4] North was the long miry lake; beyond it the mainland with brush and trees. Between the trees on a small hill could be seen the "very cheerful and American-like" Episcopal Church mission station, Spring Hill.[5] Wadé was born about 1860,[6] and that view was a part of his birthright, together with lake and bush, ocean and beach, palms, village huts and American-type housing, fishing and farming.

The probable origin of Half Graway was as a half-way camp for travellers passing between the larger settlements.[7] It was dependent on Whole Graway, five miles to the east, where the *Bodio* (or *Tape*) lived.[8] The *Bodio* was a kind of hereditary priest in whom was concentrated much of the sacral power and authority of the villagers. His residence, the *takae*, called "greegree house" by colonists and missionaries, with its sacrificial altar and village "fetish", was the most sacred edifice of the village, a place of refuge that was never closed. Its fire was never to be extinguished. With his staff and monkey-skin, *ple* or *pleko*, badges of authority and power, he mediated between parties in conflict. He was also responsible for harvests, health, trade, and

---

[3] Cf. *BR* I, 10.

[4] The May 1868 *Cavalla Messenger* reported: "Steamer day at Cape Palmas presents a scene of most peculiar interest and excitement. From 150 to 300 canoes can be seen gathering from all directions as the steamer approaches. They come to receive their relatives and friends who have been to sea, from six or eight tribes about Cape Palmas—some of them from sixty miles interior. These parties have been to Cape Coast, Lagos, Benin, Calabar, Fernando Po, Gaboon, and other places to make money and now return with the fruits of their labour."

[5] Cf. Mary B. Merriam, *Home Life in Africa*, Boston: Williams 1868, 117.

[6] The date of 1865, given by Haliburton in *The prophet Harris*, 1971, 7, is not accepted in more recent studies. Zarwan suggests "about 1850" (*Missiology* 3 (4) 1975, 433; as does Martial Sinda (*Les messianismes africains. . 200 ans de Christianisme. T. 8*, Paris: Aufedi 1976, 66.), Haliburton based his date on the *Benoît Report*, but did not know Benoît's source. The *Benoît Notes* reveal the source as S.B.K. Clarck, a friend from Whole Graway (*BN* II, 23. However, we have accepted a word from Harris to Benoît as more authoritative: "When Bishop Auer came I was in Sino" (*BN*, II, 6). Auer had returned as bishop in late 1873, and died in early February. Lowrie was transferred to Sinoe in early 1873, with the twelve-year-old Harris. This means that he would have been born *circa* 1860. We will presume this date to be correct.

[7] Cf. S. Jangaba M. Johnson, *The traditional history and folklore of the Glebo Tribe in Liberia*. Monrovia: The Bureau of Folklore, Interior Department, 1963, 20.

[8] See description by Bishop John Payne, cited in Harry H. Johnston, *Liberia* vol. II, 1906, 1074–78, and 1068–72. Payne was a missionary among the Glebo from 1837–1874.

freedom from witchcraft, which he assured by sacrifices, regularly at the time of the new moon, as well as special sacrifices, as in times of war or epidemics. He gave the signal to start the new rice-planting and fishing seasons.[9]

His judicial role has been described by Schwab:

> Whenever a person of the town gets into a quarrel with another whose vengeance he has reason to fear, he goes to the town elders and lays his case before them. They go to the Bodio, get his walking staff, summon both offenders, and lay his staff down between them. This is a sign that all difference between them must be "buried". If not the one who reopens the affair must die. The elders will see to it that "the staff gets him".[10]

After 1874 the Bodio of the Graway peoples—named Nmatee—was established in the village of Glogbale.[11]

To the west of the village lay Bigtown, but in between was the sacred rock, Tule, at which sacrifices were offered to the spirits of dead ancestors from the surrounding villages. Being central, it had become a general meeting place. There the diviners consulted the spirits, and there also a man who had returned from sea would pass to spill gin on the rock. All who passed would at least give cold water at the rock, which colonists and missionaries called "the devil rock".[12]

But Glogbale had its own smaller sacred rock. There women came to pray for fertility; rice was sprinkled and a white fowl released within the fence that surrounded the rock; if the fowl pecked the rice, the petition had been accepted.[13]

The men of Glogbale were fishermen and sailors; they also prepared the land for rice. This was on the mainland, and the women who did the actual cultivating had to walk long distances to their rice-fields. Thus the village, between sea and lake, was economically and geographically vulnerable, yet it was close to the sacred rock and to Bigtown where the Paramount chief lived. Thus there was an essential religious, social and political security.

---

[9] S. Johnson, *op. cit.*, 44f; also A. Massing, *Economic development in the Kru culture area*, Indiana University, Ph.D. dissertation 1977, 76ff.

[10] George Schwab (ed. with additional material by George W. Harley), *Tribes of the Liberian hinterland*. Cambridge, Mass.: Peabody Museum 1947, 376f.

[11] Annual Report, BMPEC, 1891 (2nd ed.), 10.

[12] S. Johnson, *op. cit.*, 83f.

[13] *Ibid.*, 93.

As well as the established leadership of the *Bodio*, there was also in the Glebo village the patriarchal structures. A senior elder, the *woraba*, kept the common treasury and provided betrothal money and paid fines. There were other heads of families, who made up a kind of court. Below them came the *sedibo* class, comprising all males over twenty who were not yet leading elders. The *sedibo* took care of village matters, and was also the warrior class. There were hereditary war leaders.

Glebo youths from about eleven to eighteen years were in the *kediba* class, subject to the *sedibo*. Little boys from six to eleven were part of the *kimbo* class; they cleaned the village and ran errands. All these classes met to talk, play and judge one another when necessary.

There was also a masked society called *kwi*, a "society of departed spirits". All males above eleven were members. It had police functions and administered the *gedu*, the poison trial which used the so-called sassy-wood potion. For the trials they usually worked with the anti-sorcerer, the *deya*. Women were excluded from the *kwi*, but had their own society and were usually consulted over major decisions.[14]

In Glebo villages the creator God, Nyesoa (or Nyswa),[15] was the background of all life. Each morning he received praise, he was called on in trouble and in rejoicing for help and for thanks. In the witchcraft trial, *gedu*, it was to Nyesoa one appealed for justice and whose verdict was accepted. In his name peace treaties were signed.

All the written sources which talk about Nyesoa do so from within a Western—and usually Christian—perspective. Agnes McAllister, a Methodist missionary, wrote in 1896:

> The natives of Liberia call God "Niswa". They believe that he is ever near and hears them and knows all they are doing. They always call upon him to witness when offering a sacrifice or judging a "palaver" . . . or a trial . . . In case of sudden death or any terrifying calamity the heathen call upon the unseen God—Niswa—not upon their idols.[16]

Father Patrick Kla Julwe, later Roman Catholic suffragan bishop of Liberia (died 1973), was growing up in Grand Cess just at the time

---

[14] *Ibid.*, 51ff. Also see Payne, *op. cit.*, (note 8).

[15] *Ibid.*, 83; also see John Payne, Journal (n.d.), in *Spirit of Missions* 15, 1950, 321f, cited by J. Martin, *op. cit.*, 1968, 31.

[16] Agnes McAllister, *A lone woman in Africa. Six years on the Kru coast* NY and Cincinnati: Eaton and Mains 1890, 116f.

the Catholic mission started there. He gives a Kru understanding of Nyesoa:

> Everything which transpires in the natural world beyond the power of man, or of spirits . . . is at once . . . ascribed to the agency of God . . . The prevailing notion seems to be that God, after having made the world and filled it with inhabitants, retired to some remote corner of the universe, and has allowed the affairs of the world to come under the control of evil spirits, hence the only religious worship that is ever performed is directed to those spirits, the object of which is to court their favour, ward off the evil effects of their displeasure.[17]

From across the French border, in Kru territory, Paul Marty wrote in 1922:

> Magic has taken the place of religion, that open and evident tie which unites man to God. The cult of Ku, "the devil" . . . if you wish the principle of evil . . . has been annexed to the worship of Nyessea "the good Lord" . . . It has even finished by replacing it. There is nothing to fear from Nyessea, who is good as a matter of principle. . . . But it is to Ku, spirit of evil, that must be given the propitiatory sacrifices and the incantations.[18]

Schwab has described Nyesoa on the basis of his fieldwork of 1928:

> He is inescapable, because he is omnipresent. He is almost omniscient. He helps people, doing them good rather than bad . . . He can become vexed with people, however, and harm them. Sometimes when things go wrong . . . the bauweo [*bodio*] finds out from Nyesoa what has caused him to be vexed and plague them so, and what must be done to put things right. When it is time for people to leave the earth, it is Nyesoa who calls them . . . Before petitions are made to Nyesoa foods are set out in cleared places . . . One may then make request for anything desired.[19]

A later description is by the Catholic missionary, Feeney, who was writing about the Sikleo people, close neighbours of the Glebo:

> All believed in the existence of God. He was one and supreme. He was the creator of all things . . . He would not do any harm and good

---

[17] Patrick Kla Julwe, *The Grebo tribe* n.d. Unpublished mimeo ms from Thomas E. Hayden collection, Institute of Liberian Studies, Philadelphia, PA.
[18] Marty, *op. cit.*, 8.
[19] Schwab, *op. cit.*, 315.

would always come to any human who tried to live a good life, unless the plans of God were thwarted by lesser, evil spirits. God's supremacy was always acknowledged at the beginning of sacrifice. . . . It was only then that the spirits to whom the sacrifice was being offered were invoked and asked to accept the sacrifice as a sign of respect and as a petition for help . . . There was a wonderful realization of the omnipresence of God.[20]

None of the testimonies about Kru or Glebo understandings of Nyesoa examine the question of Christian influence. Nor is it possible for us to discuss this question here; our interest is in the nature of the beliefs inherent in the traditional life as it was in Wadé's most formative years. The mosaic of texts gives a valid impression.

The distant—yet present—Nyesoa required the services of an intermediary. It was the *deyabo*, known by outsiders as "medicine-men", "country doctors", "devil-men" or "devil-doctors", who became for the Glebo the effective mediators in day-to-day decisions. "This most remarkable class of men" was one of men moved by the inspiration of a spirit which came upon them and possessed them. Following his call through "possession" a future *deya* underwent a novitiate dressed in a white cloth (never afterwards washed) and was "established" in his vocation after proving his powers. Thereafter, wrote Payne, the *deya* became a "most wonderful character":

[U]nder the inspiration of his demon, there is nothing which he cannot find out or do. For hundreds of miles the secrets of hearts are known and revealed. Hidden acts of witchcraft are brought to light. . . . There is not a good sought or ill deprecated for which he does not at once provide a specific greegree. But it is specifically in reference to witchcraft that the powers of the *Deyabo* are invoked. To guard against this the *Deyabo* make charms for the persons or individuals, for their houses, for the town, for the country.

By consulting their demons they are supposed to be able at once to designate the witch or wizard in any particular case, and the word of the *Deya* is taken ordinarily as sufficient ground for subjecting him to trial by *gedu*.[21]

---

[20] John Feeney, *The tribe that found the sea*, n.p. 1950, (typewritten MS), 33f.
[21] Harry H. Johnston, *Liberia*, vol. I. London: Hutchison and Co., 1906, 1076f. He cites Bishop Payne's work of "some fifty years ago". We presume it to be from the February 1851 *New York Colonisation Journal*, as cited by Etta Becker Donner in "Über zwei Kruvölkerstämme: Kran und Grebo", *Koloniale Völkerkunde* 6 (1), 1944, 58ff.

The most obvious religious expression of the people was to be found
in their application of the *deya's* prescription in the use of what had
come to be called "fetish" both by the native peoples and the Western
colonists, traders, and settlers. One description, from among the Kru,
may help to show how the word "fetish" was used in the writings
of the time.

> A fetish, strictly speaking, is little else than charm or amulet, worn about
> the person or set up at some convenient place, for the purpose of guarding
> against some . . . evil or securing some . . . good.
>
> In the Anglo-African parlance of the coast, they are variously called
> jujus or fetishes, but all signifying the same thing. [It] may be made
> of . . . metal or ivory, and needs only to pass through the consecrating
> hands of a native priest to receive all the supernatural powers which
> it is supposed to possess. They must be tried and give proof of their
> efficiency before they can be implicitly trusted.
>
> If a man, while wearing one of them, has some wonderful escape
> from danger, or has good luck in trade, it is ascribed to the agency
> of his fetish, and it is cherished henceforth as a very dear friend, and
> valued beyond price . . .
>
> There are several classes of fetishes, for each of which there is a
> separate name. One of these . . . embrace[s] such as are worn about
> the person, and are intended to shield the wearer. Another class are
> such as are kept in their dwellings . . . They also have national fetishes
> to protect their towns from fire, pestilence, and from surprise attacks
> by enemies . . .; the most important and sacred [of these] are kept in
> a house in the centre of the village where the Gbidio . . . lives and takes
> care of them; these are called national fetishes . . .
>
> The practice of using fetishes is universal, and is so completely wrought
> into the whole texture of society, that no just account can be given
> to the moral and social condition of the people that does not assign
> this a prominent place.[22]

In 1949 Geoffrey Parrinder wrote about the use of the terms "fetish"
and "fetishism":

> One would have thought that the use of the word "fetishism", as vaguely
> descriptive of West African religion had been so thoroughly trounced
> by scholars that it would by now be altogether abandoned. Unhappily
> this is not so. . . . It is best to drop this confusing and unfair word "fetish"

---

[22] [Rev] J. Thomas Moffat, "Handbook on Kudu religion", n.d., unpub. typed
MS in Thomas E. Hayden Collection, Institute of Liberian Studies, Philadelphia,
PA.

altogether, along with "juju" and "greegree". They need to be relegated to the museum of the writings of early explorers.[23]

We are not unaware of the problem involved in the use of the word; we are in fact working within "the museum of the writing of the early explorers". "Fetish" was the word used by the colonial administration, by the missionaries, and by Harris himself in the context of power encounter. We intend to use the word as historical terminology, and not as our own religious understanding. We have found it most useful to discover the ways in which the word was used and perceived, and to use the word guardedly and in quotation marks.

What is important to observe for the Glebo is the unanimity about the one creator God, the role of the *deyabo* as ministers of that one God, the "fetish" as an effective instrument of power, and that the phenomenon was bound up with all of life.

The other expression of religious belief among the Glebo was to be found in their practice of sacrifice. It has been discussed in connection with the *bodio*, and with Nyesoa; the *deya* could also prescribe appropriate sacrifices. A missionary wrote about this phenomenon among the Glebo about five years before Harris's birth:

> I alluded to the fear which the Greboes entertain of evil spirits, and proposed to describe the modes which they adopt to propitiate them. I did not use the word evil in the sense of satanic, but merely meant offended spirit. The Greboes believe that all spirits, good and bad, have great power, and that any want of attention and respect ... excites wrath ...
>
> Every heathen family professes to have a *ku*(spirit) whom they regard as their presiding genius, and to whom they are in the habit of making offerings of food, rum and ... furniture. They foolishly imagine that this *ku* has the power of conferring ... favours, and sending ... them troubles.[24]

Sickness, ill-luck, and defeat in battle could all be avoided by propitiating the *ku*, and the *deya* prescribed the manner of propitiation. There were also public spirits such as the one believed to inhabit the great rock west of Cavalla. To these spirits sacrifices of fowls, goats and bullocks were made and they were held in great reverence.

---

[23] Geoffrey Parrinder, *West African Religion*, London: Epworth Press 1969 (2nd ed. rev.), 8f (cf. also lst ed. 15–17).

[24] A.M.S., "African offerings". *Cavalla Messenger*, 3 (3), September 1854, 10.

It was the relationship of sacrifice and offering to the world of spirits which was of consequence. As a missionary described it, the Kru believed in a great diversity of character among the spirits. The good spirits were supplicated earnestly, and given all kinds of offerings, but they were even more careful to make offerings to the evil spirits and to use all possible means to expel them from their villages and homes.[25]

As well as these beliefs, the Glebo also had a body of moral and wisdom teaching, embodied in stories and proverbs.[26] Such teachings, together with the *bodio*, the village structures, Nyesoa, the *deyabo*, "fetish", spirit powers, sacrifices, made up the texture of traditional life. All these elements would have been present around the young Wadé as he grew up in the village.

But across Shepard Lake the mission station represented a new factor in the life of the village and of the boy himself. And Glogbale was only three miles from Cape Palmas, which had had a mission presence for even longer.

The first mission presence in Cape Palmas had come at the end of 1834 when Rev. J. Leighton Wilson of the American Board of Foreign Missions arrived with his family. In the next seven years "seven stations and outstations were formed" with a day school at each one. There was regular preaching at these stations, and at the central one a church was organized. A boarding school was commenced, and linguistic and translation work undertaken. But the differences between the American Negro colonists and the local people affected the work, and the central government passed laws which made evangelization and education difficult. As a result, the work was given up in Liberia, and transferred to Gabon in 1852.[27]

In 1836 the Protestant Episcopal Missionary Society appointed two colonists, Mr. and Mrs. James M. Thompson, as their first missionaries, and they opened a school not far from Cape Palmas. A doctor and several other missionaries arrived soon afterwards, and the Spring Hill Station was established in 1839. About the same time the Methodist Episcopals arrived and by 1845 had three stations among the Glebo. Roman Catholic missionaries made a start then, but illnesses and deaths curtailed their work, which did not effectively begin until well into the 20th century.

---

[25] Moffat, *op. cit.*, 68f.

[26] Melville Herskovits and Tigbwe Sie, "Kru proverbs", *The American Journal of Folklore* 43, 225–29993.

[27] J[ohn] Leighton Wilson, *Western Africa: its history, conditions and prospects.* New York: Harper 1856, 501.

Under the leadership of John Payne (bishop, 1851), the Episcopal Mission continued with church, school, translation and literacy work similar to that of Wilson. In 1856 the latter reported on the ongoing work. It was estimated that at least 1,500 youths had attended schools for shorter or longer periods; that a hundred colonists had become communicants, and that nearly as many local people since the beginning of the mission had been baptized and confirmed. Latest reports spoke of a general religious movement among the Glebos.[28]

No justification, for the missionary, was required for the attack on Glebo traditional life and religion. It was an obvious duty. John Wilson described the incongruities which the traveller would meet as he journeyed along the west coast, but "there is enough to remind him that he is not entirely beyond the pale of civilization. But on his arrival on the Kru coast, he feels that he has struck the very heart of barbarism itself."

About the Glebo themselves he wrote that

> [They] are the largest of all the families on this part of the coast. Their intercourse with the American settlement at Cape Palmas, the instruction which their children have been receiving in the mission schools of late years, and their participation in the service of foreign ships have placed them on a footing of equality, in point of general intelligence with the Kru people proper. They are poorer, however, and do not conform as readily to the habits of civilized life as might be expected.[29]

A recent study by D.A. Holt[30] has isolated the missionary assumptions of the Episcopal mission in Liberia. They may be summarized as follows:

Cultural: Western civilization was superior to African culture; Christianity and civilization were inseparable; the indigenous Liberian culture was not worth sustenance and nurture; the white man assumed a mandate to carry Christianity and civilization to Africans.

Religious: the uniqueness of Christianity; Africans were immoral, degraded, miserable heathen souls; non-Christians were deprived and damned without Christianity; Liberia was the threshhold to the whole African continent, and its conversion would signal the conversion of sub-Saharan Africa.

---

[28] *Ibid.*, 503.

[29] *Ibid.*, 101ff.

[30] Dean Arthur Holt, *Change strategies initiated by the Protestant Episcopal Church in Liberia from 1836 to 1958 and their differential effects*. Boston University: Ed.D. thesis, School of Education 1970. Cf. Chapter 4, "Missionary assumptions", 32ff.

Racial: White missionaries assumed that black people needed and required white masters; they assumed that administrative control of the mission would be in white hands.

Roles: Missionaries assumed their roles to be divinely conceived and their right to work in Africa unquestionable; contact with the Christian Gospel changed men; the Episcopal Mission assumed that collaboration between Africans and colonists was unnecessary.

Moral: American whites have a debt to pay to blacks because of slavery.

Institutional role: The model of the Protestant Episcopal Church could be exported to Africa without alteration.

This approach to the Glebo, one of the earliest missionary efforts in Africa in the modern period, is reflected in the 1837 Report by Dr. Savage, written less than a month after his arrival. Describing the main town (probably Gbenelu), he writes:

> The town has its greegree house, or place of religious ceremonies. These are said to be of the most disgusting character, and are addressed solely to the devil. Their religion is emphatically the religion of devils.[31]

Savage spoke with the head trade man in the village, and recorded a conversation about their greegree house. "They believe that atonement for sin lies in the power of Fetishism. I told them that it lay in the blood of Jesus Christ." But he found the people keen to have schools, and they pleaded for teachers to be sent. "They desire schools, that they may learn to be like the Americans, and, as they attribute the whole superiority of the whites to their knowledge of the Bible, they are most earnest to be taught 'God's book'."

The missionary—the God-man—preached, taught and practiced healing all in relation to "God's book". The Glebo saw the whites as more successful in trade, health and prosperity and freedom from sorcery with the God-man and the God-book than they were with the *bodio* and his sacrifices and the *deya* with his fetishes. This was taken from the performance of the white men and was tested over a period of decades.

A missionary doctor like Savage, theologically trained as well, would have represented in himself the most important aspects of white power.

---

[31] *History of American missions to the heathen from their commencement to the present time.* Worcester, Mass.: Spooner and Howland 1840. Reprint edition, University of Minnesota 1970, 573ff.

The first hospital in the Cape area was built in 1858, just two years before Wadé's birth. When he was eleven, there was a terrible smallpox epidemic, which the boy survived. The hospital, as it became well-established, must have been seen as in some senses undermining both the technique of the traditional healer and also his spiritual power and authority. This was what the missionaries intended. There was indeed an initial response but it did not continue. Bishop Payne in the early 1860s pondered the reasons for this apparently retrograde situation. He suggested that the material superiority of the missionaries had been like miracles in attracting and benefitting the bodies of men, but those who sought only such benefits turned away from the spiritual proclamation of the Kingdom of God.[32]

A doctor like Savage had entered quickly into open confrontation; Payne took longer but by 1842 he "began preaching directly against fetishes and in two weeks there were fifteen men of the village [Cavalla] who had put theirs on the fire. Payne realized that if such an object ceased to be considered a seat of power, it would be thrown away in any case. Thus he said it was nothing to give up a greegree which has proved to be vain, but when a man gives up all of them it must have been caused by the Word of God at work."[33]

This struggle for power is amply illustrated in the missionary records for the early years.[34] A marked example of the struggle between the two systems occurred over the keeping of the Sabbath. The use of this Old Testament name went along with missionary requirements which owed more to the Old than the New covenant. The white "Christian" crews of the ships which came into the Liberian ports, and on which Kru men worked, paid no attention to the day of the week when it came to loading or unloading cargo. In 1843 Glebo Christians challenged the observance of the Sabbath and other behaviour of the white men, and asked the missionaries why there should be one law for them and another for the whites. It was not possible for the missionary or his Glebo agent to give a very satisfactory response.[35] Issues like these must have been debated as the Glebo considered their response to this new system. As they did so, the missionaries as well came to reconsider their early judgement on Glebo

---

[32] Cited by John Walter Cason, *The growth of Christianity in the Liberian environment.* Columbia University: Ph.D. dissertation 1962, 213.

[33] *Ibid.*, 152, citing *Spirit of Missions*, 11, 82.

[34] *Ibid.*, 153, citing *Spirit of Missions*, 8, 149.

[35] *Ibid.*, 159, citing *Spirit of Missions*, 8, 20.

life and beliefs. The Episcopal bishop came to feel it would be wrong
to say "they worship the devil";[36] but the earlier impressions were
what passed over into the tradition of the Glebo Christians. One
missionary came to look at her early views, and compare them with
her later recognition of the many parallels to Old Testament practices
in Glebo life.[37]

The Christian penetration was slow, but it was visible. Glebo young
men caught the vision and initiated ventures among their own people.
One such was a certain N.S. Harris, who started work that later
developed into the Hoffman Station. Some taught at the earlier stations,
and by 1855 the Episcopalian bishop began to use them as paid
employees. One of these, who taught at Spring Hill, was John Farr.
Both Farr and N.S. Harris had attended the Episcopal Mission school
at Cavalla, and had been outstanding students. In 1854 the first Glebo
deacons were ordained. A little later the Methodist Mission also
"received on trial" two promising young men, one of whom was John
C. Lowrie, a Glebo. "I need not tell you we were much encouraged
by this event . . .".[38] Still, their "native work" progressed slowly; in
1864 they could claim only ninety-eight "native members",[39] after fifteen
years of mission work.

By 1860, the time of Wadé's birth, Bishop Payne had published
his *Dictionary of the Grebo Language*. It was to serve a population of not
more than 40,000, but he argued that the Glebo furnished a large
proportion of "Krumen", and also that the affinity of the Glebo language
with other Kru dialects would make it valuable in spreading the Gospel
in West Africa.[40]

So Glogbale Village was directly and indirectly involved in the coming of the new faith and culture. Village children—how many cannot
now be estimated—went to the school at Spring Hill Mission. A young
man from the village was ordained deacon in 1878—Owen E. Hemie.
But the Christian impact on the life of the village seemed limited.
A German missionary from the Basel Mission in the Gold Coast
blamed the lack of impact on short and superficial preaching visits,

---

[36] *Ibid.*, 214.
[37] McAllister, *op. cit.*, 116–129. The parallels are so striking that one anthropologist
(following Wilhelm Schmidt) could write a book entitled *Hebrewisms of West Africa*,
NY 1930 (author, Joseph J. Williams).
[38] *Missionary Advocate* 17, August 1861, 36.
[39] *Ibid.*, 20, July 1864, 28.
[40] [Rt. Rev.] John Payne, *A Dictionary of the Grebo language*. NY: Ed. O. Jenkins
1860, 4f.

and insufficient regard for the vernacular.[41] Hurried excursions could not substitute for the depth of long consistent contact.

Still, the visits of missionaries like G.W. Gibson, R. Miles and C. Hoffman and local deacon Thomas Toomey[42] undoubtedly helped to encourage a local leader like John Farr, who as catechist led regular services in and around Glogbale.[43] And the mission school provided a model of order, system and law, where cleanliness and economy were demonstrated, and where works of charity and mercy were practiced daily.[44] But the solidity of the traditional life, culture and religion were not easily penetrated, even though white and black missionaries had worked there from 1839. In the 1868. Report on Spring Hill Station, tribute was paid to the work and the consistent life of John Farr, but it is obvious that progress was fairly slow.[45]

In the life of the young Wadé Harris, however, there was a second strand of Christian influence. Although he spoke of his "heathen father",[46] he told Pierre Benoît in 1926 that he was "born Methodist". It is most likely that he was born of a Christian mother in a traditional and polygamous family.[47] At that time (and it caused the missionaries much dismay) a non-Christian family might still dispose of their mission-influenced daughter as a wife in such an environment. When we learn that the Methodist minister John C. Lowrie was uncle to Wadé Harris, it seems possible that his sister would have been influenced by her brother, who was highly educated by the standards of the time and who led an "unblemished life".[48]

---

[41] Correspondence, J.G. Auer to S.D. Denison, 8 February 1868. Archives of CHS:EBFM, Liberia.

[42] Gibson, in *Cavalla Messenger*, 4 (10), April 1856, 3; Miles in *ibid*, 10 (7), January 1864; Hoffman in *Spirit of Missions* 29, 1864, 242f; Toomey in *ibid*, 31, 1866, 642.

[43] Annual Report, BMPEC 1865, 497.

[44] F.A. Price, *Liberian Odyssey*, NY 1954, 141f. Price was Methodist superintendent in the Cape Palmas area after 1917, and was speaking from the perspective of that place, though somewhat later than the period under study.

[45] Annual Report, BMPEC, 1868, 120.

[46] *BN*, I, 14; *BR* I, 6; and *BN*, I, 26.

[47] This is contrary to Haliburton, *op. cit.*, 7, "born of Grebo parents uneducated and unacquainted with Christianity." His source was the *Benoît Report* I, 25, but Benoît himself states that when being interviewed "Harris did not reply directly to the point" when asked about his parents. In a later conversation he referred to "my father, a heathen . . ." (*BN* I, 26). We might be suspicious of Harris's "born Methodist (*BN* I, 14) because of the difficulties to which Benoît refers, if Harris's daughter, Mrs. Neal, had not given precisely the same information to Benoît prior to his conversation with Harris.

[48] *Spirit of Missions*, 29, 1864, 185. The Methodists in 1856 had twenty day schools with "upwards of 500 pupils." (J. Leighton Wilson, *op. cit.*, 500.)

At his birth the child was named "Wadé",[49] which means "comfort or "consolation". Since his home environment was not fully Christian, he could not be baptised in the Methodist tradition. But, especially considering the strong emotional link between mother and child,[50] we may presume that his Christian mother had considerable influence on him. It seems he had an older brother, who also left the village as Wadé did, to live with their uncle Lowrie in 1873.[51]

If this understanding of Harris's parents is correct, it means that the first years of his life were lived in the presence of a conflict between the traditional life and religious practice of the Glebo father, and that of the Christian faith as perceived by his Glebo "Methodist" mother. This situation would have complicated the usual pattern of child-parent relationships. It had, however, an advantage for young Wadé in that he saw his mother living as a Christian within the traditional context. He was not removed into the sheltered environment of a Christian village. For this his mother may well have paid a high price.[52] She would not have been able to attend a church regularly, but was presumably able to join in services when the missionaries made "excursions" into Glogbale.[53]

The 1860s was for the Nyomowe Glebo a decade of internecine strife with the Kudemowe Glebo who were supported most of the time by the Liberian authorities. Armed conflict between various Glebo groupings, and especially between the two main divisions, were not new. The "First Grebo War", such a conflict, took place in 1856, and the Kudemoye were supported by the colonists, who tried to exploit the struggle to their own advantage. At this time and later

---

[49] "Wade" in the Glebo transcriptions is always written "Wadé", signifying a long vowel. The pronunciation is "Waddy", as it was sometimes written. We have decided to write it with the French accute accent, "Wadé", to avoid a one-syllable pronunciation as "waid".

[50] Wilson, *op. cit.*, 116f.

[51] *BN* II, 6.

[52] Letter, NS. Bastin, Thursday 20 June 1850. Archives of Methodist Church: Board of Foreign Missions, Liberian Letters 1846–1912. (Microfilm 2509).

[53] R. Miles, "Reports", in *Cavalla Messenger*, 10 (7), January 1864, 2: "Each month I have visited both Graway and Half Graway, generally alternately every two weeks and preaching in each of the two towns at the two different places. The attendance is not very large, generally from ten to twelve adults and many children. There are always some who pay particular attention to what is said and will afterwards ask questions on the subject. On a few occasions there were no men to be found in the town so the few women who were willing have been called together to hear. Knowing that what was said must be particularly for them, they have manifested particular interest. The young men of the station have always accompanied me as interpreters. They have also visited the towns without my company."

(1860, 1868) the Liberian central authorities failed to fulfill any kind of mediating or arbitrating role between hostile groups. This was a cause of bitterness among literate Glebo.

The black American settlers, the "colonists", began to arrive at Cape Palmas in 1834. Originally assisted by the Maryland Colonization Society, they called their colony Maryland, and it was not until 1856 that Maryland became an integral part of the Republic of Liberia. Conflict over land was another source of bitterness between the colonist-settlers and the "aboriginal population", as an Episcopalian missionary termed them. "The colonists . . . imagine they have a right to any land which they choose to take," she wrote. "It is the old tragedy which was acted on the western continent between our forefathers and the Indians".[54]

The missionaries tried to distance themselves politically from both the government and the Glebo peoples. They were sympathetic to the Glebo position, and this helped the educated Glebo to commit themselves to the unification of their own people, which led to the open conflict of 1875 with the colonial Blacks.

Bishop Payne had been succeeded in 1873 by the German missionary linguist, John Auer, who died suddenly in February 1874. He had brought back from the USA several trade teachers recruited to teach skills to the local people. This was unpopular with the colonists. Having had disputes over land, they now saw their skills in danger of being taken over and another source of livelihood gone. Auer's death was attributed to the Liberians, and the role of the trade teachers was said to have been a major cause of the 1875 war.[55] Auer had desired to take the mission thrust into the villages, and his reports on the village schools showed his concern.[56] He did not see the catechists as providing what was needed for their pupils. He had started a new consolidated boarding school at Hoffmann Institute.[57] He had also improved Wilson's and Payne's translations; in the schools he replaced older teachers and catechists with younger and better-trained men. He sent students to Accra and as far as Germany for trade training.[58]

His policy was to encourage Glebo initiative, and with his concern

---

[54] Merriam, *op. cit.*, 160.

[55] Martin, *op. cit.*, 160.

[56] School report of J.G. Auer, pp 9–10, filed in Auer Papers, February–December 1872. Archives of CHS:EBFM, Liberia.

[57] Martin, *op. cit.*, 231–236.

[58] *Ibid.*, 229. Martin gives a full discussion of the role of Auer in a section entitled "John Gottlieb Auer changes mission policy", 227–236.

of permitting Christian faith to reach deeply into the traditional communities, he was in favour of allowing the baptism of polygamists. This had been considered by earlier missionaries such as Hoffman, who wondered if the Episcopal Mission's policy at Cape Palmas might not "make the door to the kingdom narrower than the scripture".[59] He also encouraged some of the educated Glebo to take the initiative in peace-making between the rival Glebo sections. They had some success in 1871, and in 1873 their "G'debo United Kingdom" was organized to provide a structure for unity between the clans.

It is easy to see in all of this why the Protestant Episcopals earned the opposition of the colonists. Although Wadé had left the area in 1873 to live in Sinoe his family would have been involved both in the on-going conflicts and the 1875 "Protestant Episcopal War". The existing feelings of discrimination on the part of the young Glebo elite were increased by unwise actions on the part of a new young superintendent of Maryland County.[60]

Thus we may see that during Wadé's childhood in Glogbale he would have experienced conflict at several levels. Within his family there were the differences between the Christian mother and the traditional father; there were the on-going conflicts between the two Glebo sections; the conflict between the Glebo and the Liberians; and also the conflict between Liberians and the Episcopal mission. All of this was taking place within a sacral society in which things were indeed starting to fall apart.

An important commentator on the processes of change in the area was the Liberian deacon, R.H. Gibson, who had been ordained in 1868. Born in 1830 and having come to Liberia as a child, he had known the first Episcopal missionaries and been educated in their homes and schools. Bishop Auer had appointed him "Travelling missionary to Graway", and thus he was responsible for the services at Half-Graway and at Spring Hill station. His letters, written from a distinctive perspective, help us to understand the environment to which the young Harris would return. In 1874 he was undoubtedly working in a difficult situation, but waiting and praying till "Ethiopia stretches out her hands unto God".[61] By the end of 1874 he felt he was seeing some change for good.[62] But in 1875 with the problems

[59] *Ibid.*, 233.
[60] *Ibid.*, 271ff.
[61] Correspondence, R.H. Gibson to Dr. Duane, 12 April 1874: CHS:EBFM, Liberia.
[62] Gibson to Duane, 28 December 1874.

stemming from the "G'debo Reunited Kingdom", he was musing over the need in Liberia to "build up, in time, a great Negro Republic" uniting the colonists and "the native Africans, who are really our brethren ... but if every two or three tribes, as soon as they become half-civilized, combine and form petty governments—hence confusion and trouble would ensue and blast our future hopes of success".[63]

He had practical problems, like replacing his white gown with a black one, preferable in his situation;[64] a more serious problem faced him when war broke out on September 11, 1875. He could no longer visit the Graway settlements,[65] and indeed during the war became chaplain to the Liberian colonists. Only after the war was over (a treaty of peace was signed on 1 March 1876) could he return to his missionary work, visiting Half-Graway and Whole-Graway while living near Harper.[66]

Later in 1876 he wrote of the need for a chapel at Graway; he was evidently instructing the children out-of-doors. The war had caused poverty and hardship, and the "poor Grawaians ... avow it as their belief that the present trouble came directly from the hand of God as punishment for their late conduct."[67]

The peace treaty had been signed under threat of the guns of the American man-of-war *U.S.S. Alaska*, at a time when the Glebo had the upper hand in the conflict. They were forced to capitulate ... after having won. John Farr at Spring Hill Station recorded the difficulties he experienced during the war: he had to cease teaching school, but was able to continue services. Food had been very short, but despite the troubles he saw "no Country doctor" (i.e., a *deya*) brought in to direct the people. He took this to mean that faith in the traditional religion was weakening.[68]

Less than a year later it was reported that a Glebo town (probably Bigtown) had passed its own "law for a strict observance of the Sabbath Day", partly in consequence of a defeat that the Liberians had suffered when they had launched an attack on a Sunday morning".[69] Other signs of the Christian thrust were that sassywood trials were less frequent;

[63] Gibson to Duane, 11 February 1875.
[64] Gibson to Duane, 12 March 1875.
[65] Gibson to Duane, 5 October 1875.
[66] Gibson to S.D. Denison, 25 March 1876.
[67] Gibson to Denison, 19 August 1876.
[68] Report of John Farr, 23 June 1876.
[69] *An historical sketch of the African mission of the P.E. Church of the U.S.A.* n.a., New York 1889, 2nd edition. (Through the courtesy of Bishop G. Browne of the Episcopal Church of Liberia.)

that the number of "devil-doctors" had greatly decreased; that earth
burial instead of exposure of the corpse was common; that faith in
"greegrees" had lessened; that fewer girls were betrothed in infancy.
An increased openness to literacy was also a positive indication, as
the deacon, Gibson, observed in 1877. He noted also the use of the
G'debo dialect in services, though English literacy was also popular.[70]
Civilization and Christianity were breaking through the cracks of the
traditional culture. Gibson, comparing the Glebo with the Webbo
people, some sixty miles to the interior, commented:

> The G'debo people are a long way ahead of the interior tribes as regards
> intelligence, and they [the latter] begin to see their disadvantages.[71]

Yet Wadé, at Sinoe, was well in advance of his own class, for the
Spring Hill station and two adjoining villages could report as late
as 1884 only four communicants, and these must have included the
local teacher and his family.

Indeed, at the age of about twelve the young Wadé, by then a
member of the *kedibo* class, had with his brother left Glogbale to
live with his mother's brother,[72] Rev. John C. Lowrie, the Glebo
Methodist minister.[73] He went in 1873 to Sinoe, or Greenville, a
hundred miles west from Cape Palmas.

"Brother Lowrie" had been employed by the Methodist mission
from 1860, originally as a teacher, and was thought of highly by the
missionaries.[74] As early as 1861 he had "several children living in
his family", and seems to have continued this practice, with good
results for the youths concerned.[75] This was a plan much approved
of by the Methodist Episcopal Church, who regarded it as better than

---

[70] Correspondence: Gibson to J. Kimber, 9 February 1877, *op. cit.*.

[71] Gibson to Kimber, 13 March 1878.

[72] Cf. S. Johnson, *op. cit.*, 119.

[73] All of the accounts, following *BR* of 1926, speak of "Jesse" "Lawry". Benoît
heard Harris and Mrs. Johnson say "Jesse" when they apparently had said "J.C.".
In the Methodist reports he is quite consistently mentioned as John C. Lowrie.

[74] *Missionary Advocate*, 16, December 1860, 71. Also: "A few years ago it pleased
God to convert a Grebo young man who had been recaptured in a slaver, and
was landed at Sierra Leone and there fell under the influence of the Wesleyan Mission.
After a pretty good religious training, and a fair trial of his piety, he returned to
the vicinity of Cape Palmas and began to preach to his own countrymen in their
own language. This was the foundation of the extension of the mission of the Liberian
Conference to the Greboes. This young man's Christian name is Rev. C. [sic for
J.] C. Lowrey." 1861 Annual Report of the Methodist Missionary Society.

[75] *Missionary Advocate*, 20, May 1864, 10.

a boarding school. The plan was promoted by Bishop Scott, so the custom became known as "Scott schools". They were thought to produce young men more likely to work hard and identify themselves with the Christian community.[76]

Wadé had now moved from the conflict-conditioned childhood towards the new "civilization" represented by new role models other than his father—John Farr, the village teacher, the Liberian deacon Gibson, and now his Methodist minister uncle, John Lowrie. He was on the way to becoming one of the second wave of "civilized natives".

B. Youth, 1873–1881: "Civilization"

When John C. Lowrie in 1873 took his two nephews to Sinoe he removed them from troubled Maryland County where the terrible conflict between the "G'debo United Kingdom" and the colonist-settlers was to take place. But he also removed them from the Glebo people, traditional village life with its age classes, extended family, and the religious climate and practice.

Lowrie had been transferred from Cape Palmas district to Nimo country of the "Sinou [sic] District",[77] an area where he had earlier worked. The Methodist Episcopal Mission already had a strong tradition of work among the Liberian colonists in preference to the "native" populations. Lowrie's own successful work among the Glebo (like Bishop Auer's), may have represented a threat to the colonists; the Methodists in 1873 made a decision to concentrate on work among the immigrant population, with the intention of creating a model of "civilized" people for the indigenous peoples to follow.[78] This may have been behind Lowrie's transfer.

The "Scott schools" were still being promoted with mission funds, and the support received for the children placed in his home became all the more vital to Lowrie as the Methodist Mission moved to make their churches self-supporting. This trend became official policy in 1884, and by 1894 the Bishop, Taylor, was able to claim that forty

---

[76] *Missionary Advocate*, 17, August 1861, 36.
[77] Annual Report, MSMEC, 1873, 39. Cf. also 1872, 1.
[78] *Ibid.*, 41, where the Hon. and Rev. D.F. Smith is cited from a report to Bishop Roberts: "With regard to *African* natives, whatever may be thought or said to the contrary, the most feasible method of promoting their interests, in a religious as well as a political point of view, is to sustain and strengthen the Churches in the civilised portion of our community".

Liberian ministers "are in the main self-supporting . . . and give most of their time to the work of effective ministers.[79]

In January 1875 Lowrie was named "Presiding Elder" for the Sinoe District, and this in fact meant supervising a circuit of some five churches, only one of which had a resident minister.[80] Under his leadership Greenville Circuit "enjoyed a revival season, and thirty-eight converts were received on probation. It had a day and a Sunday School".[81] Lowrie himself had to raise all but $275 of his $600 salary from his "stations". He was also enjoined by a conference decision in 1874 to apply strict discipline with regard to the use of alcohol by church members. Alcohol, declared the resolution, "is the bane of our national and religious life".[82]

In this home the young Wadé remained from the age of twelve to eighteen. He later attributed his basic education to this period, claiming that his Uncle Lowrie had taught him to read and write both G'debo and English. His knowledge of the Bible, also, was begun at this time.[83] When he went later to the Protestant Episcopal School he was "already taught". This included skill in the Glebo language, which a colleague later recalled he knew and wrote "very well".[84]

When one considers the contribution Harris later made to the Methodist Mission churches, the contribution made then to his training was a good investment. It is difficult to judge, as one missionary wrote, how much real education the pupils in the Scott schools received.[85] Yet many years later the Irish missionary, Father Harrington, was astonished at the quality of Harris's spoken English. "He spoke in perfect English, a very remarkable acquisition for a Kruman".[86] This indicates the ability not only of the pupil but also of the teacher.

Lowrie had from early in his service been highly praised by his missionary supervisors. His own response when offered the chance to receive more pupils was positive and he saw it as a means of evangelism.[87]

---

[79] Cf. Cason, *op. cit.*, 256, where he cited the 76th Annual Report of 1894, 32.
[80] Annual Report, MSMEC 1875, 37.
[81] *Ibid.*, 1876, 37.
[82] *Ibid.*, 1875, 44.
[83] *BN*, II, 14f., 6.
[84] *BN*, II, 23f.
[85] Cason, *op. cit.*, 204.
[86] Father Peter Harrington, S.M.A., "An interview with the 'Black Prophet'". *The African Missionary*, 18 (March–April) 1917, 13–16.
[87] Quoted in *Missionary Advocate* 16, December 1860, 71.

Thus it is not suprising that, during his time with Lowrie, the nephew was baptised by the uncle.[88] The significance of the baptism is debatable, because as one Liberian witness later said, "Rev. Lawry [sic] would not have kept him without baptising him".[89] In a church which accepted the baptism of infants and children into "the household of faith", it is not necessary to think that the boy had experienced conversion, which indeed he himself attributed to a later period of his life. What the meaning of the sacrament was to him at that time we cannot now know, except that during his later ministry he was to interpret it as a kind of preventive against a return to "fetish" worship.

It was probably at this time, since baptism was seen to include the taking on of (Western) "civilization", and a shift away from "heathenism",[90] that Wadé took the names "William" and "Harris". The name "Harris" may perhaps have been suggested by that of a very early Glebo Christian, N.S. Harris, who became an evangelist.[91] A local chief who was a "modernizer" was called "William"[92] Although both men had died by 1860, they represented pioneers in the path young Wadé was now following.

Although we do not know much of what Harris's baptism represented to him, we do know that it occurred at the same period that he was immersed in a new environment, the Lowrie household and the school. Each weeekday there were lessons; later an apprenticeship, probably as a mason, and then on Sunday the Sunday school, morning and evening worship, with a mid-week prayer meeting. In the family there were morning and evening prayers, and grace at meals. New religious and cultural values were being absorbed through this activity and discipline.

His Uncle Lowrie was at the centre of authority in home, church, and school. He was a preacher and minister in a congregation of Liberians, represented as superior to the Glebo. His power and authority in this "civilized" world was based on the Bible. Even a missionary recognised him as an excellent preacher.[93]

Outsiders found the religious world of the Americo-Liberians hard

---

[88] *BN* I, 25. This was confirmed by Clarck; *cf. BN*, II, 23.
[89] *BN*, I, 5.
[90] Merriam, *op. cit.*, 90: "I was told that it was point gained when they were called by any civilised appellation."
[91] Martin, *op. cit.*, 210.
[92] *Ibid.*, 99f.
[93] *Missionary Advocate*, 16, December 1860, 71.

to comprehend. Sir Harry Johnston, the British entrepreneur and
explorer, thought they had a fault—"excess of religion". He wrote
of their attachment to Protestant churches, but felt that "they have
erected the Bible into a sort of fetish. They exhibit the Puritanism
of New England in the eighteenth century almost unabated." He made
some fun of their emphasis on dress, which led them to despise the
"naked savage". "The Americo-Liberian . . . shares with our fathers
the religion of the tall hat and frock coat." And he saw in their religion
too much of the Old Testament, too much of the Anglo-Saxon, too
much of mortification of the flesh.[94]

The best of the scene from within the culture itself is described
by a distinguished Liberian of the late 19th century, C.L. Simpson.
His father had come as a child to Liberia, and his mother was a
Vai woman from Western Liberia. Of his home life he wrote:

> I cannot speak of my childhood without mentioning the large part which
> religion played in it. Ours was not the formal kind of Christianity which
> is taken out once a week for airing and ignored in between times. It
> was a genuine part of our daily service . . . the everyday problems of
> life were met by my parents in a Christian spirit which naturally
> communicated itself to us in our formative years.[95]

The Christianity of the Americo-Liberian settlers, who had come out
of the African slave context, was in its own way as much of an African
religious movement as the later "new religious movements" which
have more recently been studied.[96] Although the American blacks often
appeared to observers to be "apeing" the white man, they were in
fact integrating into what they already were certain external elements
of a culture which was slowly assimilating them.

Such a religious creation, lived out by an internal commitment,
can cause the very elements seen by outsiders as inappropriate,
incongruous and alienating to be perceived by the participants as
significant, necessary and liberating. So-called legalistic structures and
taboos can become effective new patterns and symbols to the participants, replacing those which have been removed, destroyed or
become non-functional. Outsiders see the rigidity; the slow changes

---

[94] H. Johnston, *op. cit.*, vol. I, 352–370.
[95] C.L. Simpson, *The symbol of Liberia. The memoirs of C.L. Simpson*. London: The
Diplomatic Press and Publishing Co., 1961, 76f.
[96] Harold W. Turner, "New tribal religious movements", in *Encyclopedia Britannica*
1974, 697.

are more obvious to those within the situation. Such was the situation of the Liberian settlers, and the two descriptions, by Johnston and by Simpson, are both necessary to understand the religious climate which was the background to Harris's life in Sinoe.

That religious life also had political overtones which would not be lost on the boy. A recent study by J.M. Sullivan gives a broad view of that life:

> Competition for land, trade or political office often centred on divisions in the country based on religion, arrival time, and settlement patterns. Settlers used alliances of family ties, church membership, and settlement patterns to advance their self interest . . . Church membership became an element in political competition. Churches were often identified with a particular community. . . . Not unlike their role in the slave communities of the U.S. South, Liberian preachers had more education than their contemporaries, they gained leadership through experience in their congregations and were skilled in oratory.[97]

Thus it was not unusual for churchmen to participate in Sinoe politics with support from their mission boards. And politics and preaching became a Liberian tradition; in the 20th century those who sought political office usually sought church leadership first.[98] From 1876 to 1878 the president of Liberia was James S. Payne, who had been an active minister in the Methodist Episcopal Church. And in Sinoe there was only a small political constituency; in 1901 there were only 265 adult males.

This is the situation in which we find the Glebo convert Lowrie, pastor of a Methodist congregation of "converted" Liberians, where probation was a condition of membership. In many ways Lowrie was closer to the missionaries than he was to the Liberians among whom he was working; he seems to have been a man of deep faith and strong character, in a church in which a general feeling of *laisser aller* seemed to predominate.[99] In this household William Wadé Harris was assimilating much of the religious and moral materials which were to come alive when he was later converted. At that time those materials were part of a whole new external culture which conditioned his existence and only foreshadowed a later crisis. R. Allier has called

---

[97] Jo Mary Sullivan, *Settlers in Sinoe County, Liberia, and their relations with the Kru, c. 1835–1920*. Boston University, Ph.D. thesis 1978, 229–231.
[98] *Ibid.*
[99] Cason (*op. cit.*) writes of "lax local supervision".

this the *prodromes de la crise*[100]—foretokens of the crisis. His older brother was in fact converted while they were at Sinoe; Wadé was not, as he told Benoît.[101] This consciousness of *not* being converted was doubtless as significant as the conversion itself. But he was "civilised".

1. *Kruboy view of the world, 1879–1880*

In January 1879 Rev. John Lowrie was transferred from Sinoe back to the Cape Palmas area.[102] This move took the eighteen-year-old Wadé back to his home region. But his father removed him from the Lowrie home to the village, from the "civilized" to the "heathen" context. He himself said of this, "My father, a heathen, came and stole me before Rev. Lawry's [sic] death".[103] His mother's part in this is not mentioned.

During the six years Harris had been with his uncle his father would have had no financial benefit from the son, such as the usual tradition of sending an adolescent son to sea as a kruboy.[104] It seems that now he was sent from the village almost as soon as he arrived.[105]

There has been a good deal of conjecture about his time as a kruboy, but he spoke about it quite simply in 1926.

> I went four times to sea as a common labourer. Two times Lagos, two times Gabon—French coast. I have never been in Nigeria.[106]
> When I went to Lagos it was with a German boat .... I went to Gabon ... with an Aden and foster factory ... English from Angola. I was put in prison under a French administrator because I sung during the night ... Ogoone River. Never labored in Lagos for Elder Dempster but for Kiel Geissa. Never joined any church in Lagos, nor learned to read there. Never to French Guinea.[107]

---

[100] Cf. Raoul Allier, *La psychologie de la conversion chez les peuples non-civilisés*. Paris: Payot 1925, 2 vols. See the whole first volume.
[101] *BN* II, 6.
[102] Annual Report, MSMEC, 1879, 40.
[103] *BN* II, 6.
[104] Ronald W. Davis dates the tradition to the late 18th century, and beginning probably in the Settra Kru region near Sinoe. Cf. his "Trade and relations with the Liberian government", in *Ethno-historical studies on the Kru coast*. Newark, Delaware: University of Delaware 1976, 35.
[105] *BN*, I, 26.
[106] *Ibid.*, Lagos was at that time an autonomous island independent of Nigeria.
[107] *BN*, II, 6. In the second paragraph the prophet was answering questions put to him by Pierre Benoît precisely to clear up issues raised by F.D. Walker's reports in 1926. In the second edition of a popular account of Harris's mission Walker did not correct errors which could have been clarified by reference to the *Benoît Notes*,

A typical voyage from Cape Palmas to Gabon and back would have taken about forty days. Stops would have been made at ports in Liberia, the Ivory Coast, Gold Coast, Dahomey, at Lagos, Nigeria, Cameroons, and islands before reaching Gabon.[108] So it would have been easily possible for Harris to make four such trips in the year or so between his return to Cape Palmas and the death of Lowrie sometime in 1880.

The story of the Krumen has been well told elsewhere,[109] and here all that is necessary is to give some idea of the life Harris lived and the break this represented with life in his uncle's home. J. Leighton Wilson, writing in 1856, described the tradition which he entered. Boys were taken on board at ages between twelve and twenty, and engaged to serve as long as the ship remained on the coast. Part of the lad's wages were paid in advance to the guardian, and that was all the family would receive in the event of his death or non-return. If discharged at a distant port he would often join another ship, and so be away for several years.[110] When a kruboy did return, there was feasting in the village, and he would parade the streets for several days in his best attire. It was common after the first return for the young man to take his first wife.

Life was fairly hard, and the treatment harsh, but not unbearably so. They were fed reasonably, and often given rum; physical punishment was fairly regular.[111] Harris's time as a "kruboy" was to become for him a constant frame of reference, seen in sharp contrast to his identity as a prophet.[112]

The labour, the low wages, the drinking, brawling and fighting in the port cities must have marked Harris in many ways. He spent two nights in prison for singing popular songs late at night, and his

---

which he had then seen. See F.D. Walker, *The Story of the Ivory Coast*. London: Cargate Press 1926 (2nd impression), 13.

[108] This information is from copies of boat schedules for the S.S. Biafra and the S.S. Soudan. These were generously shared by Professor P.N. Davies of the University of Liverpool, the leading authority on maritime history of that period. Cf. P.N. Davies (ed.), *Trading in West Africa, 1840–1926*. London: Croon Helm 1976.

[109] Cf. George E. Brooks, Jr., *The Kru mariner in the nineteenth century. An historical compendium*. Newark, Delaware: Liberian Studies Association in America Inc., 1972. See also Christine Behrens, *Les Kroumen de la côte occidentale d'Afrique*. Tolence: Centre d'Etudes de Géographie Tropicale 1974.

[110] J. Leighton Wilson, *Western Africa . . .* (1856), 106.

[111] In W. Winwoode Reade, *Savage Africa*. London: Elder Smith 1864 (2nd ed.), 36.

[112] See Casely Hayford, *William Waddy Harris, the West African Reformer. The man and his message*. London: C.M. Phillips 1915, 8–9.

Christian education must have been severely tested.[113] Missionaries regarded krumen as exceptionally resistant to the gospel.[114]

But these voyages as a kruboy meant that Harris saw a good deal more of West Africa than just the eastern coast of Liberia. At the very least he would have become aware of different ethnic groups along the coast, and of the differences among the colonial powers, British, German and French.

It was said at Harris's trial, in 1909, that he had claimed to have been at the Coast "when the English capture Almia" [sic].[115] That he was at Elmina (in the Gold Coast) in 1879 when the British headed off an Ashanti revolt is a possibility. This could have influenced his later pro-British attitudes.[116]

His time as a kruboy would also have given him the opportunity to observe the religious professions of white men, and discern which of them possessed genuine faith—that "white" did not mean "Christian". An observer writing in 1865 felt that the "Kroomen" were often hardened against Christianity "because the sailors are often wicked men".[117]

When Harris went home from his time at sea it seems he went, not to his native village, but to the home of his uncle Lowrie near Cape Palmas. Mrs. Hannah Johnson of Harper remembered his being there not only at the time of his uncle's death, but for some time afterwards staying with the widow "until he was a man and started for himself".[118]

---

[113] *BN* II, 6f. Benoît edited his note with: Ce souvenir met le vieux prophète en joie, il rit très fort. "Non, ce n'était pas un cantique, mais un chant populaire." Harris was probably not a kruboy after his conversion as Zarwan suggests, *op. cit.*, except for the Tarkwa experience (Cf. p. 56 below).

[114] Cf. Brooks, *op. cit.*, 7. Also, in a source unknown to Brooks, George Thompson, *The palm lands of West Africa illustrated*, Cincinnati 1858; London: Dawsons of Pall Mall 1969, cf. p. 190: "One [kruman] in Sierra Leone became a preacher; and the thing was so novel that crowds flocked to 'hear a krooman preach.' It was an unheard of thing before . . . if one of their number does become educated or converted, he is expelled from their midst."

[115] See *Records of the Court of Quarterly Sessions and Common Pleas, Maryland County, Book 187, 1907–1909*, pages 186 to 222.

[116] The incident may also have been a part of the fabrication needed to give him status among his people. We have discovered Harris's statements from his prophetic period to correspond remarkably with situations, events and dates. But the very ambiguous situation in which he was operating in his last year prior to the "Union Jack" incident of 1909 makes us somewhat suspicious of such statements from his pre-prophetic period.

[117] Merriam, *op. cit.*, 45.

[118] Mrs. Hannah Johnson (washerwoman at Grand Bassam), interviewed by Benoît in 1926. *BN* II, 1–5.

2. Cape Palmas, after 1880

Cape Palmas was at this time an important port of call, and it maintained some independence from Monrovia. When Dr. Blyden, Secretary of the Interior, found himself in difficulties in Monrovia (in 1882), he took refuge at Cape Palmas. He stayed there for a month, giving an address explaining his reason for leaving the capital,[119] and doubtless other addresses. Young Harris would have been a witness of these events.

In this period missionary work, especially that of the Episcopalians, was under attack by colonial Liberians, largely because of the relationship of missions to Glebo development and the war of 1875–76. An act of the legislature passed in 1881–82 made it treasonable for any Liberian citizen—which included the tribal people—to engage in acts of war against the Republic, or to aid her enemies. Although the "G'debo United Kingdom" had after the treaty of 1876 been reduced to political nonentity, its general council still continued a conciliation function, especially in mediating between the two Glebo sections.[120]

Educated Glebo were at this time beginning to realise that their future wealth might lie in the soil, and agriculture was being developed, including coffee plantations. These developments and the modernizing trend in the air could not fail to interest the apprentice mason who had spent six years in a "civilized" home and then travelled to and fro along the coast of West Africa. His future political interests did not come out of a vacuum, for indeed there was plenty of such in Cape Palmas.

The Wadé who had left Glogbale in 1870 had returned as William Wade Harris, now literate, now a baptized Methodist, sophisticated by local standards, having become aware of national as well as local politics; aware also of the ways in which "civilization" exploited Africans, all along the West African coast. He said much later, "Mammon has used the Krooman all these years [filling] your ships with cargo and your coffers with gold.[121] He had been through a period of unsettledness; it was now time to settle down in adult life. Although "civilized" and baptized, he was not yet "converted".

---

[119] Cf. letter from Blyden to Coppinger, 26 April 1882, cited in Edith Holden, *Blyden of Liberia*, New York: Vantage Press 1960, 493.
[120] This and the following paragraph are based on sources quoted in Merriam, *op. cit.*, 321ff.
[121] Casely Hayford, *op. cit.*, 9.

A final possible experience in these "pre-Christian" years must be mentioned. Some witnesses of his prophetic ministry claimed that he had spent time in the gold mines of Ghana. One of these was Father Stauffer who heard that he had been "headman of the Kruboys at Tarkwa".[122] When he himself preached in Axim in 1914 he seemed familiar with local expressions.[123] There were English concessions around Tarkwa from 1881, and it is possible that after his sea-going period Harris spent time there, for kruboys were employed, and all materials and labour went inland from Axim.[124] His literacy and experience would have made him suitable for work as a "headman", an intermediary between the workers and the European overseers. If such were the case, it would have possibly been as "converted", some time between 1881 and 1885 when, as Mrs. Johnson had put it, he "started for himself".

---

[122] Note made in the diary of Fr. Stauffer, priest at Axim in 1914, some time in or around 1926. General Archives, S.M.A., Rome.

[123] *HN*, J.P. Ephson, 1964, who also mentioned the "legend that he was a steward boy in the gold mines at Tarkwa."

[124] *Cf.* W. Walton Claridge, *A History of the Gold Coast and Ashanti. . . .*, London: Frank Cass & Co. 1964 (2nd ed.), 203f. and 246f.

CHAPTER THREE

PREPROPHETIC ADULTHOOD, I: 1881–1899

1. Christian Idealism

a. Conversion, ca 1881 or 1882

When he was twenty-one or twenty-two years of age, Harris was converted in the Methodist Episcopal Church at Cape Palmas. It seems that after Lowrie's death he had stayed for some time with his widowed aunt in the Cape Palmas area. He was not at this time a "converted" Christian in his own thinking. He described his conversion to Pierre Benoît:

> The first I converted it was under Rev. Thompson—Liberian—in Methodist Church—I converted under the summon.
> T[hompson] was preaching on Revelation 2:5—I was 21 or 22. Rev. Lawry [sic] was dead—my brother older than me was converted the time I was in Sino. But me not . . . I was converted there—the Holy Ghost come on me. The very year of my conversion I start preaching— I was baptised already by my uncle Lawry in Sino—I was confirmed in 1888 by Bishop Ferguson in Cape Palmas.[1]

If he was born ca 1860, his conversion would be dated ca 1881 or 1882. The event was certainly more crucial for him than the historian Haliburton would seem to indicate.[2] In a dozen short phrases, he uses the word "conversion" half a dozen times. He was speaking of an event which had occurred over forty years before, and several things must be underlined.

First, it was under the ministry of a Liberian, Thompson, who had

---

[1] *BN* II, 6. The singular "summon" could be understood as "suh-man" for "sermon". Benoît's citation of the English "I was converted under the summon" in his French synthesis (*BN* III, 9) underscores for us the crucial character of the "summon[s]" as Benoît perceived it in Harris's recital. "I was converted *there*" was apparently spoken while Harris was either referring to or pointing to the Methodist Episcopal Church of Harper.

[2] Haliburton, *The Prophet Harris*, 1971, 13.

replaced Lowrie after the latter's death in 1880. For the conversion experience the usual antagonistic ethnic categories of "Glebo" and "Americo-Liberian" became unimportant, and the new category of "converted" Christian was all important.

Secondly, Harris speaks of being converted "under the summon"— the preaching from the Bible. He responded to an experience of the "power of the Word".

In addition there was the special meaning of the preacher's text, which Harris cited spontaneously many years later:

> Remember therefore from whence thou art fallen, and repent, and do the first works; or else I will come unto thee quickly and will remove thy candlestick out of his place, except thou repent. [Rev. 2,5.)

Even though in his own understanding he had not been converted when he left for sea, he had been baptized into a new Christian cultural pattern of life. But it had not been personally appropriated as his own. It had remained as a model for him, and from that model he had probably often fallen in his time away at sea. There was a "model" to return to, and in view of which he was summoned to "repent".

Finally, there is his description of the experience, in New Testament language,[3] "the Holy Ghost came upon me". With a confrontation of wills—indicated by "the summon"—came also a sensible experience, an empirical appropriation of power and authority which was felt and internalized.

This experience owed something to the Methodist tradition; it also owed something to the traditional Glebo experience of the *deya* who ministered from a state of "possession". Missionary observers like Wilson and Payne called it a "demon or spirit", and not the Holy Spirit, but there was a strong cultural similarity. Wilson in his description mentions that the *deya* "sometimes has communications from God".[4] The cultural context defined what it meant to have an experience of "spirit" and from it derive power and authority for responding to new problems and situations.[5] This resembled, at least superficially,

---

[3] E.g., Acts 2.17f; 8.16; 10.44.
[4] J.L. Wilson, *Western Africa . . .*, 1886, 13.
[5] This is reported for the Isoko of Western Nigeria by Simon Barrington-Ward in "'The centre cannot hold': spirit possession as redefinition", in Edward Fasholé-Luke *et al*, (eds.), *Christianity in independent Africa*. London: Rex Collings 1978, 455–470.

the Judeo-Christian situation where prophets functioned as a special class;[6] it also reminded the subject of the promise that "in the last days I will pour out my spirit upon all flesh."[7]

It was probably the cultural context rather than the missionary or catechist or Scripture which dictated the form of the experience.[8] This cultural form had also been carried to the New World by African captives and had been brought back to Liberia by the American settlers in new and Christianized forms. Winwood Reade described in such terms a visit to the Monrovia Baptist Church in 1868, where the minister was also the U.S. Minister to Liberia. He observed also that at the Episcopalian Church the service was quieter and more tranquil, and thus not acceptable to what he called the "slave classes".[9] In fact the Episcopalians in the early days of their mission had experienced such phenomena,[10] but had gradually become more decorous. These differences would have been keenly felt in Harris's later move from the more "spiritual" Methodists to the more formal Episcopalians.

A visiting woman evangelist, Amanda Smith, described meetings held at Cape Palmas in the 1880s. She noted that Bishop Ferguson seemed to be embarassed by the "spirit-filled" style,[11] and described also the conversion of "Sister Sharper", who was "struck" by the Holy

---

[6] *Cf.* J. Lindblom, *Prophecy in ancient Israel.* Philadelphia: Fortress Press 1965, 65ff.

[7] Joel 2.28 for the prophecy, and Acts 2.17 interpreted as its fulfillment.

[8] Agnes McAllister, *A lone woman in Africa.* New York: Jennings & Pye 1896, 275. "We had the old time Methodist shouting. Surely the Spirit came down from heaven, for there was no one there who knew anything about shouting in meeting or had ever attended a revival and seen other people saved. . . . Jacob was the first saved; and he was sweetly saved and testified to it. He fell over the bench and lay so for a time; but when he had the witness of his salvation he was on his feet shouting the praises of God." The cultural model would have been the way the "spirit" came upon the *deya.*

The same phenomenon was reported from Nana Kru by the Methodists Walter B. and Maude W. Williams in *Adventures with the Krus in West Africa.* New York: Vantage Press 1955, 79. ". . . as soon as the opening chapel service began, the power of the Spirit would fall. Our students would be prostrate on the ground, praying and praising." The Williams arrived in Nana Kru in 1909, coming from Angola. Nana Kru is west of Garraway, and about twenty-five miles east of Greenville (Sinoe).

[9] Winwood Reade, *The African sketchbook* II. London: Smith, Elder & Son 1873, 250. The distinction between the two types of religiosity, here described casually by Reade in 1868, is described by the scientific observer in Luc de Heusch, "Cultes de possession et religions initiatiques de salut en Afrique", in Luc de Heusch *et. al., Religions de Salut.* Brussels: Free University of Brussels 1962, 127–167. See especially the introductory pages, 128ff.

[10] John Walter Cason, *The growth of Christianity in the Liberian environment.* Columbia University, Ph.D. thesis 1962. University Microfilms 1975, 134. (henceforth Cason).

[11] Amanda Smith, *An autobiography: the story of the Lord's own dealings with Mrs. Amanda Smith, the colored evangelist.* Chicago: Mayer & Bres 1893, 437.

Ghost at her conversion.[12] Harris's conversion may not have been as incident-filled, but it was of the same *genre*.

"Conversion" meant the intervention of the Holy Spirit in a sensible experience which introduced one into the elite class of Christianity. In such an experience, moral and religious structures become thoroughly internalised in a process which has physiological[13] as well as psychological[14] implications. Forgiveness, purification, repentance, are all dimensions of that transition.

When Harris in 1926 spoke of his conversion to Benoît, the latter reflected: "Unfortunately, one thing is lacking to us: what is it that he repented of? fetishes? dishonesty? religious coldness?"[15] The answer probably is that he repented of his whole African past, and started a whole new Christian future, as defined by American and Western Christians. But he did it through a typically African medium . . . This was "the first I converted". Thirty years later there would be in different—yet parallel—circumstances a second conversion.

We have underlined the great importance of his conversion for Harris, and we have no intention of minimizing its christological inspiration and orientation. Nevertheless, it was also very typical in its time and place. Compare it with this description:

> Native children enter the families of the colonists. Here they are clothed. In a little time clothing becomes a necessity. They have thus learned a want; they soon learn others. They at first go to church because it is the white man's fashion . . . Afterwards they go because they find pleasure in it. Finally, they go as Christians.[16]

---

[12] *Ibid.*, 449.

[13] See William Sargant, *Battle for the mind. A physiology of conversion and brain washing.* London: Heinemann 1957. Cf. especially 78ff. where the Wesleyan tradition of conversion in the 18th century is seen to make everything clear to the convert— a truly total starting again. The phenomenon is seen by Sargant, however, as potentially negative and dangerous.

[14] See Raoul Allier, *La psychologie de la conversion chez les non-civilisés I.* Paris: Payot 1925, where the phenomenon is described positively in the context of a century of Protestant missions; a new ego is seen to replace totally an old ego in a death-resurrection syndrome. The weakness in Allier's approach, as Roger Bastide points out, is that it implies that the new ego among tribal peoples of the earth necessarily had to include—for Allier—Western categories of logic, rationality, etc. Bastide rightly asks what the new ego might look like if one did not have to exit from a culture of "participation". Cf. Roger Bastide, "Sociologies (au pluriel) des missions Protestantes", in *Les missions Protestantes et l'histoire.* Paris: Société du Protestantisme Français 1971, 47–62, esp. 58ff. The Prophet Harris, after his 1910 vision, may well be an illustration of an answer to Bastide's question.

[15] *BR*, II, 8.

[16] In Charles Henry Huberich, *The political and legislative history of Liberia I.* New

Harris's conversion, though intensely and spiritually crucial for him, was indeed part of a pattern ... of acculturation.

b. Mission

"The very year of my conversion I start preaching," Harris told Benoît. There is clearly a close relationship between his conversion and his preaching. His uncle Lowrie had actually died in the pulpit while preaching on faithfulness, which left a deep mark on his young nephew.[17] William's preaching would have been in the Methodist Episcopal Church in which he was "born", baptized and converted. Lay preaching and lay witnessing was encouraged in that church, as it was not in the Protestant Episcopal Church. Harris probably had no official position in the Methodist Church, but preached as a volunteer.

He worked for his aunt, Mrs. Lowrie; he worked as a mason; he no doubt worked at raising food.[18] He was "starting for himself", as Mrs. Johnson put it. It was necessary to earn a living, but, in retrospect, Harris saw this time as a period of mission through preaching. The Liberian missionary, Gibson, in 1890 described the people of Graway as still tenaciously attached to their old "heathen habits".[19] Harris, in this as in much else was ahead of his peers.

c. Marriage, 1885–86

Typically, a kruboy married on his return from sea. Harris did not follow this pattern. After his conversion he worked for several years, and then married. He was following the "civilised" pattern, and had a Christian wedding to a Christian wife.

The Glebo minister, Rev. O.H. Shannon of the Protestant Episcopal

---

York: Central Book Co. 1947, 48. Cited in Hannah Abeodu Bowen Jones, *The struggle for political and cultural unification in Liberia, 1847–1930*. Northwestern University, Ph.D. thesis 1962, 160. R.H. Gibson, superintendent of the Graway work, wrote (12 April 1874), "To merge [*sic*, for emerge] out of heathenism into the marvellous light of the Gospel is a burden of self-denial, and an assumption of moral courage which few heathen, as yet, are bold enough to undertake ... Many will say to the missionary, "Your words are true—I feel them—they touch my heart; but my friends will laugh at me. My companions will forsake me and call me 'Godman', which I have not yet the courage to hear." (Gibson to Duane, ECHS Archives). Our emphasis on "acculturation" is concerning the process and is not a value judgement.

[17] Mrs. Hannah Johnson, interviewed by P. Benoît, October 1926. *BN* II, 1–5.

[18] In April 1978 Harris's grandchildren recalled spontaneously how their grandfather prided himself for raising all his own food.

[19] In *Journal of the Second Convocation*. New York: A.G. Sherwood & Co. 1896, 38.

Church performed the ceremony in church;[20] he was superintendent of the Graway work, which included Spring Hill. The bride was Rose Bedo Wlede Farr,[21] daughter of John Farr, former catechist and teacher at Spring Hill. Rose's deceased father had been replaced by his son, Nathaniel Sie Farr, who would have been responsible for arrangements for his sister's marriage.

Rose and Harris had both been brought up in the Graway area, but on opposite sides of the lake-lagoon. After the wedding they lived on Spring Hill station, where Harris built a house.[22] It is difficult to judge what the home was like, for the only descriptions and one photo are from some forty years later. Benoît described it in his notes when it was derelict.[23] But it was a two-storied house with cement and stone walls, with windows and shutters, a staircase and a hearth with chimney. In 1890 such a house must have been a marvel. Harris was living out the cultural model which he had accepted.

Such a respectable house would have been approved by the missionaries. One wrote of the building of such houses to replace "rude huts" as being a testimony to the "true light of the gospel."[24]

2. Protestant Episcopal Period, 1888–1909

a. Orientation

After his marriage, Harris did not stay long within the Methodist Episcopal milieu in which he was "born", baptized, educated and converted. In 1888 he was confirmed by Bishop Ferguson of the Protestant Episcopal Church at St. Mark's Church, Harper.[25] Six from Half-Graway were confirmed that year.

Samuel David Ferguson, born in 1842 of a Roman Catholic mother and a Baptist father, had arrived in Liberia as a colonist child in

---

[20] *BN* I, 2 and *BR* I.6: *BN* I.14; *BN* II, 21.
[21] Benoît (*BN* I.7) writes "Rose Bodock Farr"; Rev. Killen (*BN* II, 21) spelled it Bôdodê; Harris's grandchildren in April 1978 spelled it Bedo Wlede.
[22] Robert Neal, Mrs. Betty Smith, and Mrs. Rose Horace, children of Harris's second daughter, Grace Neal, reported in April 1978 that the Harris family had only ever lived in one house, and that Harris had built it by himself. The picture of Harris taken in 1928 with John Ahui and Solomon Dagri shows the façade of that house.
[23] *BR* I, 10f.
[24] Agnes McAllister, *op. cit.*, 264.
[25] *BN* II. 6.

the late 1840s. Educated in Episcopalian institutions, he became a school teacher and catechist, and then was ordained deacon in 1865, priest in 1868. He was a light-skinned black who tried to prove his unlimited loyalty to white American values. In 1885 he was consecrated in the United States as the fourth "missionary bishop to Cape Palmas and to parts adjacent." The first Liberian to hold the post, he continued in it till his death in 1916, and was the builder of the present-day Protestant Episcopal Church in Liberia. His period in office coincided with the "pre-prophetic" period of Harris's life, and with the period of Christian outreach to the indigenous, from 1875 to 1915.

He was described as a "conscientious Christian" who believed that the Western forms of Christianity were essential to true belief. His attitude to the Glebo was a typically Western one; he saw them as degraded and needing to acquire Western habits of industry.[26] Yet at a time when the larger Methodist Episcopal Church was structurally weak, and concentrating its work on the settlers, Bishop Ferguson led a church "characterised by administrative stability",[27] which he pushed forward into missions for the indigenous people. With strong American backing, the Episcopal Church was able to promote leadership training, while still enjoying a considerable measure of self-government.

> Ferguson had a genius for driving young men into the ministry. And he saw the connections between the expansion of the church and the need for well-trained priests. One of his outstanding achievements was the establishment of Cuttington College at Cape Palmas and the training of a number of capable preachers and spiritual pastors.[28]

At much the same time the Methodists had closed their Cape Palmas seminary because of the hostility of the Liberian government and difficulties arising from the settler community nearby.[29]

Harris was confirmed at a time of great economic and political strain in Liberia. He now had a wife and baby daughter to consider. His teaching and preaching within Methodist structures did not offer him much for a future in which he would continue a civilized lifestyle. Bishop Ferguson, who confirmed him, would have seen a

---

[26] Martin, *op. cit.*, 322f.
[27] Cason, *op. cit.*, 267.
[28] Joseph Wold, *God's impatience with Liberia.* Grand Rapids: Eerdmans 1968, 85.
[29] Methodist Annual Report 1881. Cited by Cason, 253.

promising young Christian lay-man now married to the daughter of
one of his church's most faithful catechists. He would have fitted in
with the Bishop's vision. But Harris responded with realism and honesty
when asked why he changed churches. "I run away for money from
Methodist and enter Episcopal Church to make money . . . I was
married to Rose Harris."[30]

We should not take lightly this statement about why he left the
Methodist Church for the Episcopal Church, even though it was made
forty years later, after his "prophetic" work. He saw himself as having
acted not out of faith but out of self-interest; and although he served
the Episcopal Church for twenty years he seems to have seen that
period as one of disloyalty to an earlier call. After his prophetic calling
he often spoke of himself as a Wesleyan or a Methodist, but never
as an Episcopalian.

He was, however, not the only one to make such a shift. Indeed,
an observant missionary in the 1880s noted how many workers in
the Episcopal churches had been educated and trained by the Methodist mission.[31] Yet regardless of reasons why others did it, for Harris
it clearly raised an internal conflict, and when he became a prophet
he refused to take money for his ministry.

His confirmation opened the way for employment by the Episcopal
Church; he was in fact appointed to a post four years later.[32] In the
interim it seems he received some further training at a Protestant
Episcopal school,[33] where he went as "a full-grown man."[34] While
receiving this schooling, it seems he also worked as a mason, and
probably helped in the Sunday School at Spring Hill. His second
daughter Grace was born in 1889. A time of change in the family,
it was also a period of change and conflict among the Grebo. As
early as 1886 the ten-year Cavalla rebellion had started.

The Episcopal Church's Cavalla Station was by 1884 one of its
showpieces, with a large well-organised "native congregation . . .
ministered to by its own (native) clergyman."[35] But this very kind of
development could appear to contribute to rebellion, which could then
be blamed on the Episcopal Church. Unlike his predecessors, Bishop

---

[30] *BN* I, 11; cf. *BN* III, 1 and *BR* II, 1.
[31] Amanda Smith, *op. cit.*, 437.
[32] Annual Report, BMPEC, 1891–92, 159.
[33] *BN* I, 25f.
[34] *BN* I, 24.
[35] *An historical sketch of the African mission.* New York: no pub., 2nd. ed. 1889, 75.

Ferguson was completely loyal to the Liberian government, and now had to prove that loyalty, against Glebo recriminations.

The Christians at Half Cavalla attempted to remain neutral, but when they were attacked by the rebels early in 1887 some 250 refugees went through the Spring Hill Station en route to Harper and its vicinity. The Cavalla refugees belonged to the Kudemowe moiety, while the Harper Glebo belonged to the Nyomowe. The situation proved impossible, and eventually they rejoined the rebels. Meanwhile the French were looking for what advantage they could make out of the Liberian weakness, and they finally annexed the territory east of the Cavalla River in 1892. For the Episcopal Mission it meant a loss of thirty-five preaching stations.

Wadé Harris's confirmation and eventual posting as an Episcopal teacher required him to be as loyal to the Liberian central and local government as was the bishop. Since the rebels were Kudemowe, this was not difficult. The station at Half Cavalla was eventually put under a ban, and four teachers and a priest were excommunicated.

Stirred up by the French annexation, the Kudemowe rebels attacked the settlements near Harper, and in some cases proved stronger than the Liberian troops. In 1893 a temporary peace was established between the Kudemowe and the Nyomowe, and the Cavalla chiefs signed a treaty of submission to the Liberian authorities. But French influence was still strong, and French authorities collected taxes and levies. Eventually Nyomowe Glebo from Cape Palmas, including a hundred students and workmen from the Episcopalian Cuttington College, defeated the rebels in 1896. The college principal, Rev. M.P.K. Valentine, was killed in the battle.

Bishop Ferguson supported the bearing of arms by mission employees and the final war initiative of 1896, though it was forbidden by church canons and disapproved of by the Liberian president.[36] What was Harris's attitude to this?

Harris later spoke of three Liberian imprisonments, and F.D. Walker conjectured that they must have been connected with the Glebo rebellions of 1893, 1896, and 1910.[37] This assumption has never been questioned.[38] But Harris during the 1890s was a firm Episcopalian

---

[36] Martin, *op. cit*, 364. This whole section is dependent upon Dr. Martin's research.
[37] Frank Deaville Walker, "More about the prophet Harris." *The Foreign Field*, March 1927, 138.
[38] E.g., Jean Rouch, "Introduction à l'étude de la communauté de Bregbo," *Journal*

and a supporter of Bishop Ferguson, as well as being a member of
the Nyomowe moiety. If he was involved in the conflict (which is
likely), it would have been on the side of the establishment, ecclesiastical
and secular. Ferguson in 1893 specifically mentioned the loyalty of
the Nyomowe, who were "fighting side by side with the Americo-
Liberians".[39] In 1896 the bishop complained of the difficulties caused
by the continuing rebellion, which meant that older students and
teachers were being called up for military duty.[40] Harris, then thirty-
six, without doubt was included among those fighting the rebels under
the bishop's initiative.

At the time of Harris's marriage Bishop Ferguson's regime had
just begun, and in the next decade there was considerable expansion
in the Protestant Episcopal work. This expansion was almost all among
the indigenous populations.[41] Ferguson was co-operating with the
Liberian government in their effort to make "one nationality", Liberian
and christianized, out of the diverse groups. We have reason to believe
that Harris fully supported and worked towards this end, as we shall
observe below.

b. Mission Employee, 1892–1898

In 1892 there was a break-through in the Mission's work at Half-
Graway. An old man, the former *bodio* of the whole group, was baptized
as a Christian.[42] At nearby Hoffman Station the whole population[43]
had finally agreed to give up their "fetish house"; the whole tribe
agreed to replace the "greegrees" with a Bible which would be placed
in a chapel built in Bigtown in front of the Bodio's house "where
sacrifice had regularly been offered to the devil.". The people at Half
Graway also asked for a chapel, and the bishop agreed providing
that "they would make a law to observe the Lord's Day".[44] In his
next budget proposal he asked for funds, among other plans, to employ
"Wm. Wade Harris" for the small wages of five dollars a month,

de la Société des Africanistes 33 (1), 1963, 113. His source was the 1931 French translation
of F.D. Walker's work of 1926, page 31. Also see Bohumil Holas, *Le séparatisme religieux
en Afrique noire*. Paris: P.U.F. 1965, 262,
[39] Annual Report, BMPEC 1892–93, 141.
[40] *Ibid.*, 1895–96, 152f.
[41] *Ibid.*, 1894–95, 187.
[42] *Ibid.*, 1891–92, 10 (R.H. Gibson report).
[43] *Ibid.*, 166–68.
[44] *Ibid.*, 167. "We have made this (the Sunday law) the sharp edge of our Gospel
wedge."

"to lend a hand".[45] In fact some ten days before he had appointed Harris as "assistant teacher and catechist at Half Graway."[46]

The Cape Palmas district was the largest of the three districts under the jurisdiction of the missionary bishop, and the total budget was between $3,000 and $4,000. Of this $2,000 was the bishop's own annual allowance,[47] and the head teachers at Spring Hill School and Whole Graway earned $300 a year each.[48] Harris's $60 a year was not much for someone who had changed churches for financial reasons. In fact a cook in Monrovia would receive three times as much, besides rations. One suspects that the bishop may have appointed Harris for lack of someone with better qualifications, and wanted to see how he would get on.[49]

In any event, he had pleasant working conditions, with his brother-in-law as headmaster. The work appeared to be advancing, despite set-backs caused by the war. Harris had charge of a Sunday School in an outlying village, as well as teaching in the day school.[50] There were coffee trees at Spring Hill, and the assistant schoolmaster supervised the schoolboys who cared for them.[51]

In 1895 the Liberian deacon in charge retired, and his replacement was a Glebo deacon, Rev. O.E.H. Shannon, who himself came from the Graway area.[52] His father had been a prominent elder of Glogbale, and was buried at Tule Rock.[53] Now he was a Christian minister among his own people; the former village *bodio* was in his congregation, and one of his teachers was Harris, also a native of the area. In Shannon's Annual Report of 1894–95 he mentioned the "promising

---

[45] ECHS Archives: Ferguson to Langford, 16 May 1892,

[46] Annual Report, BMPEC, 1891–92, 159.

[47] For comparison, in the acts of the 1908–09 legislature, the vice-president of Liberia was attributed a salary of $1,200 a year; a member of the legislature received $800 a year. At that same time the president of Liberia College received a salary of $1,500 a year.

[48] *Cf* note 45 above.

[49] Annual Report, BMPEC 1892–93, 166: "There are vacancies in the mission at this moment that cannot be filled for lack of competent men. I will warrant that by the blessing of God in a few years there will be no lack of qualified men for such positions. Without such provisions for training men, the Church will have to bear the disgrace of an unlearned priesthood, and the Mission that of commissioning ignorant catechists and teachers."

[50] *Ibid.*, 111.

[51] Annual Report, BMPEC, 1983–94, 119.

[52] Annual Report, BMPEC, 1894–95, 191.

[53] S. Jangaba M. Johnson, *The traditional history. . . .* , Monrovia: The Bureau of Folklore 1963, 84.

Christian community at Half Graway made up of some forty pupils
of the school and the families of the pastor and teachers."[54] Harris's
own family was increased that year (1895) by the arrival of a son,
John.

At that time there was no building for worship in the Graway-
Spring Hill area. Meetings were held outside, in fine weather, or in
a room of Nathaniel Farr's home.[55] In early 1897 the bishop planned
a chapel for Half-Graway, and a spot was chosen with Harris's
participation mid-way between the two native villages. During that
same visit the bishop also confirmed eleven young people, and forty
communicants participated in the celebration of Holy Communion.[56]
The Half-Graway station was starting to show growth.

The chapel, completed in 1897, was called the Wolfe Memorial
Chapel, after an American donor; the chief of Whole Graway
subsequently also asked for a *Nyesoa a kai*[57] (house of God) to be built
in his village.

Even with these and other advances, there were only forty-six
communicants in 1898,[58] including the families of the staff. Wolfe
Chapel was in 1898 the site of the annual convocation.[59] At the end
of 1897 Harris had been licensed as a lay reader for Graway Station,
with Nathanael Farr as the lay reader for Wolfe Chapel.[60] A lay reader,
as well as being a good reader, needed to be familiar with the Prayer
Book and able to select the readings and prayers for the church year.
Growth of the work and a shortage of clergy made it necessary for
the bishop to use lay readers in some numbers.[61] The ordained minister,
Shannon, had to return to Hoffman when the priest there died, and
could only come to Half-Graway for a monthly communion. So Farr
and his colleagues—including Harris—led and preached at most of
the services.

Shannon's report in 1899 was not encouraging. He himself had
been ill, and the affairs of Half Graway were in a state "of spiritual

---

[54] Annual Report, BMPEC, 1894–95, 195.
[55] ECHS Archives: O.E.H. Shannon, written report of 9 July 1895.
[56] ECHS Archives: Ferguson (Monrovia) to Langford, 27 February 1897.
[57] The language was that used to speak of the Creator God, and *kai* was the
word used to describe the house of the *bodio*, the famous "greegree house" in missionary
language.
[58] Annual Report, BMPEC, 1897–98, 202.
[59] *Ibid.*, 231.
[60] *Ibid.*, 235.
[61] *Ibid.*

torpitude" [sic]. The local King "had brought demon worship" back into the town, and there was also "political partizanship". Shannon and others were preaching "of the wrath of God" and calling them to repentance, and they had seen some change in their attitudes.[62] Harris was as a lay reader involved in this work and style of ministry.

c. Parallel Thought Currents

During the decade of Episcopal expansion, in which Harris was involved, there were signs that the traditional foreign mission organisations and their work were not fully satisfactory.[63] One of the leading Glebo Episcopalian priests, S.W. Seton, set up an independent church in Cape Palmas in 1887. This was but part of a larger tendency, articulated by the educator-statesman-thinker, Edward W. Blyden.[64] Both men were working within a yet larger pattern of cultural conflict.

i. Cultural conflict between Glebo and Liberians

The Liberian president who took over in 1904 claimed that past difficulties in the Glebo area had been cleared up, with the "Christian natives" enjoying the right of suffrage, and peace and lack of conflict between the various tribal groups.[65] But the cultural conflict between the two major communities, for many years the country's major problem,[66] was ignored by him.

The Episcopal Church had worked diligently at a policy of inte-

---

[62] *Journal of the fifth general convocation of February 1899.* Cape Palmas, 1900, 67f.

[63] See Martin, *op. cit.,* 314ff. E.g., already in 1878 there was an attempted Union Christian Convention in favour of one general body. Again, in 1887 J.W. Howard was working at a Home Missionary Society in view of "the great African church of the future." The openness to "Russellism" was due to this same current.

[64] The principal sources for understanding Blyden are: Blyden, Edward W., *Christianity, Islam and the Negro race.* Reprinted, Edinburgh: Edinburgh University Press 1967 (1st ed., London, 1887); Holden, Edith, *Blyden of Liberia.* New York: Vantage Press 1966; Lynch, Hollis R., *Black spokesman.* London: Frank Cass 1971. The introduction, pp. xi–xxxvi, constitutes the best brief summary of the man's life and work. Details are then to be found in Lynch, Hollis R., *Edward Wilmot Blyden, Pan-Negro patriot, 1832–1912.* London: OUP 1967. His educational work is discussed in Livingstone, Thomas W., *Education and race: a biography of Edward Wilmot Blyden.* San Francisco: Glendessary Press 1975. A bibliography of the primary sources is to be found in both Holden and Lynch 1967. A collection of some primary sources is in Holden, and Lynch 1967, and in Lynch, Hollis R. (ed.), *Selected letters of Edward Wilmot Blyden.* Millwood, N.J.: KTO Press 1978.

[65] *Inaugural address of his excellency, Arthur Barclay.* Monrovia: Phillips and Government Printing Office, 1904, 11.

[66] George W. Brown, *An economic history of Liberia.* Washington D.C.: Associated Publishers Inc., 1941, cited in Hannah Jones, *op. cit.,* 20f.

gration, especially under Bishop Ferguson, but despite signs of hope
the barriers were still there. "Native converts", although present at
worship services in larger towns, occupied a separate section;[67] colonist
ladies condescended to visit in the native quarters, but their patronising
attitudes showed "so much contempt" for the people "that they do
little good".[68]

Such was the situation inside the church; outside there were
conditions which were very much worse. Americo-Liberians treated
the Africans "as if they had no rights worthy of respect".[69] As late
as 1909 a mission employee (a Liberian himself) complained of the
arrogance with which the Africans were treated.[70] He also spoke of
the faults of the Africans, especially in relation to granting land rights;[71]
but it was the immigrant who had introduced the conflict. During
the forty years previous to Dunbar's statement, the indigenous people
had found a spokesman in Edward W. Blyden.

ii. "Blydenism"

Edward Blyden arrived in Liberia as a colonist in 1851, when he
was nineteen. He was editor of the *Liberian Herald* 1855–56, ordained
as a Presbyterian minister in 1858, and worked in secondary and
higher education from 1858. At the same time he was active in politics,
unsuccessfully running for the presidency in 1885. He was praised
and blamed; scorned and accepted; at times he had to take refuge
in Sierra Leone. He went to Lagos for a brief time; he took refuge
in Cape Palmas in 1882 and 1886;[72] in 1901 he went to Sierra Leone
as director of Islamic education.

Much of the conflict in his educational and political career sprang
from the fact that, although himself a colonist, he was on the side
of the indigenous people in most of the differences that arose. He
supported polygamy; he was dissatisfied with the cultural impact of
Western Christian missions on the African population; he was sympathetic to Islam. As early as 1875 his critique of the Christian missions
was based on his perception of their hostility to African cultural

---

[67] Mary B. Merriam, *Home life in Africa*. Boston: A. Williams 1868, 113.

[68] *Ibid.*, 166.

[69] Hannah Jones, *op. cit.*, 152ff.

[70] J. Fulton Dunbar, *Liberia, a commonwealth of a peculiar character*. Liberia [Harper]
1909, 26f.; cited in Hannah Jones, *op. cit.*, 154f.

[71] *Ibid.*

[72] See Thomas Livingstone, cited in note 64 above, pp. 129 and 145. Also Hollis
Lynch, 1967, pp. 158 and 165.

expressions. He saw Islam as respecting indigenous values more than Christianity, and although he believed that "paganism and devil-worship" would eventually die out, he felt they could be best replaced by an Islam-like Christianity. Moreover, he saw the African himself as the agent of change, rather than the young Western missionary. For him, such men "regarded everything with contempt" for being so un-European, and preached a crusade against harmless customs, striving to replace them with inappropriate European practices. The result was that "we as a people, think more of everything that is foreign, and less of that which is purely native; have lost our self-respect and love for our own race, are become a sort of nondescript people . . ."[73]

This was written in 1876; similar ideas were given wide circulation through Blyden's *magnum opus* of 1887, *Christianity, Islam and the Negro race*. During the 1875–76 war he had been outspokenly in favour of the indigenous peoples; he had no sympathy for the mulattoes in power who were intent on imposing American cultural and legal patterns. When he resigned from the Presbyterian ministry in 1887 he defended himself: "I have not left Christ . . . once a minister always a minister."[74] With Islam as a model, and African custom as a background, he felt the need to build respect for the polygamous family, and wished to see a United West African Church which could establish its own disciplines without Western pressures. In Lagos in the 1890s his influence upon ecclesiastical independency was for a short while very strong.[75] But in Liberia as well his ideas were gaining ground, and he did not hide his enthusiasm for Seton's independent congregation at Cape Palmas in 1887.

iii. "Russellism": an influence in religio-cultural synthesis
Samuel W. Seton was a part of the first wave of Glebo Christian leaders.[76] Converted in 1856, he had been ordained at the same time

---

[73] In Edward W. Blyden, *Christianity* . . . , 1887, 63. The text was first published in *Fraser's Magazine*, October 1876, in an article entitled "Christian missions in West Africa."
[74] Cited in Holden, *op. cit.*, 1978, 581, from letter of Blyden to Coppinger, 13 April 1887.
[75] He defended the idea in Lagos in January 1891 ; "Proposals for a West African church" was published in London in 1891 as *The return of the exiles and the West African church*. Extracts are to be found in Hollis R. Lynch, *Black spokesman, op. cit.*, 191–194. Blyden's role in the provocation of church "independency" among African Christians in 1890–91 is discussed in James Bertin Webster, *The African churches among the Yoruba, 1888–1922*. Oxford: the Clarendon Press 1964.
[76] An excellent study of Seton has been made by Jane J. Martin: "Samuel

as Ferguson, in 1865, priested in 1868, and was put in charge of Hoffman Station. After his wife's death his personal life was subjected to criticism, and he was suspended from his work in 1878. He was a prime mover in the 1873–76 "G'debo Reunited Kingdom" and while he continued to be active in the Episcopalian Church he also carried on numerous political involvements. In early 1887 he was the first Glebo elected to the national legislature.

Later in the same year he vociferously withdrew from the Episcopal Church and created his own church, called "The African Evangelical Church of Christ". The church authorised polygamy. But it also became a distribution point for printed matter coming from the United Sates, and the new "Russellite" movement, later to become better known as Jehovah's Witnesses. When Seton wrote to Bishop Ferguson to sever his connections with the Episcopal Church, his long letter was obviously influenced by Russelite material, though doubtless many of their criticisms of "Babylonian confusion" coincided with his own. He wrote, "I dare remain no longer to dapple with you in the human teachings, . . . I have already united myself with the Church of Christ . . . I shall endeavour to win you all to Christ and into his Church.[77]

Bishop Ferguson was quick to react. He soon had a tract, *A warning!* printed for wide distribution.[78] Edward Blyden and Seton had known one another for some time, and Blyden's reaction was, needless to say, very different to Bishop Ferguson's. He wrote to a friend a month later, stressing the mistake which had been made in appointing "a mulatto" as bishop. He regarded the common opposition of the mulatto to emigration as "providential", and asked the secretary of the American Colonization Society not to try and counter it.[79] For Blyden, the racial-cultural issue was enough in itself to justify the creation of an independent church. Blyden's close relationship with Seton added the other racial argument to the biblical and ecclesiastical ones Seton had already used to the bishop.

Seton quite clearly derived his arguments from Russellite literature. He was the Maryland agent of the American Colonization Society,

W. Seton, Liberian citizen." Indiana University, Bloomington, Indiana: second annual conference on social science work in Liberia, 1–2 May 1970, unpublished paper, 28pp.

[77] ACS Archives, No. 109583–4: Seton to Ferguson, 1 September 1887 (MS Division, Library of Congress, Washington D.C.).

[78] ACS Archives, No. 109595.

[79] ACS Archives, No. 109611: Blyden (Sierra Leone) to Coppinger, 3 October 1887, p. 4.

and in writing to the Monrovian agent, C.T.O. King, he mentioned the paper, *Zion Watch Tower*, and sent King a copy.[80] Charles Taze Russell had only founded his movement in 1884, as the Watch Tower Bible and Tract Society, though *Zion's Watch Tower* had been begun in 1879. Speculation about the coming of Christ and of his kingdom was central to the teachings. A rejection of institutional Christianity was emphasised. Those who gathered together to study the Bible in its purity would constitute an "Elijah-people" to announce the imminent coming of Christ on earth, starting in 1914.[81]

During 1887 Seton was in correspondence with Russell, who reported the founding of the new Liberian church in *Zion's Watch Tower* (henceforth *ZWT*) of December 1887. Russell sent Seton a number of his publications, and gave news about the Liberian work in later numbers of *ZWT*,[82] which Seton shared with King in Monrovia.

But Seton was also closely in touch with influential local people, who met with him to discuss the organisation of the "Ecclesia" as set out in the *ZWT*. There was weekly Bible reading, and preaching at several different places. "I believe we have the presence of the Lord with us."[83]

Seton was not the only Liberian leader to show that he was influenced by Blyden and found Russell's teaching attractive. A Baptist minister, Robert Richardson, who later became president of Liberia College and an associate justice of the Supreme Court was writing in not very dissimilar terms to Coppinger (the American-based secretary of the American Colonization Society) in early 1888. He quotes an article from *ZWT* and like Seton attacks the institutional church and Western imperialism, calling for a return to the Bible for the "pure, unadulterated word of God".[84]

In Seton's personal history, we see that he was first a committed Episcopalian Christian, and then a dedicated politician. After the defeat of the "G'debo Reunited Kingdom", he continued to work for a united

---

[80] ACS Archives: S.W. Seton to Hon. C.T.O. King, 30 September 1887.

[81] A good résumé of Russell's early career and thought is found in Alan Rogerson, *Millions now living will never die*. London: Constable & Co., 1969. However for full understanding it is necessary to read the literature of Russell written in the 1880s and 1890s.

[82] Cited on p. 12 in Sholto Cross, *The Watch Tower Movement in South Central Africa 1908–1945*. Oxford University, Ph.D. thesis 1973. We have not been able to locate a copy of January 1888 *ZWT*.

[83] *ZWT*, 9 (6), February 1888, 7f.

[84] ACS Archives: R.B. Richardson to Coppinger, 17 February 1888.

Liberia, but found himself fully at home neither in Liberian society
nor in Glebo society. "We are like the bats—we are neither beasts
or birds," wrote the civilised Glebo of Cavalla in 1885.[85] For men
struggling in such a situation the simple and forceful interpretation
of the Scriptures by Russell, and the appeal of the holistic theocratic
kingdom, was very great.

The Episcopalians took the challenge of the Russellites seriously.
In July 1888 Bishop Ferguson organised a conference of Baptists,
Methodists and Episcopalians at Harper, attended by over forty
representatives. They drew up a four-page printed document entitled
A Letter to the Churches. To all the Christian Churches of Liberia.[86] It was
printed and distributed because the delegates expected a deluge of
Russell's tracts and publications within the country. They listed a
number of doctrinal errors, including teaching about death, heaven,
and final judgement, and also specifically noted the false teaching that
"polygamy is no barrier to Christian baptism."[87] Bishop Ferguson's
views were reflected in the document, where it stated:

> This is the greatest danger that has ever threatened Liberia. War and
> pestilence and famine bear no comparison to it; they but kill the body
> while this ruins immortal souls; not only of the present generation, but
> the evil will descend to generations yet unborn.

Shannon, Gibson and Farr from Half Graway were all at the meeting,
which took place in the very year that Harris was confirmed. At that
time Seton's teaching would have had little relevance to Harris, who
was in the position of Seton thirty years earlier. In another twenty-
five years, however, Harris was to be troubled by similar disillusionment,
but his response was rather different.

In late 1888 Zion's Watch Tower reported both the meeting, and
progress in Seton's church. There were over fifty regular subscribers
to the magazine in the country.[88]

---

[85] Cited by Martin, p. 209, from Memorandum to Special Committee, 17 September
1885, in ACS Archives. Also from J. Martin, *op. cit.*, note 76 above, "He was not
considered a social equal by the Americo-Liberians at Cape Palmas, where Western-
dressed Glebo had sometimes been referred to openly as 'native dogs', and no Americo-
Liberian ever asked educated Glebo, 'not even Rev. Seton' to dinner, according
to one observer." (p. 5)

[86] *A letter to the churches.* Cape Palmas, 28 July 1888, in ECHS archives.

[87] *Ibid.*, 2.

[88] *ZWT*, 10 (4), October 1888, "The cause in Africa", 1f.

Bishop Ferguson was not pleased, and sent a copy of the article to Langford, General Secretary of his mission board, in a letter dated 8 November 1888.[89] He felt that Seton's claims were exaggerated, but was still anxious about the situation.

> The circulation of Russell's book and papers is enormous. Every mail brings them, and they are in most cases, given gratuitously. Now the majority of our people attach great weight to what comes in print from the mother country.[90]

Seton, on the other hand, was seeking support for his independent church through North American contacts, some of whom came through Dr. Blyden. We find him, for instance, in correspondence with a Rev. John Miller of New Jersey, whose church was also named "The African Evangelical Church of Christ".[91]

It has been necessary to show the existence of this stream of thought, which provided an alternative for Seton. He had rejected his traditional African ("heathen") past; he could no longer go along with the missionary and Evangelical thought of the time in Liberia. Edward Blyden, and the apocalyptic kingdom teaching of Russell provided a viable alternative, though it is probable that neither Blyden nor Seton fully accepted all Russell's teachings. Seton remained active in Liberian politics, and became Commissioner of Education and later a judge in Maryland County, offices he was still holding when he died in 1908.

His congregation maintained its existence at least until the late 1890s. It was even claimed that the future president of Liberia, William Tubman, remembered such a Bible Class in Harper when "just a boy". But independent of a church congregation, the literature with which the country was "deluged" would have taken aspects of Russellite teaching to a wide range of people, especially in a country where literacy was equated with elitism, and where the written word was closely associated with the source of power. In the report made by N. Farr on the work of Spring Hill Mission, in June 1900, he lists "Russell's Church" as "another organization" in his field.[92] and W.W.

---

[89] ECHS Archives: Ferguson to Langford, 8 November 1888.
[90] *Ibid.*
[91] S.W. Seton to Rev. John Miller, 1 February 1889. In John Miller Collection, Princeton University Library.
[92] Nathaniel H. Farr, Annual Report, June 30, 1900. RG-72-C-87 (ECHS Archives).

Harris as one of his teachers. It is thus more than likely that Harris
was studying Russellite literature by the end of the century. In his
1914 narrative to Father Hartz, the prophet described his pre-prophetic
period.

> Wesleyan teacher and preacher in the minister's absence, I now prepare
> myself for my prophetic role by prayer, and by reading and study of
> the Bible. The Angel teaches me about the times of the future: the
> actions of Gog and Magog, the wiles of the great dragon . . . which
> will be bound for a thousand years.[93]

The themes Harris reports, although taken from Revelation 20, were
also important themes in the dispensational patterns taught in the
literature distributed by Russell. Indeed, he seems clearly to have been
concerned about those very themes at the time when Russell's influence
was still strong in the immediate area.

---

[93] G. van Bulck, "Le prophète Harris vu par lui-même (Côte d'Ivoire 1914)" in
Museum Lessianum, *Devant les sectes non-chrétiennes*. Louvain: Desclée de Brouwer n.d.
[1962], 121.

CHAPTER FOUR

PREPROPHETIC ADULTHOOD, II: 1899–1910

1. In The Service of Two Masters

In 1899 Harris was still carrying on a double ministry; he was day-school teacher at Half Graway school and was also a lay reader in the church.. This involved leading regular services using the *Book of Common Prayer.* The layreader had to be able to follow the official "Table of Readings" from both the Old and New Testaments. A small chapel had been built "for the heathen" across the lake from the mission house—"a rough structure".[1] But he was still receiving only $5 a month as a mission employee. A letter of protest sent about the bishop in December 1899 reveals that this situation was clearly the bishop's own decision. The letter, from local agents of the mission to the Board of Managers of the Episcopal Board of Missions in response to a circular about "misdirected monies", complained that as clergy and lay workers they had never had any access to church monies to "misdirect, nor were they consulted in the use of funds."[2] The letter, written by the Rev. E. Shannon, was signed by twenty local agents, including "Wm. Wadé Harris". He was thus obviously recognised as part of the "clergy men and lay workers of the mission".

Harris had by then worked for seven years at the mission, gaining much experience even if not well-paid. His work had included the teaching of carpentry and building skills, and of brickmaking.[3]

In addition, connections made through his work had led to a further job. At some time in 1899 he had become the official interpreter of Maryland County. For this position he received $200 a year.[4] He was recommended for the job by "King" Bulu of the "Graway tribe",[5]

---

[1] Annual Report, BMPEC 1899, 161.
[2] ECHS Archives, Shannon *et al* to Board of Managers, 2 Dec. 1899.
[3] Annual Report BMPEC 1899, 194.
[4] *BN*, 24. We know from other sources that Harris was interpreter but did not know when he had begun.
[5] See the record of his trial, to be found in *Records of the Court of Quarterly Sessions*

and he saw his role as that of a middle man between the Glebo population and local Liberian authorities "to settle matters." It was a political function, and his salary came from the Liberian central government. Since in his mission work he earned only $60 a year, his government work doubtless took priority.

In his 1901 Annual Report, Shannon listed N. Farr and P.B.N. Seton as lay readers, and W.W. Harris as rendering efficient help[6] as "teacher of day school amongst the heathen."[7] In that year there had been no new adult members in the church, although six infants had been baptised. These doubtless included the Harrises' youngest daughter Ella, who was born that year. Harris, now forty, had six children, the oldest of whom was fifteen. There were now fifty "native communicants" for the Graway district. Shannon was now living on the Spring Hill station, where he was building his own house. He used the Montgomery Ward catalogue to order American furniture and materials for his house;[8] he also ordered numerous books from America.[9] Cultural models were all from overseas.

In 1897 the bishop had moved his headquarters from Harper to Monrovia, and his attention was increasingly given to development of the mission outside of Maryland County. His perspective on local happenings inevitably changed, and the numerous local conflicts seemed no longer acceptable.[10] His visits were now rare, and his authority mediated through local superintendents. For Graway District this was through the Glebo, Shannon.

In 1901, on 14 July, Rose Harris's brother Nathaniel Farr died. It was a serious blow, as he had been in charge of the boarding school and was one of the mission's "most efficient workers".[11] It was difficult to replace him; several different substitutes were appointed.[12] The work in general was discouraging; there were no new members in 1901, and the "heathen" were said to have lapsed into practices they had

---

and Common Pleas, Maryland County, Book 187, 1907–1909, from pages 186–232. A transcript is to be found in Volume III of the dissertation filed at the University of Aberdeen, pp. 882–904.

  [6] ECHS Archives: Shannon, Annual Report, 1901.
  [7] ECHS Archives: Shannon, 30 June 1901, "Graway District".
  [8] ECHS Archives: Shannon to Kimber, 11 Dec 1899; 26 June 1900; 3 May 1901; 28 Oct 1901.
  [9] ECHS Archives: Shannon to Kimber, 5 June 1899.
  [10] Annual Report, BMPEC 1901, 219.
  [11] *Ibid.*
  [12] Annual Report BMPEC 1902, 185.

once given up.[13] Shannon's health was very poor. It was a low point in the Graway District.

Shannon's report in February 1903 bears out the gloomy picture. He reports Farr's death, and names his replacement at the time of writing—T.K. Hammond. He mentions those who were helping him in the pastoral work, and, to our specific concern, omits the name of W.W. Harris. He notes that the Sunday School "does not show the life in it that is desired". Two adults were recorded as baptized, and two as confirmed, since the preceding report.[14] Just before Farr's death Shannon had commended Harris's "efficient help in the work", and so the omission of his name now is the more surprising.

Harris must have expected promotion to replace his brother-in-law, but two outsiders, J. Russell and then Hammond, were brought in. In the pastoral work Shannon's son, an ordinand, was also used. But shortly after the report was written, in March 1903, Hammond was transferred elsewhere and "Mr. W. Wadé Harris . . . succeeded him". Farr's widow was appointed assistant teacher, to replace Harris.[15]

During 1903 Shannon had been to Lagos on sick leave and "[t]hough not quite restored he returned much improved in health."[16] While he was away other staff, who had in any case been taking on most of the responsibilities, were of course left to run things at Spring Hill mission. The Harris-Farr families seem to have used the situation to "take over" from the outsiders, and the bishop's decision to promote Harris may not have been with the local superintendent's approval.

Be that as it may, Harris was now "Master of the Boarding School" and next in authority, among the Episcopalians, to Shannon, the only local ordained man. His salary was $200 a year, and Farr's widow as assistant teacher received $60.[17] Harris's salary was less than the $300 which Farr had received; his educational qualifications were lower.

Day schools, as set up in the villages, had the continual problem of irregularity when scholars were kept out of school to help on the farms. A boarding school avoided this difficulty. Practical trades were taught, and the "usual exercises" included Bible history, reading,

---

[13] *Ibid.*

[14] *Journal of the seventh general convocation . . . February 1903.* Cape Palmas: Mission Printing Press, 1904, 61f.

[15] Annual Report BMPEC 1903, 202f.

[16] *Ibid.*

[17] ECHS Archives: Ferguson's budget for 1903–04.

writing, arithmetic, and singing.[18] It seems that by the time Harris took on the Master's role, teaching in the Grebo language had been removed from the curriculum. Harris later denied he had ever taught "that way of writing",[19] and another report claimed that Bishop Ferguson and the government had forbidden it.[20] This may have happened during the Cavallan rebellion. The Spring Hill school was a preparatory school for Cuttington College, and Harris's own sons, who later went to Cuttington, were taught by their father there.[21]

Harris was now "second in authority" in the local Episcopalian Church, and official government interpreter for the Graway people. In relation to both church and state—the structures of the modern sector—he had achieved a good deal. But if we look at the path he had taken, we find a complex trail. He had left his Methodist origins, admitting himself that it was "for money". After his confirmation he improved his qualifications with extra education, apparently encouraged by the bishop.[22] But it was four years before he was hired as an assistant teacher at a very low salary, and for nine years his position did not change, although he took on extra unpaid work for the church. Even when Farr died he was not at first considered for the vacant position. It would seem that, in 1888, in 1892, and again in 1903, the bishop did not consider his formal qualifications sufficient for the work required. But he had other qualities and, in 1903, grass-roots support from the local population.

a. Conflict with ecclesiatical authority, 1904–1905

With the bishop now in Monrovia, and Shannon still ailing, Harris, now older and the father of six, found himself with more and more responsibility. This situation led him into conflict with ecclesiastical authority, which lasted for a year. The bishop was a strict disciplinarian, and consistent in this, even when (with the rebellion of older students) it resulted in their loss to the church.[23]

The reports from both Shannon and Bishop Ferguson are discreet

---

[18] Annual Report BMPEC, 1888–89, 37.
[19] *BN* II, 6.
[20] *BN* I, 18.
[21] Conversation at Harper, April 1978, with Mr. Edward Brookes, fellow student with Harris's son Edward at Cuttington College.
[22] The question of where is not resolved, since Harris also told Benoît, "I never went to school here [Cape Palmas], nor in Cavalla, nor in Cuttington." *BN* II, 14.
[23] Cason, *The growth of Christianity in the Liberian environment*, 1975, 273ff.

and guarded, but they reveal the same situation. "Satan has been unusually active" and two church employees had "fallen into his snares." One was S.B.K. Clarck, in charge of the Whole Graway station, who was suspended; "Mr. W. Wadé Harris . . . has also been guilty of improper conduct" though not to the same extent. He was suspended conditionally.[24]

Later Shannon reported the temporary closure of the boarding school, and the appointment of his son, now ordained, to help with the evangelistic work but finding it impossible to carry on because of the "recent troubles".[25]

In July of the same year Bishop Ferguson wrote that Clarck had been restored to the work and that "Mr. W. Wadé Harris has resumed his charge at Half-Graway." But the deacon, Rev. Edward Shannon, "has left without leave or notice, and his whereabouts are not known."[26]

Unfortunately we do not have access to the bishop's diaries, which might help us to illuminate this situation. But from what we know, and from incidents occurring in other parts of Liberia at the same time, it is clear that local political conflict and apostasy from the "civilised world" was the activity of Satan referred to. During a time of such distance from Liberian authority, traditional and non-Christian customs like the *sassy-wood* trial, witchcraft, and consulting traditional healers tended to be resumed by those who had dropped them. This is documented for Bigtown, the Nyomowe "capital", in 1903.[27] Political initiatives, including a proposed *coup d'état*, were taking place at the same time.[28] But with the deposition of the chief, there was also a return to the church. Fetishes and charms were burned while the *Gloria in Excelsis* was being sung.[29]

The bishop had in his report of 1904 quoted with approval from the inaugural address of President Barclay, made in January 1904. Barclay saw the church "as the balance wheel of the civilised world". Every convert was also a political recruit. He spoke appreciatively of the educational and religious work of the Protestant Episcopal

---

[24] Annual Report BMPEC 1904, 251.

[25] *Journal of the eighth convocation . . . February 1905* p. 69. Report of Graway District. Courtesy of Bishop Browne of the Liberian Episcopal Church.

[26] *Twentieth annual report to the Board of Missions.* Cape Palmas: P.E. Mission Printing Press, 1906, 29f. Courtesy of New York Public Library.

[27] Annual Report BMPEC 1903–04, 201.

[28] Wallis to Foreign Office, 16 April 1903. F.O. 47/38, cited by Haliburton, *PH*, 23.

[29] *Op. cit.,* note 26 above, p. 27.

Mission, and its enormous political usefulness, specifically in Maryland County. "The Republic has no more loyal and devoted citizens than among the Christian Greboes of the county of Maryland, and we must thank the Episcopal Mission for it".[30]

So, after Harris had been headmaster of the boarding school for only a year, he too went through this period of religious and political "lapse". Liberian loyalty required for religious reasons was totally opposed to Glebo political interests. There is evidence to show that while Harris was in difficulty with his church superiors, he was supported by local chiefs. At the time that Ferguson had been appointed in 1885 Blyden had forseen his probable future stance, and the warning now was being fulfilled. Ferguson supported Liberian central authority. Harris did not give in quickly, despite his suspension. But in 1905 there was a shift in political loyalties with a new king more in favour of Christianity and civilization. It was at that point that the Graway leaders were reconciled with their ecclesiastical superiors.

President Barclay, who was married to a Glebo woman, had in 1904–05 led the legislature in setting up a system of indirect rule for the administration of the interior. This made it possible for the local Glebo king to support the central Liberian authority without abandoning his own prerogatives. Harris likewise could at this time come to terms with the religious and political authorities without abandoning his loyalty to Glebo concerns. At this time his political concerns seem to have taken priority over his religious interests. He was launched on a new role as part of the second wave of "civilized" Glebo.[31] His problem was similar to that of Seton, who had however greater educational advantages. But both of them saw clearly the dichotomy created when one feels the injustice to one's people of a regime which one is expected to support simply as a result of shared Christianity and civilization. Although Harris's official position in the civil government was that of interpreter, he could not abandon his own kinfolk, even though as a "civilized" Christian he no longer fully shared their life and beliefs.

Indeed his role as interpreter had thrust him into the mainstream of Liberian politics at a local level. It is important to see this in context.

---

[30] Annual Report, BMPEC, 1903–04, 243.

[31] Harris, restored to a relationship with the mission, on 26 August 1905 ordered from Montgomery Ward a dozen and a half wooden chairs, two ladies' rockers, a hand sewing machine and soap. The payment was to be taken from his next quarter's allowance.

Bishop Ferguson had, at the elections of 1895 and 1899, been concerned about corruption and distortion. Such corruption involved not only "heathen" and "unconverted" Americo-Liberians, but also Christians, including ordained ministers. The clergy were being sought after as political candidates, and one man, G.W. Gibson, an Episcopal clergyman, became in 1896 Secretary of State and later president of the Republic. The bishop wrote of election frauds, bribery, and disregard of moral constraints,[32] and the dangers for clergymen and layworkers, specifically in Maryland County.[33] 1899 was the year when Harris was appointed interpreter; during the election campaign that year Hoffman station was partially destroyed.

In 1901 the bishop again issued a pastoral letter speaking of the "election evils" accompanying the national biennial elections.[34] At this time more and more high officials, including President Coleman, a number of judges, senior army officers, and members of the ruling party, were Episcopalians. In 1903 two catechist/teachers were elected to the national legislature and had to resign their mission posts.[35] The Episcopalian Church was becoming more and more identified with the Liberian political establishment.

In his annual report of 1905 the bishop summarized his ideal position—not much different from the vision he had had when first consecrated in 1885. He saw a nation where government and mission harmonized, and in which the aborigines were incorporated into the body politic. Mission and government would each succeed best as they sought to support and strengthen the other.[36] After twenty years his vision was becoming a reality.

Problems remained. In 1901 the government had passed laxer legislation on divorce, and on this question the bishop would not compromise.[37] In 1907 a bill was passed reverting to a stricter position, due mainly to the bishop's influence.[38] Another ongoing evil, that of the liquor traffic, continued, and the legislative assembly asked for the bishop's help in fighting this also.[39]

---

[32] Annual Report BMPEC 1894–95, 190.
[33] Annual Report BMPEC 1898–99, 191.
[34] Annual Report BMPEC 1900–01, 219.
[35] Annual Report BMPEC 1902–03, 202.
[36] *Op. cit.*, note 26 above, p. 7.
[37] Annual Report BMPEC 1902–03, 200.
[38] *Journal of the ninth convocation ... February 1907*, 18.
[39] *Ibid.*, 44.

On these questions of divorce and the liquor traffic the bishop was unbending, but he was prepared to compromise when violence was required for putting down rebellion, even of his own members. In fact he encouraged his members to participate by armed intervention, as in the Cavalla affair, even against government directions. In 1887 he had stated his unswerving conviction that "heathen minds that cannot be affected by moral suasion must needs be brought under subjection by physical force."[40] In this he was no different from most other Western colonisers, even Christian ones, of his time. His son, in Lagos in 1914, justified Liberian action against the indigenous population in a similar way, claiming that the settlers were only "doing evil that good may come". For him, the good was evident all over Liberia where the aborigines of the country were "benefitting by the introduction of Western civilization."[41]

It was into a religious institution with this political orientation that Harris had taken work, in 1892. On the one hand he faced a hoped-for holistic harmony of religion and politics, with a militant Western Christianity and civilization supported by American gun-boats. On the other hand, Harris was identifying more and more with his own people and their concerns. And outside Liberia other nations were considering what actions they should take in her time of growing chaos and anarchy.[42]

There was considerable pro-British sympathy within the country, and as early as 1888 President Coleman had even envisioned an Anglo-American protectorate. The French, with their neighbouring colony, were in the late 1890s contemplating a take-over. Their vice-consul in Liberia, Delafosse, saw both Germany and Britain as ready to

---

[40] Cited in Martin, *The dual legacy: government authority and mission influence among the Glebo of Eastern Liberia, 1834–1910*, 1968, 294, from Ferguson to Langford, 20 January 1887. ECHS Archives.

[41] A report on a lecture, 6 November 1914, at Breadfruit Schoolroom, in the *Lagos Standard* of 25 November 1914. The lecture by young Ferguson "cleared up" misundertandings for the Christians at Lagos. "We must confess that before this lecture the unfortunate Gribbo war [sic] was one that presented the Liberian settlers in a very bad light to the civilised world. We were once again led to believe that this was one of undue agression but the lecturer . . . has aquitted Liberia of a once popular misapprehension that the Liberian settlers were Liberia's greatest enemy and the stumbling block to the country's progress."

[42] French National Archives, 200 Mi 629 (7 F47): Ponty to Baret. 17 June 1909: "L'état d'anarchie de la République Noire que vous avez pu constater pendant la durée de vos fonctions de Vice Consul s'est perpétré les années suivantes [1905–08]. La situation intérieure continue à être déplorable."

intervene, and thought that France should get in first.[43] In 1902 the vice-consul of France wrote of how he saw the Republic becoming, "little by little", a sort of English protectorate.[44] Earlier we have reported the 1903 offer to the British Consul of a *coup d'état* in favour of the colonial office.

In 1905, at the time of boundary negotiations with France, the diplomatic plenipotentiary for Liberia was Dr. Edward Blyden. He himself favoured an Anglo-French protectorate, as a foundation for financial security and as a defence against a threatened German takeover. He had stated, in a speech in London in 1905, "Liberia is a British colony in everything but the flag."[45] This was in clear opposition to the views of Bishop Ferguson.

Blyden's differences with Ferguson were not merely political; they held deeply divergent views over questions of the religious and social identity of Liberia. Blyden, at this time, gave at the request of leaders in Monrovia a lecture in which he attempted to indicate his vision of Liberia's mission. It was not a conventional Western Christian view. The head of the new Roman Catholic mission in Liberia summarized Blyden's ideas and influence at that time. Blyden propounded the idea that we—Africans—needed a "religion of our own—an African religion." From Islam, from traditional indigenous religions, with the essential of Christianity, "let us make our own religion."[46]

The Catholic writer went on to report that he had seen the effects of these ideas—straying, he called it—in national public and private life over two years. He dated a rejection of them to a "National Sermon" given by Bishop Ferguson in July 1908. But of course not all who had accepted these ideas necessarily rejected them as result of the bishop's "National Sermon". For Harris, who had been in trouble with the bishop in 1904–05, Blyden's views clearly represented another option.

We have independent evidence that Blyden's religious ideas continued to be influential in Liberian elite circles, in an anonymous typed letter dated May 1908 and sent from Monrovia to the General Secretary of the Episcopalian Mission in the United States. It commented upon

---

[43] FNA 200 Mi 1642 (7 F87).

[44] FNA 200 Mi 1642: Delafosse to Governor of French West Africa, 2 January 1899.

[45] Edward Blyden, *West Africa before Europe*. London, 1905, 23.

[46] SMA Archives 14/812.97:16.982: Préfet Apostolique Jean Ogé to Cardinal Préfet de Propagande, September 1911.

a church trial of two well-known Episcopalian priests accused of adultery. The anonymous writer justified the men:

> My opinion is that the people are only gendering [sic] back to laws, customs and usages of our fore Fathers, from which we have been led away blindly and ignorantly by the teachings of the white man who has himself found out that his teachings to the Africans are wrong and contrary to the laws of the GOD of Africa.[47]

b. Conflict with local Glebo and Liberian authorities, 1907–08

In May 1906, back in Half Graway, the Rev. E. Shannon died suddenly. The deacon, the Rev. M.P.K. Killen, who was temporarily in the area, was appointed "for the time being" to look after Graway District. Harris, Clarck, R.N. Killen (father of the deacon) and Mrs. Farr were all reported as at their places.[48]

Killen, as shown by his purchase in 1906 of clerical and domestic goods from USA catalogues, was clearly following the American and Episcopalian models. He was also studying the "Thirty-Nine Articles" and the church creeds.[49] At the same time his elderly father was concerned that Glebo was no longer being taught and that the lack of Glebo materials made evangelism very difficult.

In his report to the local convocation of February 1907, Killen spoke of "William W. Harris" as rendering "very valuable assistance as a Lay Reader."[50] Harris (no longer "Wadé" but "William") seems at this time to have been reintegrated into the imported Christian ethos. The 1904–05 crisis seems to have been fully healed.

In May 1907 Killen was replaced at Spring Hill by the Rev. B.K. Speare, who had been assistant minister at Hoffman Station. Ordained priest in 1906, he was young and energetic. He reorganised the parish and started to hold weekday services. The bishop saw the work as "promising".[51] But in July there was a violent setback, which was reported in *The Silver Trumpet*.

> ... on the 4th of July, the day of the opening of convocation ... the catechist W.W. Harris was seized by the Natives (heathen) at Graway

[47] ECHS Archives, Liberia.
[48] Annual Report BMPEC 1905–06, 191.
[49] ECHS Archives: Killen, annual report, 1905–06.
[50] ECHS Archives: Killen to Kimber, 19 July 1906; 8 April 1907.
[51] Annual Report BMPEC 1906–07, 305.

and was compelled to drink *sassiwood*; and that the natives were so determined that remonstrance and even threats were unavailing.

The cause of the trouble appeared to be accusations of "witchey" against a Graway man named Bhne. He was said to have cast a spell which prevented people from catching fish, and was judged and condemned to drink *sassiwood*. Harris was asked to intervene, and the result was that he was told to drink the *sassiwood* instead. Even the intervention of the chief and the *bodio* could not calm the people, and it was only by the appearance of white missionaries and the chief from Whole Graway that Harris was rescued.

The editor (who wrote the account for the church journal) commented that, since church officials were not always available to save people in such circumstances, "the government should really do something to prevent this compulsory poisoning of innocent sufferers." He compared it with the situation in neighbouring Sierra Leone, where "all such practices are suppressed by resident district commissioners throughout the colony. . . . in this way both missionaries and natives find protection throughout the exterior and peace is maintained."[52]

Harris is again, in this incident, on the side of "Christianity and civilization", and is maintaining the reputation of the Episcopalian Church. But it also reveals local opposition to Harris. Later it seems that the people invited Harris to "spew waters",[53] which was a symbolic act of reconciliation.[54] We do not know the reasons for local animosity against Harris, but in view of the suspension from church duties in 1904–05, when it seems he was deeply involved with the local chiefs, and possibly in certain compromises with "native customs", it may be that his now very uncompromising attitude had led to a reaction against him.

---

[52] *The Silver Trumpet* (Cape Palmas), 1 (3), July 1907. The text is probably from the editor, S.F. Ferguson Jr.

[53] *Ibid.*, 12, from a résumé by Speare.

[54] Haliburton (*PH*, 16) wrongly interprets the "spewing of the waters" as being the same as drinking the sasswood, "that is, undergo the test." Martin, p. 27, with Bishop Payne as her source, indicates that the spewing of the water was to indicate that a "palaver had been set", thus leading to a cessation of hostilities. It was part of a ritual of truce following a battle. Agnes McAllister, *op. cit.* 84 wrote: "One rite that has to be performed as a part of any reconciliation is what is called 'the spewing of the water.' All parties concerned meet together, fill a basin with cold water, and each in turn lifts some of the water in his hands to his mouth. Then he blows it out upon the palms of the hands of the other party. This is done by each party three times, these words being repeated: 'I do this to show that I wash myself from all the past. We shall be friends from this day.'"

Shortly after this incident Harris, following Killen's lead, wrote to the Episcopal Mission secretary in New York ordering a new Church Hymnbook and prayerbook, and, from the Montgomery Ward catalogue, two trunks, two sewing machines, two pairs of "men's stylish shoes" and three pairs of ladies shoes.[55] He was surely "keeping up with the [Episcopal] clergy", "the best-dressed, best-educated and most intelligent-looking body of Coloured ministers in the country."[56] A witness to the events of some eighteen months later reported that Harris at the time was dressed "in a long frock coat."[57]

The cleavage earlier reported was due not only to Harris's return to the Episcopalian discipline; there had also been a return to more traditional ways on the part of the population. The bishop specifically mentioned this in his report of 1907.[58] The shift also involved a move from acceptance of centralised Liberian authority in favour of local authority. The local chief, King Gyude, was to be a major leader in the Glebo war of independence in 1910. Harris made a shift back towards supporting local Glebo opposition, probably early in 1908.

The bishop's report, in that same year, indicated grave developments: ". . . serious political trouble among the heathen at Half Graway". The king and seven chiefs had had to abdicate; "such upheavals always retard the progress of missionary work." But further difficulties for the small church came from immorality among members; seven persons had been excommunicated. Notwithstanding, "the superintendent speaks hopefully of the work. . . . Messers. Harris and Clarck are still at their posts in charge of boarding schools . . ."[59] The bishop visited Wolfe Memorial Chapel in June 1908, and celebrated Holy Communion "with a number of people from among the heathen being present."

What the bishop did not know was the involvement of the Junior Warden of the congregation in the political developments and troubles. Harris, the interpreter, was using his official position to build up an opposition to the local chief of Whole Graway, King Bulu, because of his (Bulu's) loyalty to the Liberian central authority. Harris was

[55] ECHS Archives: W.W. Harris to Kimber, 14 Oct 1907.
[56] So wrote the visitor Edgar Allen Forbes in 1909 at the time of his visit to Liberia. The secretary of the Episcopal Mission cited the text with evident satisfaction. BMPEC Annual Report 1909–10, 284.
[57] Conversation with Edwin G. Hodge, Hoffman Station, April 1978.
[58] Annual Report BMPEC 1906–07, 303.
[59] Annual Report BMPEC 1907–08, 201.

also working with Gyude of Bigtown to establish as the local king one Holo, who was anti-Liberian, at least at the local level. Such political involvements also meant that Harris was of necessity favouring traditional religion against the Christianity/civilization favoured by the Episcopalians. Elections were scheduled for 1909, and it seems that Harris was using common electoral tactics to build up a constituency. But the questions being asked related not only to local issues; it became clear in 1909 that opposition to Liberian authority had gone as far as the consideration of a British takeover, probably in the form of a protectorate. And in 1909, Harris was tried and found guilty of treason.

The exact charges against him were that he had "between the first day of July and the 31st of December 1908 traitorously expressed, declared and imagined by divers covert acts meeting with the Whole and Half Graway people . . . and did counsel with the Whole Graway people to disregard the supremacy of the Republic of Liberia with force and arms . . . and traitorously did insist and persuade the Cape Palmas tribe subjects of Liberia to set themselves up in a warlike attitude against the Republic of Liberia . . . brought a country band on the 13th day of February 1909 with force and arms in a warlike attitude and hoisted the Union Jack of Great Britain and Ireland . . . with treachery planned to levy war against the Republic of Liberia contrary to his allegiance . . ."[60]

The events of the second half of 1908 must be interpreted in the light of these charges, and of his conviction by a jury who accepted them.

In June 1908 there were conflicts between the Glebo and Cape Palmas Liberians over a local tax of $5 for each kruboy. There was such tension that two members of the Liberian cabinet were sent to Cape Palmas to clear up the problem, and to the mind of the Monrovian government "hostilities were averted";[61] they visited villages where they had "loyal and warm receptions", and received a very favourable impression.[62] In fact at that time the Glebo were more

---

[60] The records from Harris's trial of 11–14 May 1909 provide the details for these events of 1908. *Cf.* footnote 5, above.

[61] Commander Fletcher (U.S.S. *Birmingham*) to Navy Department, 12 April 1910. USN Archives: Department of State, Internal Affairs of Liberia, 1910–29 (military and naval affairs): 12083/359, enclosure.

[62] FNA: 200 Mi 629(7 F49), Vice Consul at Monrovia to Governor General of French West Africa at Dakar, 4 March 1909.

sympathetic to the national than to local authorities, who had passed the tax in question, and who employed some notoriously brutal officials.[63] President Barclay's pro-British alignment during 1908 was one which the Glebo welcomed.

In a confrontation with the French vice-consul, Hantz, on 31 July, Barclay gave Hantz the impression that he was "leading Liberia consciously to an English protectorate or to its being annexed, and I [Hantz] have no doubt that he has a personal interest in such a venture."[64] In Harper, in late July, a mass meeting charged Cadell, British officer in charge of the Frontier Force, with being a puppet of the British consul, and both of being in league with Barclay in plotting to establish a British protectorate.[65] This open opposition, in Cape Palmas, to the British alignment, would have served also to polarize the issue for the indigenous populations. This is where we can understand Harris working with "native politics" to build up pro-British support for the Barclay—and Blyden—policy.

Harris was dabbling in deep waters, and the person most able to give him guidance, the pro-British, pro-Blyden politician S.W. Seton, a judge of Maryland County, had died in February 1908. Most of the other "civilized" Glebo were Episcopalians committed to the Bishop's policies.

A number of facts are clear from the record of Harris's 1909 trial. During 1908 there were plots and secret meetings; attempts to eliminate local leadership loyal to local Liberian authority; arming with ammunition of the anti-Liberian constituency; death-threats against the catechist Clarck because he refused to participate in the planning, and against King Bulu; slaying of cattle as a punishment; Bulu fleeing for his life in the "bush", pursued by Harris—and all of this under the leadership of Harris. While pretending to be pro-Bulu (in order to receive money) he was working to depose him. Speare, who was pro-Liberian, had to flee for his life to Harper, and Killen again replaced him. Harris began to call himself "secretary of the Graway people". When Thorne, the county supervisor, called him to his office to explain what was going on, he refused to go; he was then dismissed from

[63] Haliburton, thesis 1966, 42f., citing F.O. 458/10, Baldwin to Grey, 13 April 1910.
[64] FNA: 200 Mi 629: Vice Consul Hantz to Minister of Foreign Affairs, 3 August 1908.
[65] David Michael Foley, *British policy in Liberia 1962–1912*. University of London, Ph.D. thesis 1965, 277. (Hereafter cited as Foley).

his position as interpreter. President Barclay endorsed the suspension, and finally Harris travelled to Monrovia to complain in person.

A witness said of him at this period:

> He himself was well-known in the villages around Harper, where he went not only to proclaim the word of God but to inflame resentment against the Liberian authorities, and to tell his fellow tribesmen that they were the rightful owners of the land, had the right to rule it themselves, or if they wished, invite whom they would to rule them.[66]

Now, in 1908, we get a very different picture from the Harris of 1907; he now seems to be promoting what a year earlier he had been fighting.

Meanwhile at Harper, in November, a citizens' meeting adopted a resolution against the alignment of Liberia with Britain, and questioned the British-sponsored and British-led Frontier Force, created with President Barclay's approval.[67] Although the Glebo in this case may have approved of Monrovian policies, they were still opposed to the local authorities.

2. Conflict with National Authority: The Rebel

a. Treason, 1909.

During the rest of the year 1908 President Barclay continued his attempts to save Liberia through an alignment with Britain. A French officer observed in April 1909 that this had developed favourably, "in spite of the affair of February 1909."[68] At the end of 1908 the Frontier Force was in place, commanded by three British officers; there were English officials in charge of Liberian customs, and two English judges in Monrovia overhauling the system of justice; an English-built gunboat, the *Lark*, bought with English money and manned by an English crew, had been acquired. Barclay publicly defended his pro-British policy. But this was before February and the so-called "Cadell incident".

---

[66] Rev. J.D. Kwee Baker (Monrovia) to G. Haliburton, 2 July 1963, in Haliburton, thesis, 1966, 54.

[67] Foley, 289.

[68] FNA: 200 Mi 612 (7F2): Capt. Thévenin to Dakar, HQ of French West Africa, 21 April 1909.

The Liberian legislature were not accepting without struggle the Barclay-Blyden policy. Nor was the pro-American Bishop Ferguson. Early in 1909 President Theodore Roosevelt made some attempt to obtain funds from Congress for a U.S. commission to examine the situation in Liberia. But nothing was forthcoming, and the view from Washington was that "annexation by Great Britain" was to be the "manifest destiny" of the Republic.[69]

In line with their anti-British fears, the Liberian legislature on 13 January 1909 appointed a Liberian officer (Colonel Lomax) to take over from the British officer, Major Cadell, as commander of the Frontier Force.

Behind the pro- and anti-British stances of the various Liberian leaders was the British consul, Braithwaite Wallis. He, contrary to the policy of the British Foreign Office, was resolutely working towards the establishment of a British protectorate over Liberia, at least up to 9 January 1909.[70] He had brought Major Cadell to Liberia and within the Frontier Force were a number of Sierra Leone enlisted men "under oath to its British commandant rather than to the Liberian government."[71] Further, Cadell was acting all the time under the impression that he was to be involved in a *coup* led by Wallis acting under secret orders from the Foreign Office.[72] Anti-British feeling growing in Monrovia during January required a shift in position; a shift that Wallis may at least officially have made but which Cadell, it appears, did not.

And now in mid-January Cadell had been removed from his command. But initially he refused to give it up. On 18 January Dr. Blyden gave a strongly pro-British discourse in which he warned that it was possible that "in the present crisis of our history, the Star of the Republic will for the time being be obscured."[73] It is possible that Harris was present in person at the lecture; he was at that time in Monrovia protesting about the loss of his job as an interpreter. He had gone as far as President Barclay who, it was testified at Harris's later trial, "did not take any part in his acts in what he was to do, that is to fly the Union Jack . . . on the 13th day of February 1909."[74]

---

[69] From *African Mail,* cited in *Liberia* 34, February 1909, 76.
[70] Foley, 249, 294.
[71] *Ibid.,* 274.
[72] *Ibid.,* 252.
[73] Edward Wilmot Blyden, *The problems before Liberia.* London: C.M. Phillips 1909, 3.
[74] See account of trial: cf. footnote 5 above.

This evidence from Superintendent Thorne suggests that Harris had indeed tried to involve President Barclay, but without success. By 12 January Barclay had made a complete shift.[75] When Harris left Monrovia it was said that he had a number of Union Jacks with him, indicating that he was prepared for his later act. On the morning that he made his public act of treason, he used the expression, "I am going back into heathenism." This appears to correspond with Blyden's closing remarks in his speech on 18 January: "Acquaint yourselves now with God—the God of Africa—and be at peace."[76]

Blyden was in touch with Cadell during his stay in Monrovia, and later kept in constant touch with Wallis, the British consul. He wrote of the leaders of Liberia as "a gang of thieves",[77] and welcomed the possible impeachment of Barclay and a take-over of power by England, as representative of "the Powers".[78] After finding out that the legislature were authorising armed action against Kru centres, unless they paid heavy fines for customs violations, he wrote to Wallis (30 January): "The crisis has arrived. . . . It is evident that H.B.M. Government should at once *require* that Liberia should make these reforms."[79]

Four days earlier, Wallis had cabled for a gunboat, and had also asked for all British supplied arms and ammunition not paid for to

---

[75] Foley, 296.

[76] Blyden, *op. cit.*, 32. What Blyden meant by this may be determined by a text of 1910.

"The Bible is constantly pointing out that the dispensations of Jehovah are not restricted to the Hebrew course of history—that Jehovah makes no distinctions. The Ethiopian is as dear to him as the Israelites, or rather, that the Israelites are as dear to Jehovah as the Ethiopians (Amos IX 7). We are also taught that in all parts of the earth Jehovah is worshipped though under different names . . . His ways are past finding out. We cannot limit him to sects and parties . . .

Islam or Christianity [Western Christian system as structured in the Anglo-Saxon culture] for Africa is not the only alternative. Christ told the woman of Samaria that the worship of Jehovah should be confined neither to Mt. Gerizim nor to Jerusalem. The ultimate fate of Africa does not depend exclusively upon Jerusalem, Rome, or Mecca. It may be that from some height yet undiscerned the river of Salvation may flow through Africa and may quench the thirst of other nations also. It will not be the first time that Africa has given religion to the outside world. Then will come the end, when all things shall be delivered up to Jehovah, when, as Zechariah predicted, the Lord (Jehovah) shall be one Jehovah and HIS NAME ONE. Sierra Leone, West Africa, June 1910." In Edward Wilmot Blyden, *The Arabic Bible in the Soudan: a plea for transliteration*. London: C.M. Phillips 1910, 18f.

[77] Blyden to Wallis, 23 Jan. 1909, encl. with Wallis to Grey, 10 Feb. 1909. F.O. 367/160/8334. Cited in Foley, 300.

[78] Blyden to Wallis, 27 January 1909. Cited in Foley, 301.

[79] Blyden to Wallis, 30 January 1909. Cited in Foley, 301f.

be returned. The arms and ammunition were on 31 January handed over to the Elder Dempster agent in Monrovia for shipping back to the War Office. The Liberian secretary of state protested against Wallis's actions, and on 4 February told an American visitor that Cadell's former troops were "on the verge of mutiny" and that other disaffected discharged soldiers were demanding back pay.[80] On 10 February the British gunboat *H.M.S. Mutine* with a company of Sierra Leone troops arrived in the harbour. On 11 February Cadell wrote to the president asking for back pay for his men, and warning that they were threatening mutiny.[81]

Barclay then appealed to the Liberian militia to remain in readiness, and brought in a company of the Frontier Force to try and recover the stored arms. When the dean of the diplomatic corps called a meeting of the foreign representatives, Wallis was absent, but when informed about the mutiny he offered the Sierra Leone troops from the gunboat. This was refused. A detachment of Liberian militia was sent to the barracks of the mutinous Frontier Force, only to find that Cadell had fortified all the approaches to the camp and refused to vacate it. But when warned through Wallis (on 12 February) of a pending attack, there was a rapid and orderly evacuation into the city.[82] Cadell retired to the British consulate. Within a week the troops were dismissed; Wallis was re-assigned, and Cadell had returned to London under a false name.

Meanwhile, back in Cape Palmas, on 13 February—the day after the expected mutiny—Harris went out on Puduke Beach across from Harper and hoisted the Union Jack on a flagpole. He ridiculed the Liberian flag[83] and insulted Liberians watching from across the river, telling them they should get out of Liberia.[84] Witnesses later claimed that violence had only been avoided by the wise actions of Thorne, the county superintendent. Harris repeated the flag-raising the next day and was also said to have painted the Union Jack on a large

---

[80] See Edgar Allen Forbes, *Land of the White Helmet.* London and Edinburgh: Fleming Revell 1910, 233–235. Forbes arrived in Monrovia from the U.S. on 13 January 1909 and was eyewitness to the events.

[81] The text of the letter was published in the *African League*, 10 (8), Feb. 1909, 1–3.

[82] These details are taken from "Liberia and the Frontier Force" in *Liberia and West Africa* 11 (2), 4.

[83] Rev. W.B. Williams, in interview of 26 January 1966. See Haliburton, *PH*, 30, note 3.

[84] Judge Edward G. Hodge, April 1978.

rock which was on the boundary between the Nyomowe and Kude-mowe Glebo.

In Monrovia a government board of inquiry investigated the events, and revealed that Cadell had urged the soldiers to mutiny. The whole was seen as a larger plot of Wallis and Blyden to place British interests in control. Blyden, as a result, lost his pension; two teachers at Liberia College were dismissed because of their involvement.

It has been argued convincingly that the British Foreign Office was not behind any plot or *coup d'état*. But the argument that it was only a Cadell-inspired mutiny is less convincing.[85] There are numerous facts which point to a degree of pre-arranged plotting and careful coordination. These include the timing of the gunboat's arrival; the presence of the Sierra Leone troops on the gunboat; Blyden's speech; his correspondence with Wallis; his activities during the mutiny; and also Harris's raising of the Union Jack, perfectly coordinated with the other developments. Wallis also sent cables to London informing of the mutiny before it took place, and the Foreign Office informed the U.S.A. ambassador in London that a revolt had broken out in Monrovia on the 10th of February.[86]

There are additional considerations which favour the probability of a Blyden-Wallis-Cadell-Harris coup attempt, including Wallis's tight control of British subjects at the time; the fact that British arms dealers were supplying arms to Glebo in the Cape Palmas area, and the later reaction of French officials to what took place.[87] Both the American ambassador in Monrovia[88] and the French *chargé d'affaires*[89] accepted the official Monrovian interpretation of a *coup d'état* which failed.

Blyden himself seems to have recognised the fact of an attempted *coup*, when in a letter a year later he spoke openly of "taking a step in advance of what was bound to come," adding that the "Negro . . .

---

[85] Foley, 315f.

[86] Foley, 307; also Ponty (Monrovia) to Minister of Colonies (Paris), 22 April 1909, in FNA 200 Mi 629 (7F47): "superficial troubles falsely represented in Europe by English cablegrams as a veritable revolution against the president."

[87] Vice Consul Baret (Monrovia) to Minister of Foreign Affairs (Paris), 15 February 1910: ". . . it appears that the question of Liberia is a cause of divergence of views between the Foreign Office and the Colonial Office of London; the latter would purely and simply like to take over Liberia, in part at least."

[88] The report of the U.S. Commission is cited in R.L. Buell, *The native problem in Africa II.* New York: Macmillan 1928, 788. Buell gave 1 February as the date of the mutiny; it is probably a typographical error but it led Haliburton (*PH* 29) to move up the date of the mutiny ten days, confusing the events.

[89] *Op. cit.*, note 68 above.

will not attain his highest development under his own rule."[90] The *African League*, an anti-Blyden publication from Buchanan, openly linked Harris's name with that of Blyden. "It is said that the man [who raised the British flag] gives as an excuse that he was directed and advised to do so by one who is called Liberia's greatest and most learned man . . ."[91] And Bishop Ferguson's son, the Rev. S.D. Ferguson Jr., made the same connection when writing about the war of 1910.

> . . . one Harris, a civilised Grebo of the same Cape Palmas tribe . . . was tutored it was said by the English conspirators to return home and induce his people to go under English rule, and that on a certain date Monrovia the capital would fall into the English's hands . . .[92]

President Barclay himself made the same connection, reported during the 1910 war by the U.S. Minister Resident in Monrovia:

> . . . the present uprising is, in [the President's] opinion, due to outside influence, and dates back to the Cadell's incident when the natives all along the coast . . . were told that Liberia had become a British colony. Believing this to be true a native Liberian, who is now imprisoned hoisted the British flag on Liberian territory. It is claimed he was influenced to do so by Dr. Blyden . . .[93]

All these three sources are polemical, and it is always possible that the connection made was not a real one. But the timing of Harris's own actions during the *coup* period, coupled with his behaviour in the year preceding, seem to make the probability of his deliberate involvement in the attempt very strong.

b. *Prison, trial and punishment*[94]

Harris was now, at Cape Palmas, in prison for almost three months pending his trial for treason, which lasted from 11 to 14 May. The charges have been listed above (page 89). The court was presided over by Judge James L. Cox; the prosecution was in charge of the

---

[90] Holden, *op. cit.*, 858; from Blyden to J.O. Wilson, 10 January 1910.
[91] *African League*, 10 (1), June 1909, 14.
[92] S.D. Ferguson Jr., *Letter from King Yado Gyude of the Cape Palmas Grebo, and Reply to King Gyude's Indictment*. Cape Palmas 1910, June 20, 26.
[93] USN Archives: 882.00 No. 367, Record Group No. 59, Ernest Lyon to the Secretary of State, 6 April 1910.
[94] Record of trial (cf. footnote 5).

County Attorney, S.J. Dossen, and the District Attorney, A.F. Tubman, and Harris was defended by Attorneys S.B. Nelson and J.K. Gibson. Leading witnesses for the prosecution included King Bulu, the teacher-catechist S.B.K. Clarck, and the County Superintendent, Thorne. A Glebo man gave evidence as to the flag raising, and the County Treasurer witnessed to Harris's accusations against Bulu and Clarck, "that they were devils and King Bulu was a witch and Clarck was one also." It was to Cooper (the Treasurer) that Harris had reportedly said just before the flag-raising ". . . I am going back into heathenism. I am going to take off all these cloths."

The only witness for the defence was Harris himself. He denied the charges or said that actions had been committed "in ignorance". He did admit that he had not yielded obedience to King Bulu. But in putting up the Union Jack "he was only playing."

On the final day of the trial Harris's attorney gave notice that owing to his own allegiance to the Republic of Liberia he was abandoning the case. The jury met and gave the verdict "in favor of the state." Harris remained in prison until 21 May when he was sentenced to two years in prison and a fine of $500.

Harris did not however remain in prison. On the same day he was released to the Episcopalian priest, F.A.K. Russell, who paid off Harris's time in prison at $6 a month, or $144 in total. The fine was paid immediately, probably by local sympathizers; there is no firm evidence for the source of this large sum for a man now without a salary.

It is important for what follows to know that Harris was not in prison in the months that led up to the war of 1910. Moreover, on 15 July Russell himself was fined $15 "for not conforming to the law" in his responsibility for W.W. Harris.

> Harris was very active, going around stirring things up, making big speeches—thundering speeches, for he was a stout man. He emphasized things to make us see that it was necessary to rule our country; "It is time for these people to get out of here and let us aborigines rule over this country; it belongs to us. If they stay the aborigines should rule over them."[95]

---

[95] Edwin G. Hodge, April 1978.

c. The war of 1910

It has been—in our opinion wrongly—surmised that, as Harris had little to do with the "Cadell incident", he also had little to do with the war of 1910, because he was in prison.[96]

Hostilities began on 12 January 1910, after a Liberian guard at Cape Palmas fired on a canoe in the Hoffman river. It was essentially a war between the Nyomowe Glebo and the Liberians.[97] But its origins lay buried deep in "traditional antagonisms".[98] President Barclay blamed the external influences of the "Cadell incident", but there was also the long conflict over land between the Nyomowe Glebo and the Kudemowe Glebo, specifically over land around Bolobo, forty miles up the Cavalla River. In 1909 Lomax, the Liberian commander of the Frontier Force, had intervened injudiciously at Bolobo, resulting in the deaths of several of his men. When the Cape Palmas Glebo (under King Gyude) were asked for an "explanation" of their allies' actions, they began to fortify their towns and appealed direct to President Barclay. He responded by sending a special commission from Monrovia. This was early in January. But before the commission had arrived, during the night of 11 January, two educated Glebo were killed, one being the Episcopal minister, Speare. The Glebo claimed that the Americo-Liberians were responsible. When the commission arrived with 150 reinforcements for the Frontier Force, the situation was already completely out of hand, and its Glebo secretary, Nathaniel

---

[96] Cf. Haliburton, *PH*, 31; 33; 36. See also Gordon M. Haliburton, "The Prophet Harris and the Grebo Rising of 1910." *Liberian Studies Journal*, 3 (1), 1970–71, 31–39. "Summing up the available evidence, it may be said, therefore, that contrary to what has been said in the past, the Prophet Harris did not bring on the 1910 Grebo War by his raising of the Union Jack, nor did he participate actively in it." p. 39.

[97] President Barclay, memo to Ernest Lyon, 5 April 1910, in *op. cit.*, note 195 below. Also in Wm. V.S. Tubman, "Reminiscences of the Grebo War of 1910", *The Liberian Historical Review*, 2, 1965, 10–14."It was almost a holocaust with only the Hoffman River as dividing line between the Nyemowe living in Puduke, Wuuke, Bigtown, and all the surrounding area on the one side, and the Government and people in Harper, Middlesex, Jacksonville, Tubmantown, and Philadelphia on the other. The sound of gunfire ran throughout the night and part of the next day." Page 11.

[98] Martin, 390. Most details in this section were gleaned from her research. Also Commander Fletcher, U.S.S. *Birmingham*, 30 April 1910: "The hatred and distrust of the native for the Liberian is so sincere, and has apparently grown from such just causes [wanton killing of Glebo fisherman by Americo-Liberian clergyman, 17 April] that I can see no solution of the matter short of a concert of the Powers who have interests here with a view to investigating the state of the country and arranging for its regulation." in Secretary of Navy to Secretary of State, 28 May 1910, USN Archives, 882.00/364.

Seton, himself left to join his fellows at Cape Palmas, claiming that his own life was threatened. The Glebo living in Harper withdrew to outlying towns; after the exchange of fire on 12 February hostilities continued till the Glebo surrender on May 18, but the troubles at Bolobo were not settled until late in June.

On 15 February a "Memorial of Grebo chiefs" was sent to the British government specifically requesting Britain to take over their country.[99] A revised form of the memo, entitled "Letter from King Yado Gyude", was sent to the U.S. Department of State and other American bodies (including the Protestant Episcopal Mission) and to the *Washington Star* and the *Lagos Weekly News*, who both published it. Where was Harris during this period and at the beginning of the war? We have no details except that he was "stirring things up", and it would certainly be likely that he would have been involved in the war preparations by the Cape Palmas Glebo, said to have been the most extensive ever made.[100] A friend of his sons later recalled how he went around "preaching sedition" and "inciting people to fight."[101]

By late March, according to President Barclay, Harris was indeed in prison.[102] But he also seems to be one of seven "civilised Greboes involved in the present insurrection" whose names were recalled in a 12 April memorandum from the commander of the U.S. *Birmingham*.[103] Nathaniel Seton was recognised to be the amanuensis of the "letter . . ." of 15 February, but it is more than likely that William Harris, one of the Glebo elite, would have been involved in the drafting of the letter as with other preparations.

The grievances against the Liberians had been building up over several generations. They included the two wars of 1856 and 1875; the effects of a master-slave relationship imposed by the settlers upon the Glebo; the excessive taxes levied on returning kruboys; the Liberian powerlessness to stop intertribal wars; the irresponsibility of soldiers

---

[99] F.O. 367/184, Memorial of Grebo Chiefs, 15 February 1910. Cited in Haliburton, *PH*, 33.

[100] Martin, 402.

[101] Conversation with Edward Brookes, 15 April 1978, at Harper. The Glebo were armed by the British through smuggling. Cf. Ellis to Secretary of State, 10 Feb. 1910. USN Archives 882.00.

[102] Cf. Note 93 above.

[103] USN Archives 882.00/364, enclosure. "Civilised Grebos involved in present insurrection. These number about forty, principally among whom, as far as my knowledge goes, are: H.R. Scott, V.E.B. Seton, Henry Baker, S.B. Seton, S.B. Clarke and W.W. Harris, the man who raised the British flag at Puduke and Graway about fourteen months ago. There may be others whose names I do not recall, Jeremiah Scott."

in the Frontier Force, and the wanton killing of Glebo; the limited educational opportunities and even more limited work opportunities for trained Glebo; and the refusal of the government to issue title deeds for land owned by Glebo. "We are therefore constrained to offer our country to some European power—preferably England, whose methods of colonization are less onerous—for their government."[104]

King Gyude later denied that the letter was from him, and the Liberians refuted the charges it contained, but clearly it was the issues mentioned which had impelled William Wadé Harris when he hoisted the Union Jack one year earlier. Here there is continuity with the Cadell incident, and also with the involvement of Seton, Harris, and Gyude.

Nathaniel Seton was, like his father, a disciple of Blyden, and he was one of two teachers dismissed from Liberia College because of being implicated in the Cadell incident. King Gyude had by this time been defined as "defiant and revolutionary . . . and hostile to such of his chiefs whose attitude is friendly and conciliatory towards the government."[105] Behind the plots and intrigue stands the figure of Harris.

The war of three months did not involve great loss of life, but nevertheless it was disastrous for the Glebo. Without any support from the United States, King Gyude was forced to surrender, and the Glebo people had to settle for an imposed *pax americana*. The Glebo towns were occupied by Liberian soldiers out of the control of their officers; the Kudemowe who had been "loyal" were able to profit by looting and burning in the Nyomowe towns. The villagers themselves fled into the bush. But the terms of the settlement were particularly severe.[106] They included forced resettlement, property seizure, and heavy fines; chiefs were deposed but King Bulu of Half Graway was named as paramount. Eleven men were charged with treason; this did not include Harris, who was already in prison.

But the Commission did recognise that there had been a major failure.

> To those of us who have labored with so much zeal and assiduity to effect a strong national bond with this tribe, we feel forced to declare our cause a lost one.[107]

---

[104] Letter from King Yado Gyude, 15 Feb 1910 (cf. footnote 92, above).
[105] Cf. source in note 103 above.
[106] See Martin, her appendix VII, 439ff.
[107] *Ibid.*, 439.

In 1910, S.D. Ferguson Jr. represented Harris as having become involved almost accidentally in the 1909 plot which failed. This is possible. But all of the evidence suggests that his involvement was the end of a logical process which can be observed in other Western-educated African Christians. The same shift from an initial enthusiasm to a resignation and disillusionment is expressed.

In Harris's case he had served for twenty-five years in the Episcopal Church, and his bishop had become one of the Liberian counsellors to the American commission of inquiry in 1909. Ferguson saw involvement with the U.S.A. as the only road to national salvation with independence. This was not the view of Barclay, Blyden—or Harris. As for Harris, Bishop Ferguson in 1909 thought he had seen the end of a local problem—Harris was in prison "and his connection with our work has ceased."[108] But it was not the end of the problem, even after the end of the war of 1910, which cost the poverty-stricken republic £25,000.[109] And the church had again to bear accusations that it trained disloyal Africans.

One Glebo who recalled Harris from the days of his youth was Edwin G. Hodge, who was grandson of the former king of Bigtown, and had been a judge. He felt, speaking in his own old age, that Harris's arrests, imprisonments, and the defeat of the 1910 war had served to make Harris wiser in the ways he expressed his patriotism. But they did not extinguish his feelings about his own people, and he believed that Harris remained a Glebo patriot to the end of his life.[110] Harris's basic stand was neither anti-white or anti-Christian; he was anti-Liberian and opposed those whites who supported the settlers against the just claims of the Glebo. Likewise he opposed missionaries (like Bishop Ferguson) who seemed to him to be using American power to that end. His aims were justice and peace.

d. The Blyden influence

The relationship of Harris to Blyden during the Cadell incident of 1909 raises the longer-term question of Blyden's influence on Harris. The facts of Blyden's life, and his writings, which make such an influence possible, need to be briefly narrated.

Blyden took political refuge at Cape Palmas in 1882, when Harris

---

[108] Annual Report BMPEC 1908–09, 205.
[109] F.O. 458/11: Parks (Acting Consul) to Grey, 16 August 1910, cited in G. Haliburton *op. cit.*, note 198 above, 38.
[110] Conversation of 15 April 1978 at Hoffman Station.

was an adult and probably visiting Harper frequently; his conversion (in Harper Methodist Church) is dated to 1881. In 1885 Blyden ran for president, and the nature of the campaign would be such that a Christianized and civilised Glebo like Harris would have to consider his claims. Blyden had taken a pro-Grebo stand in the war of 1875 and was known to be anti-settler in his views. His major work, *Christianity, Islam and the Negro Race*, first appeared in 1887.

Samuel W. Seton, perhaps the leading Glebo of Cape Palmas, was a friend and disciple of Blyden. He was not the only friend of Blyden in the Cape Palmas area, and at Cuttington College there was in 1904 (and perhaps earlier) a "Dr. Blyden Literary Union".[111] Blyden withdrew from the Presbyterian ministry in the same year that Seton separated himself from the Episcopalians, and they had similar justifications.

After 1892, Blyden's appointment as Liberian ambassador to Great Britain would have been important to the pro-British Glebo. Harris's son, born about that time, was named "Edward".

In March 1901 Blyden again took refuge at Cape Palmas. He had been teaching at Liberia College and some faculty had taken exception to his instruction on "the principles of polygamy and Mohammedanism"; because he had favoured a protectorate he was no longer considered eligible for government posts.[112]

The broader influence of Blyden was such that one could speak of "Blydenic" thought.[113] Fifteen major concerns, for Blyden, may be isolated from his writings:

> He supported aboriginal rights and indigenous values.
> He gave open support to the Glebo against the Americo-Liberians in Maryland County.
> He criticized Christian missions for their aggressive cultural Christianity.
> He rejected western Christian denominationalism as "sectarianism".
> He supported polygamy as a social institution.
> He admired the simple religious approach of Islam with its apparent

---

[111] S.D. Ferguson Jr. (ed.) *The Living Chronicle for 1904*, Vol. III, Cape Palmas, 48. A copy of this is to be found in FNA 200 Mi 612.

[112] Cited in Holden, *op. cit.*, 273, from J.S. Steven, agent at Monrovia of the American Colonization Society, to Mr. Wilson, 18 June 1901.

[113] During the dedication of the "Blyden Club" in Sierra Leone in 1907, Blyden was hailed as "the leading husbandman in the intellectual cultivation of the mind of Liberian youth." A year later at its first anniversary there was the exhortation to be "Blydenistic" and to conduct oneself "Blydenistically". See H. Lynch, *Pan-African Patriot*, 239.

respect for native institutions.
He believed in the spiritual and servant role of the African races as
  compared to the political, imperial role of Westerners.
He held to the concept of a pan-African spiritual empire, and encouraged
  the creation of an autonomous African church.
He opposed the drink traffic in West Africa.
He had a very strong sense of the "destiny" and "special calling" of
  the African peoples.
He had an intense racist rejection of the "hybrid mulatto".
For Liberia he favoured a British protectorate.
He was convinced of the inaptitude of the African for the exercise of
  political power along Western lines.
He perceived Christianity more as a way of being a servant, than as
  an ideology; practice took priority over doctrine.
He affirmed the existence of an undistorted African religion, and a faith
  in the African Creator-God of all of Africa.

Blyden had sailed to West Africa in 1850, when he was only eighteen
years of age. His vision then was the diffusion of the "knowledge
of the Lord" in the dark places of Africa.[114] His African experience
led him to a major shift in understanding. His contemporary, Bishop
Ferguson, who arrived in Africa with a similar vision, never wavered
in his "imported concerns".

Ferguson believed in a crusade for Christianity and civilization into
which the aboriginal would be converted and totally integrated.

He believed in total support of Americo-Liberian institutions.
He believed the Episcopal Church to be both "catholic" and "apostolic"
  and thus above sectarianism.
He was pro-American both culturally and politically.
He percieved African religion as demon-worship and idolatry, and
  polygamy as immoral.
Islam was seen as an enemy to Christianity.
Christianity itself was perceived as ordered hierarchy, ordered doctrine,
  and ordered morality.
He supported the anti-liquor forces.
He saw the church as a training ground for Western political processes,
  and church convocations as small legislatures.
He believed in the importance of education along Western (American)
  lines in view of learning Western trades.

Ferguson announced his policies at the beginning of his bishopric,

---

[114] Blyden to Rev. J.B. Pinney. 26 November 1850, cited in Holden, *op. cit.*, 23.

in 1885, and remained faithful to them throughout his time of leadership. It will be seen that the two men seem to agree only over the question of the liquor trade.

Although Harris worked from 1888 to 1908 in a structure dominated by Ferguson, his views at least from 1908 and throughout his prophetic period were very clearly "Blydenic". He was also obviously influenced by the Seton-Russellite relationship, emphasising the Russellite biblicism including the doctrine of Elijah with its apocalypticism and eschatological predictions including the 1914 war and the theocratic and millennial kingdom of peace. All these may be discovered, though often used in a different way, in Harris's prophetic thought.

CHAPTER FIVE

THE TRANCE-VISITATION OF 1910

Commenting on the "extraordinary physical and mental sensations" which preceded Harris's prophetic mission, Haliburton wrote: "In a way there seems to be no sharp break between what he was and what he became. After a long journey he had reached his goal."[1] Was that goal indeed the same as "going back into heathenism" which Harris had (in 1909) declared as his intention? Or was it something different? Would he have reached his goal—as prophet—without the vision? It is important to attempt an understanding of this from the perspective of the person in question.

For Harris there is no doubt that the trance-visitation during his imprisonment of 1910[2] was most crucial. Of his Christian conversion at the age of 21 or 22 he said "the first I was converted"; the 1910 experience was a second conversion. After both of them he began preaching missions. For something so crucial it is necessary that we examine the experience in depth.

A. The context

It is established that Harris was in prison in 1910, and was perceived in Monrovia as one of the civilised Glebo responsible for leading the insurrection and war early in that year. It can be accepted that the conditions in Crafton Prison, Harper, were not good.[3] Harris's colleague Clarck reported to Benoît that Harris was "badly treated in prison"

---

[1] Gordon M. Haliburton, *The prophet Harris*. London: Longmans 1971, 211.

[2] The dating of the trance-visitation, like other events in Harris's life, is problematical. Some witnesses (Harrington, Killen, Clarck), make statements which would indicate that it occurred during his imprisonment after planting the Union Jack on the beach. But President Barclay reported him to be in prison in early April; we can assume he was already there in late March. Since the war ended in May 1910, and since his wife is said to have died in June 1910, after his vision, we have dated his vision at the end of the war, during a second imprisonment. On the basis of the Harrington narrative, we assume a third imprisonment, following his prophetic vocation.

[3] *Cf.* the remarks of President King in 1924, cited in Raymond L. Buell, *The native problem, II.* New York: Macmillan 1928, 719.

but was "not sick when coming out."[4] However, he was allowed visitors, one being his own wife Rose, according to his daughter Grace.

He was in a complicated moral and spiritual situation. For over a year he had been without employment either as a teacher or as interpreter for the county. For the same period he had no longer been active in church as a catechist or lay reader, and probably no longer attended church. Prior to his flag-raising he had spoken of his determination to go back into heathenism, for his attempts to work within the civilised framework had failed. And as for his twenty years' service under the Episcopal Church Mission, he was later to acknowledge that he had gone there "for money". In the year preceding his first trial he had been using the traditional pre-Christian spiritual powers. In prison he was told to "burn the fetishes *beginning with his own;*" the report, from his own daughter, is evidence that in prison—if not earlier—he had reverted to what he had discarded at his conversion twenty-eight years earlier.

The Western "god" and Western "civilization" were not enough; not even simple justice had been achieved. Historical evidence bears this out.[5] Dr. Blyden had said "Acquaint yourself with God—the God of Africa—and be at peace."[6] What that meant to a much less sophisticated man than Blyden seems to have been a pure and simple intention to return to traditional African life and practice.

Oral tradition (as recorded by Haliburton) confirms this view.[7] He was described as "a fetisher", "a great fetisher", a "fetish worshipper." In 1964 the Methodist preacher Abraham Nandjué had reported to Claude-Hélène Perrot, "*Harris était un grand féticheur, un brigand.*"[8] Others made similar observations. Williams, an American missionary, recorded that when he visited Harris in prison he had "begged him to change his ways."[9] What was the change? To non-revolt, or to return to

---

[4] *BN* II, 24.

[5] *Cf.* Jane Jackson Martin, *The dual legacy: govenrment authority and mission influence among the Glebo of Eastern Liberia, 1834–1910.* Boston University Ph.D. thesis, 1968 (henceforth Martin), *passim.*

[6] Edward W. Blyden, *The problem before Liberia.* London: Phillips 1909.

[7] We feel that Sheila Walker assumes too easily that the popular oral tradition about Harris being a "fetisher" was deduced purely and simply from his evident powers as a prophet. Cf. her *Christianity African style,* University of Chicago Ph.D. thesis 1976.

[8] *René Bureau Notes* (henceforth *RBN.* (To be found in the Centre for the Study of New Religious Movements, Selly Oak Colleges, Birmingham).

[9] See p. 63 in Gordon M. Haliburton, *The Prophet Harris and his work in Ivory Coast and western Ghana.* SOAS, University of London, Ph. D. thesis 1986. Also his *PH,* p. 192.

Christianity? It would seem both. He was far away from his first Christian faith; he was imprisoned in very poor conditions; the news he would be receiving of the war, the surrender, the harsh conditions imposed, showed that the revolt had proved futile. That for which he had laboured and fought in view of the liberation of his people had brought them instead to the darkest moment of their history, and Harris to his. He was fifty years old when, in a second conversion, he "saw Gabriel and start preaching."

B. Sources for study of the event

1. Introduction

Two of our sources were in close contact with Harris in 1910. Mrs. Neal, Harris's daughter, reported the events to Benoît in 1926, as did S.B.K. Clarck, who although threatened by Harris in 1908 was said to be one of the "civilised Glebo" with Harris behind the 1910 insurrection. Two other important African sources are those of Casely Hayford, the Gold Coast politician, who wrote at the time of Harris's visit to Axim, and the Gambian merchant Campbell, who told his story in 1922. Roman Catholic missionary clergy, Fathers Hartz, Harrington, O'Herlihy and Gorju, all reported with some cynicism, humour and scorn. Pierre Benoît took the testimony of Harris quite seriously; he had recently studied religious psychology with Professor Raoul Allier at the University of Paris[10] and was thus particularly interested in the phenomenon.

There is little else in the sources, and in fact there is one contradictory witness, an acquaintance in Axim who said, "He didn't mention Gabriel or say anything about receiving messages at night."[11] In texts originating from within the "orthodox Harris" (Ahui) tradition, there is a passage which says simply, "*par l'ordre de Dieu . . . l'ange Gabriel commanda ce vieillard par l'intermédiaire de Dieu [sic] d'aller convertir les fétichistes*".[12] There is a well-known tradition which places Harris under the call and the service of the angel.[13] But such hints tell us little about the event itself.

An early distortion entered through field reports picked up by F.D.

---

[10] Letter of Mme Renée Benoît-Meffre to Shank, 29 September 1977.
[11] *HN*
[12] *RBN*: La biographie du prophète William Wadé Harris . . ., Bregbo, le 5 mai, 1966.
[13] There was at one time (observed in 1973–74) a statue of the angel Gabriel outside a Harrist temple in Petit Bassam, but it has since been removed.

Walker in his 1926 visit to the Ivory Coast. He reported, "It was rumoured that Harris had seen visions, that angels had spoken to him, that a vulture had brought him special messages from the sky."[14]

The narration of his prophetic call seems thus to have been given to various authority figures rather than to the masses, for whom his powers were self-authenticating. Not that the narration was created for such a purpose; on the contrary, its authenticity is assured precisely by its use in situations where it was received with derision. In his own self-understanding his visitation by Gabriel—precisely because of its reality[15]—was the most important way of validating his ministry.

We will first report the sources, then attempt to develop a harmonization of their themes, and finally offer a *résumé* of the whole.

2. *The texts*

2a. Mrs. Grace Neal, Harris's second daughter, to Benoît in 1926, following Benoît's rapid notes.

> En 1909 affaire pr son drapeau
> En prison il a une vision
> Dieu lui ordonne de quitter ses vetements. Il est oint
> a Crafton Sa femme lui porte un pagne
> un trou pr passe la tête.
> En juin 1910 sa femme le croyant fou mourut de chagrin.
> A partir de ce moment il emmène avec lui 3 femmes pour
> l'aider ds sa predication——mais "Dieu dit il lui a ordonne
> de ne pas se marier."[16]

These notes of Benoît were then expanded into the following:

> In 1910, after the affair of his banner, Harris was imprisoned by the Liberian government. In prison he had the vision which decided his missionary career.
> According to Mrs. Neal, he saw the Lord in a great wave of light, and was, he said, anointed by him. He felt the water pour on his head. God told him to burn the fetiches beginning with his own, and to preach

---

[14] Frank Deaville Walker, *The story of the Ivory Coast.* London: the Cargate Press 1926, 12.

[15] A parallel that might well be kept in mind during the analyses in this chapter is from John J. Neihardt, *Black Elk speaks.* New York: Simon and Schuster 1977. See especially page 41, where Black Elk told the author about his vision as a nine-year-old child. "I did not have to remember these things; they have remembered themselves all these years."

[16] *BN*, I, 12.

everywhere Christian baptism; he must, by divine command, leave off all the European clothes he was wearing and his patent leather shoes, to reclothe himself in a kind of togo [sic, for toga] made of a single piece of stuff with a hole for his head. It was no later than the next day that he had this dress made by his wife.

He seemed so exalted and talked so incoherently that all the world thought him mad.

Released some time after, he began in 1910 his ministry and baptisms.

His wife, believing him really mad, died of grief the same year, his daughter told me.

He began from that time to take on his rounds of preaching three women who sang the hymns. These three women have made an effective charge of polygamy against him; from that time he does not seem to have respected the vows of Christian marriage. God, he said, had shown him a better way of living.[17]

2b. Mr. S.B.K. Clarck, friend and colleague of Harris, teacher at Whole Graway in 1926, to Benoît.

When he start preaching, 'people suppose him that he must be crazy'.
[Benoît] What did he say you about the vision?
[Clarck] The angel tell him that he would be a prophet.
... a light ... angel in the light ... badly treated in the prison ... but was not sick coming out ... but boldly speaking to the people.[18]

2c. Mr. Campbell, wealthy Gambian merchant, English-speaking; as a nominal Christian was in the Ivory Coast at the end of 1913 and early 1914, and was "converted" by Harris at the time of his first passage at Bingerville.

He was a great fetishist. One day while carrying out his rites as usual he heard someone behind him speaking, and looking around he saw a man standing who said to him: 'You must not believe in this rod or in these amulets which are in front of you, because they are powerless as you well know. Therefore take this (a long cane is given to him) and go here and there from place to place and preach Christ. Tell first of all your family to believe in the same way, to abandon the fetishes (stone, wood and amulets) which are nothing at all of what they represent. A great power is upon you.

The cane was accepted. His wife was sick at that time but in accepting the faith she was healed and they left at that moment for their mission. And they are still at that labour, even now [1922].[19]

---

[17] *BR*, I, 8f.
[18] *BN*, II, 24.
[19] Jean Bianquis, *Le prophète Harris ou dix ans d'histoire religieuse à la Côte d'Ivoire* Paris: Société des Missions Évangéliques 1924, Appendix I, 33.

2d. J.E. Casely Hayford, barrister at Axim, and newspaper publisher.
Casely Hayford took Harris seriously, as friends reported to Haliburton
during the course of his research, and it was even rumoured that
he had been baptized by Harris.[20] His book about Harris was published
in 1915 and he probably wrote the following in 1914, at the time
of Harris's visit to Axim.

> Of his call he speaks with awe . . . It seems as if God made the soul
> of Harris a soul of fire. You cannot be in his presence for long without
> realising that you are in contact with a great personality. He began
> as a reformer in the state. He ended as a reformer in the spiritual
> realm. But I anticipate. One day in his own State in Liberia he hoisted
> up the Union Jack as a protest. He was had up for treason and imprisoned.
> In prison, as he puts it, he fell into a trance. Thrice was he visited
> by strange visitants, and thrice he received his call. He was quick to
> understand. He was eager to obey. He began "prophesying and preaching
> rebellion", to put it in his own words. Thrice was he imprisoned, and
> thrice was he released. By then it began to dawn on men that this
> thing was of God. From then the spirit had its way with him until
> today he is a force to reckon with. [. . .] According to Harris he saw
> a light in his dungeon. Then he built this cross and carried it about.
> Is it possible that same light follows him and causes souls to tremble
> in his presence.[21]

2e. Father Joseph Hartz, temporary Superior at Bingerville, interviewed
Harris at Governor Angoulvant's request in September 1914.

> I am a prophet; above all religions and freed from the control of men.
> I depend only on God through the intermediary of the angel Gabriel.
> Four years ago [i.e. in 1910] I was rudely awakened during the night.
> I saw the guardian angel in a sensible form above my bed. Three times
> he struck me on the crown of the head and said to me, 'I ask of you
> the sacrifice of your wife. She will die, but I will give you others who
> will help you in the work which you must establish. Before her death
> your wife will give you six shillings; this will be your fortune; you will
> never have need of anything more. With these six shillings you will
> get around everywhere, and they will never be lacking. I will accompany
> you everywhere and will reveal to you the mission to which you are
> destined by God, the Master of the Universe whom men no longer
> respect. After this revelation the angel renews his apparitions and little

---

[20] *HN*
[21] Casely Hayford, *William Waddy Harris: the West African reformer*. London: C.M.
Phillips 1915, 10. On p. 8 Hayford wrote: "He means I came to preach against
rebellion. He denounces authorities and powers without fear."

by little initiates me to my mission of prophet of modern times, of the Era of Peace about which Saint John speaks in the 20th chapter of revelation: peace of a thousand years whose arrival is at hand.

In fact, shortly thereafter my wife died, she also having been informed of my mission by the Angel. Before leaving me, she predicted a laborious success for my mission.[22]

2f. Father Peter Harrington, Irish missionary recently arrived at Grand Cess in 1916, where he had a visit in May with Harris, accompanied by one woman, whom Harrington referred to as "his better half".

He described how he was imprisoned by the Liberian authorities at Cape Palmas, he and other young Krumen, for attempting to plant the Union Jack on the sand beach; how through the intervention of the Angel Gabriel, he had escaped from prison, leaving his old clothes behind, and was miraculously clothed in his present garb; how he was re-imprisoned and again released as soon as his visions were acknowledged by the people and the authorities; how he visited the Ivory Coast and the Gold Coast; preaching the destruction of fetishes and the reign of Jesus. His Kru name was Wadé—his Liberian or assumed name was Gabriel Harris, the Archangel Gabriel being his defender, and as one would imagine a kind of travelling mentor. [. . .]

When I was in *trance* [sic in original text] the Archangel Gabriel said to me, "Harris, you must not touch wine or such things, neither must you follow the frivolities of the world; you must not wear boots or trousers or collar—you are a prophet of Christ, of God the Mysterious. This is a favourite phrase of his and inclines me to think that he must have been in touch with some phase of Mahomedanism, for the Koran and the conversation of Mahomedan preachers is full of similar expressions, "God the compassionate, the merciful, the abundant, etc."[23]

2g. M. Gaston Joseph, *Chef du Cabinet* of Governor Angoulvant, perhaps present for the interview of the latter with Harris in late September 1914.

He said that he was the envoy of God. The angel Gabriel had appeared to him and had guided him towards the animistic countries.[24]

---

[22] Rev. Joseph Hartz, Superior at Bingerville, Ivory Coast. Extracts from his journal, published in G. van Bulck, s.j., "Le Prophète Harris vu par lui-même (Côte d'Ivoire, 1914)", in *Devant les Sectes Non-Chrétiennes*. Louvain: XXXème Semaine de Missiologie [1961], 120–124.

[23] Rev. Peter Harrington, S.M.A. (missionary at Grand Cess, Liberia), "An interview with the 'Black Prophet'". *The African Missionary* 18 (March–April), 1917, 13–16.

[24] Gaston Joseph, "Une atteinte à l'animisme chez les populations de la Côte d'Ivoire", in *Annuaire et Mémoires du Comité d'Etudes Historiques et Scientifiques de l'Afrique Occidentale Française*. Gorée: Imprimerie du Gouvernement Général, 1916, 344–348.

2h. Captain Paul Marty, colonial administrator, probably writing from administrative reports.

> He was summoned to Bingerville. There he made some declaration which one might summarize thus: being master of a protestant school of Cape Palmas, and given the title of 'reverend', he saw in a dream the angel Gabriel who in the name of God invited him to go to the fetishists to destroy the emblems of their worship, to stir them up to a more moral life through work, and to hinder them from giving themselves to their bent on drunkenness.[25]

2i. Father Joseph Gorju, provicar of the Ivory Coast mission, absent at the time of the Hartz and Angoulvant conversations. He returned to the Ivory Coast in November; eye-witnesses reported to Haliburton in 1963 that Gorju had contacts with Harris. As provicar he also had access to the governor and his administration.

> [...] this sly fox, putting to profit a similarity in names, recognized an incarnation of the archangel Gabriel, his ordinary guardian, in the person of the Governor of the colony [Gabriel Angoulvant] who was quite astonished by this celestial origin which he had never suspected.[26]

2j. Rev. Pierre Benoît, missionary pastor from Grand Lahou, to Cape Palmas, end of September 1926. The text given is our edition, based on the *Benoît Notes* and filled out with the *Benoît Report* III, which is here placed in parentheses, and following our translation.[27]

> The Angel Gabriel is my teacher; when he teach me I am in trance. He show me the verses ... St. Mark 9. Jesus Christ must reign: I am his prophet.
> Q. When did the angel Gabriel begin to speak to you?
> A. Liberia man put me in prison 1908 [sic]. But in prison Angel Gabriel came and told me you are not in prison (you are in heaven).

(I then try to learn what this expression means to him,—"the angel Gabriel"—which he has evidently found in his Bible).

> Q. How do you recognize the angel Gabriel?
> A. I know it is he. I was in trance and I saw him spiritually.

---

[25] Paul Marty, "L'impressionabilité religieuse des populations maritimes et lagunaires", chapter 1 in *Etudes sur l'Islam en Côte d'Ivoire*. Paris: Editions Ernest Leroux 1922.
[26] J. Gorju, "Un prophète à la Côte d'Ivoire", *Echo* 14 (4), September–October 1915, 116.
[27] *BN* I, 10ff; *BR* III, 6ff.

Q. Did you see him with your eyes?
A. Not with my eyes; (I see him inside myself,) spiritually. I was in a trance.
Q. What did he tell you?
A. You are not in prison. God will come and anoint you. (You will be a prophet). Your case resembles Shadrach, Meshach and Abednego. You are like Daniel (thrown into prison to be tested, then to become a great prophet.)
Q. How did you feel that God was anointing you?
A. At that time God anointed me; (the spirit came down with a noise on my head). It was like that: shie! (he imitates the noise of a jet of water) . . . three times. It was like ice on my head and all my skin. My case is like Rev. 20:4. Now I (will have a throne and) am going to be judge.
Q. How do you know that all that is really true?
A. It is like Hebrews 11:1. You do not see those things but they possess you . . . like prophet Moses.
Q. How do you know all the verses you give me?
A. Angel Gabriel tell me: search so-and-so. . such verses. The spirit in me is the spirit of Pentecost. (It is the spirit which makes speak in tongues as it is in) I Cor 14:2. (These are mysteries which men do not understand.) Your questions are a spiritual examination so you see I am the prophet.

C. The Event

1. *What happened?*

   - had a vision (Neal).
   - heard someone behind him speaking (Campbell).
   - fell into a trance; thrice visited (Hayford).
   - intervention of the archangel (Harrington).
   - angel appeared to him (Joseph).
   - angel came to me . . . I was in trance (Benoît).
   - in dream he saw an angel (Marty).

2. *Where?*

   - in prison (Neal, Hayford, Harrington, Clarck)
   - in his dungeon (Hayford)
   - above my bed (Hartz).

   The prison context does not appear in sources coming from the French administration, to whom Harris did not mention his prison experiences.

3. When?

   − during the night (Hartz).
   − while carrying out his [fetish] rites as usual (Campbell).
   ["One day while" translates the French *un jour*, which does not imply daytime, but rather "once", "when".]

4. How?

4a. Saw . . .

   − a vision . . . the Lord in a great wave of light (Neal).
   − a light . . . angel in the light (Clarck).
   − a light in his dungeon (Hayford).
   − the guardian angel (Hartz).
   − in a dream the angel Gabriel (Marty).
   − [Gabriel] spiritually . . . not with my eyes but spiritually; I was in trances (Benoît).

4b. Heard

   − orders . . . to abandon his clothes, not to marry, burn the fetishes beginning with his own, preach everywhere Christian baptism, leave off all European clothing . . . and his patent-leather shoes, reclothe himself in kind of toga (Neal).
   − he would be a prophet (Clarck)
   − call to preach (against) rebellion (Hayford)
   − need to sacrifice wife who would die, give him six shillings first for provision; others would be given to help in work; angel will accompany and reveal a mission (Hartz).
   − abandon rod and charms, take long cane, go here and there from place to place and preach Christ; tell family to abandon fetishes; power is upon you (Campbell).
   − must not touch wine or such things nor follow frivolities of the world; not wear boots and trousers or collar; you are prophet of God the Mysterious (Harrington).
   − invited in the name of God to go to the fetishers to destroy the emblems of their worship, to stir them up to a more moral life through work, to hinder them from giving themselves to their bent on drunkenness (Marty).
   − you are not in prison but in heaven. God will come and anoint you. You will be a prophet . . . a great prophet (Benoît).
   − thrice was he called (Hayford).

4c. Felt . . .
- he is anointed. . felt the water pour on his head (Neal).
- three times struck on the crown of the head (Hartz).
- a long cane is given to him (Campbell).
- The spirit descended upon my head, like water, three times, like ice on my head) and my skin (Benoît).

It may be noted in this synopsis that Harris chooses to emphasize certain elements in his narrative according to his audience (missionary, administrator, nominal Christian) and to omit others. Superficially this may give the impression that he is describing different events, but it actually shows his remarkable sensitivity. A *résumé* of the whole might read:

> Disillusioned with Christianity and civilization, William Wadé Harris was ready to use any of the traditional methods to seek out justice and peace for his people. Demoralized completely because of failure, even in war, to obtain his goals, and because of the dark future resulting from the war of 1910, he turned again in prison to fetish practice. Some time before June 1910 he was awakened at night and in bed—during a trance—was called by God (of the Bible) through the visitation of the Archangel Gabriel who appeared to him spiritually as a man in a great wave of light. He was told that he was in heaven, and that God was going to anoint him prophet, like Daniel, but of a modern time of peace. This God-destined mission was to consist of preaching, fetish-destruction, and Christian baptism. He was to destroy his own fetishes as well as those of his family and accept new patterns. Details of his future behaviour and dress were revealed. He was told that his wife would die, after helping him to make his new costume, and that she would leave him six shillings as a precise sign of future provision. The visitation concluded with a triune anointing by God, which came to him as a physical sensation of cold water and ice. He was given a promise of great power. Through the angel's intervention he escaped from prison and began preaching, but although re-imprisoned was later released. The whole experience was such that he could describe it as "seeing the Lord", "God told", or "God ordered". It constituted his prophetic vocation.

The result of what others called his "vision" but which Harris himself described as a trance-visitation was to change his identity and mission and his relationship to God and other people. One student of Harris concluded that Harris did not appear to be "anything extraordinary" and "was not unique". He went on to say, "Harris was not doing anything very different [from other white or black missionaries]; he is only exceptional . . . in his vision, his departure from Liberia and the resulting success."[28] This view ignores the evidence which makes it clear that the visitation was essential to Harris's mission, and without any doubt responsible for his departure from Liberia and the resulting success.[29] With such an understanding one misses completely the essential inspiration of the religious dynamics which set off the movement within the Ivory Coast, the Gold Coast, and Liberia. In spite of all the colonially imposed political and social *dégradation*[30] in West Africa which indeed helped to precipitate the movement, it can yet not be understood without this inspirational factor. It is the inspirational factor which "suddenly makes a movement". It is as "condensation nuclei are to the formation of rain; the rallying point, its stimulative center."[31] When African church history comes to be written by Africans for Africans, no doubt the significance of Harris's trance-visitation will be properly evaluated.[32]

D. *The content of the vision*

This is not the place to give way to the temptation to analyse the possible mental mechanisms[33] of the "vision", and to reduce it to some

---

[28] John Zarwan, "The genesis of an African religious movement." *Missiology* 3 (4), 1975, 445.

[29] Zarwan underestimates the religious dimension of Harris's success, attributing it to the demoralized populations of the Ivory Coast. Thus the Gold Coast success, where the economic, social and political conditions were quite different from those of the recently "pacified" Ivory Coast, is seen by Zarwan to be "peripheral". In reality it was a major breakthrough.

[30] See for the Ivory Coast in particular Simon-Pierre Ekanza, *Colonisation et sociétés traditionelles. Un quart de siècle de dégradation du monde traditionel ivoirien, 1893–1920.* University of Provence, Aix-en-Provence, thesis of the 3rd cycle, 1972 (2 vols).

[31] Gottfried Oosterwal, *Modern messianic movements. . . .* Elkhart, Indiana: Institute of Mennonite Studies 1973, 34.

[32] This is made quite clear by the African theologian John Mbiti in his "God, dreams and prophetic militancy", in John S. Pobee (ed.), *Religion in a pluralistic society.* Leiden: E.J. Brill 1976, 38–47. Harris's vision is there cited as a prime example of the crucial character of the vision for prophetic vocation. A more general discussion of the transcendant significance of dreams and visions in West Africa may be found in "Dreams as charismatic significants: their bearing on the rise of new religious movements" in W.T. Williams (ed.), *Psychological anthropology*, 1975, 221–235. Bengt Sundkler, *The Christian mission in Africa*, London: SCM Press 1960, illustrates the important role of dreams for ministerial vocations in Africa.

[33] Particularly as discussed by M.J. Field in *Search for security*, London: Faber, 1960; more recently in her "Relevant mental mechanisms", in M.J. Field, *Angels and ministers of grace.* London: Longman 1971, 65–83. Zarwan, *op. cit.* 346, writes of the vision as "an appropriate psychological device for the answer to come in a dream."

fuller awareness of a newly-acquired "super-ego" in the developmental process from tribalism to individualism.[34] Jung's analyses might be more fruitful,[35] but it seems more pertinent, and more helpful, to examine some of the raw materials of the visitation. Whatever the attitude towards it of outside observers, we dare never forget the transcendental, supernatural and authoritative character that it had for him.[36]

1. The Angel Gabriel

Numerous writers have pointed out parallels between the simple patterns adopted by Harris and the simple but effective impact of Islam in sub-Saharan Africa. Blyden's known interest in Islam could possibly have influenced Harris. Points of comparison are, first, Harris's simple message: "Jesus Christ must reign; I am his prophet"; his headress is sometimes noted as a second, at least external, Islamic note. Father Harrington noted a third, in Harris's Muslim-sounding expression, "God the mysterious". Is it possible that the Angel Gabriel tradition in Mohammad's experience had influence upon Harris? Although not wholly impossible,[37] no evidence but the Blyden connection can be found for this kind of influence.

However, it would appear more faithful to Harris himself to look where he pointed to the angel's own teaching ministry—that is, to the Bible.

Harris himself related to Benoît that the angel said, "You are like Daniel." The story of Daniel would have been well-known to Harris both as a student, and as a school teacher. Bishop Ferguson used a sketch of Daniel on his personal envelope for some time.[38] The book of Daniel, after recounting supernatural presence and deliverance in times of imprisonment, finally relates three appearances of the angel Gabriel to the man Daniel.

---

[34] Cf. Raoul Allier, La psychologie de conversion chex les peuples non-civilisés, I. Paris: Payot 1925, especially 349–397.

[35] Cf. Carl Jung, Man and his symbols. London: Pan Books 1978 (lst ed., 1964).

[36] Cf. V. Lanternari, "Dreams as charismatic significants" in W.T. Williams (ed.) Psychological anthropology, 1975, 221–235.

[37] Such a claim, without evidence, was made by the then recent Harrist convert, Egny Pégard Michel, in a public lecture at Groguida, Grand Lahou, 12 August 1979 : Fondation et pratique de la religion Harris, unpublished ms., 3: "[Harris] entreprit une étude comparée de la Bible et du Coran" [. . .].

[38] See in the archives of the Episcopal bishop Browne, in Monrovia in April 1978, in volume of Missionary Reports 1903–1907.

In the first vision Gabriel addresses Daniel when he is in a deep sleep, and gives him the interpretation of a previous vision. (Daniel 8.16–27). In the second vision the angel comes while Daniel is speaking, praying and confessing his sin and the sins of his people Israel. He addresses Daniel as "greatly beloved" and tells him that he will receive "skill and understanding". (Daniel 9.21–27). In the third vision Daniel is again addressed as a "man greatly beloved" (Daniel 10.11), and in chapter 11 various revelations are given to him.

Daniel was seeking meaning for himself and his people in the midst of events which were causing distress to the people of God, under imperial pressures of cultural and religious repression, which he saw as caused largely by their own unfaithfulness.

This distress called forth Daniel's prayer of confession, found in chapter 9: "To the Lord our God belong mercies and forgivenesses, though we have rebelled against him; . . ." In this situation the angel Gabriel was sent to Daniel to help him to understand the present, and to give him a promise of future vision in the "time of the end" (11.35). Here the "Ethiopians" are temporarily submitted to a "king of the North" who finally comes to his end (11.43).

To Harris in his prison cell the creative power of the Daniel narrative is not difficult to grasp. One can indeed see within it the background for the affirmation, "You are like Daniel".

The book of Daniel is not, of course, the only biblical source describing the activity of Gabriel; he is the messenger of God to the Virgin Mary and to the father of John the Baptist; the ministry of angels to Jesus is specifically mentioned in the story of the Temptation and Gethsemane. In the early church angels are mentioned as helpers in times of crisis, such as when Peter was imprisoned. (See also Acts 8.26ff; Acts 10; Acts 27.33).

So from the perspective of Holy Scripture, the intervention of an angel is no strange or inappropriate event, but nevertheless was extraordinary and supernatural. A reading of Bede's history of the early English church will demonstrate the same attitude.[39]

It was the exceptional occurrence which made it marvellous, and made it become an accepted medium for guidance, warning and revelation to individuals, and often to a community through them.

---

[39] Bede, *A history of the English Church and people*. Penguin Books, 1976. E.g., Bishop Germanus of Auxerre during his mission to Britain in 429, cf. p. 62; the monk Fursey in 633, p. 173ff.; the nun Earcongata, a generation later, p. 154; etc.

2. *The trance*

We use the word "trance" rather than "vision" because Harris preferred it. From the beginning it seems to have been the word he used to refer to his experience, although other sources have often used "vision". Because of the importance of what happened to Harris himself, it is necessary to examine the phenomenon carefully.

First, as regards Harris's religio-cultural heritage, we must recall the reports of the *deyabo*, the Glebo doctors or "devil-men", as Bishop Payne described them.

> They suppose themselves possessed by a demon or spirit under whose inspiration they act and give their responses. They exhibit the peculiarities of those mentioned in Scriptures as 'possessed'. . . . an individual [who] is said to be possessed . . . is at once placed with an old 'Deya' to be instructed in the arts and mysteries of the profession.[40]

The child Wadé would have been conditioned to believe that supernatural spiritual powers were available and obtainable, although the source, in his understanding, would not be that of the *Deyabo*.

Harris had also been open to conditioning by the Bible, where he found accounts of supernatural powers being used effectively by "men of God", the Old Testament prophets and the New Testament apostles. Such men used the powers they were granted against the powers of the *deyabo* of their world, as Elijah against the priests of Baal, Peter against the magician Simon Magus, and Paul against Elymas the sorcerer.

The Biblical phenomena have been discussed by Lindblom;[41] one point especially worth noting is that Harris possessed and used the English King James Version of the Bible.[42] In that version the word "trance" is used in, for example, Numbers 24.4 and 24.16. In the New Testament also the term "trance" is used, as in Acts 10.10 (Peter's vision). The trance phenomenon is in fact a real part of Harris's own traditional background, and also to be found in the Bible which he read.

---

[40] Rt. Rev. John Payne, cited in Harry H. Johnston, *Liberia*, vol. II. London: Hutchinson 1906, 1074–78, and 1068–72.

[41] J. Lindblom, *Prophecy in Ancient Israel*. Philadelphia: Fortress Press 1965, 47ff.

[42] "I saw that the book he placed in my hands was the Authorized Version of the Bible, so I warmly welcomed him." Ernest Bruce, "I grew up with history." *African Challenge*, 7 (4), April 1957, 6.

I.M. Lewis has simply stated the implications of trance: it is, in the circumstances in which it occurs, "open to different cultural controls and to various cultural interpretations."[43] Therefore we must look not merely at the cultural and biblical background but at Harris's own usage.

In addition to the texts already cited, we may gain light from other texts in Benoît's record. From the *Benoît Report*:

Benoît: How is it that you hear God speaking to you?

Harris: It is mysterious. I do not hear with my ears. It is stronger. I hear spiritually. God speaks to me in an unknown tongue.

Benoît: Is it not your own voice?

Harris: [He is scandalized and opens his eyes wide] No never. How could I believe? They are unknown voices and I understand them. I also reply to God in an unknown tongue. Moses, the Angel Gabriel, and Elijah, these three great prophets come and I alone speak with them. See Apoc. 5.8.[44]

It seems clear from the texts that the word "spiritually" and the reality of the trance are closely linked. Harris "sees" the Angel Gabriel "not physically but spiritually". Benoît's curiosity about these phenomena is seen as a "spiritual" examination, and the spiritual phenomena are evidence of a prophetic status. "Spiritual" appears to connote what Western categories might describe as "psychic".

Harris claimed his trance experience (for instance in speaking to the French colonial authorities) as evidence of his exceptional and gifted status. The trance was for him a non-verbal yet conceptual communication; nor was it wholly passive. Harris speaks with Gabriel, Elijah or Moses, and replies to God when in a trance.

Father Hartz reported that during his conversation with Harris in September 1914, Harris "went into a trance. A cataleptic crisis threw him to the ground. When he recovered, I resumed the conversation."[45] Bureau, who noted the testimony, indicated that it needed to be received with caution.[46] However, we have no reason to think that Hartz was doing anything but describing faithfully what he saw; but it was in any case only one form of trance. Benoît, when he met with Harris

---

[43] I.M. Lewis, *Ecstatic religion: an anthropological study of spirit possession and shamanism.* Harmondsworth: Penguin Books 1974, 44.

[44] *BN* II 12; *BR* III 5f.

[45] See Hartz (as footnote 22 above).

[46] René Bureau, "William Wadé Harris et le harrisme." *Annales de l'Université d'Abidjan,* Série F., t.3, 1971, 38.

in 1926, found Harris "trembling"; but what Harris said was "in trances" Benoît saw only as the trembling of old age.[47] Hartz's testimony reminds us that the possibility of occasional possession trances was not outside the whole experience of Harris;[48] it is not clear, however, that the Western category of "psychological dis-equilibrium" is an adequate appreciation of the phenomenon.[49]

There is independent evidence to show that Harris came from an area known for its cultural acceptance of possession-state trances compared with simple trance or spirit possession.[50] We do not have enough evidence to justify the idea that he was culturally bound to that type of experience. But it seems clear that, whatever form the trance took, it provided Harris not only with the cultural understanding of "election" or "vocation", but also with the spiritual context for ongoing spiritual guidance and revelation.

The biblical cultural contribution confirmed this understanding for Harris, and the Bible also furnished most of the contents of his trances. An expert on trance and possession states has commented that "in possession-trance we find a very clear expression of the influence of learning and expectation on the behaviour of the trances."[51] This is consonant with the Messiah's word that the Spirit "shall teach you all things, and bring to your remembrance whatsoever I have said to you" (John 14.26). Harris was on solid biblical ground for trances and angel visitations in the midst of persecutions, and guidance through angelic messages and healing.

But such patterns were acceptable neither with the teachings of

---

[47] *BR* I 22

[48] John Howe, 92 years old in 1978, was Harris's nephew and neighbour. He reported in Cape Palmas in April 1978 that Harris often had trances in which he appeared to be absent, and in which he saw people who had "already gone to heaven", like Shannon, Harris's old Episcopal superintendent. Cf. also Paul Breidenbach, "Ritual interrogation and the communication of belief in a West African religious movement", in *Journal of Religion in Africa* 9 (2), 96. The tradition among the Church of the Twelve Apostles in western Ghana was, according to Breidenbach, that: "Aside from his message and this simple ritual action, Harris appeared to enter into possession states during which he expelled evil *sunsum* from others. It was this aspect of what my informants called the *tum* of Harris that seems to have most impressed Tani and Nackabah and their followers."

[49] Cf. Roger Bastide, *Le rêve, la trance, et la folie.* Paris: Flammarion, 1972. See esp. "La trance", pp. 55–104, where Bastide contests the validity of western psychiatric concepts to describe phenomena which appear as "ordered corporal liturgy", etc.

[50] Cf. Erika Bourguignon, "'World distribution' and patterns of possession states", in Raymond Price (ed.), *Trance and possession states.* Montreal: R.M. Buck Memorial Society 1966, 3–32; see esp. 19.

[51] *Ibid.*, 12.

the Methodist Episcopal Church, nor with those of the Episcopal Church. Harris had been the agent of both churches, but it is an African and biblical pattern which emerges in his prison cell. He himself applies to his experience the Pauline criterion of spirit experiences— does it build up others in the church?[52] He twice cited its context— I Corinthians 14—to Benoît in 1926.[53]

Benoît—a modern Westerner—sought to understand Harris's explanations:

> [they] show Harris's experience to be very like other mystical experiences already studied. Rational knowledge and mystical knowledge mingle and help each other to terminate in a state in which the subject feels himself dominated by an outside power higher than himself.[54]

Lindblom, in discussing the primitive prophets of the Old Testament, can make a singular and fuller contribution to our understanding of Harris.

> If ecstasy is understood as the well-known state in which the ego fully loses the consciousness of itself and becomes completely absorbed in the Divine, ... there can be no talk of ecstasy in connection with the Israelite prophets. Psychologists also use the term ecstacy, however, in another sense denoting a mental state in which the human consciousness is so concentrated on a particular idea or feeling that the normal current of thoughts and perceptions is broken off and the senses temporarily cease to function in a normal way ... which may also be called 'concentration ecstasy'. Ecstasy in the [second] sense is not in any way at variance with personal religion. To use the language of religious experience, God can speak to men during a state of ecstasy as well as during a state of prayer. It is a fact that men whose awareness of the external world is temporarily inhibited can have religious experiences and receive divine revelations and spiritual impulses which by far surpass what can be given in a normal state of mind.[55]

Harris must have observed the close relationship of the trance and the angelic presence in the life of Elijah, one of the Old Testament prophets he refers to (I Kings 19.5ff. and II Kings 1.3, 13ff). Lindblom's comment is helpful: "The 'angel' illustrates the 'extension of personality'

---

[52] I Corinthians 14.3, 4, 5, 12, 17.
[53] *BN* I, 12; II, 12.
[54] *BR* II, 8.
[55] Lindblom, *op. cit.*, 106ff.

which, according to Johnson, played so great a part in Israelite thinking."[56] This is helpful in understanding how Harris, in his experience of angelic visitation, could "see the Lord". But it is also an interesting suggestion for a better understanding in Harris of what has been seen by many observers to be an unmitigated monotheism. Harris's religious pilgrimage from Glebo traditional religion to that of his "only true God" must have been not unlike that of the Palestinian peoples in their transition from *baals* to prophetic ethical monotheism in Israel; Harris himself made the parallel. It may also remind us of the caution against a too facile identification of phenomena as specifically "African"; it may rather be typical "primal" religious experience but in an African context with an African expression.

3. The Anointing

Grace Neal reported to Benoît that her father had been "anointed" in the Grafton prison. Then Harris explained for him the angelic promise of his "anointing" as well as his experience: "the spirit came down with a noise on my head. . . ." We have already observed the importance of the "spirit" in Harris's first conversion and we meet it again on this second occasion. If he can speak of the spiritual nature of the prophetic call in terms that suggest psychic reality, he also speaks of it in biblical terms, identifying it with Acts: "the spirit in me is the spirit of Pentecost" (BN I.12). We note here its importance but will examine its significance in Chapter VIII.

E. The prophetic mission and message

In May 1916, the prophet Harris told Father Harrington that in the Ivory Coast and the Gold Coast he had been "preaching the destruction of fetishes and the reign of Jesus." Ten years later he told Pastor Benoît, "Jesus Christ must reign; I am his prophet." Thus his message and mission are set within a clear Christological and eschatological pattern. The evidence seems to date that pattern specifically from the first visitation in prison.

When Harris presented himself to Father Hartz with "I am a prophet", this eschatological, Christological pattern gave explicit content

---

[56] *Ibid.*, citing A.R. Johnson, *The one and the many in the Israelite conception of God.* Cardiff: University of Cardiff Press 1942, 32ff.

to "prophet". Again, when Father Harrington addressed him as "Mr. Harris", he confirmed with "Yes, I am Harris; Harris the prophet." It is quite clear that "prophet" is a title given him and not a self-designation; but it is also a title which is orientated essentially to Christ and the "last times".

A second observation in connection with the title and role of prophet is that, contrary to many later "prophets", he did not appear to have any apparent model or prototype from within West Africa. There had certainly been occasional appearances of prophets or prophetesses prior to Harris, but not in West Africa. Such independent churches as had appeared were within the so-called "Ethiopian tradition", which can scarcely be called a prophet movement.[57] From the perspective of Schlosser's and Sundkler's studies of 1948, [58] and the post-Kimbangu studies from the Congoes prior to independence, one is easily tempted to read the presence of such models back into Harris's situation. And the contemporary student has often been given a clear image of an "African prophet" since Balandier's sociological study of 1955; there the dynamics of the prophetic phenomena are laid bare from a uniquely socio-political perspective.[59] If it is apparent that the pre-prophetic Harris tends to fit that typology, it is not obvious that the prophet Harris conforms to Balandier's canon. Even in his pre-prophetic period he was protesting in favour of a strong white colonial regime. Indeed, Harris himself deserves the appellation of *prototype*, as it is used by René Bureau, especially as far as West Africa is concerned.[60]

In discussing Harris's declared role as a prophet, we need first of all to understand what the term meant to Harris himself. Haliburton notes the now accepted definition of Old Testament prophets as "forthtellers rather than foretellers"—"not seers of the future in any specific sense, though in common usage we tend to assume so."[61] But we cannot be certain that this was Harris's own self-understanding.

[57] See Maurice Leenhardt, *Le mouvement Ethiopien au Sud de l'Afrique de 1896 à 1899.* Montauban: Cahors, 1902. Réimpression: Paris: Académie des Sciences d'Outre-mer, 1976.

[58] Katesa Schlosser, *Propheten in Afrika.* Braunschweig: A. Limbach 1949; Bengt Sundkler, *Bantu prophets in South Africa.* London: Oxford University Press 1961 (2nd ed.); 1st ed., London: Lutterworth Press, 1948.

[59] See George Balandier, *Sociologie actuelle de l'Afrique Noire.* Paris: Presses Universitaires de France, 1955.

[60] *Cf.* René Bureau and Jean-Pierre Lehmann, "Le prophète, pouvoir et guérison en Côte d'Ivoire." Unpublished ms., 1973, 9.

[61] *PH*, xiv f.

There are certainly indications in the *Benoît Notes* that Harris believed that he "knew" the future.[62] Such evidence is convincing proof of the inappropriateness of examining the Harris saga strictly in the light of its socio-political intent or effectiveness.[63]

"You will be prophet . . . like Daniel,"said the angel. The biblical book of Daniel is, peculiarly, a predictive, apocalyptic, book. There, the Angel Gabriel opens up the future to Daniel. Following his first visitation, Harris—like Daniel—is "initiated little by little into my mission of modern times, of the era of peace . . . of a thousand years . . . whose coming is nigh. The angel instructs me on the time of the future." Harris is a predictive prophet functioning within the pattern of eschatological and apocalyptic thought patterns. An oral tradition several times confirmed reports his prediction of the First World War as well as the times of peace that were to follow. We are not here concerned with the accuracy of Harris's predictions; we insist simply upon the role of those predictions and Harris's own faith in them as a motor for his own activity.

Father Harrington was surely not the only person who asked himself what motivated Harris to brave so many difficulties, as in the time of the Kru wars of 1916 when he continued his foot journeys despite warfare and exceedingly bad conditions of movement.[64] "But the Prophet seemed undaunted."

Of course, when the future has been revealed, one is undaunted; particularly is this true if one is oneself not only identified with that future but is, as well, the instrument of its appearing. Such was the import of the identity and mission which Harris received through his prison visitation; his predictive message was a fuller expression of that basic understanding. His task was to announce the soon-coming reign of Christ and to prepare others for it in the present.

When Benoît interviewed him in 1926 this was still his first reaction.

> He knows, he says, that the people of the Ivory Coast still worship fetishes. Someone must speak to them all. The time is short . . . Jesus Christ is coming again, he will soon be here. He will bring fire everywhere he is not known—that they may serve the true God only.[65]

---

[62] See for example *BN* II, 8f.

[63] As Ekanza has done in *Le messianisme en Côte d'Ivoire au début du siècle* in *Annales de l'Université d'Abidjan* Série I, t.3, 1974. This is an adaptation of a chapter from his thesis; see note 30 above.

[64] Harrington (as in note 23 above).

[65] *BR* I, 14f.

Here the thrust of his message is part of a larger pattern of the soon-coming of Christ in judgement, in view of blessing. This eschatological pattern did not fit Benoît's pre-conceptions of him as the simple "fetish-destroying" Elijah. In fact, the French missionary could not accept that this was part of the "genuine" or "original" Harris, and attributed the eschatological views to "a pamphlet of an adventist sect. . . . The old prophet has based on this a whole series of eschatological convictions."[66]

Benoît was totally misinformed; it was not this pamphlet[67] nor Harris's age that were responsible for "the whole series of eschatological convictions." They had been expressed to witnesses who spoke to him already in 1914 and 1916; rather, according to Harris himself, the real source was the trance-visitation of 1910. Christ's imminent reign was the horizon of his mission; "fetish-worship" had to be rooted out because it was seen as the greatest hindrance to that reign.

The missionary message he had received in his youth was an appeal to abandon Africanness; his prophetic message is not anti-African, but anti-"fetish". His later adherents have sometimes interpreted him as anti-white, and anti-European. But his message was that of the coming reign of Christ, which cut across all human polarizations, whether heathen/civilized, black/white, or African/European. It called for a new polarization of disobedient/obedient and rebellion against/respect for the authority of Christ. "Fetishism" was a form of rebellion characteristic of blacks, but the whites too had their own forms of rebellion, and both were equally subject to divine judgement.

All this has been obscured in the contemporary accounts, and Benoît's bias, which accentuated the "fetish-burning and baptizing", and almost reduced Harris to a kind of "white magic" artist and hypnotist. A more recent analysis totally underestimates the eschatological dimension: "Harris's millennial ideas do not appeared to have played an

---

[66] *BR* I, 20.

[67] The *Benoît Notes* reported the title of the newspaper as *The Christian Herald*. It was in fact an "adventist" paper from within the main evangelical stream of British Protestantism. However, a careful perusal of the edition which Harris had reveals no particular "adventist" concerns; there is hardly any eschatological reference in that number. It is *The Christian Herald and Signs of our Times* 59 (26), Thursday 25 June 1925. There is a first page headline: AN AFRICAN "ELIJAH" AND HIS 20,000 CONVERTS. Page 726 has an article: The African Elijah. Missionary Discovers 22,000 Black Christians. There are photos of Platt in clerical dress, and of Harris, "The Black 'Elijah' who has been the leader of a remarkable revival in West Africa."

important role, . . . and they were not picked up," wrote Zarwan in 1975.[68]

The French missionary de Billy did not find this the case when he went to the Ivory Coast in 1925. He wrote of

> the enthusiasm of the beginning, where messianic hopes were being added to the natural joy of churches who were naturally famished [and where] the Whites with the Bible, the successors of Harris, were to institute a new era [. . .][69]

The Methodist missionaries' problem was that they were not able to satisfy the expectations which Harris's message had created. When the secretary of the Wesleyan Missionary Society returned from his visit to the Gold Coast in March 1915, scarcely seven months after Harris's visit to the Axim area, he wrote,

> He had taught them that there was one God and Jesus Christ the Saviour of men. And he had called upon the people in God's name to abandon fetishism and become Christians. . . . There had been a touch of fanaticism about him, no doubt preaching a simple elementary Gospel.[70]

His apocalyptic eschatology might appear as "fanaticism" to many observers. And it was indeed a simple elementary gospel which Harris was preaching—it might even be compared, as Harris himself did, with the preaching of John the Baptist.

> I am not a minister. I am only a voice crying in the wilderness. Repent for the Kingdom of Heaven is at hand.[71]

Harris was not simply quoting Scripture when, at Axim, he said that he was "forerunner of one greater than he"; he totally identified with the message and its urgency. A witness interviewed in 1964 had heard him speak in this way in 1914, and had been amused by him. He

---

[68] Zarwan, *op. cit.*, p. 440.

[69] Edmond de Billy, *En Côte d'Ivoire*. Paris: Société des Missions Evangéliques [1931], 39f (Our translation).

[70] Quoted in "Missions and the changed outlook." *The Methodist Recorder*, 6 May 1915, 5.

[71] Quoted in C.W. Armstrong, *The winning of West Africa*. London: Wesleyan Methodist Missionary Society 1920, 39. Armstrong visited the Axim area in late July and early August 1914, only ten days after Harris had left the area to return towards the west.

did not even know to whom Harris referred; yet he remembered the saying fifty years later.[72]

How effectively he communicated the Christological, eschatological message, and how it was interpreted, is a question for further study, which goes beyond the present analysis of Harris's thought.

F. The immediate consequences of the trance-visitation

The trance-visitation was the genesis of Harris's prophetic message and mission, and these were its most obvious consequences.

But his on-going relationship with the Angel Gabriel must be noted. "I am under the control of the angel. This is something I cannot resist; I must do all that he puts into my mind," he told Father Hartz. "One day I shall be the companion in heaven of that angel who now commands me."[73]

According to Hayford, in June 1914 at Axim, "The Angel Gabriel's name is constantly on his lips, and he talks of receiving telegrams from heaven."[74] Father Stauffer at Axim confirmed this. "It's the Angel Gabriel who dictates to him whatever he has to do." But Stauffer, who was not on good terms with Hayford, added: "The prophet left to himself would have done a lot of good. He did a lot of good, but would have done a lot more if some people had not been taking upon themselves the role of angel towards him."[75] It was precisely Hayford among others whom Stauffer saw giving guidance in the daytime which would then, in the priest's view, be confirmed to Harris by the "angel" during the night time visitations.

There are other references which help to build up the tradition of Harris's receiving messages from the Angel Gabriel, as in notes sent to *l'Afrique Française* in 1922 with a photo of Harris. Harris is "holding a calabash surrounded by a net carrying shells, by means of which the Angel Gabriel was supposed to give him revelations."[76] Father Harrington reports his reliance on Gabriel as ". . . a kind of travelling mentor",[77] and a similar report was published in the *Sierra Leone Weekly News* of August 1917.

[72] J.P. Ephson, in *HN.*
[73] Hartz (see footnote 22 above).
[74] Hayford (see footnote 21 above).
[75] Father Stauffer, missionary at Axim in 1914. Notes made in a diary sometime around or after 1914. General Archives, S.M.A. Rome, 3A4.
[76] *L'Afrique Française* 32 (6), June 1922, 281.
[77] Harrington (see footnote 23 above).

Harris continued to the end of his life to acknowledge the control of the angel, who replaced all the other authorities to whom he had been subject in his life. "I am prophet. Above all religion and freed from the control of men, I am under God only through the intermediary of the Angel Gabriel."[78] He told Benoît in 1926, "Angel Gabriel is my teacher."

Another consequence of the prison visitation was the death of the prophet's wife, Rose. According to Father Hartz, it was the original visitation which asked of him "the sacrifice of your wife."[79] His daughter told Benoît that "it was not later than the next day that he had this dress made by his wife."[80] In his abandonment of western clothing (a topic which was in his mind earlier) he seems to have confused his wife with the angel. This suggests that in the time immediately following his first visitation he was no longer totally aware of what was going on around him. "His wife thought him to be mad," Mrs. Neal told Benoît; from his notes one concludes that she must have died soon thereafter in June 1910.[81]

Harris had married Rose Farr in the Episcopalian Church in around 1885, when he was preaching with the Methodist Church. Within a few years he had shifted to his wife's church, "for money", as he later admitted. He later seemed to see his time in the Episcopal Church as a period of infidelity, and perhaps saw his Episcopalian wife as a hindrance to his earlier preaching mission. Rose Harris was probably told of the angel's word concerning her, and it must have seemed a "mad" word; shortly thereafter she died.

This can help us to understand the word he reported to Father Hartz, "I will give you others who will help you in the work you must establish." Benoît interpreted from Mrs. Neal's conversation that, from that time, he had not respected the vows of Christian marriage. He reported it negatively: "God, said he, had ordered him not to marry."[82] If his marriage had been a cause of infidelity to his early mission calling, conjugal relationships without vows might have been seen by him as less disobedient than his previous respect of Christian marriage vows.

---

[78] Hartz (see footnote 22 above).
[79] *Ibid.*
[80] *BN* I, 8.
[81] *Ibid.*; *BN* I, 2.
[82] *BN* I, 2: "Dieu dit il lui a ordonné de ne pas se marier." *Cf.* with "I run away for money from Methodist and enter Episcopal Church to make money. I teach school in Graway. I was married with Rose Harris." (*BN* I, 14.)

Such an understanding could place his view of polygamy, later a cause of discussion, in its context. His openness on this question was bound to the 1910 angel visitation and was a direct consequence of it.

G. Re-imprisonment after the prison-visitation of 1910

Six years after the event Harris told Father Harrington that he had miraculously escaped from prison but had been re-imprisoned. From this imprisonment he had been released as soon as his visitations were acknowledged by the people and the authorities.[83]

This is the only evidence we have of Harris's imprisonment by the Liberian authorities after his prophetic calling. But it does account for a third imprisonment to which he had referred in conversation with Hayford. All three periods were grouped around the *coup d'état* of 1909 and the war of 1910, and confirm his non-involvement in earlier Glebo armed uprisings. His anti-Liberian stance developed slowly, and reached its climax in the crises of 1908, 1909 and 1910.

Later in 1910 young Hodge heard him preaching in Monrovia, "Repent! from all your sins, or . . . fire!"[84] In 1915 the French vice-consul in Monrovia recalled having seen him there two or three years earlier, "dressed in white with a white turban, carrying a staff topped with a cross, gesturing and crying . . . At that time no one attached any importance to him; his stay in the Negro captital was not of long duration."[85]

Shortly thereafter he was found in the Ivory Coast, following his July 1913 departure from Cape Palmas with Helen Valentine and Mary Pioka. It is that mission which made him a historically significant personality.

---

[83] Harrington (see footnote 23 above).
[84] In conversation of April 1978 at Cape Palmas.
[85] E. Baret, French Vice-Consul at Monrovia, to the Minister of Foreign Affairs, 19 February 1915.

ILLUSTRATIONS I–IX

A Glebo chief and family, in front of traditional *takae*, Maryland County, Liberia ca. 1900.
om Sir Harry Johnston *Liberia II* London: Hutchison & Co. 1906; figure 360, p. 957.

II. The town of Harper at Cape Palmas, Liberia, after 1900. From R.C.F. Maugham *The Republic of Liberia* London: George Allen and Unwin, 1920.

III. Upper: Methodist Episcopal Church, Harper, Cape Palmas. From Sir Harry
Johnston *Liberia I* London: Hutchison & Co., 1906; figure 131, p. 376.
Lower: Protestant Episcopal Church, Harper, Cape Palmas. From *Liberia I*,
figure 132, p. 376.

IV. Barrister Casely Hayford, politician at Axim, Gold Coast (present Ghana)
and contemporary author of *William Waddy Harris. The West African Reformer:
the man and his message* London: C.M. Phillips, 1915. Photo from Robert W. July
The Origins of Modern African Thought... London: Faber and Faber, 1968.

V. Prophet Harris with Singers, and (presumably) John Swatson after Assinie mission, Côte d'Ivoire, 1914.
Courtesy of Archives of Société des Missions Africaines, Rome.

VI. Prophet Harris with Singers, at height of Côte d'Ivoire mission at Grand Bassam, November 1914. Photo by Fanti photographer, Ignatius Phorson. Courtesy of Mme. Renée Benoît-Meffre, Antony, France.

VII. Twelve Apostles and Preacher in front of church building, more than fifty kilometers in the interior, at Katadji, Côte d'Ivoire, 1926. Photo by Frank Deaville Walker from his *The Story of the Ivory Coast* London: The Cargate Press, 1926; opposite p. 17.

VIII.   Prophet Harris at Harper, Cape Palmas, September 1926; his daughter Grace Neal and her children Rose and Betty; with missionary Pierre Benoît and his interpreter Tano. Courtesy of Mme. Renée Benoît-Meffre, Antony, France.

IX. Prophet Harris, December 1928, at Spring Hill (Half Graway) home, just four months before his death; at time of visit of John Ahui (second from right), Solomon Dagri (extreme left), and their interpreter John Djibo (extreme right); with wife of Harris's nephew and neighbour John Howe, Mrs. Lue Howe, and her children (back row). From *Premier Livret d'Instruction Religieuse à l'Usage des Missions Harristes*, Petit Bassam, 1956.

PART THREE

PROPHETIC THOUGHT PATTERNS

CHAPTER SIX

BIBLICAL ESCHATOLOGY: THE KEY TO HARRIS'S PATTERNS OF THOUGHT

Harris began his prophetic ministry at the age of fifty, in 1910. An examination of the sources which describe the experience has made it clear that there was an essential Christological and eschatological orientation to Harris's understanding of his role as a prophet, as a result of his initial trance-visitation. But the sources also indicate that further understanding and development followed.

> After this revelation, the angel renews his apparitions and little by little initiates me to my mission of prophet of modern times of the Era of Peace about which Saint John speaks in the 20th chapter of Revelation: peace of a thousand years whose arrival is at hand.[1]

This chapter will attempt to understand the fully developed thought emerging out of the gradual initiation of which the prophet speaks.

Our major sources are first of all eyewitnesses to his preaching who wrote their accounts during or soon after meeting him—the missionary priests Stauffer, Harrington and Hartz; the notes and records of the French Methodist, Rev. Pierre Benoît, who met Harris in his old age; and two African men who met Harris and recorded their impressions in interviews many years later. There is variety in these sources, which together build up a fuller understanding of Harris's thought, despite the biases and prejudices of the witnesses.

A. War in 1914

An early element in Harris's predictions was that of a war in Europe in 1914. This was not just a prediction arising out of political awareness,

---

[1] Rev. Joseph Hartz, Superior at Bingerville, Ivory Coast. Extracts from his journal, published in G. van Bulck, s.j., "Le Prophète Harris vu par lui-même (Côte d'Ivoire, 1914)" in *Devant les Sectes Non-Chrétiennes*. Louvain: XXXème Semaine de Missiologie [1961], 120–124.

but an element of an eschatological framework. It is a question of religious prophecy.

> He said that two years before the European war he had predicted to a European that such a catastrophe would occur in Europe. The one to whom the prophecy was made laughed him to scorn. He had however asked him to make a note of what he said . . . at the same time telling [him] that when the war broke out he would think of him.[2]

At this point it is tempting to discern the influence of Russellite teaching, since Russell had become convinced that 1914 was to be a crucial year in the final events of the unfolding of history, and had written of it in his 1891 publication, distributed at Harper, *Thy Kingdom come*.[3] Indeed, the events at Cape Palmas at the end of the century would appear to make it highly probable. In some Evangelical circles in England similar teachings had given rise to emphasis on the importance of 1914.[4]

If Harris saw the war as a part of the prophetic unrolling of history, he also saw it as a result of a "misknowing . . . of God's law".[5] It was "godless bloodshed",[6] yet through which "God speaks by the cannon and the horrors of the war".[7] Harris predicted in late 1914 that the war would last three years; in this he differed from Russell who said that the end of 1915 would bring about the end of "all present governments . . .".[8] According to Harris, the horrors at the end of the war would be worse than those at the beginning.[9]

It would also appear that for Harris the reign of Christ was bound up with the ending of the war and the period which was to follow.

---

[2] *Sierra Leone Weekly* 33 (49), 4 August 1917, 13.

[3] *Cf.* p. 314 in 1960 edition by Laymen's Home Mission Movement, Philadelphia.

[4] See, e.g., Marr Murray, *Bible prophecies and the present war*. London: Hodder & Stoughton 1915, 130ff. Cf. p. 150: "So the Great Pyramid indicates that the year 1914 when the great war broke out was the end of the Christian dispensation, and that we are now at the beginning of the 'Great Day of the Lord' Day when all the prophecies contained in the Book of Revelation are to be fulfilled."

[5] Hartz, *op. cit.*, (as note 1 above).

[6] Rev. Peter Harrington, SMA (missionary at Grand Cess, Liberia, 1914). "An interview with the 'Black Prophet'". *The African Missionary* 18 (March–April 1917), 13–16.

[7] Hartz *op. cit.*, (as note 1 above).

[8] Cited by Alan Rogerson, *Millions now living will never die*. London: Constable 1969, 21f. From *The time is at hand*, 1889, in 1960 edition of Laymen's Home Mission Movement, Philadelphia.

[9] Hartz, *op. cit.*, (as note 1 above).

That reign was to be an "Era of Peace . . . of a thousand years" in which the "face of the world" would be changed.[10] Europe would become powerless,[11] and the "new dispensation of Christ", "a future reign of Christ on earth" would follow.[12] It is not clear from the text that Harris himself used the term "millennium", but it is clear that the millennial expectation was there. It was that of which Saint John speaks in Revelation 20 "whose coming is nigh."[13]

B. Intermediate period

Careful reading of the texts shows that for Harris there was to be an intermediate period between the end of the war and the time when "the reign of Christ is *fully* established"[14] (our italics). A group of prophets, including Harris, were to give guidance during this time through their work of conversion and through granting certain dispensations (for example regarding polygamy). In some senses the intermediary period was already under way through the work of these prophets. "I preach the gospel, the first resurrection now."[15] Quoting from Revelation 20.4–5, he was suggesting the condition of those who, once having been persecuted, would in a short time reign with Christ. This was "the last day" where the "new ways" of the special dispensation were already operating, and in that scheme he was "the last prophet".[16]

The authenicating evidence for his role was to be found first in the war which he had predicted, and second in the fact that "the crowds have understood me, that they have changed [their] life, and that I am sought everywhere". But these evidences were not available till the latter part of 1914, after the war broke out on 4 August, and especially after his notable reception in the Gold Coast in May, June and July 1914. Although the Ivorian historian Ekanza writes that "[p]artout il rencontre un accueil enthousiaste",[17] other evidence, for instance from Haliburton, indicates that his reception even around

---

[10] *Ibid.*
[11] *Ibid.*
[12] *Ibid.*
[13] Harrington, *op. cit.*, (as note 6 above).
[14] Rev. Pierre Benoît, *Benoît Notes* II, 12.
[15] *Ibid.*, I, 26.
[16] Hartz, *op. cit.*, note 1.
[17] Simon-Pierre Ekanza, "Le messianisme en Côte d'Ivoire au début du siècle . . ." *Annales de l'Université d'Abidjan*, S.I. (Histoire), T.3, 1975, 59.

Bingerville was sometimes hostile.[18] Even where the crowds were convinced, it was clearly not yet evidence which would convince the ecclesiastical authorities.

Over the four years from his trance-visitation to the successes of late 1914 we can—later—see the progression through initial rejection from his family, prison, chains, bannings, attacks and threats from traditional religious practitioners, to the period of mass conversions. These in the end confirmed the belief which he had held all along— that he was at work in that period between the time of war and the time when the "reign of Christ is fully established." The "last times" were indeed being fulfilled.

The recent account from an eyewitness, John Ahui, indicates that Harris saw the intermediary period as of seven years, four years of war and three to four years following before the reign of Christ on earth.[19] "I told you it was necessary to pray, and after seven years you would accomplish things you have never known and which will astonish you." Ahui himself did not see the greater eschatological context, nor did Jean Ekra of Bonoua. But he reported that Harris

> told the villagers to pray well, to listen to the Word of God, not to sin, and to shun fetishes above all, and they would see born a flourishing prosperity.[20]

As we know, events did not, in fact, follow the schema. But despite that failure and opposition his own conviction was confirmed to him through the obedience of thousands who accepted his baptism as the

---

[18] *PH*, 98f.

[19] John Ahui, Spiritual Head of the Harrist Church, Petit Bassam, Ivory "Coast, in interview with Robert Arnaut of *Radiotélévision Française*, Bregbo, 1976. (See Appendix L in Vol. III of Shank, thesis.) One cannot avoid the problematical character of a witness so long after the event. Dominique Desanti (*Côte d'Ivoire*. Lausanne: Rencontre, 1962, 71f.) tells of her visit in 1961 to Ahui who told the story of his visit to Harris in 1928. But he was interrupted by other Harrist listeners: "At this point in the story, a tumult occurs in an attempt to know whether their guide came from Tabou or Graway. I saw happening before my eyes the phenomenon of a historic truth being tread upon by a gilded legend; the only witness attempted to re-establish the facts but his disciples did not wish to contradict what they had so often affirmed. John Ahui shrugged his shoulders and took up [again, another preacher enters the discussion]. From now on each episode, each word of the prophet will provoke strong scholastic discussion in which John Ahui throws sometimes his authoritative argument, 'After all, who lived this, you or me?'" The most recent published material makes no allusion to the "seven years", but allows for it. See Paul William Ahui, *Le Prophète William Wadé Harris* . . . Abidjan: NEA 1988, 190ff.

[20] *HN.*

beginning of a new life in Christ. In 1928 Solomon Dagri and John Ahui openly confessed to him that they had lapsed into apostasy in the seven years following their baptism.[21] This he saw as only temporarily delaying the coming reign, and his message to the Petit Bassam delegation was "Begin over again . . .".[22]

In his conversations with Benoît in 1926, Harris acknowledged that disobedience on the part of Ivorians and rebellion to God on the part of the French authorities were hindering the expected reign of Christ. The prophet would re-order the situation through judgement, but the intermediate period was indeed prolonged. Yet for those who had believed and obeyed a new era had come.

Although Harris in 1926 showed no particular sympathy for white civilization, particularly for the French regime, there was sympathy for Platt and Benoît, "whites with the Bible." He told Benoît, "You [are] like Aaron—Platt like Gideon."[23] Christ's mission in the light of his immediate return was the real issue. In the messages he sent through Benoît Harris constantly stressed the theme of obedience and disobedience. To Loa: "Christ is coming—no more disobedient." "For my people in Tiegba and Yocoboué, Jesus Christ reign—do not remain disobedient. I want to keep you apart. Men who disobey will be punished. Learn the Bible and believe in Jesus Christ alone."[24]

So the intermediate period was seen as prolonged through disobedience, and it stretched up to 1921, to 1926, and up to 1928. In that year he reminded Ahui and his uncle of their apostate situation, which he knew.[25] He let them know that they had not received the promises, after seven years, because of their disobedience. But he himself was already "near the throne" and, just beyond physical sight, was the Christ, holding out his hands ready to make it all happen, if they would just obey.

Prophetic self-understanding

Harris's self-understanding was tied initially to his prophetic call of 1910 through the trance-visitation. But what was his developed self-

---

[21] John Ahui, as cited in note 19 above.
[22] *Ibid.*
[23] *BN* II, 11.
[24] *BN* I, 8; *BR* II.
[25] John Ahui, as cited in note 19 above.

understanding emerging out of that call?

He believed that a group of prophets,[26] both white and black, from the four corners of the earth, were to be sent by Christ to convert the world and bring in the Kingdom. Harris saw himself as one of the four black prophets who were to work in each of the regions of Africa. Harrington understood him to think that he was the prophet of West Africa, and the greatest of the four.[27] In Freetown, in 1917, he learned of another prophet in the Niger Delta region of Eastern Nigeria. This was Garrick Braide. In Freetown a disciple of Braide, the "Rev. M'Carthy", collaborated with Harris, and the Freetown press reported:

> [. . .] that though he [McCarthy] had been suspended for no other cause than believing and following Prophet Garrick (Elijah II) who sometime ago was preaching and making many converts to the Christian faith, and healing many who were sick, yet he has not been daunted but has identified himself with him [Harris] since his arrival in Freetown.[28]

We do not know if Harris ever heard of Oppong in the Gold Coast, or Kimbangu in the Belgian Congo, in the 1920s, but the connection with Braide must have served to confirm Harris's view about the four African prophets.

1. "Elijah II"

Garrick Sokari Braide was born about 1884 in Obonoma, New Calabar. Baptised in 1906 and confirmed as an Anglican in 1908, he began a ministry of prayer and healing from about 1909. There were new spectacular visible manifestations from 1912, and by November 1915 this had become a mass movement.

With this mass movement, it soon became impossible for the existing ecclesiastical structures to assimilate those who responded. One of Braide's "ordained" disciples presented a large number of converts to the Sierra Leonean pastor at Bonny, the Rev. S.S. McCarthy, who by mid-November was holding nightly baptisms of "people who had not been instructed and who knew practically nothing of the rudiments

---

[26] Stauffer reported nine; Hartz, ten; Harrington, twelve.

[27] Harrington, *op. cit.*, (as cited in note 6 above).

[28] *Sierra Leone Guardian and Foreign Mail* 12 (37), 24 August 1917. The Braide story is well told in G.O.M. Tasie, *Christian Missionary Enterprise in the Niger Delta, 1864–1918.* Leiden: E.J. Brill 1978, chapter 5.

of Christianity."[29] McCarthy's wife had earlier been cured by another disciple of Braide, and he refused to denounce Braide when all the Anglican clergy in the Delta were asked to do so. For this McCarthy was temporarily suspended and so went back to Sierra Leone. He was there before March 1917 when his case was discussed *in absentia* by the Delta Pastorate authorities.[30] In 1918 McCarthy was tried by an ecclesiastical court for (1) identifying himself with the "Prophet Garrick movement" and thus being schismatic; (2) having baptized about 396 adults in connection with the movement; (3) maintaining his connection with the movement despite episcopal warnings. Although he pleaded guilty he failed to express regret "in terms which the court could accept", and was deprived of his license as a priest of the Anglican communion.[31]

Samuel Silvanus McCarthy, from Sierra Leone, had been ordained priest on 25 July 1905 for the Bishop of Western Equatorial Africa. After serving at Opobo in Calabar he was assigned to St. Stephen's Cathedral in Bonny in 1913, and he was still there at the time of the "Garrick movement".[32] Back in Freetown he collaborated with Harris, and told him about "the prophet in the east". Braide's movement was condemned by the ecclesiastical authorities, and Braide was taken to court.[33] The opposition led to the rise of the separatist *Christ Army Church*, while Braide himself died in November 1918.

Apart from this connection with McCarthy we cannot determine any direct relationship between Harris and Braide. But their very similar ministries began and peaked at much the same times—Braide began in 1909 and Harris in 1910; Harris's ministry began to "peak" at Axim in June 1914, and Braide's movement reached its height in November 1915. It is possible that they could have heard of one another,[34] but their relationship seems to have been one of parallel patterns rather than of reciprocal influences. Both denounced "fetish"

---

[29] Rev. J.A. Pratt in Minutes of February 1916, *Niger Delta Church Board Reports*, 64. Courtesy of Dr. H.W. Turner, Centre for the Study of New Religious Movements, Selly Oak Colleges, Birmingham. For the full story see G.O.M. Tasie, *Christian Missionary Enterprise in the Niger Delta, 1864–1918*. Leiden: E.J. Brill, 1978, 166–201.

[30] Report of Commission, 17, in Proceedings of Church Missionary Society 1916–17, in *Western Equatorial Diocesan Magazine* 23, August 1918, 194.

[31] *Niger Delta Church Board Report*, 1918, 8–9.

[32] *Register of Missionaries and Native Clergy*. [London]: Church Missionary Society, [ca 1906]. *Cf.* no. 582, List III, 485.

[33] *Cf.* H.W. Turner, "Prophets and politics: a Nigerian test case," *Bulletin of the Society for African Church History* (Nsukka), 2 (1), December 1965, 112–17.

[34] *The Gold Coast Leader* was reporting Harris's work as early as 27 June 1914;

worship and practiced destruction of "idols"; both also denounced the consumption of alcohol. Braide's influence in this area was so great that colonial fiscal income from the sale of alcohol dropped sharply. Both used the title of Elijah to denote their ministries, Braide calling himself "Elijah II". It was apparently for this reason that Harris, who also called himself Elijah, accepted McCarthy as a collaborator.

2. "Elijah—the last prophet"

It is from the *Benoît Notes*, rather than the *Benoît Report*, that we glean Harris's self-understanding of himself as that of Elijah. To the colonial administrator Corbière he had said in 1914: "I am the prophet like Elijah to destroy the fetishes."[BR III, 2.] But as Benoît recorded in the *Notes*:

> Kruman become prophet—big prophet—you must fear—fire will fall upon you [to the Governor of the Ivory Coast] Rev 5.1. Who is worthy? I a Kruboy will come and open it [*BN* I.9].
> I will be Heliha and convert all people. This case is the last case— Angel Gabriel is my teacher, when he teach me I am in trance—he show me the verses—St. Mark 9 [where in verses 4–5 and 11–13 Elias (i.e. Elijah) is referred to.] Jesus Christ must reign; I am his prophet.[BN I.10][35]

The story of Elijah is told in I Kings 17ff. and II Kings 1 and 2. He was prophet during the reigns of the corrupt and unjust Ahab and his son Ahaziah, both kings of the northern kingdom of Israel. Both died during Elijah's time, the latter following a judgement pronounced by the prophet. In the story, the prophet is seen by others to be a "man of God"; this was confirmed because "the fire of God came down from heaven and consumed . . ." (I Kings 17.18; II Kings 1.10, 12, 14.) The principal event was the great confrontation on Mount Carmel between Elijah and the "prophets of Baal" and the "prophets of the groves." Elijah is presented as a unique figure in his struggle in the name of the one God against the baals of Caanan; he struggled not only against the priests of the fertility cults but also against the political authorities who were using the cults as part of a political strategy.

The Lagos Weekly Record was reporting on the Garrick Braide movement by 10 February 1917.
[35] See also *BN* I, 12.

When Harris met Benoît in 1926 he was carrying on his person an English weekly paper with the headline: **"An African 'Elijah' and his 22,000 converts."** Was his Elijah model suggested by the journal? Benoît imagined that it was this article which gave him his eschatological emphasis. But in 1924 Ivorians reported to the Methodist missionary Platt that Harris was the "black Elijah".[36] Thus Harris must have used the term of himself as early as 1914, before he had been connected with Garrick Braide. However, in the major primary sources (Campbell, Hayford, Hartz, Harrington, Stauffer, Joseph, Marty, Armstrong, Bruce) there is no reference to the Elijah model. Are we justified, then, in attaching such importance to it?

There are in fact other connections. A current rumour was referred to in a letter to the Provincial Commissioner of Western Province, Gold Coast, in April 1915, some nine months after Harris had left Axim.

> Harris being unusually holy has undergone an "ante mortum" translation to heaven and presumably the mantle of Elijah has fallen on Swatson's shoulders.[37]

The allusion is to the prophet Elijah casting his mantle on Elisha, who was to take up his work, before Elijah's miraculous disappearance into heaven (I Kings 19.19 and II Kings 2.11).

The Liberian informant of another recent researcher recalled seeing a prophet "Wualé" when he was about thirteen years old.

> Wualé is a Grebo who worked before the First World War, at any rate before 1920. He used to walk from town to town with a stick in his hand carrying his bag on his back. The stick had on the top a cross of red cloth. He was not tall, a stout man, not too slim. The people called him prophet Elijah.[38]

Since Harris carried on his ministry among the non-Christianised population, who would not have had the biblical knowledge to make

---

[36] *Christian Herald and Signs of the Times* 59 (26), 25 June 1925, 726. "Led by their 'Black Elijah' *as he is called*, they have built 150 churches . . ." [our italics]. "The Rev. W.J. Platt was received by them with great rejoicing, the 'Black Elijah' having told them he was but a forerunner."

[37] Cited in *PH* 220, from Ghana Archives, Accra: Correspondence, "Conf. 9/15, D.C. Sefwi [Howard Ross] to Commissioner, Western Province, 16 April 1915".

[38] Werner Korte, "A note on independent churches in Liberia", *Liberian Studies Journal* 4 (1), 1971–72, 85f.

the association, the name must have come from the prophet Harris
himself.

A critic of Harris's disciple McCarthy, who had previously been
a follower of Garrick Braide, "Elijah II", used the name Elijah of
Harris when writing to warn McCarthy, in a Freetown paper, in 1917.[39]

But the most convincing use of the term "Elijah" comes in the
dictated letter which Harris sent to Chief Akadja Nanghui through
his son John Ahui, in 1928. He specifically cites Malachi chapter 4
(the last chapter of the last book of the Old Testament). The verses
4–6 read

> 4. Remember ye the law of Moses my servant which I commanded
> unto him in Horeb for all Israel, with the statutes and judgements. 5.
> Behold, I will send you Elijah the prophet before the coming of the
> great and dreadful day of the Lord. 6. And he shall turn the heart
> of the fathers to the children, and the heart of the children to their
> fathers, lest I come and smite the earth with a curse.

Before the coming of "the day of the Lord" Elijah was to come and
convert all men. In Harris's appeal to the chief of Petit Bassam (Akadja)
he commended the chapter and underlined the importance of keeping
the "law of Moses". It is our understanding that he saw himself as
the promised Elijah, and was known as such to the local populations,
as is witnessed by *The Christian Herald* of 1925. It was a theme found
in all the areas Harris visited (Ivory Coast, Gold Coast and Liberia.)
In 1926, therefore, it was not a new theme; it is the notes of Benoît
which permit us to enter into Harris's understanding of an old theme.

The morning after Benoît had met Harris, the latter dictated messages
for the missionary to take back to the Ivory Coast. The last of these
was addressed to the Governor of the Ivory Coast. It is here that
we find the expression already cited:

> Kruman become prophet—big prophet—you must fear—fire will fall
> upon you—no more fetishes—worship the only true God. Rev. 5/1.
> Who is worthy? I a Kruboy will come and open it.[40]

The Governor himself was not, of course, a worshipper of fetishes,
but he was permitting it under his authority, and so hindering the

---

[39] *Sierra Leone Guardian and Foreign Mail* 12 (39), 7 September 1917, 5.
[40] *BN* I, 9.

one—the prophet Harris—who had shown that he could eradicate it. In 1916 the *chef de cabinet* in the Ivory Coast administration had written of the "strict neutrality of our administration in religious matters . . . [purging out of] trials and fanaticism [but] respect for cultic practices . . . as long as they have nothing contrary to our mores, to good order and the social as well as the judicial organization . . ."[41]

The French administration thus attacked traditional religion where it had political dimensions, but not at all in its "cultic" dimensions— which was precisely where Harris considered change necessary.

As a "big prophet" he could threaten with fire, and he gives evidence of his own self-identification as the great eschatological prophet who was to come before the end—the day of the Lord when the Sun of righteousness was to arise with healing in his wings (Mal 4.2).

His citing of Revelation 5:1 and his interpretation of the context confirm this crucial role.

> 1. And I saw in the right hand of him that sat on the throne a book written within and on the backside, sealed with seven seals. 2. And I saw a strong angel proclaiming with a loud voice, who is worthy to open the book, and to loose the seals thereof?

The elder's answer was (v.5)

> Behold the Lion of the tribe of Judah, the Root of David, hath prevailed to open the book and to loose the seven seals thereof.

In the Biblical text, this is a clear reference to Christ, who in the context of the vision is seen to open the book and thus "opens up" the final chapters of history and its consummation.

Do we at this point see Harris, as "a kruboy [who] will come and open it", putting himself in the place of Christ himself? Did he see himself as a "black Christ"?[42] This is not how one should interpret

---

[41] Gaston Joseph, "Une atteinte à l'animisme chez les populations de la Côte d'Ivoire." *Annuaire et mémoires du comité d'études historiques et scientifiques de l'Afrique occidentale française.* Gorée (Dakar): Imprimerie du Gouvernement Général, 1916, 344.

[42] As is implied by Roger Bastide in "Les Christs noirs", in Martial Sinda, *Les Messianismes congolais et ses incidences politiques*, Paris: Payot, 1972, 12. Just because it may occur with orthodox Harrism that one occasionally hears a kind of "black Christ" thought, one dare not automatically attribute such "Christ claims" to Harris himself. But there is indeed an explicit messianism in his self-understanding as this chapter attempts to indicate; it is tied however to that of the coming Christ. Henri Desroche, in *Sociologie de l'Espérance* (Paris: Calmann-Lévy, 1972; Eng. trans. in *The Sociology of*

it. Harris had too much Christ-centred authority in his language,
perspective and message to even suggest that he saw himself as taking
the place of Christ. Indeed he could speak of himself as the "footmat
of Christ."

The context in the book of Revelation is one where a situation
is sealed up with no one to open it up. Harris had lived through
such a situation in Liberia. Blyden in 1909, in an address before the
Liberian legislature, spoke of the situation of Christian missions in
West Africa as "[without] the slightest success" over eighty years of
expenditure of life and treasure.[43] He was making a call for a new
breakthrough. In the Ivory Coast and the Gold Coast such a
breakthrough did occur, and it was Harris, the Kruboy, who was
responsible. We may also note that the theme of a sealed book to
be opened in the last times also appears in one of Harris's favourite
books, Daniel (chapter 12.4,9). But he does not claim to be the Christ,
yet he was clearly identified with the "Lamb" who in the vision took
the book and opened its seals. It is apostolic identification with the
Lamb, not Christological substitution for the Lamb ... who opens
the book. The dynamics are clearly messianic in their import; only
it is the Elijah who precedes the Christ that is intended, and not
the Christ himself. "I will be Heliha and convert all the people."

It is as commissioned by Christ: "Here is my commission: Jesus
Christ tell me—Matt. 28.19." [Matthew 28.19: "Go ye therefore and
teach all nations, baptizing them in the name of the Father, and of
the Son, and of the Holy Ghost."] All of his ministry as Elijah, as
the "big prophet", was under the commission of Jesus Christ, who
was coming to reign over—and on—the earth.

Benoît, when he interviewed Harris, asked him, "Who spoke to
you to teach you all these things?" The answer, as recorded in the
Benoît Notes, was:

> Angel Gabriel is my teacher;
> When he teach me I am in trance

Hope, London: Routledge & Kegan Paul 1972) 110ff., has developed a typology of
messianisms which would situate Harris clearly in a messianism of the type where
the messianic personage is historically absent; where he has come, gone, and is waiting
to reappear; and where an intermediary solution is found in a kind of vicarial function
of prophet and/or precursor. All of this, according to Desroche, is messianic in its
dynamic, and we would concur totally in the case of Harris.

[43] Edward W. Blyden, *The problem before Liberia*. London: Phillips 1909, 15f.

He show me the verses—St. Marc 9
Jesus Christ must reign—I am his prophet.[44]

Mark chapter 9 refers to the transfiguration of Christ in which Moses and [Elias] Elijah "appear [...] and they were talking with Jesus." In another reported conversation, Harris cited another verse which referred to Elijah. Further, in chapter 9, verses 11 and 12 are significant:

And [the disciples of Jesus] asked him saying, "Why say the scribes that Elias must first come?" And he answered... them "Elias verily cometh first, and restoreth all things; and how it is written of the Son of man, that he must suffere many things, and be set at nought. But I say unto you, that Elias is indeed come, and they have done unto him whatsoever they listed, as it is written of him.

This was Jesus' response to his disciples concerning the Elijah promise of Malachai 4, which we have already cited. It is clear from Matthew 17:13 that Jesus' disciples understood him to be referring to John the Baptist. This is omitted from Mark, and Harris understands this text as referring to his own situation. He was the final prophet who was to precede the Christ at the coming of the eschatological reign about to be established on the earth.

Confirmation may be found in Harris's repeated use of *last*[45] in his reported words and in correspondence. To the governor, "This is the *last* case;" in speaking of polygamy, "the *last* day"; in a new warning to France which follows: "I am the *last* prophet"; in his conversation with Benoît in the Mt. Vaughan cemetery: "I am the *last* prophet, fire—God sent me." This corresponds with what Benoît heard in his first contact with Harris:

The time is short—God will send fire upon all rebels, yes his fire; and the prophet himself will send fire upon Abidjan and Bingerville because the French government serves the devil and not the true God. Jesus

---

[44] *BN* I, 10. The textual reference in the *Notes* was not put into the *Report;* Benoît surely did not perceive its significance.

[45] We recall again that in 1914, Father Hartz reported that Harris attributed to himself the mission of *"prophète des derniers temps"*. Further, Governor Angoulvant in his (now missing) letter of 30 September 1914 to Gov. General Ponty at Dakar, spoke of Harris as a *"sorte de Mormon Libérien"*; the expression is found in two letters which respond to Angoulvant. What distinguished the Mormons, of course, was that they called themselves "the latter-day saints", in addition to their openness to polygamy. Harris's conviction about the "last days" was driving him, in 1914, clearly; this was not, we insist, a late development in his thinking.

Christ is coming again. He will soon be here. He will bring fire everywhere where he is not known—that they may serve the true God only.[46]

There is evidence that Harris interpreted bubonic plague in Lagos, 1924–1926[47] as "pestilence" predicted in the "last days" of the "little apocalypse" of Luke 21. In this and other incidents he is clearly interpreting current events in the light of "the last times" which condition his thinking.

So the Elijah ministry was somehow telescoped into the John-the-Baptist ministry, and both into the ministry of the Kruboy who was to be the *last* prophet of the *last* days, ushering in the reign of Christ. This became reality to Harris through the "trances":

Prophet no man like you. He is in transes. Moses and Helajah come to visit me. [and earlier:] God talk me unknown tongues. Moses—Angel Gabriel Helaja—three to one: Harris Rev 5: chap: palabre est great for me. Il rit [He laughs][48]

It is the Elijah content of the trances that is of interest. For Harris, the Angel Gabriel not only pointed out the text (Mark 9) which identified him with the prophet, but visited him in the way that Jesus was visited by Moses and Elijah. The visitations were probably the origin of Harris's 1914 remark, "I am like Heliah."[49] There he uses the language of analogy rather than of fulfillment—"*like* Elijah." In his ministry there is clear evidence of Elijah-like events. This included calling down fire, and the power to call down rain.[50] In fact, many localities today remember Harris as a "rainmaker". Even if we dismiss such oral traditions as popular exaggerations, we have to take seriously Harris's own claim. Father Hartz reported:

At a certain moment I asked him for a *sign*. "I can make it rain." he said, "but the principal sign is that already the masses have understood me; they are changing their life, and they are seeking me from all around."[51]

---

[46] *BR* I, 15.

[47] "Luc 21/10 angles stroke Lagos with pestilence." [*BN* II, 11] See J.D.Y. Peel, *Aladura: a religious movement among the Yoruba*. London: Oxford University Press 1968, 73, where Peel cites Nicholson, *Plague in Nigeria*. Lagos, 1926.

[48] *BN*, II, 12, 13.

[49] *BN* I, 26.

[50] *HN*.

[51] Hartz, *op. cit.*, (as in note 1 above).

Although Harris saw this as a "sign" of his prophetic vocation, he sees as more important that this final Elijah should show that God was alive and active, and powerful in changing lives, in preparation for the coming reign of Christ.

There are also reports about those who died due to opposition, mistreatment or disobedience, following pronouncements of Harris. His words were seen to have life-or-death consequences. How did he discover his power expressed through these signs? We believe that his "try"—which proved efficacious—was based on the certainty of his own identity. He did not become like Elijah because he had discovered he had these powers; rather because of his convinced identity as Elijah he made the pronouncements and gestures which were efficacious.

The Elijah-like eschatological prophet of the last times contained within it, for Harris, an additional Moses-like dimension. Moses as well as Elijah had come to him in trances, and he spoke to Benoît several times of "the prophet Moses".[52] In Deuteronomy 18.15–22 the prophet Moses speaks of a coming prophet "like unto me".

> I will raise them up a Prophet from among their brethren, like unto thee, and will put my words in his mouth . . . And if thou say in thy heart. How shall we know the word which the Lord hath not spoken? When a prophet speaketh in the name of the Lord, if the thing follow not, nor come to pass, that is the thing which the Lord hath not spoken, but the prophet has spoken presumptuously: thou shalt not be afraid of him.

This passage is commented on twice in Acts—by Peter in Acts 3.22–23, and by Stephen in Acts 7.37. Harris often quoted the Book of Acts, and he must have known the verses and their origin in Deuteronomy. There is reason to believe that as the final Elijah he saw himself fulfilling the role of the prophet "like unto Moses". "You ought to tremble. It's Moses and Elijah who have come to visit you," he said to Benoît, in a word intended for the French authorities.[53]

One might question this self-understanding as the *final* eschatological prophet, since he spoke of an "assembly" of prophets, to which he

---

[52] *BN* I, 13; *BN* 1, 12.

[53] The Benoît rewrite is not conformed to the original notes; this appears therefore as an "interpretation" of Benoît. That he did so perceive it, in spite of his notes, would suggest that Harris indeed gave an impression in conformity with what we have discovered elsewhere in the texts.

belongs.[54] And his open acceptance of Garrick Braide as Elijah II might also be perceived as negative evidence. Harris, however, presented himself as the "greatest" in the assembly, and as "the head of them all." According to his perception, then, we would understand him to be "Elijah I", and Braide to be "Elijah II".

3. Carpet of Christ

Looking back, it is not difficult to understand Father Harrington's reaction: "Poor prophet! He evidently looks on Kaiser, Czar and Sultan as some petty native rulers."[55] What appeared as illusory pretence could scarcely avoid provoking such a response. In 1926 Benoît reacted similarly: "Notice the authority he gives himself. He rules humanity."[56] In citing Rev. 20.4 he sees himself as one of those seated on a throne of judgement in the future kingdom. Observers, whether Western or Westernized Africans, are obviously ambivalent about the enormity of these claims and the contradictory impression of the prophet's humility. Both Casely Hayford and Benoît mention this humility, and his astonishment at being chosen; he is "the carpet on which Christ wipes his feet."[57]

A clue to understanding this apparent contradiction may be found in Harris's own astonishment. He had not "given himself authority"; he was sent by God. He was "the carpet on which Christ wipes his feet!" He repeats this expression in his discussion with the French official Corbière: "I am J.C. carpet. I am J.C. horse. He takes the foolish things in the world to confound the wise."[58] That which is in itself humiliating and lowly becomes transformed because of its identification with Christ.

4. Horse of Christ

Jesus Christ's horse? He had been a kruboy, good only for carrying cargo and serving people; but he heard Christ telling him, "You will carry me!" This commission was the highest of honours, and it gives us a perspective of understanding of Harris's estimate of Christ, and

---

[54] Stauffer, nine; Hartz, ten; Harrington, twelve.
[55] Rev. Peter Harrington, S.M.A., as in note 6, above.
[56] *Benoît Report*, II, 1; II, 9.
[57] Casely Hayford, *William Waddy Harris the West African Reformer*. London: C.M. Phillips 1915, 9; 13. See also *BR* II, 10–11.
[58] *BN* II, 29.

of Christ's attitude towards him. Through it we see how close Harris could come to apostolic identification with the Lamb without saying of himself, "I am the Lamb of God." This would have been impossible for him.[59] But as carrier of Christ, Christ's horse, he comes as close as it is possible without eliminating the distinction between Christ the Commissioner, and the Christ-commissioned prophet.

What is the origin of the image? As the writer of BR III observed, Harris had never seen a horse.[60] We must return to Harris's textbook, the Bible. In Rev 6.1–2 (after the Lamb has opened the seals) there is a vision of a horse:

> And I saw and behold a white horse
> And he that sat on him had a bow;
> And a crown was given unto him;
> And he went forth conquering and to conquer.

And preceding Harris's favourite chapter, Revelation 20, we read in Rev 19:

> I saw the heaven opened and behold a white horse, and he that sat upon him was called Faithful and True, and in righteousness doth he judge and make war. . . . And the armies which were in heaven followed him on white horses, clothed in white linen white and clean. . . . And he hath on his vesture and his thigh a name written, KING OF KINGS AND LORD OF LORDS. (Rev 19.11–16)

In Harris's self-understanding, he himself was *the* white horse of the Apocalypse, the bearer of the conquering Christ as he moves into the last days of conflict before the final apocalyptic judgement with fire, before his ultimate reign comes.

We have already observed that "trance" was important for Harris in his daily guidance. This was not something exclusively passive, nor was it seen to be spirit possession. Within the trance phenomena are a broad range of possibilities of expression.[61] Bastide has insisted on

---

[59] When Father Harrington asked whether he would change the doctrine of Christ, his answer was: "Oh man, what do you say? Change the doctrine of Christ! . . . Of God the Mysterious!" and indeed he seemed greatly perturbed at the mere suggestion. In Harrington (as cited in note 6).

[60] BR III, 6.

[61] E.g. Erika Bourguignon and Louanna Pettay, "Spirit possession, trance, and cross-cultural research" in *Proceedings, American Ethnological Society*, Annual Spring Meeting 1964, 38–49.

differential degrees due to Christianizing influences, or "the baptism of the 'god'", in which culturally conditioned models are adopted by what are seen to be—in forms of possession—the "horses" mounted by the "god".[62] And in the West African cultural context we find the horse image specifically used in relation to a god and his worshipper.[63]

Those who met Harris, during the time of his early ministry and later, have recorded their impressions of his openness to spiritual realities, and his receptiveness. "His whole soul is open to God."[64] "He lives in a supernatural world in which the people, the ideas, the affirmations . . . are more real than those which he sees and hears materially."[65] And other observers testified to Harris's personal appearance as providing visible evidence of this identity. Especially stressed are the flashing eyes,[66] reminding those he met of the one "whose eyes were as a flame of fire" (Rev 19.4). Another spoke of "his terrible voice" which made "a visible impression on his hearers"[67]; was it not also a reflection of "a sharp sword . . . from his mouth"?

These witnesses confirm for us that the expression "Christ's horse" was, for Harris, more than a figure of speech. Christ was in the prophet's perception riding Harris to victory before his ultimate reign was established. The expression "victory" is not too strong. When in 1928 he gave his Bible and Cross-staff to John Ahui, the latter reported that Harris told him, "Take your cross; take these effects— the arm with which I conquered the world of Africa".[68]

5. Conclusion

We thus see factors in Harris's self-understanding which constitute for him a vision and a dynamic which makes his incredible ministry

---

[62] See Roger Bastide, "Le château intérieur de l'homme noir", in *Le rêve, la transe, la folie*. Paris: Flammarion 1972, 61ff.

[63] Erika Bourguignon, "The self and the behavioural environment and the theory of spirit possession", in E.E. Spiro (ed.), *Context and meaning in cultural anthropology*. Glencoe, N.Y.: Free Press 1965, 38–45.

[64] Hayford, *op. cit.*, 13.

[65] *BR* II, 9.

[66] *Cf.* Jacques Boga Sako; see Appendix XXIV in Shank, thesis, vol. III. See also De Billy in note 67.

[67] Edmond de Billy (French Reformed missionary), *En Côte d'Ivoire. Mission Protestante d'A.O.F.* Paris: Société des Missions Evangéliques [1931], 16; Donald Ching, *Ivory Tales*. London: Epworth Press 1950, 126; Walter E. Williams and Maude Wigfield Williams, *Adventures with the Krus in West Africa*. New York: Vantage Press 1955, 141–42; Harrington, as cited in note 5 above. .

[68] John Ahui (as cited in note 19, above).

understandable. These include the prediction of a world war followed by an intermediary period when a dozen prophets, led by Harris, will create conditions of peace, to be followed by Christ's thousand-year reign. We have seen also Harris's self-understanding as the final prophet of the last days.

All this gives us a picture very different from the traditional Protestant missionary understanding of Harris, as mediated through the writings of Platt, Benoît and F.D. Walker. Other witnesses—Stauffer, Hartz, Harrington, and the Freetown press reports—confirm for us Harris's major eschatological orientation. The Harrist oral tradition preserves the "seven years of obedience", unknown to the Methodist missionaries, but which "fits" with the larger eschatological structure. There is, as we have seen, also that unused evidence in the *Benoît Notes* and the *Benoît Report* which go far beyond the simple analogical use of scripture. The missionaries, biased as they were by Harris's age and the effects of his stroke (unknown to them), had neither the time nor the motivation to attempt to penetrate this dimension of the prophet's thought.

We would suggest that in fact the (orthodox) Harrist interpretation of Harris's eschatological thrust—seen as a "prophet"—is one other form of a deviation of which the Methodist one is the better known: the arrival of the Methodist Mission was perceived by the Methodists to be the promised fulfillment of what was for Harris a much larger eschatological hope—the imminent peaceful reign of Christ.[69] In spite of its eccentricities the Harris vision seems much more likely than the other two; in any case, Harris's concern was faithfulness to the vision and not credibility.

It is worth recalling here the existence in Cape Palmas between 1887 and 1900 of the Russellite doctrine which was widely spread by literature within Liberia—and present in Spring Hill where Harris was teacher and catechist—which included a systematic teaching of: world cataclysm in 1914 tied to the return of Christ; the imminent establishment of a theocratic kingdom of peace under Christ; an Elijah class, outside the churches, responsible for bringing in that theocratic

---

[69] See note 36 above. In one of W.J. Platt's texts prepared for *The Nigerian Methodist* apparently some time in 1924, his writing reflected Harris's eschatological message as recorded in oral tradition: "Scores of thousands of followers were told to go to Church for Light and teaching; he claimed to be only the *forerunner of a new era*. He proclaimed his Bible." (Our italics) From "News on the new Methodist District of French West Africa", in MMS Archives, London. The "new era" for Harris was the imminent Kingdom of Christ; for Platt it was the Methodist missionary opportunity. But it is important to note that Harris had clearly announced this new era, and it was still "in the oral tradition" when Platt arrived ten years later, in 1924.

kingdom. It would appear to us that Harris was strongly influenced by this literature; we can assert that what appear as some of his eccentricities were in fact being defended literally at the time as a rational view of Holy Scripture.

6. Individual eschatology

We have seen Harris's general understanding of the last times, but we have not examined how he perceived his own death, his own last days. Did he believe that as the last prophet he was somehow immune to death, but was to be translated into the Kingdom without death? Such a belief was in fact current in the western Gold Coast shortly after his departure. Was this his own conviction? There are some suggestions latent in the *Benoît Notes*, and they are the only source we can draw on.

To Benoît in 1926:

> I go work for God and if they kill me that's all right; I go heaven.[70]

To Benoît when speaking about his 1914 ministry in Apollonia, when asked if he did not fear imprisonment by the French authorities:

> Yes, but I couldn't disobey. I had to go—God asked me to do so. If God asked me tonight to go again, I will go. And if they kill me all right. I will raise again. Here the face of the old man shines. He laugh quite loud—full of joy. Raise with Christ.[71]

When speaking of his arrest and mistreatment:

> If the spirit of God direct me to go I go. I don't fear to die. If I die I go heaven. All the commandants and bishops live like Pharisees, but prophet live near the throne.[72]

There are other similar remarks,[73] and together they build up a picture, not of a man who thinks he will not die, but rather of one who does not fear to die, and who believes that he will not die until his work is accomplished. At the same time there is clearly the note of

---

[70] *BN* I, 4.
[71] *BN* II, 8f.
[72] *BN* II, 10.
[73] *BN* II, 13; *BR* III.

eschatological urgency to be found, as illustrated by his remarks to Pasteur Benoît in September 1926.

> And I asked here [in the Mount Vaughan cemetery] shall I die. He said: No you work more, you will never die. I am the last prophet fire God sent me.[74]

He very clearly understood that Benoît would not die, but would enter into the imminent reign of Christ . . . without seeing death. This too was Russellite conviction. And given the self-understanding related to Moses and Elijah, it is quite possible that he saw his own martyr death in the light of Revelation 11 and the two slain witnesses.

Be that as it may, he seems at the end to have been clearly reconciled to his departure. In his dictated message of December 1928, only about four months before his death, he said: "The prophet bids you goodbye—he is about to go home." Further on he added: "I am now old and sick and God says I must remain home to wait my time. It may be soon or late." It is the pious language of an aged man of faith; though an eschatological note may appear to be missing, John Ahui testifies that at the same time he asked his visitors to look at the heavens to see the appearance of Christ who was reaching out his hand to them . . .

A recent study of Harris, echoing the Methodist tradition, totally missed this perspective of Harris.

> Harris, the preacher and evangelist, does not appear to be anything extraordinary . . . Millenial ideas played only a minor role in Harris's preaching . . . Harris was not unique. He was an evangelist preaching in the same manner as white (and black) missionaries and other Grebo lay preachers. . . . Descriptions such as 'prophet movement' or 'Messianic movement' tell us little about the movement and its dynamics.[75]

A careful sifting of all of the evidence in fact presents a very different view. And what we learn from Harris himself is that whether or not he met with success his sense of mission and his self-understanding and eschatological faith and hope would have pushed him anyhow up and down the coasts of West Africa in faithfulness to his God whose Messiah had called him to be his prophet.

---

[74] *BN* I, 28; see footnote 8 above.
[75] John Zarwan, "The genesis of an African religious movement". *Missiology* 3 (4), October 1975, *passim*.

CHAPTER SEVEN

PATTERNS IN BIBLICAL UNDERSTANDING

The prophet Harris was commonly to be seen with a Bible in his hand, as most of the extant photographs show. Father Hartz described him as "equipped with the traditional Bible of the Wesleyans." In baptism, he was observed to "lay a tattered Bible on your head before dismissing you." He read verses from it before baptism, but he also used the Bible without opening it. Thus he used the Bible symbolically, liturgically and sacramentally. Here we wish to explore how Harris employed the Bible as a source for his own thought patterns. As it was for Harris, so it must be for us, a kind of starting place for understanding him.

Observers noticed how he could spontaneously quote the Bible, and he himself claimed to have prepared for his prophetic role through prayer and through reading and study of the Bible.

> ... his account of himself seemed to imply that his knowledge of English, which seemed perfect, and of the Bible, especially the Old Testament, which seemed equally so, was to be ascribed to the gift of tongues and divine inspiration.[1]
>
> Then he searched for the verse in his English Bible, which he is ever turning over and which he knows through and through.[2]

Harris himself claimed this "divine inspiration" after his 1910 prophetic vision, and there appears to be a change in his use of scripture before and after that date. We will therefore look at the pre-prophetic and then at the post-prophetic use.

A. Pre-prophetic use of Scripture

Throughout the greater part of Harris's early life, the study of the Scriptures had played a part. When he lived with his uncle John Lowrie

---

[1] Rev. P[eter] Harrington, S.M.A. "An interview with the 'Black Prophet'." *The African Missionary* 18 (March-April) 1917, 13–16.
[2] *Benoît Report* I, 17.

he encountered it at home, at school and in church. This was not at all unusual in Liberia. From 1892 to 1908 he was daily teaching the Bible to schoolchildren, and after 1897 as a lay-reader he was using the Bible when he led services, and when preaching and catechising in the villages. Earlier, he had been a Methodist lay preacher. His canons of interpretation would have come first from the Methodist Episcopal Church and later from the Episcopalian Church. In the latter church the influence of the bishop, combined with church structures, was important. Bishop Ferguson was a strong personality who in the last decade of the 19th century was using his authority to combat the threat of a new Biblical interpretation from the Russellites.

However, there does not appear to have been anything unusual in Bishop Ferguson's patterns of interpretation. There was Episcopalian orthodoxy, evangelical piety, and a belief in clear hierarchical structures. These were to condition Harris's understanding of the Bible.

B. Shift of 1910

Harris's faith in Episcopalian structures, however was to weaken and this showed up as early as 1904. He spent a year under discipline, and this may have brought him back again to previously rejected patterns. But between 1906 and 1908 he seems to have been oscillating between his committment to Western (Episcopalian) Christianity and traditional Glebo patterns, which led in February 1909 to his declared intention to "return to heathenism". This intention seems to have been carried out by the time he was imprisoned in the war of 1910.

Nevertheless, the spiritual, psychological and social conditioning of his Biblical foundations could not be completely rejected overnight, after thirty years. The Episcopalian frame of reference was wiped out, after the trance-visitation of 1910, which took him away again from the traditional patterns. There was now a new interpretative grid: "I am a prophet; above all religions and freed from the control of men, I depend only upon God through the intermediary of the Angel Gabriel," as Father Hartz reported his words. He had a new key to understanding. From at least 1872 to 1885 his uncle Lowrie had been the key; from at least 1888 to 1904 Bishop Ferguson had been that key.

It is thus not inappropriate to examine Harris's use of the Bible after having studied the essential eschatological key into which he

began to fit the biblical materials. It was not complete in 1910, but
we have been unable to observe major shifts after 1914. Once the
key was provided, even the eschatological materials in the Bible would
fit into the framework, and reinforce it.

Despite his dependence on the one book, we have earlier seen that
there may have been some influence of Russellite teachings. The role
of the book of Daniel prior to the vision, and of the book of Revelation
after the vision, are crucial. They were particularly important to Harris
in his human context.

C. Biblical apocalyptic: inspirational factors in a messianic dynamic

Commentators have seen three main themes in the book of Daniel:
cultural protest, end times, and a divine intervention with the establishment of the kingdom.[3] All these themes are major items in Harris's
prophetic agenda. The importance of Daniel's message for the imprisoned
Harris is easily understood, for Daniel was writing of a people also
displaced by an alien culture, and Harris's own life had been completely
dislocated, with no possibility of returning to his previous roles as
school-master or as interpreter. But neither could he return to the
traditional patterns. Going back was impossible; the only route was
before him, with the horizon of the coming kingdom that God would
install. The book of Revelation contributed to this consciousness and
was, little by little, fed into this new pattern.

The book of Revelation itself contains the principal themes of
Daniel, but christianizes those themes by making Jesus of Nazareth
the Christ-agent who presides over the events of the final days and
brings in the kingdom. Its major image is that of "the Lamb that
was slain", an image which first appears in ch.5 and then reappears
in later chapters—6, 7, 12, 13, 15, 17, 19, 21, and 22. This image
of a defenceless lamb engaged in mortal combat who nevertheless
overcomes all evil is an inescapable Christian element of those same
apocalyptic dimensions.

In Harris, at this point, we discover the basic elements of what
has been described by Henri Desroche as the classic "scenario" of

[3] See for example D.S. Russell, *Apocalyptic: ancient and modern*. London: SCM Press
1978, 10; H.H. Rowley, *The relevance of apocalyptic*. N.Y.: Harpers 1945 (rev. ed.),
48; Archibald Robertson, *The origins of Christianity*. London: Laurence and Wishart
1953.

a messianic movement, as he has extracted it from his study of hundreds of them.[4] Such movements are defined as:

> primarily the religious belief in the coming of a redeemer who will end the present order of things, either universally or for a single group and institute a new order of justice and happiness.[5]

Within the area of Christian messianism, Desroche cites as the "royal" text for such movements Revelation chapter 20; seven other passages in Revelation are seen as basic sources.[6] After the book of Revelation, the second major source is the book of Daniel. According to Desroche, the classic scenario for such a movement is a shift from a time of oppression to a time of resistance to a time of liberation. It offers a prospect of action in the midst of despair. It is easy to recognise that this was indeed Harris's situation.

If we follow the analysis of Oosterwal,[7] we find it fits the case of the Ivory Coast very well. Harris appears exactly as the "inspirational factor" which sparked off a movement in the midst of "precipitating factors" such as "social disintegration, catastrophes, economic deprivation, political oppression, culture clash", et cetera. All these were present in the Ivory Coast, and Harris undoubtedly provided the "inspirational factor." In Liberia the same precipitating factors were present. What was, in that case, the inspirational factor in the messianic dynamic which came to birth in Harris's trance-visitation of 1910 and which developed in the following months? It was the Bible, and particularly Daniel and the book of Revelation—the major apocalyptic writings—under the guidance of the Angel Gabriel.

D. Angelic hermeneutics

We have looked at the role of the Angel Gabriel in Harris's calling; here our task is to look carefully at the fact that Gabriel was perceived

---

[4] Henri Desroche, *Sociologie de l'espérance* Paris: Calmann-Lévy 1973, 132–137; (English translation: *The Sociology of Hope*, London: Routledge and Kegan Paul 1979); Desroche, *Dieux d'hommes. Dictionnaire des messianismes et millénarismes de l'ère chrétienne.* Paris: Mouton 1969.

[5] Hans Kohn, "Messianism", in *Encyclopedia of Social Sciences*, 10. New York: Macmillan 1933, 358.

[6] See Revelation 7.1–14; 11.1–17; 12.1–14; 13.1–18; 16.17–20; 18.1–4; 17.1–6.

[7] Gottfried Oosterwal, *Modern messianic movements as a theological and missionary challenge.* Elkhaart, Indiana: Institute of Mennonite Studies 1973, 32–33.

by Harris to be his major interpreter of Scripture during his time
of prophecy. His angelic hermeneutics were seen to be part of the
immediate consequences of the 1910 visitation, and the documents
from Hayford, Stauffer, Hartz, Harrington, the newspaper reports from
Freetown, and in Benoît, all testify to this. In the Bible, Gabriel appears
to Daniel, to Zechariah and Elisabeth (parents of John the Baptist),
and to Joseph and Mary, announcing and effecting the events of "the
last time." In seeing how this operated for Harris, we will examine
his references to Scripture, in chronological order, following his
pilgrimage along the coasts.

1. Ebonou, September 1913

Our first evidence comes from one of the interpreters used by Harris,
Jacques Boga Sako, an Avikam clerk from Ebonou, who was later
to become a mainstay of the Methodist Church in that place. His
1963 testimony was influenced by his later Methodist experiences,
but we must still take seriously his account of the original experience
of Harris.

> In the course of his sermons, for their first time, he announced them
> the gospel in the book of the prophet Ezekiel: Chap. 37 at the verses
> 1–14, exhorting them to love his neighbour as himself. He predicted
> a luminous future of the work of our Methodist Protestant mission in
> the whole world. He revealed to them also the events of the wars of
> 1914–18 and the realization of the community between whites and blacks.[8]

This took place some time in September 1913, before the start of
the passage through the lagoon areas at the "beginning of October"
after "about one month" at Lozoua following time at Ebonou.[9] This
is our earliest sample of Harris's preaching, aside from the simple
"repent . . . or fire" of his earliest years in Liberia.

The Ezekiel passage, chapter 37.1–14, is that which contains the
well-known image of the "valley of dry bones", given to the prophet
in a vision. Through his obedience in prophesying, the dry bones
take on life. It was for Ezekiel a vision of Israel in captivity being
brought back to its own land, and was thus a message of hope in

---

[8] Jacques Boga Sako, typed memoir, Ebonou, 29 August 1963, in *Haliburton Notes*
[our translation]; Appendix xxiv in volume III of Shank thesis.
[9] *The prophet Harris*, 53–55.

a time of despair. It announces resurrection. Sako also noted that Harris was

> ... announcing to them the good news of the Kingdom of heaven, the existence and the power of God the creator of all things and his son the Lord Jesus Christ.[10]

Although Sako spoke of the announcement of "a luminous future of the work of our Methodist Protestant Mission in the whole world", there was at that time no Methodist Mission at Ebonou, although there were clerks with Methodist backgrounds who were later to carry on Harris's ministry after his departure. But we can trace in Harris's preaching the main themes which he was to carry on throughout his ministry: the judgement of a catastrophic war in 1914 followed by the coming of the Kingdom with peace between black and white— and the call to live out the life of peace in love even in the time before the Kingdom has come, and even in a time of world-wide conflict.

How did Harris come to use this particular text at this particular time? A year later the colonial administrator Gaston Joseph observed that Harris in his ministry was "reading some-times from an English book of prayers."[11] We know that in 1907 he had ordered through the Episcopal offices in New York "one Church hymnal and Prayer Book combined",[12] and such Prayer Books contain a lectionary. For evening prayers on September 19 the first lesson is Ezekiel 37 "to v. 15". Harris the lay reader and catechist must have been accustomed to using the lectionary, and it is altogether likely that he continued to use the lectionary to guide his Bible reading, with the passages then interpreted as he said by the Angel Gabriel.

2. Axim, June–July 1914

a. Casely Hayford at Axim referred to Scripture numerous times in his description of Harris, but it is not clear that Harris himself was

---

[10] Boga Sako, as in note 8, above.

[11] Gaston Joseph, "Une atteinte à l'animisme chez les populations de la Côte d'Ivoire", in *Annuaire et Mémoires du Comité d'Etudes Historiques et Scientifiques de l'Afrique Occidentale Française*. Gorée: Imprimerie du Gouvernement Général, 1916, 344–348.

[12] Correspondence of Harris to Kimber, 4 October 1907, in Archives and Historical Collections, Episcopal Church, Austin, Texas.

the author of those allusions. One reference which is clear occurs when he reports:

> I have spoken of humility. It is a word that he was always using. He says of the Christ that he took the form of a babe in order that by his helplessness he might indicate the true nature of humility.[13]

There is no specific passage of Scripture to which this refers. Several verses in the gospels give Jesus' teaching on humility, and indicate through that teaching an eschatological reversal of roles:

> Luke 18.14 he that humbleth hmself shall be highly exalted (also 14.11; cf. Matt 23.12).
> Matt 5.5 Blessed are the meek for they shall inherit the earth,
> Matt 18.4 Whosoever shall humble himself as this little child, the same is the greatest in the kingdom of heaven.

Christ also attributed this quality to himself.

> Matt 11.29 Take my yoke upon you and learn of me; for I am meek and lowly in heart: and you shall find rest for your souls.

Later writers of Scripture interpret humility and meekness in Christological terms.

> Philippians 2.5–11 Let this mind be in you which was also in Christ Jesus ... who made himself of no reputation and took upon him the form of a servant and was made in the likeness of men, and being found in fashion as a man he humbled himself ... wherefore God hath highly exalted him ...

The Apostle Paul refers to the meekness of Christ (II Cor 10.1), defines it as a fruit of the [Holy] Spirit (Gal 5.23), and writes of the Christian vocation as one of "lowliness and meekness". The Apostle Peter made a general exhortation:

> I Peter 5.5–6 Be clothed with humility, for God resisteth the proud, and giveth grace to the humble. Humble yourselves therefore under the mighty hand of God that he may exalt you in due time.

---

[13] Casely Hayford, *William Waddy Harris: the West African reformer*. London: C.M. Phillipps 1915, 9.

Harris, in relating the teaching on humility to the doctrine of incarnation gives a special "twist" to the teaching. How far it is original, and whether he had ever heard it in a Christian sermon, we cannot know. That it was a recurrent theme of Harris is suggested by the echo found in Campbell's words of 1921:

> [The Ivorian populations] see the moment when their villages will also be consecrated to the child of Bethlehem.[14]

Rather than a specific interpretation of specific texts, Harris gave a general interpretation of a generally accepted fact of Christian doctrine: God's way of working is intended to be also that of his people. As God humbled himself into helplessness—as seen in the Babe of Bethlehem—so his people will also humble themselves as an essential pattern of faith and life.

b. Father Stauffer at Axim reported on the way in which he perceived the angelic hermeneutic at work:

> One day the black angels [meaning "Messrs Casely Hayford, Hamilton, W.B. and a few others" who gave Harris "bad advice"] came to the prophet complaining that they, big men, were surely not bound like poor men to keep only one woman. That might be God's law for the white people, but was surely not meant for the blacks. The answer came: "You have nothing to say . . . the arch-angel . . ." and the next morning came the result. "God did not intend to make the same law for blacks and white people. Blacks could take as many wives as they could keep." And setting the action to his words he took several fetish women he had converted, as his wives—and then these women, when Harris left the country, remained behind him and were the founders of the water carriers, one at Osimfokrum at Ankobra and at Atuabo.[15]

We do not know who Father Stauffer's informants were, and his report was written a decade after the event. But in confirmation we have Harris's own word to Benoît, "At Axim, I had six [wives]." J.P. Ephson

---

[14] Text from Campbell, Gambian merchant in Bingerville, Ivory Coast, cited in Jean Bianquis, *Le prophète Harris ou dix ans d'histoire religieuse à la Côte d'Ivoire (1914–1924)*. Paris: Société des Missions Evangéliques 1924, 26–27; 33–35 [our translation].

[15] Father Stauffer, 1914, Axim. Notes made in a diary around or after 1926. General Archives, S.M.A. Rome: 3A4 (translation and paraphrase by Rev. J. van Heesewijk, S.M.A.)

also told Haliburton in 1964, "He said no harm in marrying many wives—he had five with him at Axim."[16]

The evidence points to a change of attitude towards polygamy while at Axim. Previously his position had been of non-condemnation of plural wives and encouragement of monogamy allied to a condemnation of adultery. His new position was of his taking several wives himself, yet condemning adultery. For Harris this change had come about by angelic intervention; Stauffer saw it as controlled by the pressures of the day, including the "big men" of Axim, including Casely Hayford. Stauffer had recently been involved in a court case defended by Hayford, which Hayford had won, and his evidence must therefore be treated with caution.

What Stauffer would not have been aware of was the Liberian background, including the conflict between Bishop Ferguson and Seton (who had left the mission church for the Russellites) over polygamy. Nor would he have known of the legal battles within Liberia as to whether a "civilised" native Liberian could have several wives, nor of the pressures from Blyden which had caused Bishop Ferguson to preach and publish a sermon at Christmas 1912 to assert that there were not different ways for white and black Christians.[17] Nor did Stauffer know of the pressures on Harris caused by solicitation from numerous women, many being converted priestesses, who no longer had a social *raison d'être*.[18] This is not a defence of Harris's shift, but an indication that his change was by no means the result of one night's consideration. In addition, it is likely that Harris's own mother, with a Christian orientation, had been married by her parents to a Glebo traditional polygamist, and that he knew firsthand that it was possible for a woman to continue as a Christian in such a situation. In any case, his own apostolic strategy apparently shifted following the overnight guidance from the angel. In later records of 1916, 1926 and 1964 we gain further insight into his views on polygamy.

---

[16] *Haliburton Notes.*

[17] See Bishop Ferguson, *Our mission in Africa*, Annual Report, BMPEC, 1912–13, 174ff.

[18] In *BN* I, 13, Harris said of women, "I raise in behalf of Ethiopian—many more come and ask me." Stauffer reports that the wives he had taken were ex-"fetish priestesses".

(1) Grand Cess, Liberia: May 1916

Father Peter Harrington, after hearing Harris's story and claims, asked the prophet:

> "Are you going to change anything in the doctrine of Christ?"
> "Oh, man, what do you say? Change the doctrine of Christ—God the Mysterious?" and indeed he seemed greatly perturbed by the question.
> "But, Prophet," I persisted, "if you allow polygamy for instance, will that not be introducing a change into Christ's doctrines?"
> "Man, don't you see? The prophets can dispense—they cannot change. When all the prophets of Christ meet we shall get heavenly light from above—from God the Mysterious—and like the prophets in the Old Law we may grant certain dispensations until the reign of Christ is fully established on earth...[19]

Here then is a basic interpretative principal: the prophets can dispense, but they cannot change. Regarding polygamy, Harris's answer is: the prophets can grant a dispensation regarding polygamy in this instance, until the reign of Christ is fully established. The application is temporary, and in expectation of the final dispensation of Christ's earthly reign. "Like the prophets in the Old Law" suggests a reference to Jesus' words in Matthew 10.2–12, when Jesus replied to questions put to him by the Pharisees regarding divorce.

Harris's reasoning seems to be that just as Christ recognised a dispensation prior to his coming "because of the hardness of your heart", so the later prophets like Harris might grant dispensations in order to prepare the conditions for the coming of the kingdom established in West Africa. But he sets a clear limit: "until the reign of Christ is firmly established upon the earth."

(2) Harper, Liberia: September 1926

In Pierre Benoît's notes of this date we read statements of the prophet which are answers to questions asked by Benoît, although we have no record of what the questions were.

Benoît appears to have been asking Harris about his marital situation.

> Women—Isaiah 4.1. That's the case with me and we are in that day— seven women and many more come and ask me—I raise in behalf of Ethiopian. This is the day—the last day [*BN* I,2]

---

[19] Harrington (as 2 above).

I had a son named James; his mother Mary Pioka . . . . .
Samson—He died 2 days old last year. I had his mother as wife
2 years ago. Letitia Williams, . . . Sierra Leone. . . .
3 women. One live at Axim. 2 died. I had no children from them.
I had all those women as wife—at Axim I had six—I came to see
[?] Salomon. He had 900.
What shall we teach on polygamy?
Thou shalt not commit adultery—
St. Paul . . . For the hardness of your heart you shall have one woman.
that's Paul, not God—but God let us have several woman if we do
not commit adultery. (*BN* II, 13–14)

This was not included in the *Benoît Report*, but it is important for
us, since it gives a rationale, with scriptural backing, for something
going as far back as Axim in 1914.

The first verse cited is Isaiah 4.1.[20] It is a context of judgement
pronounced against Jerusalem with a predicted description of what
it will be like. Twice the expression "*in that day*" is used, indicating
a coming day of judgement, and a coming day of restoration.

Harris saw in the text a relation to the African context, and said
"I raise [i.e. stand] for the Ethiopian." And the African context in
which a woman's reproach is taken away because of her relation to
a man is seen as the criterion for plural marriage. This cultural fact,
well known to Africans, is seen by Harris to be foretold by the prophet
Isaiah. Harris does not here seem to be saying, "Take as many women
as you want," but rather, "give a name to those women who are
reproached because they have no name." It seems that it was in this
sense that Harris "took away the reproach" of several fetish women
he had converted. One outstanding example was the well-known Grace
Thannie, from Kristen Eikwe (Ghana), who followed him back to
the Ivory Coast after her baptism and deliverance.[21] After Harris's
expulsion she returned to the Gold Coast, calling herself Madam Harris
Grace Thannie, and she tried to carry on his work, calling the movement
she founded "The Church of William Waddy Harris, and Twelve
Apostles."[22]

Harris appears to see a difference between the cultural ethos of

---

[20] As a parallel, we note that the founder of the Church of the Lord Aladura
in western Nigeria, Josiah Oshitelu, utilized the same Isaiah text as a basis for his
seven wives; this was a decade following Harris. See H.W. Turner, *African Independent
Church*, vol. I. London: Oxford University Press 1967.

[21] *Haliburton Notes*.

[22] Cf. *The Prophet Harris*, 148ff.

the African and that of the Westerner. Without the anthropological tools available to modern observers, he comes to a conclusion not unlike theirs, by intuition, that in transition out of traditional life polygamy may not necessarily have to be rejected with guilt as most white missionaries in his time prescribed.

The second Biblical reference cited is to Solomon and his wives: "He had 900." [I Kings 11.1–3 reports 700 wives and 300 concubines]. This story makes it clear that in the old dispensation the question was taken out of the realm of absolute morality and placed in the context of what was economically possible/impossible. This appears to be what Harris was saying in his 1928 dictated message: "If you are able to marry two women [it] is all left with you; if you can [you] *can* [may] do so. God do not protest against it—only thing you must follow your God. Don't let anybody deceive you. If you can marry 10 women do so only follow God's laws."[23]

This is also what he meant when he said to Benoît, "God let us have several women if we do not commit adultery." To undertake what is not possible—what you can not do—is not permitted; that is unethical. But if you can (economically, socially, in keeping God's law) you may; that is the dispensation, until Christ's reign is fully established on earth . . .

The third scriptural hook for Harris's applied angelic hermeneutic, regarding polygamy, is more difficult. "For the hardness of your heart you shall have one woman. That's Paul, not God." The problem with this "Pauline" text is that there is no such text.

Harris appears to be claiming that Paul had set up a special dispensation requiring monogomy—"for the hardness of your hearts". He is synthesising several texts. ". . the hardness of your hearts", an expression found in Matthew and Mark, is used by Paul in Romans 2.5:

> But after thy hardness and impenient heart treasurest up unto thyself wrath and revelation of the righteous judgement of God; who will render to every man according to his deeds.

This follows a list of "unrighteous things", in chapter 1, which includes "fornication" (in the King James version which Harris used) as the

---

[23] Dictated message of the prophet William Wadé Harris, to the Chief Akadja Nanghui and his people at Petit Bassam, Ivory Coast, via his son, John Ahui, December 1928, 4. Copied at the home of John Ahui, Petit Bassam, 29 April 1978.

first expression of hardness. In I Corinthian 7 Paul recommends "by permission and not of commandment" one wife for one man (and *vice versa*) to avoid fornication. Perhaps this use of Pauline texts by Harris permits him to say in good faith, "That's Paul, not God; but God let us have several women if we do not commit adultery."

Such a use of Scripture is not without its problems. It is a result of a prior conviction that there is under God such a thing as a righteousness which expresses itself in a polygamous context which is ethically and morally superior to and in fulfilment of an imposed legalistic arrangement of monogamous marriage; it implies economic and social possibility and obedience to God's laws. In connection with the trance-visitation of 1910, Harris had already claimed that "God had shown him a better way."

We have by-passed earlier sources to pursue this particular hermeneutic. To these we now return.

(3) J.P. Ephson, Axim, July 1914

Ephson, the friend of Casely Hayford, was among those who did not take Harris seriously; further, his report dates from 1964. But we still need to listen to his witness, as recorded by Haliburton in *The Prophet Harris*.[24]

> He said no harm in marrying many wives—he had five with him at Axim. They asked him if it was wrong. (How could he have more than one? "There's no harm in that!" he cried, unless you take her to the altar.") Even if you have lawfully married (church), I will show you this way out of it. Tell lawful wife, "I have seen this woman and want to marry her." If she refuses [to agree] call a woman messenger and give her the same message to deliver. If the woman refuses a second time, send a second messenger. And if she refuses again you have the right to marry, because you have told her in the name of Father, Son and Holy Ghost.[25]

Given the mocking questioner, we may be somewhat suspicious of his perception of the import of Harris's answer. However, we must take seriously Harris's reported distinction between a wife married legally—in church—and one taken in the traditional way. We also note his use of the triune name, which is used to validate an action

[24] *The Prophet Harris*, 87.
[25] *Haliburton Notes*.

then binding also on the other person. We can draw no other conclusions from this text, other than that it confirms his polygamous practice at Axim, and his authorization of it for church-married monogamists.

3. Bingerville, September 1914

After Axim in July, we have the report of Father Hartz's interview with Harris sometime after mid-September. We return to this report for the Biblical interpretations it contains:

> The angel renews his appearances and initiates me little by little to my mission of prophet of modern times, of the Era of Peace, of which Saint John speaks in the twentieth chapter of the Apocalypse: Peace of a thousand years and whose coming is nigh. . . . The angel instructs me about the future times; the actions of Gog and Magog, the wiles of the great dragon . . . who will be bound for a thousand years . . .[26]

Several details should be noted. First, the expression, "Era of Peace", is not used in the Book of Revelation. In Revelation 20 the reign of a thousand years is mentioned; its imminence is not something Harris would have learned in the Episcopalian Church, but the doctrine of a millennial era of peace under Christ, at least in the future, was a common one in Western Christianity in the last half of the 19th century. However, for Harris, the reign was *proche*, which we have translated as "nigh"; it is likely that Harris used the English expression "at hand". C.W. Armstrong reported that in Axim he had announced, "Repent, for the Kingdom of heaven is at hand."[27]

Harris is here speaking not in the language of analogy, but of fulfilment. He is saying, "What John wrote is for us, and we can expect it soon." This is one of the constants in the angelic hermeneutic which we must pursue: it is the angel who gives to Harris the word of fulfillment. Harris's own personal hermeneutic pattern was much like that of his contemporaries, that of analogy; "even as [in the Bible] so also [for us today]." But it is the Angel Gabriel who goes beyond that in interpreting Scripture for Harris in terms of fulfilment.

The "Gog and Magog" reference in Hartz's report comes also from Revelation 20 and points back to Ezekiel 38 and 39 where those names are used for powers from the north being defeated by the

---

[26] Father Hartz, as cited in note 1, above.
[27] Cf. C.W. Armstrong, *The winning of West Africa*. London: Wesleyan Methodist Missionary Society 1920, 39.

God of Israel. Harris had preached on Ezekiel 37, and it is likely he saw there the European wars which he had predicted, and interpreted as judgements on the colonial regimes of godless northern countries.

The "wiles of the great dragon" is a reference to Revelation 20.2, 3, and 8, and also to chapter 12, where the dragon "went to make war with the remnant of her seed which keep the commandments of God . . ." (12.17). This may have underlined for Harris the importance of having the ten commandments respected by the colonial regime, especially in respect to prohibiting Sabbath work. Indeed, for Harris, the final opposition of the authorities could only be perceived as that of "Anti-Christ", a theme which we will pursue later (see chapter VIII below).

4. Cape Palmas, September 1926: Pierre Benoît

When in 1926 Harris reported on his Axim experiences, we have seen how the angelic hermeneutic still functioned for him. In his own words,

> Angel Gabriel is my teacher. When he teach me I am in transe. He show me the verses. [*BN* I,10]
> How you know all the verses you give me?
> Angel Gabriel tell me: search so and so—such verses. The spirit in me is the spirit of Pentecost. Corinth 14/2. [*BN* I.12]

The latter quotation is in the context of the Isaiah 4 citation, and underscores what we have called the angelic hermeneutic of fulfilment. In addition, Benoît's materials give us first-hand materials relating to Harris's use of Scripture. These include cited references, and also clear allusions, although the exact reference is not given.

a. Harris's Scriptural citations

In the Benoît *Notes* and *Report* Harris cites two Old Testament verses a total of three times, and twelve New Testament verses a total of twenty-two times.[28] During Benoît's conversations with Harris, the latter

---

[28] The verses cited are: (a) in *Benoît Notes*: Rev 5.1 (I,9); Rev 5 (II, 12); Matt 28.19 (I, 10); Matt 28 (I, 29); Mark 9 (I.10); Rev 20.4 (I, 11); Heb 11.1 (I.12); I Cor 14.2 (I. 12); I Cor 14 (II, 12); Is 4.1 (I. 12); Ez 33 (I. 13); Acts 5 (I.29); Rev 2.5 (II.6); Luke 21.10 (II.11); (b) in *Benoît Report*: Rev 5 (III, 6, where it is cited as 5.8); Matt 28.19 (II, 3 and III, 2); Rev 20.4 (II, 5,9); Heb 11.1 (II, 5 and 10, misquoted as Acts 11.1); I Cor 14.2 (III, 5); I Cor 14 (III, 8); Ez 33 (II, 6); Acts 5 (III, 2); Rev 2.5 (II, 7).

cited specific Bible references on at least fourteen occasions; three of the citations were repeated. Four of these texts did not find their way into the *Benoît Report*, and their absence reduces considerably the apocalyptic-eschatological colouring of the report, even if accidentally.

b. Harris's Scriptural allusions

These are more numerous. As many as thirty-five clear allusions are to be found in the *Notes* and *Report*, several repeated up to five times.[29] As with the references, allusions to the New Testament—including Pentecost— are more than twice as common as allusions to the Old Testament. This may come as a suprise, because of the generally wide-spread opinion that Harris was particularly well-versed in the Old Testament, and that his ministry is a reflection of the spirit of the Old Testament (Benoît, and the Methodist tradition up to as late as Yando's thesis of 1970).[30] But the evidence suggests that he spontaneously used the New Testament more than the Old, and because of his personal "Pentecost" ministry he was involved in New Testament times.

Benoît was certainly correct in his rapid appreciation of Harris's analogical use of Scripture:

> He adapts wonderfully some situations or some attitude of his adversary to a text and finds an analogy in the Scriptures (*BR* II, 9).

It is indeed one of his basic uses—for example:

> My case is like Rev 20.4; Tell Platt his case is like Gedeon; I told him I am like Heliah. Paris go call me as Pharao [*sic*] called Moses. (*BN*).

However, here also, as we have earlier perceived, there is a dimension which goes beyond the simple analogy or similitude. Harris seems to "cross over" time and time again into an actualizing or fulfilling of the biblical reality in his own experience.

---

[29] The allusions repeated as many as four or five times are: *Benoît Notes*: John 17.3 (I; 7, 8, 9, 10, 26); "Angel Gabriel (Daniel and Luke) (I; 10, 11, 12, 15). Other Old Testament references are to Ex 12.13; I Sam 11.16; II Kings 5; Judges 6f.; Exodus 4; I Kings 11.1–3; and Exodus 20.

[30] Yando Emmanuel, *L'Evolution du Harrisme en Côte d'Ivoire*. Paris: Faculté de Théologie Protestante Libre, thesis of 1970, 29.

all the commandants and bishop live *like* Pharisees but prophets *live*
near throne
　Moses and Elijah *come* to visit me
　My case is like Rev. 20:4; now I am going to be judge
　I *am* J.C. carpet I *am* J.C. horse

In Harris's perspective, this "crossing over" into actualization of the
biblical reality in his personal experience appears to be an important
dimension. There is a sense in which he "takes on" the task and
role of Moses, Elijah, and so on, but it does not appear to him as
a self-appropriation of roles. It is the Angel Gabriel—or Christ, or
Moses, or Elijah—who tells him, instructs him, commands him. He
describes this "passing-over" in different ways: "You do not see those
things; they possess you"; "the voice of God come through the Bible
and tell all that"; "Palabre ... est grand for me". It would be
presumptuous to interpret every "like" or "am" in a strict fulfilment
pattern. But there is nevertheless an important dimension which should
not be neglected. Benoît's unstudied description of what he observed
is quite revealing:

> He *lives in* a supernatural world in which the people, the ideas, the
> affirmations, the cosmogony, the eschatology of the Bible *are more real
> than* those which he hears and sees materially [*BR* II, 9; our italics].

It is this "crossing-over" dimension which seems to be particularly
characteristic of the "angel-taught prophet". Prior to 1910, the Bible
was for him the source of truth, God's Word, the revelation of God
to man. From the age of about twelve to fifty, Harris was immersed
in a world of ideas which completely repressed—at least overtly—
the old world of power and success, of ancestors and spirits, of witches
and trials, and of polygamy. His conversion at the age of twenty-
one brought him to affirm and internalize what had up to then been
largely external for him. In 1910, following his personal struggle for
money within the service of the Episcopalian Church, and his political
struggle for British supremacy over Liberian powerlessness to create
justice, Harris entered through his trance-visitation a new stage in
his religious life. He became a vital participant in the world of truth
that the Bible constituted for him. It was not merely a matter of "belief
in"; it was an African pattern of "participation in" the truth. It became
a question of involvement—as with the ancestors, the living-dead—
with Moses, with Elijah, with the Archangel Gabriel, and supremely
with Jesus Christ.

Participation as a dimension of a so-called pre-logical way of being has been thoroughly examined by Levi-Bruhl; criticism of his categories has not done away with the phenomenon.[31] The notion of vital participation has been seen by at least one African theologian as fundamental to an understanding of faith within the ecclesiastical community.[32] Harris, through "vital participation", had been "grafted in" to the "holy root" of Israel's life and faith to such an extent as to "partake of the root and fatness of the olive tree" [Romans 11.16–24]. Harris had earlier cut himself off from his Glebo life and family in a radical conversion; yet he was not now without living ancestors. He had simply changed family connections, now based on faith in Christ as known through the Scriptures, but by means of a spirituality of vital participation totally indigenous to his African way of being and which he identified with the "spirit of Pentecost."

We may point to three apparently different levels of Scriptural usage by Harris: the analogical, that of fulfilment of types, and that of participation. In his fifty years of Christian experiences, Harris had moved from the acceptance of a new culture and its inherent religious faith to what Kenelm Burridge has called a "myth-dream".

Burridge attempts a definition of "myth-dream", and sees it as a kind of community day-dream, which among literate people may become intellectualized and set down in writing. "From time to time a charismatic figure brings portions of the myth-dream out of the area of day-dream, and for a relatively short period of time, transforms—and externalizes—these portions of the myth-dreams into the word."[33]

We are not at this point concerned with the truth or non-truth of the biblical narrative, ideas, or reality; we are attempting to understand how Harris understood and interpreted Scripture and the

---

[31] E.E. Evans-Pritchard in *Theories of primitive religion. London*: Oxford University Press (1975 reprint of corrected sheets from the 1st ed. of 1965) writes: "Levy-Bruhl's discussion of the law of mystical participation is perhaps the most valuable, as well as being a highly original, part of his thesis", 86. We would not however, like Levy-Bruhl, consider "participation" as a more "primitive" condition not found among "more highly civilized". And we note, in passing, that it is inherent in Christian language and faith; *cf.* I Cor 10.16–22; Hebrews 3.1–14; II Peter 1.4; *et al.* The expression "in Christ", so common to Pauline language, carries the same note.
[32] See Vincent Mulago, *Un visage africain du christianisme. L'Union vitale bantu face à l'unité vitale ecclésiale.* Paris: Présence Africaine 1962, esp. e.g. chapter V. A brief English resumé is provided in Vincent Mulago "Vital participation", in Kwesi Dickson and Paul Ellingworth (eds.), *Biblical revelation and African beliefs.* London: Lutterworth Press 1969, 137–158.
[33] See Kenelm Burridge, *Mambu.* New York: Harper & Row 1970, 148ff.

use he made of them. The description of Burridge's "myth-dream" helps to explain how ideas—in this case Biblical ones—are culturally processed, then appropriated and used in a functional "word" by a charismatic individual. Thus it must have been with Harris and the "world of the Bible". Within certain limited areas—Liberia, Gold Coast, Freetown—it was a community affair where missions and colonies had planted deeply biblical notions. Harris saw it as his mission to share it with all of the West African peoples to make it totally one community myth-dream, over and above those of ecclesiastical and colonial powers. His use of Scripture had pointed to his unique identity and mission; whatever came after him would still require that the Bible have a central place.

His "testament" confirms this:

> Read the Bible; it is the Word of God. . . . Search out the light in the Bible. Learn your letters that you may be able to read the Bible; it will be your guide [*BR* I, 23f].

The same concern appears in the letters Harris dictated the same morning to individual churches. To "my people in Tiegba and Yocoboué" he added, "Learn the Bible and believe in Jesus Christ alone." And in what appeared in the *Notes* as a kind of final message to the churches, he again dictated:

> You all go to church, You all go to school. I prayed God to send teacher. He send you this man. Now you go hear him. All he teach you you learn. You learn Bible. They must go to school. [*BN* II, 15].

The Bible remained for Harris the essential source of truth and light for himself and his people.

5. Spring Hill, December 1928: Dagri and Ahui

In the "final" message dictated for the chief of Petit Bassam, Harris also used three scriptural citations and several other allusions. Other are found in miscellaneous records (newspaper reports, etc.) A total of sixteen references can be found in these sources, of which six are to Old Testament books (Psalms, Isaiah, Daniel and Malachi). There are ten New Testament references, of which seven are from passages in the Gospels, two from the Epistles, and one from the Book of Acts.[34]

E. Conclusion

The Bible was essential to the "making" of the prophet Harris. The analogical manner of interpretation, pre-eminent in the pre-prophetic period, was not discontinued. However, three new dimensions were added. Biblical apocalyptic in Daniel and Revelation provided him with a new eschatological key for interpreting the Bible in the light of his own identity as the last Elijah before the coming of the Kingdom. Second, a situational-dispensational interpretation was seen to be "given" to him by the Archangel Gabriel. Finally, through the "spirit of Pentecost" which he was given by God's messenger he participated in the life of the people of God in the Bible; the coming Christ assured him and commanded him in his role, while Moses and Elijah—with Gabriel—came to give day-to-day leading and encouragement. He was nourished by continual reading and study of the Bible. We have noted in passing that he did not always quote the Bible correctly, and that he could cite as Scripture his own synthesis of texts, based on socio-cultural presuppositions. So the African socio-cultural ethos was seen as a stage in fulfilment, and Western monogomy was seen as a moral requirement due to "hardness of heart".

There appears to be no doubt that he used the New Testament as much as he did the Old Testament, if not a great deal more. He found within the New Testament much of what Western Christians might call the spirit of the Old Testament. This again was no doubt conditioned by the apocalyptic passages, including even those of the gospels. Nevertheless, a major intention—based on a Christological foundation—was a life of humble obedience to God, in view of the coming fulfilled kingdom of Christ.

---

[34] For details, see Shank thesis, Vol. II, 470.

CHAPTER EIGHT

"SPIRITUAL" PHENOMENA AS THOUGHT PATTERNS

Harris's original trance-visitation of 1910 transformed Harris the rebel into Harris the prophet; the experience moved him into a new "spiritual" dimension that was to characterize his prophetic ministry. This we have examined both in chapters five and six; the study has accentuated in passing a number of different manifestations which we may call—since this is Harris's own word to describe them— "spiritual" phenomena. Bastide has discussed the difference between a "savage" trance with its dramatic, spectacular and frightful aspect, and that of a "baptized" trance which follows certain acceptable patterns in harmony with a mythological complex.[1] We have asked, during our study, whether the "spiritual" phenomena are not various forms of tamed or "baptized" trance states.

At the time of his original "savage" trance, his daughter reported sixteen years later,

> He seemed so exalted and talked so incoherently that all the world thought him mad. . . . His wife believing him really mad died of grief the same year. (*BR* I, 8).

Harris's teaching colleague gave a similar report: "When he started teaching, people suppose him that he must be crazy" (*BN* II, 23). This was certainly for Harris himself a part of the meaning of the shift into what he described as "spiritual". The impression that he gave at that time stayed with him until the end of his life, nor did he try to reduce that impression. In his conversation with Hayford he made it quite clear that following his trance "men thought him crazy . . . From then the spirit had its way with him until today he is a force to be reckoned with." The original dynamics of the trance were at work in and through the prophetic task, the Elijah mission, and the "horse of Christ" role; these dynamics express themselves

---

[1] See Roger Bastide, *Le Rêve, la transe, et la folie.* Paris: Flammarion 1972. Cf. esp. 61ff.

through continued "spiritual" phenomenon in "baptized" expressions, which can nevertheless still on occasion give the original impression of folly. It is a part of his prophetic identity of which he is fully aware, resulting from his spirit anointing—his "Pentecost".

At the Le Zoute missionary conference in Belgium in 1926, Campbell, the Episcopalian bishop of Liberia, reported to Rev. E.W. Thompson of the Wesleyan Methodist Missionary Society that "Harris was now quite mad and used to come and bellow under his window."[2] The description was unacceptable to Thompson, who hoped to present a better image of Harris to the Methodist public. But it seems to correspond in some measure with what Benoît discovered the same year: "the little children laughed at him, the grownups watch him as though to prevent him [from] doing something foolish" (*BR* I, 16). This reaction, it must be noted, was not limited only to "civilized" people. The oral tradition from Adjué, for example, reports that "all having heard Harris rejected him and his teaching. They thought he was simply a madman. They paid no heed."[3] It is the psychic— or "spiritual"—powers of the "madness" that we want to examine.

A. *Prescience*

When Benoît and Tano in 1926 first met the prophet along the road to Harper, they were struck with his expecting them. Benoît wrote that same afternoon:

> Something had warned him, he tells us, that strangers from a great distance had come to see him at Cape Palmas. For this reason he had hastened with all of his ornaments and his baptismal cross—No, not a man, it was a voice from God (*BR* I, 13).

He endorsed this when he wrote the same evening (*BR* I, 17) that Harris knew several days before that "we were coming. The Spirit had announced it to him." And Benoît went on to ask, "Has this man a gift of second sight, as all the blacks have affirmed?"

His prediction of the war of 1914 is well known, and he claimed to have predicted it two years before its coming. In 1928 he predicted

---

[2] Correspondence, Rev. E.W. Thompson to Platt, 3 January 1927. MMS Archives, London.
[3] *HN*, Adjué.

another war for France; the Ebrié Harrists have no doubt about his knowing with prescience the war of 1940, twelve years later. In Axim, too, he was known to have forewarned in 1914 of a "big sickness [to] come to the world in about four years." Locally, when the world-wide influenzaa epidemic came in 1918 it was perceived to be that which Harris had foreseen.[4]

B. Spiritual leading

The way in which Harris himself was led "spiritually" impressed a number of people. Hayford wrote:

> He talks of receiving telegrams from heaven. What he means, of course, is spiritual intuitions. One Sunday thousands flocked around him to be baptized. Suddenly he stopped and prayed a prayer I shall never forget.... When he had calmed down he said, "I received a message I must leave this place. I must turn back, I am not to go forward."[5]

To Father Hartz he said:

> I am sent by the Christ and I must irresistibly accomplish the deeds and gestures which he inspires me to do. I am going across the country pushed by the blast from on High. I speak only under the inspiration from on High.[6]

Then, also, there is his word to Benoît:

> I went with my three singers to Apollonia. I was sent by God, too.[7] After three months I turned back. [Asked about his return to the Ivory Coast] I had to go. God asked me to do so. If God asked me to go again, I will go ... if the spirit of God direct me to go, I go. (BN II, 8–9)

Father Harrington reported from May 1916 that "God the Mysterious

---

[4] HN, Axim. The witness was twelve years old at the time.

[5] Casely Hayford, William Waddy Harris. The West African Reformer: The Man and his Message. London: C.M. Phillips 1915, 9–10.

[6] Joseph Hartz, diary entry, published in G. van Bulck, "Le Prophète Harris vu par lui-même (Côte d'Ivoire, 1914)" in Devant les Sectes Non-Chrétiennes. Louvain: XXXème Semaine de Missiologie [1961], 120–124.

[7] Peter Harrington, S.M.A. "An interview with the 'Black Prophet'." The African Missionary 18, 1917, 13–16.

was then leading him by ways unknown towards the north (he was bound for Sierra Leone) to meet his northern confrère." He must have been directed back to Cape Palmas in the meantime, but in August of 1917 he did arrive in Freetown. It was reported thus:

> He came to this place from Cape Palmas touring overland, and made the journey in fifty-two days. He did this in accordance with instructions received from the Angel Gabriel, under whose directions he was, and who enjoined him not to make his journey by any other means no matter what facilities might be granted to him to proceed otherwise. It was his Angel Gabriel who told him to proceed to Sierra Leone.[8]

C. Exorcism

An additional and significant dimension of these "spiritual" phenomena was exorcism, although Harris to our knowledge never used that word. The press in Half Assinie spoke of it as "casting out devils"; this may have been Harris's own description.[9] The best single description is that given by Casely Hayford at Axim, although the phenomenon was undoubtedly repeated countless numbers of times.[10]

> Nothing has happened up to now. There has been noticed in the crowd a woman who has attempted several times to touch the cross, and held back as if she would rather not. See! she now gets nearer. At last she has touched, barely touched it. What is this that is happening? Great God, is it possible? The woman is torn as if by a violent force. Her body is convulsed. She tears at her breasts. Her eyes literally dart from her sockets. They roll completely up and then completely down. Her hair stands on end. At last she falls prone and rolls about in great agony. Harris calmly goes on baptising as if nothing is happening. After a while he goes near and utters a strange prayer. Gradually she grows somewhat calm. She is now on her feet. This strange man again approaches the agonized soul, opens the tattered Bible and holds it before her face,

---

[8] *Sierra Leone Weekly News* 33 (49), 4 August 1917.
[9] *Gold Coast Leader*, 13 (134), 3 October 1914, 2.
[10] Amos-Djoro records an incident about a woman from Abidjan by the name of Logbé, with a reputation for her activity in witchcraft. He uses the Hayford text and applies it literally to Logbé, citing as sources "Testimony of J. Mobio and D. Nanghui, preachers of the Methodist Church of the Ivory Coast, confirmed by a document furnished by E. de Billy, ex-missionary." p. 115 in *Les mouvements marginaux du protestantisme africain: les Harristes en Côte d'Ivoire*. Paris: E.P.H.E., Vème Section, 1956. We shall probably never know how the Hayford text got injected into this parallel situation.

the while uttering a prayer. She seems to be growing calmer now. But
again she is seized by—I know not what. She roars like a beast. Her
attitude is distinctly defiant. She is indeed menacing. Harris breaks into
a low laugh, turns away, and continues to baptise as before. He now
approaches her for the second time, and once more holds the Bible
to her face. She gradually calms down and then comes to herself. She
is now as helpless as a babe. She takes her seat with others of like
nature and awaits baptism.[11]

Marty gives a description of what might appear to be a collective
exorcism.

He arrives in a village, the crowds gather around him, the men at his
right hand and the women at his left. He then cries out in a thundering
voice telling them all the evil that their fetishes cause them and orders
the sorcerers to come and stand in front of him. He shows them his
cross. Then they are seized with convulsions, seek to flee but cannot,
and roll over and over while they howl. They appear at that moment
to be in a hypnotic state. Harris calms them down and traces on their
foreheads with water a sign of the cross, while having them hold his
cross. The sorcerers then go themselves and destroy their idols. The
village is then baptized.[12]

It was what Marty describes as a typical situation. Indeed, many of
the oral traditions report how "fetish priests" in particular were often
freed from their spirits in ways similar to the above description with
their writhing in the dust and foaming at the mouth. Even the
announcement of Harris's coming could be sufficient for exorcising
a village, as was reported from Abidjan-Adjamé.[13]

Harris was conscious of his specific call to exorcise: the local tradition
from Bingerville reports it thus:

I am sent by God, clothed with his power. I am coming to convert
you and to cast out from you all the influences of the fetishes and the
idols, and to make of you children of God by my baptism.[14]

---

[11] Hayford, as cited in note 5 above, p. 11.
[12] Paul Marty, "L'impressionabilité religieuse des populations maritimes et lagunaires",
chapter one in *Etudes sur l'Islam en Côte d'Ivoire*. Paris: Editions Ernest Leroux 1922.
[13] *HN*, Adjamé-Abidjan.
[14] Evidence from John Ahui, Spiritual Head of the Harrist Church, Petit Bassam,

D. Healing

Harris's ministry also involved healing, and in a way that often seemed related to exorcism; this aspect of his ministry has been overlooked. K. Schlosser, Greschat and Amos-Djoro insist in their descriptions on Harris's emphasis being upon the message of the Word; he was for them a preaching prophet and was specifically not a healing prophet. However Schlosser, following Platt, reported that "*it was said* that he performed cures of the sick."[15] It is important to know that Harris himself claimed to exercise the gift. He told Benoît: "In Kraffi I baptised the Adjoucrus—heal many women with water" (*BN* II, 10). This was close to the time of his arrival in the Ivory Coast.

Even earlier, at Lozoua, Harris's initial ministry according to local tradition involved the healing of the village's leading songstress from a long siege of paralysis; and this was followed by the healing of the chief's son.[16] Following this there was his call to conversion and baptism. From Axim comes a report indicating that Harris did present himself in this light; the following is from Haliburton's field notes:

> Tumluni Kwesi, 75 years old in 1964, reported: "Harris came to Axim saying he was a divine healer." Another person, twelve years old at the time of Harris's ministry at Axim, reported, "He came from Tabou (Kruland) but God sent him to go round and heal sickness and teach them how to worship him . . . he healed many devils."[17]

J.P. Ephson also indicated: "People came to him because he healed the sick; he had power."[18] A commentary from the local newspaper on his ministry in Axim gives insight into Harris's own understanding of that healing ministry.

> Harris was invited to cure a woman who was suffering from heart disease (when baptizing her he informed her people that he did not come to cure outwardly but inwardly) and there is hope of the woman being recovered and she was seen the following morning full of life.[19]

Ivory Coast, interviewed by Robert Arnaut of Radiotélévision Française, 25 March 1976.

[15] William J. Platt, *An African Prophet*. London: SCM [1934], 86f. (our underlining).

[16] Evidence from an eyewitness, Koadjan Gnaba, Chef-Apôtre Harrist de Braffedon. Transcribed by Lévry Modeste Beugré, 30 April 1977, at Braffedon.

[17] *HN*.

[18] *Ibid.*

[19] *Gold Coast Leader, op. cit.*

When the prophet arrived in Freetown in late July of 1917, he was
interviewed by a local journalist who reported from him that "he
could do metaphysical healing."[20] We assume simply that by the word
he meant healing through spiritual powers. But it is important to note
his own claims and not just what was public rumour. A Methodist
confirmation, however, did come from one of the second wave of
Methodist missionaries, Pastor André Roux. He wrote in the light
of his numerous contacts with those who had experienced directly
the ministry of Harris:

> On many occasions Harris had indeed shown an extraordinary power
> as healer. I met men and women, who had been paralysed during long
> years, who had been brought to him from afar on litters, and who
> were healed at his word. That is a fact, in all certainty.[21]

Since much of traditional religion had to do with cures and healing,
it was essential for Harris to act in some sense with healing if he
indeed destroyed the "fetishes" and asked the people to do so. This
is illustrated by an early reaction to his ministry at Lozoua. The people
asked him,

> "You come here to burn all de fetish . . . suppose person be sick, how
> we gone to make medicine?" Harris said: "If you believe God, all be
> nutting. Everything be fit do you." He explained that when they went
> to gather medicinal leaves they should make a small prayer to God,
> do the same while they prepared the medicine, and again when they
> administered it. A man treated in this way would be sure to get better.[22]

According to this report, confirmed by others, Harris's understanding
of healing did not eliminate the use of traditional medicines, with
medicinal leaves and herbs, but he associated his converts' prayers
with its use in gathering, preparing, and administering.

---

[20] *Sierra Leone Weekly News, op. cit.*

[21] André Roux, "Un prophète: Harris." *Présence Africaine* 8–9, 1950, 139 (our
translation).

[22] Haliburton, *PH*, 54. Note 1: "These are quotations, set down as well as I could
catch them, given by the old men of Lozoua, who speak pidgin fluently, though
not French." [summer of 1963] A similar tradition seems to be present in the Harrist
healer, Albert Atcho of Bregbo, who insists that God does the healing through prayer
even when herbs are used.

E. Speaking in tongues

Benoît reported that Harris told him:

> The spirit which is in me is the Spirit which came down at Pentecost.
> It is the Spirit which makes me talk with tongues, as it says in I Cor
> 14. v. 2. I too talk with God with tongues: there are mysteries which
> men do not understand (*BR* II, 5–6).

This section is a slight filling out of the *BN* I.12. But in *BN* II, 12, we have solid confirmation in another conversation in which Harris responded to Benoît's inquiries.

> "How is it when God speaks to you?"
> "It is mysterious—spiritually. I Cor. 14."
> "Is it not your own voice?"
> "Not never—God talk me unknown tongues. You missionaries are for
> me like Aaron for Moses—you are Aaron." (*BN* II, 12.)

Much earlier, in 1916, he had told Father Harrington that his knowledge of the Bible "was to be ascribed to the gift of tongues and divine inspiration." When Father Harrington suggested that his ministry in the Ivory Coast must have required a knowledge of French, Harris had replied:

> "Well, as a matter of fact, I cannot read it. A prophet had indeed
> the gift of tongues, but he may exercise this great gift only for the preach-
> ing of the Word and it comes and goes as the spirit wills.[23]

The accent upon the exclusive use of the "gift of tongues" for minister-ing the Gospel Word emphasizes Harris's own perception of his preaching as being under inspiration. But the message comes in "unknown tongues" which he then interprets in his preaching. From his own description we gather that it is understood to be a conceptual communication which takes place within Harris's spirit through the Spirit of God, as at Pentecost (Acts 2), since the spirit in him "is the spirit of Pentecost." The language is not totally unfamiliar to Christian readers of the New Testament. The Apostle Paul wrote in

---

[23] Harrington, as cited above, note 7.

I Corinthians 2:9–16 of the work of the Spirit of God in the heart of the spiritual man.

> ... Now we have received, not the spirit of the world, but the Spirit which is of God; that we might know the things that are freely given to us of God. ... But he that is spiritual judgeth all things, yet he himself is judged by no man. For who hath known the mind of the Lord that he may instruct him? But we have the mind of Christ....

This section of I Corinthians follows that which Harris cited in another context (Grand Lahou, December 1914): God has chosen the foolish things of the world to confound the wise (I Cor. 1.20f.) The whole was surely a well-known passage for Harris. The emphasis is upon communication from God to man by way of the spirit of each. At one level there is the identification of communion and communication which could easily be mistaken for total identification of Paul (and/ or Harris) with God. Yet this it is not, either with Paul or Harris; there remains a distinction between the apostle and the sending and inspiring God. This must be clearly understood in order properly to interpret Harris's words which follow almost immediately after his words to Benoît about "unknown tongues".

> When I say "I", I mean "God"; tell Governor, "I" want make peace with France. J.C. [Jesus Christ] said Peace I bring unto you. Peace on earth. If they want peace, "I" bring peace. If fire, "I" bring fire. X [Christ] will come. Peace on earth. (*BN* II, 12f; our quotation marks).

God's message was communicated spiritually to the prophet in unknown tongues; it is a clear concept of God's will and intention, which the prophet then communicates using the personal pronoun "I"—thus saith the Lord, "I . . ."—when addressing the governor of the Ivory Coast through Benoît.[24]

The phenomenon for Harris was certainly very important; he used the I Corinthians 14 reference to "tongues" twice in his brief conversations with Benoît; even if the citation was prompted by a question from Benoît, the facility with which he cited the passage is itself very telling. The evidence does not permit us to develop Harris's

---

[24] For comparison, we report how this was understood by the editor of *BR* II: "Men discuss me, but I speak only for God. When I say 'I' in speaking, I mean God," (p. 6). Taken from its context, it sounds as if Harris and God are indeed one and the same.

ideas on the subject more than we have done; but it is important to note the existence of the reality.

F. Signs

The "spiritual dimension" of the prophet's thought and activity found also a very important expression in his consciousness of "signs". Such an understanding of events was a part both of traditional African life in West Africa and that of Old and New Testaments which Harris knew so well. In Exodus chapter 4, Moses is given "signs" in order to impress the people with his divine calling—"that they may believe that the Lord God of our fathers . . . hath appeared unto thee" (Ex 4.5). For Harris, avid reader of the Bible, signs are given to—and by—prophets to authenticate their ministry.

With Harris, this dimension appears as a constant in his prophetic thought and ministry, going back certainly to some of his earliest prophetic statements. When Benoît asked Killen (Episcopal priest at Graway) when Harris had started preaching, Killen replied:

Many people thought he was out of his senses—that he was sick. After some time, they believe him—some because we had a hard time before famine—it came to pass and people thought it was because of the prophet (*BN* II, 20).

Another early illustration comes from Mrs. Hannah Johnson, who told of Mrs. Helen Valentine's call to accompany Harris in his prophetic ministry. Mrs. Johnson may well have heard the story direct from Mrs. Valentine, since they were friends and former classmates.

Mrs. Valentine was asked by prophet Harris to assist him in the work. She didn't at first—but she saw a vision one night, a sign in the sky near the moon—she saw it two times, and before to see it three times she made up her mind to join W. Harris and she joined him. [Benoît: Was it spiritually?] The first time she saw it with her eyes—the second time in a dream and that made her think (*BN* II, 2f.).

Benoît checked the story with Harris:

How did you know Mrs. Valentine?
God told me: go and call her. I did it—she refused. I told her, you see sign. She saw, and say I will go. (*BN* II, 11).

The two texts must be read together to understand that Mrs. Valentine was first of all warned by Harris that she would see signs if she did not respond affirmatively to his call. But that warning itself came only after God had first told Harris to call her. Thus in Harris's thought— as well as in Mrs. Valentine's—the sign was related to an original word of God concerning her. That it was a spiritual phenomenon is indicated by the question of Benoît and the answer of Mrs. Johnson. The fact that it was in a dream made it a "spiritual" (i.e. psychical) phenomenon; again we see the role of the dream in giving spiritual guidance. Mrs. Valentine, it will be remembered, was the young "civilized" Christian widow of the Episcopalian deacon, Rev. Nathaniel Valentine.

A very similar understanding is revealed in Harris's letters of 27 September 1926, dictated to Benoît:

> Harris will give signs for the disobedient—Christ is coming—no more disobedient—they go do (*BN* I, 5: Message for Loa).
> All must do according to the message or they will see things (*BN* I.7: My people in Fresco).

A similar attitude and understanding is reported as being functional at the time of the 1913 ministry in Kraffy:

> In Kraffy I baptized the Adjoucrous, heal many women with water . . . see signs (*BN* II, 10).

Or again, he reported to Benoît his experience in Half Assinie in 1914:

> Roman Catholic curse me at Half Assinie. I said, you go see signs. The next day the church fell down. The father came and offered me one pound [sterling], to go away (*BR* III, 4; (*BN* I, 29).

This is not just reporting the fact that a credulous population was prone to see signs and interpret them in ways typical of traditional patterns; Harris himself warned of signs and understood himself to be a sign-related person. The tradition about him and his signs goes back to Harris himself; that others saw signs which he did not predict, or interpreted signs which he did not give, or interpreted as signs certain events independent of Harris's own interpretations is a real probability. But from what we know, Harris did nothing to discourage that process.

An additional aspect of Harris's understanding about signs must not be overlooked; it is reported by Father Hartz from September 1914:

> At a certain moment I ask him for *a sign* [underlining in original]. I can make it rain, he said, but the principal sign is that the masses have already understood me, and that they are changing their lives, and that everywhere I am sought after.[25]

For Harris the sign is not just a warning to the incredulous, but also an indication of authenticity; the sign is evidence, proof, of his prophetic calling. But there are levels of proof; changed lives for Harris were more important than changed weather. God's power at work in him can, and does, affect both weather and people, but the latter is more significant than the former. One could conclude that the former was given in view of the latter.

G. Miracles

"I can make it rain," Harris had said, as an example of a sign. Closely related to the sign reality was that of miracle. It was discussed by Hayford in much the same manner as Harris.

> Miracles? asks one sneeringly. It is not necessary to label the works of William Waddy Harris. But to me it is a greater miracle to drive bitterness out of one's soul than to calm physical agony. It is a miracle of miracles to turn God-ward the heart's aspirations. It is a marvel of miracles to cause a soul to pant after God as does the hart after the water brooks.[26]

Nevertheless there were miracles done to bring people to a point of change.

The Gold Coast Leader of 18 July 1914 reported from Axim on the 20th June:

> [At Half Assinie] The Roman Catholic members there attempted to defy him, their church was destroyed owing to a certain prayer he made and lifted his rod up in the sky, and after this many people were converted through his instrumentality.

---

[25] Hartz, as cited above, note 6.
[26] Hayford, as cited above, note 5. I feel that Haliburton is quite right in interpreting this as Hayford's own personal experience.

This is not just popular interpretation; it was Harris's own interpretation. He said to Benoît: "Roman Catholic Church in Half Assinie I make fall down" (*BN* II, 10).

At Axim and at Grand Bassam similar incidents were reported relating to work on the Lord's Day. At Grand Bassam:

> On arrival Harris was scandalised to see the wharf working on Sunday. He pronounced the punishment of God on the boats. It was claimed that he had definitely announced that one boat would be burnt the next day on the roadstead. The foretold event took place on the said day. One of the boats took fire and the captain was obliged to run it aground on to the beach to save at least the framework. The fact was confirmed by a European. The boat, it appeared, had arrived at the port already alight. The coal in consequence of a special fermentation began to burn in the store rooms, but there was nothing to show this on the arrival of the boat. The fact was easy to explain and to verify at Bassam.[27]

Harris himself had remarked to Benoît, "The first time I was in Bassam I make the boat burn." (*BN* I, 10). Here again it is not just the incredulous masses who credit the burning of a boat to Harris; it is the man himself who claims he intentionally provoked the event.

We do not have similar confirmation from Harris himself for his prediction of the deaths of the French administrator of Grand Bassam, M. Cecaldi, and his sergeant. However, popular tradition attributed that prediction to him. According to Father Hartz, those deaths, around the 15th January 1914, occurred eight days after the prophet left. Mrs. Johnson, who was close to Harris when he arrived in Grand Bassam, told Benoît, "He told the commandant that he would die." It is highly probable that Harris did in fact predict these deaths, and understood himself to be the intermediary cause, as people reacted to him with brutal opposition. Evidence that he spoke in those terms elsewhere comes from Western Gold Coast, as found in the Haliburton notes. Indeed it is possible that his prediction and its fulfilment in Grand Bassam gave him increased boldness with similar threats in the Gold Coast. From a Biblical perspective, we must remind ourselves that this type of experience is not found only in the Elijah stories of the Old Testament, but in several New Testament incidents (Ananias and Sapphira, Acts 5; Simon the sorcerer, Acts 8; Elymas the sorcerer

---

[27] *BR* III, 4.

of Paphos, Acts 13). Such manifestations were truly seen to be miraculous, a gift of the Spirit, as is reported in I Corinthians 12.10.

Harris's execution of "wonders" earned him the title of "wonderful Harris" even in the earliest reports coming from Axim in June 1914. The press spoke of "all his mighty agencies performed"; it reported as early as 20th June that "he was arrested, mocked and put to prison; after three days through his magical acts the prison gate opened with ease to the sentinal's surprise; no one uttered a word to him and out he walked." This was reported about his stay at Assinie, but was clearly confused with Grand Bassam, since it reported also the death of the commandant. In any case we suspect that even this interpretation is Harris's own, when we compare it with his story to Father Harrington that "through the intervention of the Archangel Gabriel, he had escaped from prison." This was already in Liberia, prior to his Ivory Coast and Gold Coast missions. Harris himself interpreted his prison releases as supernatural events, even when they were "explained away", as Hayford put it.

Thus, similarly, at Grand Lahou Harris was released by the commandant Corbière after an intervention by Lambert Ackah;[28] the people interpreted the event as supernatural. We suppose again that it was Harris's own interpretation which became popular tradition. We suppose that through prayer, or use of his staff, or words of command he had either asked God or ordered men and doors to free him . . . and he was freed. Any human intervention, for example by Ackah, was only a secondary or tertiary mediation. The primary mediation of the supernatural was, for Harris, Harris himself; he had intervened with his word or act of power . . . and God had done the rest. But even this does not explain away the wonder or the miracle; the wonder or miracle is not in what happens but—as Hayford put it—in the "coincidence" of the word—or gesture—and the event.

Trance-visitations, prescience, special leading, exorcism, healing, tongues, signs and miracles are all spiritual phenomena which are an integral part of Harris's patterns of thinking. They are not absolutely compartmentalized categories, for they often interpenetrate each other as in trance and tongues, trance and leading, exorcism and healing, signs and wonders. We have observed that these are understandings of his own, and his personal claims; that others' understandings and

---

[28] *HN*, 24 August 1964.

affirmations reinforce his convictions and thinking there is little doubt. He also makes the identification with the "spiritual gifts" of 1 Corinthians 14, but the patterns originated in his own spiritual experiences, themselves native to his traditional African patterns, and confirmed, validated and made authoritative by the Scriptural ethos as a result of his own personal Pentecost.

CHAPTER NINE

SYMBOLIC PATTERNS

In 1963 Jacques Boga Sako, who had been Harris's interpreter at
Ebonou in 1913, wrote his memories of Harris's impact as he
remembered it over fifty years:

> Towards the year 1913 one heard rumours—without a well-informed
> source—of a messenger of God coming from Sassandra, Controhou,
> as far as Fresco, but that the inhabitants of these regions opposed him
> and did not at all accept his preaching. Following the coast from Sassandra
> to Fresco he had been taken in a pirogue by several inhabitants of
> Fresco who used the river route.
>
> It was in this manner he arrived at Ebonou, in a white cassock with
> two black slanting sashes, a white turban wrapped round his head, a
> staff with a cross without crucifix, the complete English Holy Bible in
> his left hand. He appeared to be a genie—this man—with his completely
> white beard and flaming eyes. As soon as he entered the village, he
> went towards the old Ekpo-Avi-Addi, the chief of the village of Ebonou
> at that time. At the same time he had as companions in mission two
> women from his place of origin (Cape Palmas). These attracted everyone
> to this man of God by the sound of their calabashes (played in castanet
> fashion).
>
> The very first day of his interview with the inhabitants of Ebonou,
> he began by announcing to them the good news of the Kingdom of
> heaven, the existence and the power of God the creator of all things
> and His son the Lord Jesus Christ. All the inhabitants of Ebonou, men,
> women and even children ran to him to ask him what it was necessary
> for them to do. "Bring me all your idols so that I can burn them in
> the fire. Thereupon," he said, "I am going to baptise you in the name
> of the Father, and of the Son, and of the Holy Ghost."[1]

Although written so long after the event it describes, the impression
which Harris made is still vivid. The symbolic language used by Harris
is important—white robe and turban, cross and Bible, calabashes to
shake, and the message of fire and baptism. This is all reflected in
the photograph taken by Ignatius Phorson at Grand Bassam in

---

[1] Jacques Boka Sako, typed memoir, Ebonou, 29 August 1963. In *Haliburton Notes*.

November 1914,[2] at what was no doubt the high point in Harris's ministry. There we see Harris with the Bible in his left hand together with a small bowl for baptizing and a calabash; there is also a small pectoral cross hanging around his neck. In his right hand he holds the cruciform staff with its white crossed ribbon. The three women with him, also dressed in white, each wear a pectoral cross. From another photo,[3] taken perhaps at Assinie, we may guess that all of them were unshod.

The symbolic impact made by the group, and particularly by Harris, can scarcely be exaggerated. As Sako wrote, "he appeared to be a genie." Other witnesses reported that Harris said, "Leave your fetishes and devils and follow me; I am able to *show you God.*"[4] At Dibrimou, an Adjukru village not far from Dabou, he was reported to have said, "Pray to the God I have *shown* you."[5] At Songon-Té the population expected "a great fetish was coming, but all men can understand it, not the devils only." They sent representatives to Grand Lahou to ask Harris, "Are you the great fetish about whom they speak?" Harris replied,

> I am not a great fetish, but a man coming in the name of the Father, Son and Holy Spirit, and you will be a people of God.[6]

What is important in all this is the prior effect that Harris made by what he was and showed and did, also through the symbols which were an integral part of his being, showing and doing. The intimate relationship between the symbolic pattern and the eschatological thought pattern dare not be neglected, since, as Victor Turner has

---

[2] The well-known photograph used by Frank Deaville Walker for the frontspiece of his June 1926 first edition of *The story of the Ivory Coast* was first published in *l'Afrique Française* 32 (6) June 1922, with the title, *Le prophète Harris et sa famille*, and was twice used in Methodist publications in 1924. From that photo Walker extracted the figure of Harris alone, with his paraphernalia; the women and the rest of the "local colour" have been cut away, isolating him totally from his real context. He has thus appeared in this and subsequent books (de Billy, 1931; Haliburton,1971) and also in the French translation of Walker's book. Unfortunately Harris's pectoral cross is not clearly shown in this photograph. Harris was not a solitary figure; he was part of a team and saw himself in relation to disciples in a manner not unlike that of Jesus. The photograph dates from Grand Bassam in the fall of 1914. (Plate viii)

[3] In this picture, taken probably at Assinie in 1914, the three women are clearly barefoot.

[4] *HN.* Chief of Harrist Church, Old Cocody, August 1963.

[5] *HN.* Dibrimou (our italics).

[6] *HN.* Songon-Té. See also *PH*, p. 66, where Haliburton situates it at Kraffy.

shown, myth and ritual are dialectically interdependent institutions, and must be a basic unit for investigation.[7] We have observed Harris's "myth-dream"; this must be completed with the symbolic or ritual content of Harris's presence and work.

A. Clothing

The first impression given by Harris and his disciples was that of the white clothing. Harris claimed they were prescribed in the trance visitation of 1910, and they were part of his prophetic identity. To Father Harrington he reported the command that he was not to wear boots, trousers or collar; his daughter told Benoît how his wife "brought him a cloth, a hole where the head went."[8] Benoît commented later after his interview, more of what Mrs. Neal had told him.

> He must, by divine command, leave off all the European clothing he was then wearing and his patent leather shoes, to reclothe himself in a kind of toga made of a single piece of stuff with a hole for his head. It was no later than the next day that he had this dress made by his wife (*BR* I, 8).

The whole experience was interpreted to Harrington as an "intervention of the Archangel Gabriel" through whom "he had escaped from prison, leaving his old clothes behind, and was miraculously clothed in his present garb."

What was the exact meaning of this change for Harris? First, and obviously, it was a rejection of the Western model, which, up to that time, had been so important to Harris, striving to become a member of the Episcopalian elite. The 1909–1910 "Report of Foreign Missions—Africa" proudly recorded that the Episcopalian clergy were "the best-dressed, best-educated, and most intelligent-looking body of Coloured ministers in the country."[9] Others, like Sir Harry Johnston, the explorer, had noted the Americo-Liberian love of clothing and outward display, witnessed in the Sunday silk topper and long frock coat.[10] Casely Hayford describes such a style in Ghana, in his *Ethiopia*

---

[7] See Victor Turner, *Forms of symbolic action*, Seattle, 1969, 20.
[8] *BN* I, 1. Our translation of "Dieu lui ordonne de quitter ses vêtements, sa femme lui porte un pagne, un trou y passe la tête."
[9] See p. 284.
[10] Harry H. Johnston, *Liberia*, vol. I. London: Hutchison and Co. 1906, 354.

Unbound of 1911. When the indigenous chiefs tried to copy this style, it was often poorly assimilated, with loin cloths accompanying the high hats.[11] The Hayford description corresponds to the "outward display" of the previous sentence.

Harris, the schoolmaster, was wearing such clothes before his imprisonment. In 1907 he ordered two pairs of "fancy men's shoes" from a USA catalogue;[12] he was ordered to abandon these and the collar, and also to abandon the ambition and pretension they represented. What he substituted was described by Father Harrington as

> ... a white flowing gown not much unlike our own cassocks, with a large black band worn exactly like a bishop's stole, and a large black wooden pectoral cross.[13]

The model had shifted, but still remained European—that of the Episcopalian clerics he knew.

The turban, on the other hand, appeared to an observer like Harrington "exactly like a Mahomedan [*sic*] sheik." Arabic dress had followed the Islamic faith into Africa; the turban was thus African yet not traditional, but related to the cultural transformation which was going on. Blyden had praised the Islamic style of mission, compared to the Christian;[14] perhaps this had influenced Harris. But primarily the robe and turban proclaimed him as "prophet", and he was copied by later West Africans who wished to make the same statement.[15] George A. Ackah from Axim, eleven years old in 1914, said simply, "He was a very wonderful man, dressed like Moses, white gown bound at the waist with blue."[16]

Indeed it was the white which was important. Harris claimed that he was "sent by God" and was a "messenger of God." Both from

---

[11] A photograph from around 1904 of "Grebo Chiefs from the Maryland Coast" shows the chiefs wearing top hats and tail coats with loin cloths (Johnston, *ibid.*, vol. II, p. 923). See also Hans Debrunner, *A history of Christianity in Ghana*, Accra: Waterville Publishing House 1967, 270f. (Cf. plate iii)

[12] Letter in Archives and Historical Collections, Episcopal Church, Austin, Texas.

[13] [Father] P[eter] Harrington, S.M.A., "An interview with the 'Black Prophet'." *The African Missionary* 18 (March-April) 1917, 13–16.

[14] Cf. E.W. Blyden, "Philip and the Eunuch", in his *Christianity, Islam and the Negro Race*. London: W.B. Whittingham & Co. 1887.

[15] This was the case for Adaï in the Ivory Coast, Grace Thanni in the Gold Coast, and Paul Nafoo in Liberia.

[16] *HN*. It is the similarity to Moses which is striking. The blue waist binding is not mentioned elsewhere.

within his Glebo tradition, and from his reading of the Bible, the use of white emphasized this calling and status. The Glebo apprentice *deyabo* clothed himself in white, the colour of the spirit or divinity; white animals were preferred as sacrificial offerings; and the white robe probably said "God-man" or "Spirit man".[17] And in Harris's favoured books, Daniel and Revelation, white is again important. The "Ancient of Days" was clothed in a "garment white as snow" (Dan. 7.9); in Revelation "white raiment" is the dress of the "worthy" and the "undefiled" (3.4); of those that "overcome" (3.5), of those that repent (3.18), of the elders around the Throne (4.4), of the redeemed of all nations (7.9, 13f), of angels (15.6); it symbolised "the righteousness of the saints" (19.8). The horse that carried Christ was also white (19.11), and the armies that followed him (19.14). White was the language of purification, of righteousness, of the heavenly. Harris himself understood it in this way.

> Let's try hard so we will conquer the devil and his people, so that when Jesus comes we will wear white robes.[18]

Harris in wearing white was dressed "already" in the "raiment" of the world that was "to come". In that sense his dress was as eschatological as his orientation. He believed in the coming kingdom, and already wore "kingdom garb".

B. The Cross

The second symbolic element was the cross, both as staff and pectoral cross; he also used the "sign of the cross" in baptism. This is classic Christian symbolism; we want to ask what Harris himself understood and implied by it.

The cross seems to have been seen first of all as an instrument. The Gambian merchant Campbell, converted by Harris at Bingerville, wrote in 1922:

---

[17] The Liberian Episcopalian missionary R.H. Gibson wrote how in 1875 the children of Half Graway were so eager just to touch his white clerical robe. He finally ordered a black one from the United States so that it would not so easily show the dirt from their hands!

[18] A "shout" of Harris, recorded and transcribed at Harper, Cape Palmas, by David A. Shank, 15 April 1978, from John Gyude Howe (1885–1978), Harris's nephew.

> ... he [Harris] saw a man standing who said to him, "You must not believe in that rod and those charms which are in front of you, for they are without power as you well know. Take therefore this (a big staff [canne] is given him) and go, here and there, from place to place, and preach Christ... a great power is upon you." The staff was accepted.[19]

This testimony places the cross in close proximity to Harris's prophetic call; it also calls the staff a *canne*, as Harrists still do. It involved the exchange of the fetish rod which was reportedly part of Harris's pre-prophetic apparatus for this staff. But the "take therefore this" is not at all unlike the Mosaic experience: "Thou shalt take this rod in thine hand, wherewith thou shalt do signs" (Exodus 4.17) This is a first indication of the importance of the cross as an instrument of the prophet; the cross-staff is also identified with power, in contrast to the powerless "fetish" rod. Yet the power is not in the staff, but in Harris, who is to use it.

We have earlier cited (page 177) Hayford's description of the cross being used in exorcism at Axim. Just before this description Hayford generalises:

> He carries a cross which they touch before they are baptised. The touching of the cross is a symbol of acceptance.[20]

This understanding, which presumably came from Harris to Hayford, shows Harris calling for decision; one said "yes" by touching the cross, instrument of the power in Harris. Baptism then becomes Harris's response to the act of acceptance. This pattern is confirmed over and over by witnesses of the moment. Jean Ekra of Bonou, who was himself baptised by Harris, reported:

> When fetishers came before Harris he held out his baton and told them to touch it. They did and were overcome with trembling. Then Harris said, "Your power is finished! Go and be good men."[21]

---

[19] Campbell [Gambian merchant], Bingerville, Ivory Coast; his testimony recorded and printed in Jean Bianquis, *Le Prophète Harris ou Dix ans d'histoire religieuse à la Côte d'Ivoire (1914–1924)*. Paris: Société des Missions Evangéliques, 1924, 35.

[20] Casely Hayford, *William Waddy Harris. The West African Reformer: the Man and his Message*. London: C.M. Philipps 1915, 10.

[21] *HN.*

In the act of acceptance, one placed himself under the power of Harris, who recognised himself that the power was not just his personal authority. The cruciform staff was the vehicle of that transfer of power.

Hayford may be cited further as he considers this phenomenon:

> Men and women flock around [Harris], and he chases out of them that which is evil. It is the Cross that does it. I have said that he carries a bamboo cross. Yesterday the crowd smashed it. . . . He simply sent to the bush for a new piece which he put together. What is there behind this cross? It is the power of the Cross. A cross implies self-surrender. It also implies consecration. When we are crossed in everyday life we never forgive. When God crosses our path and twists our purpose unto His own, He can make of a mere bamboo cross a power unto the reclaiming of souls. According to Harris he saw a light in his dungeon. Then he built his cross and carried it around. . . . God has crossed the path of the humble Grebo man, and he has had the sense to yield. He has suffered his will to be twisted out of shape, and so he carries about the symbol of the cross. That is all.[22]

Another witness, Mr. J. Barnes Christian of Axim, told Haliburton that "Casely Hayford talked a good deal to Harris in private."[23] Hayford was seriously attempting to understand Harris, and his interpretation is probably a mixture of Harris's understandings and his own. It is an attempt to understand the power of the cross. Perhaps we can compare Hayford's interpretation with that of the author of the Gospel of John, who reports the words of Jesus in such a way that we are not clear where they stop and the writer's words begin. If Hayford had asked Harris, "What is there behind this cross?" we can suggest that Harris replied: *"It is the power of the "Cross". A cross implies self-surrender. It also implies consecration. When we are crossed in everyday life we never forgive. When God crosses our path and twists our purposes unto his own, He can make of a mere bamboo cross a power. God has crossed my path, and I have yielded. I have allowed my will to be twisted out of shape and so I carry about the symbol of the cross. That is all."*

This statement can only be assumed to have been behind Hayford's writing, but it is fully in line with all we know of Harris. Just as Moses' rod became an instrument of power when he yielded—after much opposition—totally to God's purposes, so Harris's cross became an instrument of power in his hands when he yielded totally to the

---

[22] Hayford, *op. cit.*, 16–17.
[23] *HN.*

coming Lord of the Kingdom, who himself was made Lord because
he humbled himself in the cross.

Like Moses, Harris was reported to use his cross for signs of power
as well as in baptism and exorcism. He told Father Hartz, who asked
for signs, that he could make it rain; eyewitnesses in a number of
places (Akué, Bonoua) reported that he would hold up his baton to
the sky to achieve this. In other situations he used his staff when
expelled from Grand Lahou, to bring fire down when fetishes were
hidden at Ebonou; when cursing a Catholic church at Half Assinie.[24]
Did the masses read this "power of the cross" into what Harris did?
On the contrary, he himself told a Freetown newspaper reporter in
August 1917 that "with the cross he carried with him as a staff he
could do many things extraordinary."[25]

His associates and helpers certainly believed he had this power,
and we have the testimony of a Ghanaian clergyman, C.H. Elliott,
of his conversation with John Swatson (appointed as preacher by Harris)
in 1916. Swatson

> told Elliott his story and showed him how he carried on his work. He
> even showed the power in his cross which those possessed of evil spirits
> clung to until freed from the evil powers.[26]

John Ahui's testimony expresses it even more clearly.

> And when [the prophet] came with the cross, he gave him this cross;
> and when he gave him this cross, he said to his companion to leave
> the place where he was standing, and gave him another place. And
> the prophet was now directly in front of him. And he said to him,
> "That which I hand over to you is all which has permitted me to work;
> it is therefore an inheritance which I give to you. I was among you;
> I had to tell you everything. . . . Today you have come; I hand over
> to you this power, I grant to you empowering . . . That will suffice for
> your labours permitting you to continue your work. [Then followed
> the ceremony of consecration with prayer and the open Bible on Ahui's
> head.] He again handed him the things [Bible and cross] saying to
> him, "Take your cross, take these things, the arm with which I have

---

[24] *Gold Coast Leader* 13 (623) July 18, 1914.

[25] *Sierra Leone Weekly News* 33 (49), 4 August 1917.

[26] Haliburton, conversation with Canon Elliott, 17 April 1964, in Gordon M.
Haliburton, "The Anglican Church in Ghana and the Harrist Movement in 1914."
Bulletin, Society for African Church History 1 (3–4), 101–106.

conquered the world of Africa. Go be revived, believe in God; I give you my power."[27]

This perception of the cross as an arm of power is confirmed by a careful reading of the earlier accounts.

Two years earlier, when dictating messages through Benoît at the time of his September 1926 visit, Harris used his cross as his "stand-in" because of his own inability to return to the Ivory Coast. To the chief of Grand Lahou:

> You go tell chief in Gd. Lahou I live here, I live in Lahou. This (he shows his cross) is my telegraph. (*BN* I, 4).

And, as Benoît points out in his report, "Harris has sent him his cross and his Bible." (*BR* I, 19). The chief is to use Harris's cross as a source of authority and power in Harris's stead.

Harris also used "the sign of the cross" in baptism. This was according to Episcopalian usage which he must often have observed. Did it also communicate power? In a report from Ghana it was said that Harris

> in front of the Omahene's palace [at Atuabo, near Half Assinie] forestalled the fetish-workers by making the sign of the cross with his cross and reciting some incantation, so causing a supernatural thundering in the sky. That was the beginning of the fear of the man[28]

This indicated the double use of the cross—the instrument and the sign—which was apparently intended to cause effects of power. According to some reports Harris did not always baptise with water, "but made the sign of the cross on the face of the purified believer."[29] We know he did use water; one gains the impression that the signing with the cross may have replaced water-baptism during times of mass baptism.

Harris's usage of the cross and the sign of the cross did not meet with Methodist approval in Apollonia, in the Gold Coast. At Half Assinie, it was reported in 1964, "the Methodist catechist, A.P. Organ, opposed him and said he was of the devil."[30] At Axim the Methodist

---

[27] John Ahui, as recorded by Robert Arnaut, *Radiotélévision Française*, at Bregbo, 1976.
[28] *HN.*
[29] George Ackah, Axim, in *ibid.*
[30] *Ibid.*

pastor, Butler, would not permit Harris to preach in the Methodist Church.[31] Butler was replaced by Rev. Ernest Bruce, who took a more positive attitude to Harris, but who also in his early days refused to let Harris use the Methodist chapel.[32]

Bruce, the African, did indeed change his mind, and when the British missionary C.W. Armstrong arrived in Axim scarcely a week after Harris had left, he reported that "Bruce and his church leaders believe in the man." But he also reported that they were attempting to prepare people for (re-)baptism: "No one is baptized [by the Methodists] who cannot comply with the conditions."[33] The Methodists did not recognize Harris's baptism—nor the power of his cross and the sign of the cross. This is confirmed by Bruce:

> After receiving Harris's converts, we instructed them further in the Christian faith and later rebaptized them, since they were actually ignorant of the New Testament meaning of baptism. We accepted their baptism by Harris as their consent to give up idolatry and as an indication of their desire to serve God.[34]

Harris would have seen this as opposition. Originally they had seen him as "of the devil"; they had chased him from their chapel; and even after the new pastor had accepted his ministry, his baptism and the power of his cross were still not accepted. This justified his attitude, as reported by Father Stauffer:

> The catholics know the cross, they serve Christ; the Wesleyans do not know the cross, they do not know Christ.[35]

We know, of course, that the Methodists of that time in the Gold Coast did in fact preach the cross of Christ. Harris also knew it from his time in a Wesleyan pastor's home and his conversion in a Wesleyan church. But "they did not know the cross." Harris and his companions each wore a pectoral cross, as Episcopalians did; this would have been

---

[31] *Ibid.*

[32] *Gold Coast Leader* 13 (621), 4 July 1914.

[33] Letter from C.W. Armstrong, Methodist missionary at Axim, to the chairman of the Gold Coast District of the Wesleyan Missionary Society, Griffin, 2 August 1914. (Original in the archives of the Gold Coast of the Methodist Missionary Society, London).

[34] Rev. Ernest Bruce, "I lived with history." *African Challenge* 7 (4), 1957.

[35] Father Stauffer, Roman Catholic missionary at Axim: notes made in a diary sometime around or after 1926, now in General Archives, S.M.A. Rome.

considered a form of "roman fetishism" by a Wesleyan Methodist. Harris used the sign of the cross, as did Roman Catholics and Episcopalians; Wesleyans would have considered this also so much "roman hocus-pocus." They did not use the sign of the cross; they opposed its use, and they considered it necessary to re-baptize. Harris used his cross as an instrument of the power of Christ, and served Christ with it; the Wesleyans treated him as of the devil and a false prophet.

This understanding must be justified in the light of two contradictory forms of evidence. First, Harris himself often broke his cross before the crowds and made another. Second, at the time of Benoît's 1926 visit he accepted the Wesleyans.

Frank Deaville Walker reports from the Ivory Coast in 1926 that, when people mistook Harris's staff-cross for a fetish, he broke it before their eyes, threw it away, and made another.[36] This differs somewhat from Hayford's account (see page 195 above) of the crowd smashing the cross in their eagerness to get near him. Was the missionary account a "taming" of Harris, as is sometimes evident? Looking at Harris in perspective, there would seem to be little doubt that, when dealing with a "fetish-bound" people, he would if necessary break the cross to emphasize that the power lay in the Spirit given him, and not in the instrument. The difference between "fetish power" and the power of the Holy Spirit working through Harris was thus stressed and taught. Whether his disciples were able to draw the line as clearly as Harris apparently did is of course open to question.[37] The Western interpretation, however, tends to minimise the cross as an instrument of power, which was not Harris's intention either.

How then did Harris come to accept the Wesleyans at the time of Benoît's visit in 1926, when he had earlier been so sure that "they did not know the cross"? One hint may be found in the first day of conversation between the two men. Harris was talking excitedly

---

[36] See Frank Deaville Walker, *The story of the Ivory Coast.* London: the Cargate Press 1926, 14.

[37] In Etta Donner, *Hinterland Liberia* (London: Blackie 1939), the auther described, from the village of Setontuo, a village guardian who kept the village in order and under subjection by his use of an old "powerful magic staff" whose specialty was the settling of disputes. It was thus called Teu—the staff of peace. It was said to be enspirited by the "great God Z'ran". This instrument was capable of foretelling the future, and it could take revenge on whoever refused proper respect to its guardian. It is not difficult to imagine how people accustomed to such practice would have received Harris and his cross. See pp. 50ff.

"of the return of Christ and the fire of the last day. Pentecost, Pentecost" (*BR* I, 20). In that situation Benoît introduced a new dimension, the Huguenot cross. This symbol had been used by French Protestants as a rallying point in their three-century old struggle for religious freedom. The so-called Protestants in the Ivory Coast were frustrated by the Roman Catholic distribution of pious medals, and had appealed to Methodist missionaries for something which could give them an identity. An on-the-spot decision had been made to distribute the crosses, in spite of strong opposition from both the Paris Huguenot and London mission offices. Benoît asked Harris for his support in this venture. He obtained it, and in a photograph of September 1926 we see Harris wearing the Huguenot cross instead of the plain pectoral cross seen in the 1914 photographs. Benoît reported this; he wrote to his administrator:

> He has found the Huguenot cross perfect, for I explained to him that it symbolizes the Spirit (*BR* I, 20).

Harris himself added, to his message to Chief Loa of Grand Lahou:

> You must use the Wesleyan cross ... the cross the pastor give you you will wear—with Jesus Christ crown with thorns (*BN* I, 5).

Benoît transposed and completed this for his report:

> Portez aussi la croix des protestants et souvenez-vous en la regardant de la couronne d'épines qu'a portée Jésus Christ (*BN* II, 1) [Carry also the Protestant's cross, and remember when you look at it the crown of thorns which Jesus Christ wore.] (*BR* II, 2).]

So, for Harris, there was a change of attitude now that he found the Methodists themselves had changed. Benoît talked symbolically about the cross standing for "the Spirit"; Harris understood the "spirit of the cross", or its power. Paradoxically, his conclusion justifies the hesitancies of the Paris and London missionary societies. It also gives one reason why Harris was so disappointed with the Methodists in 1914, and pleased in 1926 when he rediscovered them transformed in the unsuspecting Benoît. It was only one of several misunderstandings which occurred between the two men.

C. Baptism

The symbolic expressions used by Harris were inter-related, and this is especially so with the symbol of the cross, and baptism. The sign of the cross was used particularly with baptism, and the touching of the cross meant "acceptance"—that which preceded baptism. Numerous stories from different locations indicate the relationship between the cross staff and the baptismal water. The following one from Tefredji is typical:

> On the table was a little white bowl or saucer that was empty. In the cane cross there was a hole. He raised the cross to Heaven and said, "Oh God, if thou hast sent me give water, so I can baptize the men who ask it." Then he turned the cane over and water came out of the top, into the bowl, and he baptized with it.[38]

Such impressions certainly contributed to the understanding that baptism was something involving the supernatural. But our main concern is to discover what Harris himself understood about baptism and his own actions in baptizing.

Christ's "Great Commission" was central for Harris; as he told Father Hartz in 1914:

> I am sent by Christ . . . I must bring to Christ the lost nations, and for that I must threaten them with the worst of punishments, so that they will allow themselves to be baptised, and instructed by the men of God, catholics and protestants.

Hartz' response was:

> "But you must not baptise." Immediately he retorts, "Christ asks me to do it. I must give to these crowds a preventative against the influence of the fetish which they are leaving. This preventative is the Water and the influence upon it of the touch of my cross." . . . One day I again ask him not to baptise. He therefore brings to me hundreds of persons in order that I baptise them myself. Upon my request to wait until Instruction has made of these people souls capable of grasping the virtue of Baptism, he answers me, "God will do that."
> Since I cannot do right there on the spot what he wants, he replies

---

[38] *HN*, "Old men at Tefredji, August 1963." Similar stories are found in the oral tradition of men who later became Methodists or Catholics.

telling me that, through a message made by Christ, he must baptise
during his passing through the area all those of this country who have
not yet been baptised by us, that is to say—in summary—the greater
majority of the population of the Colony.[39]

The commission of Christ took precedence over the request of the
Catholic priest who would not himself baptize those whom the prophet
brought to him. In conversations with Benoît, and this in relation
to a letter to the governor of the Ivory Coast, he established his authority
on the basis of Matthew 28, where Christ gives his commission to
the disciples. The impulse goes back to the trance-visitation of 1910:
"God told him to burn the fetishes beginning with his own and to
preach everywhere Christian baptism" (Mrs. Neal, in *BR* I, 8). Given
his eschatological perspective, there was really only one basic order:
preach repentance, the coming Kingdom, and then baptize into that
coming Kingdom. The reaction of missionaries like Father Hartz had
to be seen as replacing that basic order with another. Harris saw
the command in the same context as Karl Barth, who has written,
"The kingly ministry of the Messiah is here entrusted to the first disciples
constituting the king's troops . . . Baptizing is the priestly function of
objectively introducing others into the realm of God's reign."[40]

As for the meaning of baptism, it appears that Harris understood
it as an order to be carried out where people had broken with their
"fetish" past. But it seems clear also that he understood it to be in
some sense analogous to the "fetish" which they had renounced. The
"fetish" was perceived to exercise a spiritual influence upon the people
even after they had broken with it; the water of baptism, for Harris,
carried the "influence of the touch of my cross." In order to counteract
the "pull" of the "fetish" power, baptismal water was used to give
another kind of "pull" in another direction. An African Christian leader
like Rev. Ernest Bruce of Axim understood this meaning of baptism
communicated by Harris; he wrote: "We accepted their baptism by
Harris as their consent to give up idolatry and as an indication of
their desire to serve God."[41]

---

[39] Father Joseph Hartz, Roman Catholic missionary at Bingerville, quoted by G.
van Bulck, s.j., "Le Prophète Harris vu par Lui-même (Côte d'Ivoire, 1914)" in *Devant
les Sectes Non-Chrétiennes*. Louvain: XXXème-Semaine de Missiologie [1961], 120–124.

[40] See Karl Barth, "An exegetical study of Matthew 28.16–20" (translated by Thomas
Wieser), in Gerald H. Anderson (ed.), *The theology of the Christian mission*. Nashville:
Abingdon Press 1961, 55–71. (*Cf.* 63–67).

[41] Rev. Ernest Bruce, as cited in note 34, above.

However, this understanding was generally considered to be in-adequate by the Methodist Mission of Axim; the Catholics also saw it as inadequate: the people were not "grasping the virtue of baptism." Harris's own understanding has continued to be the practice of the Harrist Church. Its Supreme Head, John Ahui, is reported to have said (through a translator):

> Each time the whites told them to get rid of their fetishes, they tried to, but they didn't receive any replacement. Then Harris came. It was the same thing—the same words. "Abolish your fetishes. They won't get you anywhere. I'll give you something with which to replace them that will protect you—baptism. . . . Harris said that once you are baptized, the fetishes will have no more power over you. Baptism will change your life. You should build a temple and worship God.[42]

A further implication of Harris's teaching was that a return to "fetish" practice after baptism could result in death. Matthieu Adobi of Adjamé-Abidjan reported to Haliburton in August 1964:

> When Harris baptized us he said to us himself that the baptism was like knives placed on a table; the commandments I have ordained for you . . . if someone doesn't obey them he resembles a man who cuts his own throat.[43]

The merchant, Campbell, told of a man who when asking for baptism was warned by Harris about burning all of his "fetishes" first and not just a part of them. Death was predicted if he returned to a "favourite idol" after baptism. At the man's insistence Harris baptized him and in fact he did die, in front of the witness Campbell.[44]

As regards the form of baptism, we have already noticed that Harris generally traced the sign of the cross with water on the forehead of the baptized. It appears that occasionally he used the sign of the cross without water, as at Axim.[45] But always, it would appear from testimonies, the baptism took place "in the name of the Father, the

---

[42] See Sheila S. Walker, *Christianity African style: the Harrist Church of the Ivory Coast.* Ph.D. thesis, University of Chicago 1976, 104 (no source cited).
[43] *HN.*
[44] Campbell, as cited in note 19, above.
[45] One dare not draw from this such generalizations as: "Fort curieusement, le baptême administré par lui ne comportait que l'imposition des mains, à l'exclusion de toute eau." Meinard Hegba, s.j., mimeographed course given in 1975 at the Institut Supérieur Catholique Religieux, Abidjan, Ivory Coast. p. 2.

Son, and the Holy Ghost.". This is the baptismal formula most universally used by the various Christian churches. For the Roman Catholics the very correctness of the form presented a problem. The *provicaire*, Fr. Gorju, wrote:

> The number of proselytes "baptized" by the Prophet was very considerable, for the poor man did "baptize" and in what was probably a valid way, at least as to form, which fact was not the least of our worries.[46]

The Fathers of Lyon had not baptized freely in the Ivory Coast. Except for infants, they had sought to confine baptism to those who had been taught, and prior to 1914 had only about 3,000 baptized members, including Europeans. They were proud that they had not given in to the temptation to baptize the masses. Gorju himself had written in 1912:

> Many persons cannot today represent the missionary in any other way than with the characteristics of a Saint Francis Xavier, one of those great converters whose arms became tired, as it were, from pouring holy water of baptism on the bowed foreheads of the multitudes who thronged after them. . . . . such is not the ordinary pattern of the apostolate. The missionary, alas, does not see the crowds running to meet him, and every conversion—even if it does indeed trouble some souls to learn it—is achieved only at the price of obstinate travail, of a struggle at every moment.[47]

The (unconscious) parallel that Gorju makes between Xavier and the prophet Harris is striking; he could not make it, however, when confronted by the experience only two years later, because it did not fall within his structural ecclesiastical categories. Yet the form of baptism was valid.

In the Gold Coast the correctness of the form was not the major question for the Methodists. For them the baptism of an adult required an understanding of the "New Testament meaning". Therefore Harris's baptism was invalid, and the Methodists officially became "anabaptists", by present-day ecumenical standards. The missionary Charles Armstrong wrote from Axim only a few days after Harris's departure:

---

[46] Rev. Joseph Gorju, S.M.A., Roman Catholic missionary at Bingerville, "Un Prophète à la Côte d'Ivoire" in *Les Missions Catholiques*, 4 June 1915, 267ff.
[47] Gorju, *La Côte d'Ivoire Chrétienne*. Lyon: V.M. Paquet 1912, 45f.

The full responsibilities of Christianity are being pressed on the people. Polygamists are not received at all and so go to the Roman Church. Others, professing belief in Jesus Christ as their Saviour, are being carefully instructed in Christian doctrine and Methodist polity with a view to their being received on trial. No one is baptised ("Prophet" Harris's baptism is not of course recognised) who cannot comply with conditions, repeat Lord's Prayer, Creed, and Commandments, etc . . . . I have urged the advisability of keeping new converts on trial for at least twelve months and [Rev. Ernest] Bruce agrees. There must be no fictitious membership!!! I reckon there is no need to *juggle with figures* [underlining in original] of membership here!!![48]

There was an obvious difference in strategies between the Methodists and Harris.

That difference existed as well for the Roman Catholic work in Apollonia. Father Fischer, whom Harris had confronted at Half Assinie, wrote concerning the "great number of pagans who, having burned their fetishes, came to register themselves on the list of catechumens."

There was good reason to doubt the perseverance of these catechumens recruited in this way. On the counsel of my Bishop, I did not accept for baptism any catechumen during a period of three years.[49]

The Roman Catholic sacrament was administered, after monitoring by a local committee, only after the end of three years. Yet Father Fischer was astonished at the perseverance of the catechumens, and gave the credit to his own methods. We want to discover how much of the credit can go to Harris's methods.

Rev. Ernest Bruce interpreted the way in which the Gold Coast masses saw their baptism as similar to St. Paul's view of the young convert congregation of gentiles at Thessalonica, in the very earliest period of the church.

. . . you turned to God from idols, to serve a true and living God, and to wait for his Son from heaven, whom he raised from the dead, Jesus who delivers us from the wrath to come (I Thess 9, 10, RSV).

Both the Methodist and Catholic missionaries might have argued that Harris's baptised masses did not have an understanding of the second

---

[48] C.W. Armstrong, as cited in note 33, above.
[49] Father Wellinger, "Merveilleux succès de l'apostolat chez les Apolloniens", in *Les Missions Catholiques* 2714, 17, June 1921.

part of this description. Yet it was clearly part of Harris's own understanding, which he endeavoured to communicate. Certainly he saw himself as delivering them, through baptism, from the judgement of fire which would descend at the return of Jesus. This is one of his most explicit objects. Benoît reported:

> He wishes someone to tell the people of the bush to burn their fetishes that they may be baptised and worship the only true God. All those who refuse will be truly punished. Fire from heaven will descend on them. He, Harris, will make it fall by a single gesture (*BR* I, 17).

The general understanding of both Roman Catholic and Methodist workers was that Harris's baptism was superficial; "understanding" would make it deeper and more radically a break with paganism, and only then could "Christian" baptism be administered. His work was placed in a pre-Christian context; "they called me John the Baptist", Harris reported from Bingerville. He was seen by the Western missionaries to be preparing—like John the Baptist for Christ—people for the coming of the white missionary who would then properly initiate them into their churches.

What "understanding" did Harris in fact convey to those he baptised? It was indeed one of repentance, and it was strict. As Campbell reported, those who hesitated about baptism, those who were not completely honest about the destruction of their fetishes, were told they faced death.[50] One question is whether massive repentance on the part of vast crowds excluded a personal, responsible and non-superficial response. Some witnesses have emphasised the hypnotic effect which Harris seemed to have on his hearers.[51] The former governor of the Ivory Coast, Angoulvant, told the French missionary administrator Pasteur Bianquis, in 1924, "For me, he was a hypnotiser. But I found nothing for which I could reproach him".[52] The question of the Western missionaries remained: could a baptism—even of repentance—be taken seriously as Christian baptism if it occurred superficially in a context of mass hysteria?

The missiologist Alan R. Tippett, working more recently within a different—yet similar—context has a helpful comment.

---

[50] Campbell, as cited in note 19, above.
[51] As reported by Katesa Schlosser in *Propheten im Afrika*. Braunschweig: Albert Limbach 1969, 254.
[52] In Jean Bianquis, *op. cit.*, note 19 above, 11.

Iconoclasm was the indigenous symbol of the rejection of a mana repository. Throughout Polynesia and Melanesia this is the indigenous conceptualization of power encounter . . . a cultural mechanism within a social pattern, the proof of sincerity in a time of major decision-making. Again it was always a voluntary act undertaken by the approved authority within the structure, or a challenge of proof by contest within a specific frame of reference. . . . The question [of baptism without proper instruction] is whether a man should be baptised on the basis of an act of faith or on an understanding of the faith? In the eyes of the Melanesian the symbolic act is conclusive.[53]

It is this dimension which must be grasped to appreciate—retrospectively—the dynamics of Harris's baptism. How did those who received baptism from him see the matter?

One report comes from Haliburton's notes of August 1963.

When Harris passed along from Kraffi he stayed here [Addah] one night with King's agent. During the evening he called together the old men of the town. He gave them his message that the fetishes they feared were not gods; they should burn them and go to Brown at Petit Lahou to be baptized. The old men were not convinced by his words. He said, "Well, I am going on my way. There is no force upon you, but your hearts will lead you to do what I have said." Next day he continued on towards Jacqueville, but after that his words had results. The old men reported to their wives and children what he had said, and they reflected upon it. People were moved by household and group to do as he had said. It was true, the fetishes were not of God. Therefore they were discarded and burnt, and little groups began making their way to Brown at Petit Lahou (Ebonou). Soon a stream of people . . . were moving through the town in the same direction. The *Chef de Canton*, Victor Niavri, decided that he should get the power to baptize, to save these people such a long journey. He called together the elders to get their opinion and they agreed that this would be good. The *Chef* went by hammock to Grand Lahou where the Fanti "Papa" was baptizing by permission of Bron [Brown]. Papa was unable to give Victor permission, so he went on to Ebonou, where he was received and instructed by Brown for two weeks and then given full authority to baptize. Thereafter people coming from the mainland by pirogue went no further than Addah. The people of Addah built a church for themselves.[54]

---

[53] Alan R. Tippet, *Solomon Islands Christianity*. London: Lutterworth Press 1967. See especially chapter 7: "Problems of encounter", 106ff.

[54] *HN*, Addah. "King" was one of the leading trading companies. Brown was already authorized by Harris to continue the work of preaching and baptizing, and he had deputized "Papa" to carry on in his name.

Here we observe consultation and respect for authority; a remarkable illustration of what Tippett has called "multi-individual decision".

Haliburton recorded another illustration from another Alladian village, Adjué. Here, Harris had stayed overnight with the chief, and at night he spoke to the villagers who gathered, telling them to destroy their fetishes and be baptized. The chief fetisher and his assistants objected, and no one offered himself for baptism. Harris left in anger, and only a few hours later a whirlwind blew through the town and frightened the people. They took it as a sign, and many now wanted baptism, but they could not locate Harris. Some went to Ebonou to be baptized by Brown, and others to Addah to be baptized by Victor. They went in small groups over a period of time, after burning their fetishes. The first to be baptized became automatically a preacher, and eventually the leading fetishers became pillars of the church.[55]

Here the whirlwind was taken by the fetishers as a sign that Harris had more power than they, and the people followed, but not *en masse*; rather, in small groups as they made their own decisions. Harris had started the process by his visit to the chief.

If we study Acts 2—where Harris learned of Pentecost—we will observe that the spiritual nature of the religious encounter, its psychological concomitants, the climate of "fear" and "signs", and the mass response, are all to be found (as also in Acts 5.1–12). It is reported there that "masses" were being received for baptism in an atmosphere where sign and marvel and fear are seen to dominate the ethos. There, too, we know from reports what was preached; we do not know what was explicitly understood by those being baptized.

Casely Hayford, an African intellectual, described the effect of baptism in words that sound as if they are a personal testimony.

> Strangely enough this man's work begins with baptism and ends in baptism. You come to him with a heart full of bitterness, and when he has finished with you all the bitterness has gone out of your soul.

He goes on to speak of this being true for others—men and women, young and old—who moved from violence to humble composure.[56] While it needed to be worked out in its full implications in the fellowship of the church, what appeared to outsiders to be marvel, terror and

---

[55] *HN*, Adjué.
[56] Hayford, as cited in note 20 above, 6.

hypnotism produced a new climate of peace. In another "Christianized" area, similar to that of Axim, Rev. S. Renner of Freetown said simply that the people came to Harris "to find peace, as we used to say."[57]

The decisive nature of baptism involved a decision on the part of the one baptized; but its efficacy seemingly depended on the water bearing the influence of the cross. This not only prevented apostasy, but also purified those baptized. Gaston Joseph, the *aide* of Governor Angoulvant, wrote in 1916 that Harris "assured his proselytes that he purified them by baptism."[58] In the following year he corrected his article, and wrote, "and by baptism he assured his proselytes that he purified them."[59] It is likely that for Harris, and for his converts, the deliverance was more from the power of evil than from a sense of guilt, or blame. Harris explicitly cited Ezekiel 33 and 37; verses in Ez 36. 25–29 must have been part of his inspiration. "I will sprinkle clean water upon you, and you shall be clean from all your uncleanesses, and from all you idols I will cleanse you. . . . You shall be my people, and I will be your God . . ." Although the primary meaning attached to uncleaness is of ritual and moral pollution, it seems that Harris also gave instruction on simple physical hygiene, and expected that baptism would have practical effects.

In yet another perspective, Harris's baptism was seen as purifying that which had been impure, and freeing men from the "fetish" commandments which put taboos on food and action. "Harris said that as God has blessed everything, nothing was impure, so people could use those roads and eat those foods without being sick."[60] In the eastern Ivory Coast, among the Agni, the passage of the prophet Harris led to the definitive destruction of the *manza-Swa*, huts on the edge of the forest where menstruating women, considered impure, were isolated. The Ivorian anthropologist Amon d'Aby offers us a short description of the shift of the pure/impure structures among the Agni as a result of Harris's impact.[61] Haliburton received similar information from the Omahene of Atuabo, in western Ghana, in 1964.[62] Harris is echoing the teaching of Jesus and of Paul, "that there is

---

[57] From my conversation with Rev. Dr. S. Renner at Freetown, 27 April 1979.
[58] Gaston Joseph, "Une atteinte à l'animisme . . ." in *Annuaire et Mémoires du Comité d'Etudes Historiques et Scientifiques de l'Afrique Occidentale Française* (Gorée), 1916, 345.
[59] Gaston Joseph, *La Côte d'Ivoire*. Paris: Emile Larose 1917, 157.
[60] *HN*. Aizi (near Kraffy).
[61] F.J. Amon d'Aby, *Croyances religieuses et coutumes juridiques des Agni de la Côte d'Ivoire*. Paris: Larose 1960, 22f.
[62] *HN* and *PH*, 75.

nothing unclean of itself" (Romans 14.14).

A further aspect of Harris's baptism is to be found in his use of public confession as a pre-baptismal ritual. Elderly men who had been youths at the time of Harris's passage gave similar reports to Haliburton when he spoke to them in 1963–4, at Axim, Abidjin-Kouté and in Alladian territory. All spoke of public confession being required before baptism took place, and any return to sin required a new confession to combat the resulting sickness or threat of death which sin brought upon the person.[63] Similar reports came from Sierra Leone, claiming that he put a special emphasis upon personal "acknowledgement of sin".[64]

The importance of this public confession of sin in its relation to baptism and to healing after baptism was something that had found its way into local Methodist congregations through the early Harrist churches which became Methodist; it has likewise been maintained in Harrist churches. But it has also been a "technique" of the post-Harris healing prophets such as Adai or Atcho, in whose ministries confession has played a major role.[65] One suspects that the roots of public confession are more from traditional life than from rites imported with, for example, Roman Catholicism. The function of confession in life among pre-literate people has been indeed to effect a catharsis by expulsion of the deed confessed, a kind of "vomiting" of the action which was contrary to accepted practice.[66] Harris did not hesitate to use that technique, but it is probable that he gave it a new usage.

Augé has concluded that the "modern" confessions along the Ivorian coast differ from the "traditional" in that the latter never involved sorcery, while the former are often a substitute for the ordeals by sassywood.[67] When the latter is not imposed by external accusations of sorcery, the sufferer may accuse himself on the basis of the logic which says that if one is suffering he obviously has done evil to merit such consequences. One suspects that the "modern" usage dates from

---

[63] *HN*.

[64] *Sierra Leone Guardian and Foreign Mail* 12 (39), 7 September 1917. See also note 57 above.

[65] For a report of Adai's ministry, see Bohumil Holas, *Le séparatisme religieux en Afrique Noire*. Paris: P.U.F. 1965, esp. pp. 134–161; for a recent study of Atcho's ministry see Colette Piault (ed.), *Prophétisme et thérapeutique*. Paris: Hermann 1975, esp. pp. 121–152.

[66] See, e.g., Raoul Allier, "La confession publique des péchés chez les peuples non-civilisés" in *Mercure de France*, March 1935, 449–75.

[67] Marc Augé, *Théorie des pouvoirs et idéologie*. Paris: Hermann 1975, 266ff.

Harris, who opposed the ordeals so strongly, yet believed also so powerfully in imminent judgement for sin. His message at Kraffy reflected this:

> If someone becomes sick, let him confess his sins to the apostles of his church, who will pray God to ask for his healing.[68]

This reflects James 4.16–18; however, the relation between sin and sickness as absolute cause and effect is foreign to the whole thought of the New Testament, apparently following Jesus, as in John 9.1–3. In this, at least, Harris was inspired more by African traditional understandings, clearly confirmed by pre-Christian understandings of parts of the Old Testament. It also explains why Harris's baptism often had healing effects.

D. Fire

"Repent! or fire!" Such was the earliest message of the prophet Harris, as recalled from 1910 by Edwin Hodge.[69] His Elijah role required the necessary power to call down fire, and he himself was convinced that he did call it down on hidden fetishes, on boats that were unloaded on Sundays . . . When in the 1950s Debrunner was investigating in western Ghana, he discovered that in popular belief Harris, "this humble and faithful preacher", had been transformed into a great "'professor of magic', able to rise in the air and bring down fire from heaven in order to destroy the spiritual battleship of those witches who wanted to confound and kill him."[70]

Undoubtedly there were distortions about Harris in popular belief, but "bringing down fire" was not one of them. Missionary belief had tamed Harris to what Debrunner saw, a "humble and faithful preacher." In fact, the threat of fire and his expectation of it was a constant theme from 1910 at least until the end of 1926 when he spoke to Benoît of those in the bush who refused to be baptized: "Fire from

---

[68] Edmond de Billy, *En Côte d'Ivoire. Mission Protestante d'A.O.F.* Paris: Société des Missions Evangéliques [1931], 15–16. de Billy, working with the Wesleyan Methodists from 1925, had often visited Kraffy, and heard the Harris story from people he met there. He tried to faithfully reconstruct the essential elements of Harris's message.
[69] Personal conversation at Cape Palmas, 15 April 1978.
[70] Hans Debrunner, *Witchcraft in Ghana.* Kumasi: Presbyterian Book Depot 1959, 150.

heaven will descend on them. He, Harris, will make it fall by a single
gesture" (*BR* I, 17).

In addition to his claims to supernatural fire, he also used fire directly
for the destruction of "fetishes" which people continued to bring to
him, often in large quantities. His person was identified as the destroyer
of "fetishes" by fire.

It is difficult to avoid the conclusion that the burning of "fetishes",
the "fire from heaven" on boats and hidden "fetishes", the threats
upon disobedient and rebels, and the proclamation of purifying fires
of judgement, are connected. Indeed, Harris's use and proclamation
of fire fits the pattern of the purge rather than that of the vindictive
punishment. Fire and baptism together effected a purification from
past evil and occult powers and their symbols, preparing for a new
power for good and peace with its own symbols.

E. The Bible

Central in the complex of symbolic impact is the role of the Bible.
Here we are not speaking of the interpretation of its contents, already
discussed, but of its ritual usage. When Harris wanted to communicate
his power and authority he gave his Bible. This was the case even
when the recipients were known to be illiterate (as with chief Loa
of Grand Lahou in 1926 and Ahui in 1928). Even illiteracy could
not render the Bible powerless.

Nevertheless, illiteracy was to be overcome. In the message which
Benoît arranged for Harris to send, it was written:

> Read the Bible; it is the Word of God. I am sending one to you and
> I have marked the verses to be read. Search out the light in the Bible.
> Learn your letters that you may be able to read the Bible; it will be
> your guide (BR I, 23f).

Here the accent is on "light", "Word of God", and "guide". Yet Harris
used the Bible as a symbol of power.

Was it the prophet's intention to communicate to the masses that
the Bible was an arm of spiritual conquest independent of its being
read and assimilated intellectually and spiritually? It is difficult to say.
Hayford's description of the healing of a possessed woman at Axim
(cited on 177f.) could give that impression. On the preceding page
Hayford had reported:

After baptism he lays a tattered Bible twice on your head before dismissing you. It is an act of confirmation.

Walker reported similar evidence from eye-witnesses in the early 1920s.

He also carried a small Bible, apparently well-worn; he always seems to have had it with him, and often held it up for the crowds to see, but I have not come across anyone who saw him read it.[71]

Harris's manner of using the Bible had in fact led to Walker's conclusion that he was "probably illiterate" and obviously "untutored".[72] There are in fact eye-witness reports of his reading from his Bible, but it is not the usual pattern, nor the impression given to the masses. The Ivorian Methodist theologian Yando wrote in 1970:

Perhaps he judged it useless [to read the Bible to an illiterate audience], or else he preferred to practice the Oral Tradition which was the dynamic means of communication of traditional African societies. If that is true, Harris there committed an error, in that today his example stands as "sacred text" for the neo-Harrists whose preachers, following the prophet, actually carry a Bible in hand, which they place on the occasion of baptism on the head of the one baptized, but forbid to read it.[73]

In our judgement, Harris felt very clearly both that the Bible was a source of power and that literacy was the key to its full potential; but he failed to communicate effectively the second part to all his followers. This was true, apparently, in spite of the clear instructions given to John Ahui in 1928 to open schools for the children.[74]

Harris came from a society where literacy was a comparatively new phenomenon, and was seen as a form of "white power". He himself was in a minority as a youth, in that he did learn to read and write. In 1875 a Liberian woman wrote that in teaching "native children" she was "training children to be white", since the belief was that in

---

[71] F.D. Walker, *op. cit.*, 14.
[72] *Ibid.*, 11.
[73] Emmanuel Yando, *L'Evolution du Harrisme en Côte d'Ivoire: Mémoire* at the Paris Theological Faculty, 1970, 44. As early as 1973 and 1974 the writer [Shank] observed young people carrying and reading Bibles during Sunday services at Abobo-Doumé. In at least one or two churches, preachers were reading the Bible with young people in unofficial evening gatherings.
[74] *Cf.* Haliburton, *PH*, 208, where the evidence is from John Ahui, the Supreme Head of the Harrist Church, in 1963–64.

learning to read they would become white.[75] An earlier comment (1839) suggested that eagerness to read and know the Bible sprang from this belief that this was the secret of white superiority.[76] Where religion deals with control, manipulation and balance of power, which are perceived as spiritual entities, the power of the book is interpreted in spiritual—that is religious—terms. For the Westerner, literacy is a normal part of his culture, and he has generally not reflected on the religious implications of the written word for a people passing from primal religious life and experience into a monotheistic religious life and practice.

There is a remark of Durkheim's which is suggestive at this juncture. He wrote:

> Religious conceptions have as their object, before everything else, to express and explain, not that which is exceptional and abnormal in things, but on the contrary that which is regular and constant.[77]

The written word introduced a constancy into information and narrative which in itself was an indication of truth. The magic of the alphabet which formed the words of the new language brought great pleasure, but, as Sheik Hamadou Kane reports, the chiefs were conscious as they put their children in the white men's schools that they were putting an end to their own traditions; they were resigned to have them "go learn the art of conquering without being right."[78]

Jack Goody, who has made a special study of the consequences of literacy, has brought to the surface another dimension of the shift. Oral tradition, he reports, "can change its content through the homeostatic process of forgetting or transforming those parts of the tradition that cease to be either necessary or relevant";[79] but literacy

---

[75] Cited in Thomas W. Livingstone, *Education and Race . . .* , San Francisco: the Glendessary Press 1975, 239, note 11, where he quotes the *African Repository* of October 1875.

[76] See chapter II, above, pp. 38f., for comments by Dr. Savage of the Episcopalian mission staff.

[77] Emile Durkheim, *The Elementary Forms of the Religious Life*. New York: Free Press 1969, 43.

[78] [Sheik] H[amadou] Kane, *L'Aventure Ambiguë*, Paris: Juilliard 1971, 47 and 172 (cited in Charles Daniel Maire, *Dynamique Sociale des Mutations Religieuses*, Mémoire of 1975, E.P.N.S. (Paris), 50.

[79] Jack Goody, "Restricted literacy in Northern Ghana", in his *Literacy in traditional society*. Cambridge: C.U.P. 1968, 201. See also Jack Goody and Ian Watt, "The consequences of literacy." *Comparative Studies in Society and History* 5, 1962–63, 304–45.

effectively challenges this. Thus history becomes possible, and provides a way of checking the transmutation of ideas, thus creating also scepticism about all received ideas about the universe. Its long-term effect is one of desacralization and even dualistic schizophrenia.

From Harris's point of view, biblical literacy would have engendered doubt about the contemporary oral religious reality, seen to be very unstable alongside the written traditions which were immutable because enscriptured. That immutable and soldily religious reality would have provided the new alternative explanation in his effort to put together that which was falling apart in his own internal process of schizophrenic detribalizing, desacralizing, and individualizing. "It is written" could become for one in search of an alternative explanation the unchanging source to which he could always return. It was true because it always said the same thing, about the same people, the same God, the same Spirit, the same Kingdom. The Bible in itself constituted a powerful religious medium for transformation, not only in preserving a critique of the past, a new opening to another future, but also the contents of that new future.

Goody has also shown how, in northern Ghana, written scraps of paper were associated with the power of God, identified with the Allah of the Muslims and the Jehovah of the Christians. "The very fact," he wrote, "that writing enables man to communicate over space and time makes it more effective as a way of getting in touch with distant deities."[80] Islam in the midst of oral societies was seen to be the possessor of a wider communication technology. This understanding reached down to the coastal area of the Ivory Coast, where P. Marty saw Islam's appeal to be particularly strong because of its "prestige of science, of instruction, of the school, of the book, of writing."[81] This religious-cultural context was not foreign to Harris. And it is simplistic to suggest that the understanding of the Bible as a symbol of power with value in itself is only that of present-day Harrists, with no origin in Harris's own understanding. He was indeed probably further along the path of perfecting the use of the key to its power—the power of God, which was also seen to be the power of the whites. Sheila Walker has made a suggestive analysis:

---

[80] Goody, *op. cit.*, 1968, 201.
[81] Paul Marty, *Etudes sur l'Islam en Côte d'Ivoire*. Paris: Leroux 1922, 96.

> The Prophet Harris was able to bring the same message as the missionaries to the Africans because in addition to being stated in a way that was reasonable within the context of their culture and in doing so within the context of a standard role within the society, *his form of presentation was very significant*. Although his verbal message was essentially the same as that of the missionaries, his *form of presentation was entirely different*. This difference between the Prophet's verbal and behavioural messages accounts for the acceptance from him rather than from the missionaries . . .[82]

It would appear that Harris's presentation of the message—in his use of the Bible, in this case—was different, because his understanding was different from that of the missionaries. This means that ultimately his message was a different message from that of the missionaries; he attributed to the Bible a power—which he had experienced as he moved from illiteracy into literacy—which the missionary had not experienced in his individualistic and desacralized society where one was normally literate.

Harris's word to France via Benoît was: "Prophet no man like you; he is in transes. Moses and Elijah come to visit me. The voice of God come *through the Bible* and tell all that" (*BN* I, 12; my underlining). The Bible has the power to "turn on" the voice of God; it was a different kind of potency than that of his missionary mentors. The powerful book was a part of Harris's message.

F. Sheepskin

Several of the early eye-witness reports mention explicitly that Harris always carried a sheepskin. This was the case from widely separated locations in 1913 and 1914.[83]

In a society in which "everywhere where the animal appears, it is symbolical",[84] one can indeed deduce that Harris was saying something symbolical about the sheep . . . or the lamb. The first meaning which occurs to the Christian observer is the association with "the lamb of God", well-known to Harris both from the Bible and the Episcopal liturgy he knew so well. Even more important for Harris would be the central image of the lamb in his favourite book,

---

[82] Sheila Walker, *op. cit.*, 331 (my underlining).
[83] See J.P. Ephson, *HN* for Axim; also *PH*, 67 for Bingerville and 78 for Kraffy; also Collins (note 89) for Liberia.
[84] Citation from Amadou Hampaté Ba by Henri Desroche, *L'Homme et ses Religions*. Paris: Cerf 1962, 63.

Revelation (chapter 5.6; 13.8; 19.7ff.; 21.9, 22f.; 22.1). For the traditional observer, the "lamb" becomes the totem of the new people. Harris's work among people of various ethnic groups and language in West Africa was fulfilling the prophecy in the hymn to the Lamb:

> For thou wast slain, and hast redeemed us to God by thy blood out of every kindred and tongue and people and nation; and hast made us unto our God kings and priests: and we shall reign on the earth. (Rev 5.9–10)

In Harris's own traditional milieu, there was a strong preference for white animals as sacrificial offerings.[85] Among the Ebrié in the Ivory Coast and the Akan in Ghana white sheep were offered for deliverance from epidemics.[86] The sheepskin like other symbols Harris used spoke of power—but in this case it was the power of innocence, defencelessness and powerlessness in the sacrificial victim.

Harris at the time of his prophetic call was a rebel—but the sheepskin speaks of his identity with the one who "was led as a lamb to the slaughter" (Isaiah 53.7). Later in his ministry Harris specifically refused to exercise or contemplate physical violence and vengeance. At Kraffy he was reported citing the text that "to Him [God] belongs vengeance",[87] and he endured beatings from the French authorities in such a spirit.

For a parallel usage in Harris's own indigenous heritage, we recall that the Glebo bodio when he exercised his authority always carried with him his *pleko*, the monkey-skin which appeared to reflect the Glebo ethnic identity.[88] The monkey skin carried in itself the ethnic history and authority. Harris, for his part, carried a sheepskin. In June 1917 Father J. Collins of Sasstown, Liberia, received the visit of Prophet Harris who "explains all of his belongings" including "the skin of a sheep to place on the head of the baptized as some symbol of the Lamb."[89]

---

[85] See Werner Korte, "Religiöse Dissidenten, Propheten und Kultgründungen im südöstlichen Liberia in 19 und 20 Jahrhundert," *Sociologus* 26 (1), N.S. 1976, 11, note 10.

[86] See Georges Niangoran Bouah, *La division du temps et le calendrier rituel des peuples lagunaires de Côte d'Ivoire.* Paris: Institut d'Ethnologie 1964, 127f.

[87] As reported by E. de Billy (cited in note 68 above). *Cf.* Romans 12. 19–21.

[88] When they first arrived at Cape Palmas, the people who successfully made the trip were called *glebo* after the monkey (*gle-*) because they appeared as monkeys climbing trees when they rode the high waves to shore.

[89] Diary of Father J. Collins 1913–1919. (Archives of SMA Fathers, Cork, Ireland, by courtesy of the Archivist, Fr. C. Clancy).

G. Calabash rattle

Both photographs and descriptions of Harris in action stress the importance of the hollowed calabash shaken rhythmically inside the beaded net in which it was carried. The women who accompanied Harris used these instruments with him to beat out their singing of "shouts" and hymns.

Such an instrument was used traditionally, not only by the Glebo people but also among Kru peoples as a whole. It was seen to be an instrument for the convoking of spirits as well as their means of communication to the people.

Thus it is easy to understand how some of Harris's congregation saw Harris's use of the instrument in this light.

> [Harris] had a big calabash; [the women] had smaller ones. These instruments were used in the old days to call the fetish spirit and sing his praise. Harris was formerly a great fetisher, knew the power of the calabashes. He used it only when burning the fetishes, thus calling the spirits into them to be burned.[90]

Another witness (in Ghana) spoke of Harris dancing with an afflicted person to the sound of the rattles. "*When he had got the power* he stopped shaking the calabash . . ."[91]

Was this also the way in which Harris understood his use of the calabash?

The earliest report we have of Harris's own understanding comes from the *Gold Coast Leader* of 18 July 1914 when he said that the "calabash round his neck" was "his harp (three strings around it means the Holy Trinity)." He also explained to Father Collins that "the three strings around it are in honour of the three divine persons." This description comes also in other reports. He seems commonly to have spoken of his "fancy gourd" as "David's harp".[92]

To Father Hartz he spoke of his gourd as his "celestial harp which translates the message given [him] by Christ"; a similar comment comes from Freetown in July 1917:

---

[90] *HN*, old men from Tefredji, at the western end of the Ebrié lagoon; *cf. PH*, 66.

[91] *HN* (my underlining).

[92] See Walter B. Williams and Maude Winfield Williams, *Adventures with the Krus in West Africa*. New York: Vantage Press 1955, 141f. ("The real story of the 'prophet movement'").

His rattle "shake-shake" represented three things, viz., a bell to call the multitude, a harp of twelve strings to captivate the multitude, and a net to draw in the multitudes.[93]

The first significant biblical reference to prophets in Israel is in I Samuel 10 where Saul meets a band of prophets said to be in prophetic esctasy; a harp is among their instruments. Harris's reference to David's harp indicates, once again, the importance to him of the biblical model. In I Samuel 16 14–22 there is a description of David's use of harp-music to soothe and help King Saul when he was troubled by "evil spirits". Given the traditional use of the calabash in Glebo religion, it would not be surprising if this was also in the prophet Harris's mind. In any case, the calabash-rattle was a conscious spiritual technique, cunningly applied along with the white clothes, the cross, water, fire, book and baptism.

Can we say that Harris "adapted" the traditional calabash rattle and other elements to Christian use? This was the interpretation of an Ivorian Methodist Christian, E. Yando.

> There are those who have reproached Harris for having been syncretistic with reference to his white clothes, his calabashes with grains, which recalled the vestimentary stance of fetishers, and yet these people do not understand that for him these elements are desacralized.[94]

In the same paragraph Yando speaks of Harris's "adaptation to the African way of living and understanding." In fact, it would appear more correct to see Harris "expressing" his Africanity rather than "adapting" to it! And it would also seem better to fit Harris's understanding to say that the elements were indeed desacralized and then—with another Spirit—completely re-sacralized. This appears more clearly to be the case when one hears the comments of observers of Harris and his technique. Haliburton in *The Prophet Harris* comments:

> His practice of singing hymns to the rhythmic clash of calabashes alone, was sufficient to induce complete loss of conscious control in those whose minds were troubled. In that sense Harris was certainly employing hypnosis.[95]

---

[93] *Sierra Leone Weekly News*, 4 August 1917.
[94] Yando, *op. cit.*, 45f.
[95] *PH*, 116.

The Harrist Church of a later date (1966) would appear to be in harmony with Harris's own usage when they reported that

> The 'Yaka', the calabash rattle, serves to chase the evil spirits. They will be progressively eliminated when we see them clearly. Each person will then keep them at home. The less-civilized villagers will keep them longer . . . Harris said [to John Ahui] to eliminate the 'Yaka' after a while. The Yaka serves for sweeping out all that is evil.[96]

And in 1966 a Harrist preacher at Abobo-Doumé said in an interview:

> It [the rattle] is the broom which chases the fetishes from the spirit of the catechumen when he comes to adore the true God. Our supreme preacher will tell you: "One day all the children will have gone to school, science will have chased the fetishes, that will be the end of the calabash broom, perhaps also the dances and songs for which the Catholics reproach us.[97]

Song and dance were intimately linked to the use of the calabashes in the 1913–14 mission of Harris. We should here note the importance of these elements in the total impact of the team. The first impression that a village might receive of Harris and his accompanying disciples was that of the group led by Harris singing and dancing down the main street of the village to the accompaniment of the calabashes, thus attracting the crowds to hear the spoken word.

H. The Word

The final element in the Harris arsenal of instrumental symbols was the spoken word. Here we refer to the word which is seen to effect and accomplish what it says, on the one hand; and on the other it is the word seen to be effective also because it is said. This is not merely an African understanding, but a more or less universal understanding within a society where orality is the dominant means of communication. It was, then, a part of Harris's cultural equipment.

> [For the African] the spoken word not only transmits some distant information; it expresses a living reality. Pronounced in the form of a blessing, it is not a simple suggestion, but the incarnation of the blessing

---

[96] Cited in Dominique Desanti, *Côte d'Ivoire*, Lausanne: Rencontre 1962, 66.
[97] *RBN*; Bruno Abéto, Abobo-Doumé, 21 August 1966.

itself. The word [viva voce] is charged with creative power, with energy and with life. It is a force and a reality. It is the good word which reinforces and vitalises man in his whole being; it is full of reconciliation for the clan and community of men.

There is also the evil word, which thwarts the expansive power of the life of man. It is especially charged with "surreality" . . . In general the malediction/curse is a power which is possessed by [those who] also have the power to bless . . . This curse/malediction diminishes the vivifying force and hinders the blessing of the ancestors to act on the rebel member of the clan.[98]

In other words

The word is all
It cuts, flays
It models, modulates,
It troubles, makes one crazy,
It heals, or kills outright,
It amplifies, or diminishes, according to its weight,
It excites or calms the souls.[99]

Harris used the word in proclamation, in warning, in exhortation, in teaching, in blessing and in cursing, and in prayer. How did he himself perceive his use of the spoken word?

Conscious as he was of being a "messenger of God" who was "sent by God", we are not surprised when he tells Father Hartz:

Thunderbolts will talk, the angels will punish the world if it does not listen to my word, which interprets that of God.[100]

He saw himself as spokesman for God, and transmitted this conviction very clearly.

I have said that he confesses himself an instrument in the hands of God . . . This great stalwart Kroo man knows no will of his own. He has learnt the lesson of those whose lips have been touched by live coal from the altar to sink himself in God. He is receptive. His whole soul is open unto God. Is it any wonder that God should play upon it as He would?[101]

---

[98] Cited from Jean Masamba, "Une approche pastorale au problème de la sorcellerie" in *Revue du Clergé Africain* 26 (1), 6 (my translation).

[99] Cited by Masamba, *ibid.*, 5.

[100] Father Hartz, as cited in note 39 above.

[101] Casely Hayford, as cited in note 20 above.

Harris himself did not cite the Isaiah passage in reference to himself.
But his thrust undoubtedly was the same: like Isaiah his lips were
purified so that he could tell the people the message God himself
had given (cf. Isaiah 6, 1–9).

In conversation with Benoît he said explicitly:

> When I say "I" I mean "God". Tell Governor "I" [meaning "God"]
> want to make peace with France (*BN* II, 12).

The reports of the effectiveness of his word to heal, to bless, to curse,
to give signs, to cause rain, are numerous. Also numerous are expressions which even today have a continuity with the various forms of
Christianity in the lower Ivory Coast: "Christ Church", "work of God",
"way of God", "Jesus" pronounced in an English manner at the end
of prayer, the beginning of prayer with "O-o-o-o-o-h" are among
these. But the power of the word to create authoritative patterns is
also well attested.

> Don't eat on the ground. (Adjukru)
> Don't have sexual relations on the ground.(Ebrié)
> If you commit adultery, you must confess it to your marriage partner
> and compensate her with the same compensation given to the adulterous
> partner. (Abobo-Té)
>   If you are hungry you can eat from another's field but you must
> report it to him and give anything picked but not consumed. (Abobo-
> Té)
>   A funeral is to last eight days at the most and not three or four
> months. (Abidjin-Kouté)
>   If you find something valuable, it is to be taken to the nearest village
> and its owner sought. If one does not find the owner, it can be kept
> as a gift from God (id.)
>   Nubile maidens were no longer to go naked after the first week of
> womanhood. (Grand Lahou)

It is not quite accurate to put it as did Sheila Walker:

> It appears that people were impressed less by Harris's words, which
> were, after all, about the same as those of the European missionaries,
> than by the concrete demonstration of his power, which gave meaning
> to his message.[102]

---

[102] Sheila Walker, *op. cit.*, 116.

Indeed the expression of spiritual power in Harris's ministry made his words significant; they took on a very great importance because of his power, but that importance must not be minimized nor underestimated. When the Methodist missionary, Platt, arrived for his visit in early 1924, he was astonished that the people had held out in their new religious tradition, waiting hopefully for teachers, in the midst of opposition, persecution from the French authorities, and the attrition of time.

> With tenacity and patience well-nigh miraculous, they have struggled on alone, believing always that others would come as "Prophet Harris" told them, to carry on the work where he left off.[103]

Because of his power, they obeyed and waited, but they obeyed and waited according to his word[s].

In this sense Harris's words, as prophet, were indeed as important as—if not more important than—the other significant instrumental symbols which he used. Without wishing to minimize the importance of the other symbols, we need to examine further, in the following chapter, that most important prophetic word.

---

[103] Rev. William Platt, cited in *Christian Herald* 59 (26), 726 (25 June 1925).

CHAPTER TEN

THE PROPHETIC WORD

The purpose of our whole study has been to determine the thought and intent of the prophet Harris during his ministry. What part of his thought and words effectively functioned in his hearers' lives? We here want to look at those patterns emerging from his message which indicate that his prophetic word was in itself an effective arm of power.

A. The message

Harris's message, though proclaimed hundreds of times to different audiences in differing circumstances, has been known for its brief simplicity. One typical résumé has been given by the French ethnologist René Bureau, who was using the only sources available to him in 1970. He mentioned first the negative and the positive points—the necessity to leave the practice of sorcery and the worship of fetishes, and the truth of the only one true God, contained in the Bible, and the power of God in the cross of Christ.

> The God presented by Harris is rather vengeful and jealous. He sends to hell the souls of witches. Jesus Christ intervenes very little; at the most his death is cited as the source of salvation. The Bible is never opened. The whites will come to teach French; then you will be able to obtain nurture from its contents.[1]

This was indeed the essential message of Harris as conveyed in the Harrist Churches of the Ivory Coast when Bureau visited in the 1960s. And it is close to the earliest reports from Methodist missionaries in 1924:

> The teaching of Harris . . . was a simple declaration of the one-ness of God and of the sin of idolatry with its accompanying vices of cruelty

---

[1] René Bureau, "Le Prophète Harris et le harrisme." *Annales de l'Université d'Abidjan. Ethnosociologie.* Série F (3) 1971, 54f.

and debauchery ... [He] charged his followers to attach themselves to the first white missionary who should come representing the religion of the Book.[2]

Already two different perceptions of roles for the whites—and two different understandings—have emerged. But the message outlined is in both cases brief and simple. This is confirmed by the outline Harris himself gave to Father Hartz at Bingerville:

> I must bring back the lost nations to Christ, and for that must threaten them with the worst punishments so that they may allow themselves to be baptised and instructed by men of God, both Catholic and Protestant. I must here make reign the worship of Natural Law and of divine precepts, especially Sunday worship which is so much disregarded. I come to speak to everyone in this country, Black and Whites. No abuse of alcohol. Respect for authority. I tolerate polygamy, but I forbid adultery. Thunderbolts will talk, the angels will punish the world if it does not listen to my word which interprets that of God.[3]

But this word is not as simple and as lacking in precision as it has sometimes been represented. And the extent to which the word became effective in the lives of its hearers is even more complex.

Casely Hayford, British-educated and Methodist-trained, a disciple of Blyden, summarized what he heard.

> "I came to preach against rebellion" [against God and His law] ... He is strong against Sabbath-breaking ... [He] is strong on truth ... His great message is "Man, be yourself. ..." He seeks to cleanse the churches ... Humility is a word he is always using.[4]

Father Stauffer, at Axim, at the same time, reported a rather different message:

> His message was: "They [sic] are nine prophets sent to convert the world. It is the Angel Gabriel who dictates to him whatever he has to do. Everywhere he must destroy the fetishes, and bring all people

---

[2] [E.W. Thompson], "The Ivory Coast adventure." *The Methodist Recorder*, 9 October 1924, 19.

[3] Father Joseph Hartz, Roman Catholic missionary at Bingerville, quoted by G. van Bulck, s.j., "Le Prophète Harris vu par lui-même (Côte d'Ivoire 1914)", in *Devant les Sectes non-Chrétiennes*. Louvain: XXXème-Semaine de Missiologie [1961], 120–124.

[4] Casely Hayford, *William Waddy Harris. The West African Reformer: the Man and his Message*. London: C.M. Philipps 1915, 8.

to serve God. He does not baptize; he has no special church; everyone goes to the Church he likes best.[5]

Father Gorju, following his experiences around Bingerville in November and December 1914, reported rather more:

> ... the abandonment of fetishes, the belief in one unique God, the observance of Sunday, the prohibition of adultery, and that was all. Even this last article was considerably attenuated by the fact that polygamy remained unquestioned; did not the pontiff himself give the example with his disciples clothed in white? And so the natives, whom a greater terror constrained to leave their fetishes which previously they feared so much, felt no great difficulties in embracing his new religion, so little complicated in its dogmas, and so benign in its precepts.[6]

Simplicity is again seen as the characteristic of the message. But the observation of the administrator, Captain Paul Marty, puts it in a different light:

> To drink only in moderation, to work six days out of seven, to no longer give one's self over to adultery: these are deprivations and an activity which are unknown to the inhabitants of the coast, the lagunes, and of the savannahs. If these good resolutions were to endure, they would bring about a total transformation of this region.[7]

The missionary priest sees "uncomplicated dogma and benign precepts" in the place of Thomistic and Tridentine complications and current casuistics. The administrator, however, perceives the "break" experienced by populations who were not given to Western concepts of labour, to the notion of One Good Spirit, to the concept of absolute marital fidelity, or to temperance. His understanding is closer to that of the hearers of the message.

Harris's message, proclaimed initially to the coastal peoples, was taken inland in the years following by those who heard it from him. This included its ethical requirements. And they were by no means as inocuous as Father Gorju suggested. For instance, all the peoples

---

[5] Father Stauffer, Roman Catholic missionary at Axim: notes made in a diary some time around or after 1926, now in General Archives, S.M.A., Rome.

[6] J. Gorju, "Un prophète à la Côte d'Ivoire." *Echo* 14 (4), Sep-Oct 1915, 13 (dated 25 July 1915).

[7] Paul Marty, *Etudes sur l'Islam en Côte d'Ivoire*. Paris: Leroux 1922, 15.

of the lagunes traditionally observed a six-day week.[8] To accept a seven-day week with a day of rest was a veritable break from the past, and not the "simple message" that some thought. We need to try and enter into the understandings of those who heard the message.

One such hearer was the Gambian merchant Campbell, whose conversion through Harris probably took place in 1914. He wrote in 1922 not only of the message to leave the fetishes, but also of "the fountains of living water . . . flowing for all" of which Harris preached."All were invited to share its refreshing balm."[9] Casely Hayford echoed the same words, which we might otherwise think were a convert's later addition. "He [God, through Harris] is leading [men] to fountains of living water. He is doing this now."[10] Both were doubtless echoing the biblical images used by the prophet.[11]

The best record we have of the perceptions of those who heard Harris's message is undoubtedly what we have from Kraffy, where Harris ministered to hundreds, of whom very many were after 1925 in touch with the French Protestant missionary Edmond de Billy. Through his contacts with those who entered the Methodist churches de Billy was able to record and synthesize the message for a French audience. In the absence of an appendix this material needs to be given at some length:

The great God, who created heaven and earth, He whose name your fathers taught you, that your ancestors worshipped before the devilish fetishes made them blind and dead, this God has sent me to proclaim that the time has come when he wants to deliver you from the power of the devil who ruins you, makes you foolish and kills you.

The time is fulfilled, the devil is conquered here also, therefore burn all your fetishes, all your greegrees and your amulets, and I will baptize you in the name of this God who is your Father, of his Son Jesus Christ who has died for your sins, and of the Holy Spirit who will change your hearts.

In your village you will destroy all which recalls your devilish worshipping, you will cut down the sacred trees, you will destroy the bewitched stones, and you will worship God only. You will put up churches where you will gather

[8] *Cf.* Georges Niangoran Bouah, *La division du temps et le calendrier rituel des peuples lagunaires de la Côte d'Ivoire*. Paris: Institut d'Ethnographie 1964, 76.
[9] Campbell [Gambian merchant], Bingerville, Ivory Coast; his testimony recorded and printed in Jean Bianquis, *Le Prophète Harris ou dix ans d'histoire religieuse à la Côte d'Ivoire (1914–1924)*. Paris: Société des Missions Evangéliques 1924, 35.
[10] Hayford, *op. cit.*, 12.
[11] *E.g.* Revelation 7.17 or Revelation 21.6.

to pray to Him and to receive His law; in each church, twelve elders called
apostles will take care that the village serves God in holiness, according to the
doctrine contained in the Bible and which lay preachers will teach. God holds
as abomination idolatry, adultery, stealing, murder, lying and drunkenness. Obey
the ten commandments. The seventh day, everyone will [observe the] rest in honour
of God; in memory of the completion of Creation and of the Resurrection of his
Son, our Saviour, you will pray to God in your churches and you will sing
his glory three times on that day. All that which God, since the beginning, has
said to men in order for them to obtain justification in His eyes and eternal
life, is written in this Book, the Bible: it is there that you will find the teachings
of his prophets and of His Son Jesus Christ. After me will come the Whites,
servants of God, with this Book and they will teach you through preaching and
schools all that is written in this Bible. It was in the home of a pastor of your
race taught by them [Missionaries of the Methodist Church] that I myself, when
I was only a small boy, learned to read the Word of God. It is this holy word
brought by the Whites which you must receive and which you must obey without
complaint if you wish to share in Eternal Life after death.

If someone falls sick, let him confess his sins to the apostles of his church
who will then pray to God to implore healing.

Have faith, don't doubt, I speak in the name of the Living God.

Woe to those who refuse to listen to me, to fetishers and heathen who harden
their hearts, to those who stiffen their necks in order not to humble themselves! . . .
God knows the secrets of the hearts and souls, he tries the reins and the bowels
of man, and it is to Him that vengeance belongs.

Choose! Before you opens the way of life if you will listen to the call of
God the all-powerful, or the pits of death and hell if you resist, if you rebel.[12]

Jean Rouch, a French anthropologist in touch with the Harrist
Church in the early 1960s, felt that "this reconstruction was unfortunately too well contrived according to Methodist concerns (even
announcing the future arrival of Methodist pastors) for one to be able
to consider it as authentic." But he added, "Nevertheless I will cite
several phrases from it."[13] Its flavour of authenticity would indeed
prevent its total rejection. On the one hand the "Methodist tradition"
which became an element in the oral tradition of Harris-inspired
communities which joined the Methodists must be noted; likewise the
missionary "filter" which de Billy brought to the testimonies must

---

[12] Edmond de Billy, *En Côte d'Ivoire, Mission Protestante d'A.O.F.* Paris: Société des
Missions Evangéliques [1931], 15–16. [My translation]

[13] Jean Rouch, "Introduction à l'étude de la communauté de Bregbo." *Journal
de la Société des Africanistes* 33 (2), 1963, 153.

be recognized. On the other hand, Rouch reflected the strong anti-Methodist bias of the Harrist Church of the 1960s, for which he cannot be blamed.

We are able to do what Rouch could not—look at de Billy's evidence alongside that of Hartz, Hayford, Stauffer, Gorju, Bruce, Campbell, Joseph and Harrington. It is remarkable how this text pulls together elements that are found in all the others (which de Billy himself did not possess).

Harris himself told Father Hartz of his Methodist background, and this was not, as Haliburton appears to have thought, a misunderstanding on the part of the Catholic missionary, who would not have understood the term "Protestant Episcopal".[14] Harris refers scarcely at all to his Episcopalian period, but seems to have emphasised his Methodist roots, and this is not an impression of Methodist observers only. F. Deaville Walker heard of such links in 1926;[15] however, ten years earlier the Provincial Commissioner in Apollonia reported of Harris that he was a man who "seemed to have been educated in an American Methodist school on the Liberian coast."[16] The source of such information can only have been Harris himself.

As Harris progressed along the shores of the Ivory Coast during his ministry, he encountered at Fresco, Ebonou and Lauzoua young Fanti clerks from Ghana, already Methodist, to whom he entrusted a follow-up mission. In none of these places, nor in Kraffy, was there as yet any Roman Catholic presence. Given Harris's own past, and his habit of relating his past to the future of his work, the use of the Methodist connection would have been a consistent one. It was also the hinge to the coming of Whites with the Bible.[17]

Rouch, of course, indicted the Methodist text particularly for its statements about the future coming of Whites. One present-day understanding and oral tradition within the Harrist Church, which also oriented Rouch's judgement, is that Harris *never* anticipated that

---

[14] *PH*, 99. "Gorju" must here be read as "Hartz". On the preceding page, Haliburton incorrectly attributes the Hartz text to Father Gorju. The latter was in Europe at this time, because of the war, and did not return to the Ivory Coast until some time in November.

[15] F. Deaville Walker, *The story of the Ivory Coast*. London: the Cargate Press 1926, 13.

[16] *The Methodist Recorder*, 6 May 1915, 5.

[17] Significantly, the text from de Billy does not announce the coming of *Methodist* missionaries, but "whites", and de Billy later adds parenthetically the Methodist dimension.

Whites would "teach religion" to his people.[18] However, there is written evidence to the contrary, beginning with that of Father Hartz; de Billy's text conforms to the word of the prophet and must not be seen as a Methodist "contrivance."

But further, one is impressed with the number of elements in the text which are not of Methodist inspiration: the emphasis on "law" as compared to "gospel" or "grace", the relationship of sickness to sin and healing to confession, the fourfold woes, the institution of twelve apostles, and three meeting times on the seventh day—a present-day practice of the Harrist Church.

On the other hand, there are some notions which might appear to be Methodist interpretations, such as that from the Pauline tradition that evil—in this case fetish worship—was a digression from an earlier true worship of God, come into the world because of man's disobedience.[19] Whether this came from the Methodist influence which was in the Ivory Coast before Harris, or from Harris himself (coming out of his Methodist and Episcopalian experience) is not clear, but it was not a result of the arrival of Methodist missionaries in 1924. Rouch of course did not know the extent and depth of Harris's Evangelical understandings, or that he had been a mission preacher for more than twenty years before he embarked on his mission.

Harris's theological justification for strict observation of Sunday, as de Billy gives it, may also owe much to Harris's earlier grounding in Christian doctrine in Liberia, where it was perceived as the "wedge of the gospel". We should also note that this is the only text we have found in which Harris himself speaks of "hell". Elsewhere he speaks of "fire" and "destruction", usually in the sense of imminent judgement. The doctrine of an ultimate judgement in hell was certainly an integral part of Evangelical faith, and so it is certainly possible that Harris made such a statement. However, it is also possible that "hell" was

---

[18] This Harrist tradition (still current in the 1980s) is based on John Ahui's understanding in 1928 of Harris's disillusion with the Methodists following Benoît's visit. For us there is no questioning whatsoever of Harris's recognition of the Methodists' mission to his people in 1926 and after. But the understandings of that mission by Harris and by the Methodists were different. In 1928, Harris's disappointment was real. It is, in fact, this sense of Harris being misused by the Methodists which constitutes for us the evidence *within* the Harrist oral tradition that Harris had indeed been anticipating white collaboration with his people. Harris's attitude as perceived by Ahui in 1928 has conditioned the life of the Harrist Church ever since that time, and has understandably "reworked" the oral tradition concerning "the whites with the Bible" for the period from 1913 to 1928, by making it all a Methodist contrivance.

[19] Romans 1.20–32.

grafted by de Billy on to Harris's more usual proclamation of fire and destruction against those who refused his message.

With these exceptions, we feel justified in accepting the de Billy text as an authentic expression of an oral consensus which goes back to Harris at Kraffy in 1913. Although the Methodist picture is certainly incomplete—as are those of other traditions—as far as it goes the different elements of the prophetic word given in the text are considered by this writer to be genuine.[20] Indeed, the first paragraph is used by some Harrists today as an authentic word of the prophet.[21]

Having assumed such authenticity, what can we learn from this text about "the prophetic word" at Kraffy in October 1913? First, let us note that this was alive within the formative oral tradition fifteen years later. Harris's *word* had left a powerful effect, despite the brevity of his visit. Then we should note the biblical tone of what was remembered. This includes the phrases of his language—"the great God", "creator of heaven and earth", "devil is conquered", "time is fulfilled", "choose life or death"—all these and other phrases testify to the biblical character of his discourse, which left a deep imprint in the oral tradition. When missionaries came later and brought biblical literacy, his converts encountered familiar language.[22]

What themes can we isolate in the text?

(1) A clear recognition of the "great God" of the fathers
(2) A belief in an earlier time of enlightened worship of God.
(3) A belief in the "power of the devil" working in a false worship through "fetishes", an effective cause of death and destruction.
(4) God's intention of deliverance.
(5) Now is the time for the fulfilment of God's intention.
(6) Harris's God-ordained mission.
(7) Proclamation of Harris's victory, here and now, over the devil.

---

[20] In 1977, retired and apologetic about his age, E. de Billy could no longer recall the names of his informants but simply recalled that he had made the résumé "such as the oral tradition enabled me to know it." Letter from de Billy to Shank, 27 September 1977, La Salle, France.
[21] In 1966 a Harrist preacher, Augustine Aboué, communicated this paragraph to the ethnosociologist René Bureau as authentic Harrist words. It was then collected as a part of Harrist tradition (RBN). Since the authorship and source were nowhere indicated, Bureau himself had not been aware of the parallel with the de Billy text.
[22] We have on several occasions during the period April 1977 to April 1980 heard illiterate Harrist preachers express their astonishment at hearing read from the Scriptures "the very things the prophet told us."

(8) Appeal to an act of repentance and faith—"fetish" destruction and baptism.

(9) A "trinitarian" baptism.

(10) A belief in God as "Father".

(11) A belief in the death of the Son on the cross for sins.

(12) A belief in the Holy Spirit as power of transformation of the person from within.

(13) Structures for continuity of a community of faith and worship and healing.

(14) A belief in the direct relationship of sin to sickness and confession to healing.

(15) Provision in worship for continuity of a new moral structure in the ten commandments—particularly as the seventh day relates to worship and rest—and sobriety.

(16) The seventh day is to be kept because of its relation to creation and (in Christ's resurrection) re-creation.

(17) The Bible, the only key to right relation with God and eternal life (with God).

(18) Prediction about the "Whites with the Bible" and their preaching and teaching mission.

(19) Appeal to obey the Bible without complaint.

(20) Pronouncement of woes upon those refusing to listen who refuse to convert; who keep "fetishes" secretly; who are hypocrites, liars and proud.

(21) An appeal to decision, and a proclamation of its consequences.

Although some aspects of the language may not be Harris's, the themes are confirmed from other sources, and are certainly his.

However, the message is incomplete. De Billy has omitted the strong eschatological dynamic which drove Harris. Was this not conveyed to him? He himself wrote of the "enthusiasm of the beginning, where messianic hopes, illusions and even misunderstandings added to the natural joy of spiritually famished churches."

> The local opinion expected to see miracles in every domain; the Whites with the Bible, the successors of Harris, were to found a new era: the persecutors would be punished. Such was the dream.[23]

---

[23] E. de Billy, *op. cit.*, 39–40.

It was not that de Billy and other Methodist missionaries were not told of the eschatological content of Harris's preaching; they heard only what concerned themselves, the promise of "the Whites with the Bible." And this aspect of Harris's word was used to advantage in the missionary publicity of the day: "Never have I found such illiteracy in Africa as I found even down to the beach in Ivory Coast. BUT NO MISSIONARY CAME to 'remove the darkness from their eyes'."[24]

Harris did indeed in some places announce the coming of white missionaries, and those who followed put him into the place of the Baptist, the forerunner, preparing their arrival. But it was not simply the coming of missionaries he was proclaiming, but the coming of the Kingdom of God as prophet of the coming Christ. André Roux also echoed this misunderstanding.

> As the Baptist also, he only presented himself as a forerunner, and in the visual language of the Blacks often said, "When the cock crows, it is not yet day but only the first ray of dawn. However the dawn is coming. I do not bring you all of the light, I am only the cock who crows; after me will come white missionaries with the Bible. Listen to them, it is they who will instruct you in the whole light.[25]

It seems most likely that Harris's parable was originally oriented to his expectation of the Kingdom, and not just of the white missionaries.

In the autumn of 1913 Kraffy was a major centre of ministry. A year later, after the war in Europe had broken out, it was Bingerville. In Kraffy he predicted the war; in Bingerville he spoke under his awareness that the "last times" were being fulfilled. How was he heard?

We have an orally-transmitted text from the present-day head of the Harrist Church who, as a young man of about eighteen, was among the hundreds of Ebrié who heard Harris in Bingerville. Like de Billy's text, we cannot be sure that every expression was Harris's own. But it is important because of John Ahui's later status, and as the consensus of the Harrist oral tradition:

I am sent by God, endued with his power. I come to convert you and to disperse from among you all the influence of the fetishes and the idols, and to make of you children of God through my baptism. All that I have seen in your

---

[24] W.J. Platt, News on the new Methodist district of the Ivory Coast section, 1924. Archives of M.M.S., London: French West Africa, 1924. The quotation marks and capital letters are in the original text.
[25] André Roux, "Un prophète noir." *Présence Africaine*, 8–9, 1950, 136.

midst I have dispersed; the fetish conflicts, the idols you have shown me, so many things which I have seen. What was to be burned I have burned. . . . Those influences which are only the power of man, I have completely dispersed; as for the fetishes I have burned them all. . . . I will ask you never again to return to them. Continue to pray to God. And to those among you who know certain plants which can heal, take care of your friends and brethren who suffer. Do not return to polytheism; continue to pray and God will be with you. And you will see that after me—and I will give you a specific date that is seven years after me—you will see the favourable accomplishments of God. And that heavy hand—the white man—that you have today, and about which you have implored God because of the chicottes *[beatings] and all which you have endured, he will be your very friend with whom you will live hand in hand in a fraternal collaboration. I promise you; but keep my word for seven years. You will see the fulfilment which I promise because it is inspired of God.*[26]

Here the eschatological dimension is explicit; but like the missionary understanding of his message, this also is clearly incomplete. What is lacking is the Christological foundation of the kingdom which will be both inter-racial and materially prosperous. But faithfulness is here a condition for the fulfilment of this vision.

And the time of fulfilment is made clear—at the end of seven years. This word is well-known among the Ebrié in the present-day Harrist Church.[27] When the Ebrié delegation went to visit Harris in December 1928 they were aware of it, and he confirmed their conviction that their own infidelity had interrupted its fulfilment. This word is not alive in the traditions of disciples of Harris who became Methodists, and the Methodist missionaries, having arrived after 1924, insist that they never heard of it.[28]

---

[26] The text is a transcription of a recording in January 1976 by Robert Arnaut of French Radio-Television, to whom I am indebted for the tape. The text was in Ebrié, and was interpreted on the spot by Bogui Claver, one of Albert Atcho's principal aides at Bregbo. Ahui's wish that the text should have wide circulation gives full authority to use the text, though one suspects that a more careful translation of the Ebrié would be fruitful. I am alone responsible for the English translation. Ahui himself asked that God strike him if he did not tell the truth. The text is published in French in Kouassi Boussou Gôh Benoit, *Jonas Ahui.* Abidjan 1983.

[27] As an illustration, at Niangon-Loka on the Ebrié lagune west of Abidjan, René Bureau was informed by Dani Yayo, who was baptised by Harris and made preacher on the same day: "On leaving, Harris said, 'Pray seven years, you will see what will come to pass.' The people prayed during three years. During these three years, they sang for a death during one day, three days, ten days, and the dead person woke up and said what he had done (e.g., I died because I wanted to kill.) But the seven years were not reached, so that what was forseen (peace, life like the Europeans) did not come to pass." *RBN.*

[28] For example, in a letter from de Billy to Shank, September 1977, de Billy wrote

How is this seven-year period to be understood? As a rationalization by Harris—or the Harrists—for the failure of the millennial prosperity to appear? This we dismiss because of our knowledge of John Ahui's integrity; his son Paul Ahui also reported to us that he had heard the story over and over all his life.

Was it only a local tradition common to the Ebrié? But the nature of Harris's apocalypticism was neither local nor ethnic. Our own interpretation—which can never be more than a suggestion—is as follows:

> The period of seven years of fidelity for the fulfilment of God's accomplishments—prosperity and racial harmony in Christ's millennial kingdom—was announced *after* the beginning of the Great War, when he was in Ebrié territory. Prior to that date, his predictions had been more general, about the war to come.
>
> But why seven years? In Revelation 11 there is indeed a prediction of three and one-half years of war; these are followed by three and one-half years of witness by two prophets and concludes with their death, resurrection and ascension. This is followed by a series of judgements which bring about the final fulfilment: "The kingdoms of this world are become the kingdoms of our Lord and of his Christ, and He shall reign for ever and ever" (Rev 11.15).
>
> For Harris, the final "war of Armageddon" having begun (in World War I, August 4, 1914), the Kingdom of God was to be fulfilled precisely within seven years time.

The Roman Catholics could not take Harris seriously, partly because of his apocalypticism. The Methodists saw themselves as the fulfilment of his eschatological hopes. Many Harrists have condensed his Christological kingdom hope to one simply of material prosperity through prayer and faithfulness. His message then was heard differently by his hearers, according to their own pre-existing situations and beliefs, but for all of them there was a call for a new dialogue with the future, conditional upon personal and collective faithfulness. His word, however, had called the people to the reign of Christ "on earth as it is in heaven."

---

of it as "some traditions added on by improvised and ignorant preachers during the years between the apostolate of Harris and the arrival of the Methodist mission."

B. Blessing and cursing '

Blessing and cursing was a most important prophetic use of the word. In the testimonies recorded, cursing is emphasised, since it was easily seen to be efficacious. Father Gorju's summary, though probably overstated, offers an image of what some perceived:

> . . . All refusals of obedience would be punished within a brief lapse of time by death, the most cruel sicknesses, . . . etc. Certain deaths cleverly exploited and dressed up afterwards with circumstances useful to the cause, did much to heighten his prestige. They became the inevitable consequences of the curses of the Prophet, for, it must be recognized, the good fellow had a great facility for [pronouncing] maledictions.[29]

In fact, a careful reading of the sources indicates that his word of blessing was just as explicit a part of his ministry. Lambert Ackah, baptized by Harris at Kraffy in 1913, told how the people were dispersed after Harris's "having blessed all the people present."[30] Several other witnesses mention also the "blessing" of the prophet.[31] The blessings are not seen as part of a larger message, but as particularly significant because of their prophetic origin; the prophet decides in which contexts the blessing—or cursing—effects God's intention.

Harris's word of blessing or curse functioned in much the same way as did the word of the African *pater familias* at times of crisis in the life of the family. But with Harris it was with the power of God, and not just with the power of the ancestors.

Platt wrote, on the basis of the many stories reported to him after 1924:

> This man's God lived, saw, acted, punished, protected, and could be talked to. This man talked to him. God certainly answered. Many knew it to their cost—others to their credit. We heard these things from a hundred eager black folks who vowed they had been eye witnesses.[32]

In this, he exercised a role which resembled that of the Glebo *deya*, whose authority was attributed to the spirit which at times possessed and spoke through him. An African writer has placed all blessings

---

[29] Gorju, *op. cit.*, 112.
[30] *HN.*
[31] *Ibid.*; also Father Stauffer and Father Harrington.
[32] W.J. Platt, *An African prophet.* London: SCM Presss 1934, 33.

and curses in the sphere of that which is evil and thus, of sorcery and witchcraft.[33] But there is also the biblical tradition, for example the Mosaic blessings and curses (as found in Deuteronomy chapters 27–30). There are New Testament parallels, both in the Gospels, in Acts and the epistles. A biblical scholar has well situated the phenomenon when he writes:

> Such utterances are not the casual explosion of a short temper, but a serious and almost ritual invocation that divine justice will be vindicated in the world through the prevention and suppression of malice. The curse thus uttered is also a means of protection for the individual himself against the malice of his enemies.[34]

Harris without doubt saw the cause of God's righteousness bound up with his person and people's response to it; his cursing was not an expression of personal—or public—vengeance, but of the confidence that God would avenge his own cause through Harris's word. "Thunderbolts will talk, the angels will punish the world if it does not listen to my word, which interprets that of God." This word to Father Hartz in 1913 is repeated at later points in his ministry. Other sources for Harris's inspiration are very probably the Book of Revelation, where the role of angels in vindication is a major theme, and the Book of Common Prayer, used by Harris for over twenty years, with its liturgy of "Commination, or denouncing of God's anger and judgements against sinners", with its specific list of vices for which "the curse of God is due".

What is important, of course, is the fact that it is Harris's word, both in his own thinking and in its practical consequences, which is also a powerfully effective instrument of God's vindication, and anger.

---

[33] Meinrad Hegba, *Sorcellerie. Chimère dangereuse...?* Abidjan: I.N.A.D.E.S. 1979, 16.

[34] John L. McKenzie, s.j., Curse, in his *Dictionary of the Bible*. Milwaukee: the Bruce Publishing Co. 1965, 166. A brief discussion of the parallel between the Old Testament and African curses is to be found in William D. Reyburn, "Sickness, sin and curse in the Old Testament and the African church", in William D. Reyburn (ed.), *Missionary Anthropology II*. South Pasadena, Ca.: William Carey Library 1978 (reprint from *Practical Anthropology* 7 (4), 1960, 103–108.)

C. Prayer and Song

Platt, the missionary, wrote that Harris talked to God and that He
answered him. Prayer is another dimension of Harris's word which
left a permanent impact upon the population he visited. Hayford wrote:

> One Sunday thousands flocked round him to be baptized. Suddenly
> he stopped and prayed a prayer I shall never forget. . . . [T]his was
> a prayer peculiar to itself. It was short. It was staccato. It abounded
> in fiery phrases. It started with praise of "O Thou most holy eternal
> Jehovah," and it ended with praise.[35]

At Kraffy, according to the de Billy résumé, his prayer had an impressive
effect:

> A sign from him: the crowd kneels both far and near; . . . the black
> heads bow together for the prophet is going to pray to his God. He
> offers to Him the destruction of all these fetishes, hideous symbols of
> folly, of cruelty, of obscenity, of oppression, bought with the price of
> gold over the centuries. He offers him the repentance of this crowd . . . ,
> the adoration of these converts . . . He thanks Him for delivering from
> the darkness of pagan death these peoples who were ever reputed for
> their ferocity, and for showering His mercy upon them. The "Our Father"
> concludes this invocation.[36]

If many of the witnesses of 1914 are to be believed, prior to Harris
God was known by name, but He was not known in the experience
of the people. It was surely Harris's own prayer and its evident efficacity
which had brought to the masses the awareness of the presence of
God. That awareness was then maintained through the disciplines
of community prayer which he created among them.

The songs, hymns and shouts with which the women accompanied
Harris, and which he himself occasionally sang, certainly were intended
to proclaim, teach and instruct. But in practice, the word given in
song seems not to have been often understood. It is true that these
were not translatable as were his spoken word.

---

[35] Casely Hayford, *William Waddy Harris. The West African Reformer The Man and
his message*. London: C.M. Philipps 1915, 9–10. In August 1964 J.P. Ephson recalled
fifty years after the event at Axim that Harris often prefaced his prayers with "O
thou great eternal Jehovah." *HN*

[36] E. de Billy, *En Côte d'Ivoire. Mission Protestante d'A.O.F.* Paris: Société des Missions
Evangéliques [1931], 16.

Probably even those words which were not understood were preserved as important, for "no doubt it [the hymn] had something about it which would protect and help in time of need."[37] We would like to know the repertoire of English hymns which the Harris team sang. His grandchildren in 1978 recalled his favourite hymns. These included "Lo, he comes with clouds descending", "Guide me, O thou great Jehovah", "Jesus, Lover of my soul", "How firm a foundation, ye saints of the Lord", and "What a friend we have in Jesus."[38] But nothing indicates that he used them in his mission to the traditional population.

On the other hand, one of his shouts, used over and over again, in Liberia at least, was that preserved by Harris's nephew John Howe:

> Let's try hard, so we will conquer
> the devil and his people [or kingdom]
> That when Jesus comes,
> We will wear white robes.[39]

In Axim and in the Abidjan region shouts in the local languages were remembered over fifty years later. And the importance that he attached to song as a medium is most important.[40]

Little content of Harris's songs has come down to us, but this is not to say they had little effect. But the effect was probably related more to making the unknown God present, than to dogmatic teaching through the medium of sound. In this function song played a major role; it was apparently not so important for communication of a prophetic word.

D. Teaching

In addition to the essential proclaimed message, the continuity of the prophetic word was to be found in a considerable number of under-

---

[37] Thomas Fenton, *Black Harvest*. London: the Cargate Press 1956, 43.

[38] These hymns were spontaneously mentioned by his grandchildren in an interview on April 13, 1978.

[39] The Shout was sung by Harris's nephew, John Gyude Howe, at the same time, and was recorded and transcribed by David A. Shank. It has been translated from the Glebo.

[40] See especially James R. Krabill, "William Wadé Harris (1860–1929: African evangelist and 'ethnologist'." *Mission Focus* 18 (4), 1990. pp. 56–59.

standings which we have chosen to call "teachings". Harris was asked
to respond in a wide variety of situations, and because of his contacts
with Western patterns in Liberia, his literacy and education, and his
capacity to communicate with the *chefs de cercles*, with the governor,
with the Catholic missionaries, he became a trusted authority for people
struggling to adapt to new ways.

It is obviously not possible to list all his teachings here. We can
only give some examples of types of teaching, indicating the sources.

1. Biblical teaching, in an African context

Harris told Benoît in 1926: "I taught the ten commandments, the
Lord's prayer, [to] sing—and to praise God because Christ is coming"
(*BN* III, 8). Some of the commandments received more attention than
others.

There was specific and detailed teaching, for example, on what
could be done on the Sabbath, allowing for necessities and emergencies,
but seeking to preserve the Sabbath rest.[41] In the case of adultery
confession and repentance towards one's partner is necessary, and
a husband must also give to his wife the equivalent of any gift he
has given his partner.[42] Theft was condemned, but taking food in
dire necessity allowed for; however in such a case and if anything
was found, strict honesty was called for.[43]

2. Marriage practices

We have observed elsewhere that prior to Axim, Harris seemed to
encourage monogamy, and after Axim practiced and encouraged
polygamy. But he was at all times tolerant of polygamy, even when
he encouraged monogamous practice. He gave many counsels concerning plural wives which, as Amos-Djoro remarks, were those which
"Africans have always observed."[44]

Such counsels repeated the African traditional requirements that
both wives should be treated equally, both in material terms and in
the amount of attention paid by the husband. Both wives must be

---

[41] Ernest Amos-Djoro, *Prophétisme et nationalisme africains. Les Harristes en Côte d'Ivoire*,
unpublished study seen at the author's home, Abidjan, p. 129.
[42] *Ibid.*, 131.
[43] *HN*, Abidjin-Kouté.
[44] Amos-Djoro, *op. cit.*, 131.

present when gifts were being shared out.[45] The women were to be treated with love, and not as slaves.

His teaching on divorce was understood as strict. It was to be avoided. But if it proved to be necessary, witnesses were to be called in, and the husband was to provide for the ex-spouse.[46]

Harris also gave specific orders relating to sexual commerce, which were dictated by concern for conjugal fidelity and public decency.[47]

3. Ancestors

On one clear occasion (at Axim) Harris gave specific orders not to pour libations for the spirits of the dead. He made exceptions for official rituals,[48] which seems to have been typical of his attitude.

4. Transformation of codes of purity and impurity

Among the Aizi people, Harris reportedly said that as God had blessed everything there was nothing impure; as a result the people began to disregard food taboos and to use forest paths previously shunned.[49] In other places, for the same reasons, other taboos (such as those applied to menstruating women and to recently bereaved spouses) were likewise disregarded.[50] Harris opposed wakes and elaborate funerals and various other funeral practices.[51] He ordered people to pity a suicide, and abortion was proclaimed as a crime.[52]

5. Hygienic and health prescriptions

Harris did not discourage the practice of traditional medicine. He appeared to distinguish between authentic healers and "sorcerers, fetishers and charlatans."

According to Amos-Djoro:

---

[45] *Ibid.*
[46] *Ibid.*
[47] *Ibid.*, 131; HN., passim.; *cf.* Sheila Walker, *op. cit.*, 287f.
[48] *PH*, 82.
[49] *Ibid.*, 67f.
[50] *Ibid.*, 65; *cf. HN.*
[51] *Ibid.*, Abidjin-Kouté.
[52] M. Corbière, Commandant, Grand Lahou: report on the Harrists at the end of 1916. [National Archives of the Ivory Coast].

He counselled Christians to reject all those who would treat sickness
by having resource to sacrifices, or to diabolical demonstrations reflecting
the animist past . . .[53]

He was believed to have authorized several of the older people to
practice healing through plants. This included some who became
Methodists at Bingerville and Adjamé-Abidjan, and also people at
Adjué and Lozoua.[54]

Harris forbade eating on the ground; also the consumption of any
animal or fish which had died of itself.[55] In Axim he took cigarettes
out of men's mouths, and opposed the use of alcoholic drinks. The
District Commissioner in Axim (Gold Coast) reported that "He
impressed upon them also that next to Godliness is cleanliness."[56]

Without attempting to be complete, we have discovered from within
the traditions and practices of his hearers the variety and extent of
the prophetic word. Important as were the symbolic patterns which
he presented, and which are for the most part alive today, he was
primarily a man of the word. The symbolic patterns helped to render
that word effective.

[53] Amos-Djoro, *op. cit.*, 137.
[54] *HN.*
[55] *Ibid.*, Bingerville-Adjamé.
[56] Record Book of Axim District, 1914–1930: National Archives of Ghana, cited
in *PH*, 90.

CHAPTER ELEVEN

PATTERNS OF THOUGHT RELATING TO MISSIONS AND CHURCHES

Because of the way in which appeal to Harris's attitudes and authority were later made by protagonists within differing religious streams, it becomes necessary to examine very carefully the evidence relating to his attitudes towards the missions and churches.

After his trance-visitation of 1910, as we have earlier seen, Harris seems to have seen the period of over twenty years which he had spent as an Episcopalian as a kind of betrayal. He looked back to his earlier commitment as a Methodist. His vision was a "second conversion"; the first conversion had been a total acceptance of the Western missionaries' synthesized Christianity-civilization; the second was to an African prophet's mission of power to convert Africa to the kingdom of Christ. Henceforth he emphasized his former Methodist training and experience—but he was never subject to Methodist organization. As he himself said at Bingerville in 1914, he was "above all religions and freed from the control of men."[1]

Two administrators, who had to classify him for their reports, saw him as claiming "to convert the natives to a kind of Protestantism",[2] and as "affiliated with the Salvation Army."[3] He himself seemed to relate knowingly to those with a Methodist background, but he transcended all denominational understandings in his role as a "messenger of God." This is the perspective from which we will trace his journeys, starting in Petit Lahou (Ebonou).

---

[1] Father Joseph Hartz, Bingerville, cited in G. van Bulck, s.j., "Le Prophète Harris vu par lui-même (Côte d'Ivoire, 1914)," in *Devant les Sectes Non-Chrétiennes.* Louvain: XXXème-Semaine de Missiologie, [1961], 120–124.
[2] *PH*, 55, citing Rapport du poste G. Lahou, 4th Quarter, 1913.
[3] ICN Archives: IEE 25 (1/3) 2nd Quarterly Report G. Lahou, 11 July 1914. There was, of course, no Salvation Army work either in the Ivory Coast or Liberia. Harris may have introduced and used the hymn, "Onward, Christian soldiers" which the Methodists heard sung in 1924 at the time of their arrival. It could have suggested the Salvation Army to the *Chef de Cercle*.

1. En route east, in the Ivory Coast and Gold Coast

From the very beginning of his ministry Harris was faced with the problem of a follow-through of instruction for his converts. In the Ebonou area he discovered Christian clerks, and he gave them the responsibility for continuity. He "ordained" A.E.M. Brown, a Fanti Methodist,[4] and Samuel Reffel, also a Methodist, from Sierra Leone.[5] The third leader chosen was a local literate clerk, Jacques Boga Sako, told to continue with the others until the white man with the Bible was to come and show them "how to do."[6] When Platt arrived in 1924 Sako spontaneously turned over to him and the Methodist society nine congregations around Ebonou.

In Grand Lahou also, where Harris preached very briefly in the fall of 1913, Brown was the representative of Harris, together with a certain Thomas, from Bathurst.[7] At a later period, converts from Addah, whom Harris had sent to Ebonou to be baptised by Brown, were actually baptised at Grand Lahou by another helper, known as "papa".[8] The people claimed to have been baptised into the "Church of England"—that is, the Protestant church of the English, rather than the church of the French.[9] But they did not join the Fanti Methodist congregation.

At Kraffy, where masses of people from different ethnic groups came to him, and where there was then neither church nor mission, Harris established the pattern of "twelve apostles" in order to give continuity to his mission. We have already noted that a part of his message at Kraffy concerned the coming of whites with the Bible and the need for the creation of schools.[10]

When Harris arrived at Jacqueville he reached the most western post of the Catholic mission, in charge of Father L. Moly. In 1922 Moly described Harris's attendance, "with all his wives", at the parish

---

[4] *PH*, 50, note 6. See also Barry T. Morris, *Some early Protestant responses to the Harrist movement in the Ivory Coast. The work of the "clerks": 1913–1924.* S.O.A.S., University of London: M.A. thesis 1983.

[5] Typed memoir of Jacques Boga Sako, *Haliburton Notes*, 1963.

[6] *PH*, 53, citing "a large group [of men] at Lozoua,. . August 1963." In testimonies from Lauzoua and Ebonou in 1977, Harrist tradition indicates that Sako was charged by Harris to baptize the village of Kokou. The word "ordain" [*ordonne*] was used to describe the charge.

[7] *PH*, 57, and 161.

[8] *PH*, 93f.

[9] *PH*, 58.

[10] *HN*, Aizi, Kraffy.

mass, and "accompanied by almost the whole population." And also "at the end of the mass he came to find me, accompanied by the principle notables of the village, in order to decide the construction of a much larger church."[11] His attitude towards the Roman Catholic mission seems to have been identical with that towards the "clerks".

A late (1963) report from an Orbaf Methodist adds another perspective.

> At Jacqueville it was Harris who prayed in the presence of all the priests of the region, then he returned to the residence and it was there that we were baptized . . . He predicted the arrival of white missionaries who would carry the Bible. He said this in the presence of the Catholic priests.[12]

The suggestion here is that there is another kind of white missionary than those already present in the Catholic mission. We are meeting for the first time the opinions which reflect the conflict between Protestants and Catholics about Harris's understandings. Reports from the Methodists after 1924 tell how Harris converts who went to the Catholic missions were disappointed to find there was no emphasis on the Bible.[13]

At this time, we should note that Brown, after giving him two weeks of instruction, authorized a Catholic, Victor Nivri of Addah, to baptize. Nivri ministered at Addah, wearing a white robe with a turban, using the sign of the cross as he baptized in the name of the Trinity. He did not go to the Catholic priest at Jacqueville, but to Brown, after having consulted his village elders. Some old men at Orbaf said in 1963:

> Before Harris came there was a Catholic Church, but it did no effective work because fetishism was still more powerful. That is why when he delivered us from sin we judged him stronger.[15]

At Audouin, where Harris himself never went, another important

---

[11] L. Moly, "Les Aladians", *Echo* 21 (12), December 1922, 179. We place the incident in 1914; it may have been in 1915, since the expression 'all his wives' suggests the group of three rather than the original two singers.

[12] *HN*, Orbaf.

[13] Cf. Report of Léthel to the Société des Missions Evangéliques de Paris, 20 October 1924: *Registre des procès verbaux*. Archives of D.E.F.A.P., Paris. See also note 42 below.

[14] *PH*, 94f.

[15] *HN*, Orbaf.

centre for baptizing was established by a Methodist called Goodman, who had heard of Harris and invited him there. Harris responded by sending a Bible and a message authorizing Goodman himself to baptize.[16]

At Grand Bassam, where Harris was arrested, his women companions were "turned over to the Catholic sisters" for interrogation. The sisters searched them and returned them to the commandant, and themselves intervened to obtain Harris's freedom.[17]

From all of these Ivory Coast reports we can see clearly that there was introduced with Harris a "new religion of power", which appeared to transcend both Catholic and Methodist structures. But Harris was willing to use those from any tradition who were willing to function in those terms, that is, in the light of Harris's personal power. And in one case Nivri—a Catholic—used his symbolism as an effective part of the message.

At Half Assinie his Methodist host asked him, "I am a Methodist, but what are you with your calabashes?" Harris replied:

> that he was messenger from God. God had told him to go abroad to preach the good news. All those who were Methodists didn't approve Harris.

Harris's reply to such was:

> "d'attendre un peu et ils verront la puissance de Dieu."[18] [Wait a little and they will see the power of God.]

But the Methodist catechist, Organ, opposed Harris and said he was of the devil.[19]

It was also at Half Assinie that Harris first met Catholic opposition. As he told Benoît in 1926,

> Roman Catholic curse me at Half Assinie. I said you go see signs. The next day the church fell down. The Father came and offered me one pound.[20]

---

[16] *HN*, PH, 70.
[17] *HN*; Pierre Agbangu, Orbaf, was witness at Grand Bassam.
[18] *HN*; son of former king of Krinjabo.
[19] *HN*; one of the town captains of Half Assinie.
[20] *BN* I, 29. See also the *Gold Coast Leader* for 18 July 1914 (Axim, 20 June).

It was reported to Axim that he had cursed Father Fischer at Half Assinie and made him blind; such exaggerated stories frequently preceded him as he went from place to place.

2. At Axim

When Harris arrived at Axim he contacted first the Catholic missionary, Father Stauffer, and then later the Rev. Ernest Bruce of the Methodist Church.[21] Both received the impression that he was encouraging converts to go to their particular church; Bruce reported that after "baptizing his converts he would urge them to join the Christian Church nearest them."[22]

Bruce's initial reception of Harris was negative since his predecessor, Rev. Elias Butler, who had just left, had urged the Methodists to have nothing to do with Harris; and Harris had countered with:

> So you don't take the advice of a Prophet. God will show you a lesson! You are my servant. You should come and hold the bowl with which I baptize.[23]

He thus exhibited his spiritual ascendancy over ministers, whether Catholic or Protestant, which is consistent with what we have already observed.

In fact, during his time in Axim Harris and his followers acted freely towards the Methodist Church, to the extent that Father Stauffer reported that "Harris took all liberties with the Wesleyans."[24] The prophet did not find such freedom in the Catholic Church, and the tensions which arose were not so easily resolved. Stauffer felt that Harris's attitude was conditioned by the black élite of Axim—who included Casely Hayford. Harris when turned away by Stauffer from the pulpit of the Catholic Church is reported to have said, "Send away all the people I brought you. I am going to make my own church."[25] Nearly a thousand people had come to the small church because of the prophet. Harris did indeed go, and before leaving Axim cursed anyone who would dare go to the Catholic church. For this

---

[21] Rev. Ernest Bruce, "I lived with history", *African Challenge* 7 (4), 1957.

[22] *HN*; J.P. Ephson, Axim.

[23] *Gold Coast Leader* 4 July 1914 (Axim, 16 June).

[24] Father Stauffer, Axim 1914: diary entry made sometime around 1926. General Archives, S.M.A., Rome.

[25] This is confirmed by remarks of Ephson in 1964,

Stauffer blamed Hayford; we have no information as to his sources. Later he was said to have changed his mind, and the report to Stauffer was that he said,

> The Father has done right. I am a prophet. I have to preach in the streets. I have not to preach in the churches. It is Hayford who deceived me. Also the Catholics know the cross, they serve Christ; the Wesleyans do not know the cross, they do not know Christ.

These successive incidents reveal a kind of jousting for authority and recognition. The Methodists, after an initial refusal, finally allowed Harris freedom to minister in their churches. The Catholics, although they early recognised the good Harris was doing, were unable to do anything publicly but to reject it. Harris's shift towards polygamy increased the public denunciations. Harris, on the other hand, saw both churches as auxiliaries in his work, and apparently made little distinction between them. Later, the attempts of the Methodist élite to use Harris caused him to turn from them, and the Methodist Hayford, who had tried to persuade him that he should create his own church, reported his refusal: "He said he did not come to found a church; he belongs to no church. Or if you like, he belongs to the church of which the universal God is both priest and king."[26] Although he then changed his intention, it is possible that it was always a potential option for him.

3. The appointment of John Swatson

After leaving Axim, following the incident with Fr. Stauffer, Harris continued westwards, arriving at Half Assinie on Monday 5 September. On the preceding day a Methodist catechist from Aboisso in the Ivory Coast had preached in the local Methodist church. He was John Swatson, originally from Beyin in Apollonia, who had been an official Methodist "agent" since his retirement in 1912 from work as a clerk in Nigeria.[27] He had by the time Harris met him worked in the area of Half Assinie for a couple of years. These two older men met and quickly appreciated one another. Harris found one who could carry on his work; Swatson for his part found a new and better model.

---

[26] Casely Hayford, *William Waddy Harris. The West African Reformer: The Man and his Message*. London: C.M. Phillips 1915, 6–7.
[27] *PH*, 217f., citing ICN Archives: Abidjan x–27–14.

Harris told Benoît how he took "Swanson" to Bingerville to get authority from the governor to work in the Ivory Coast (*BN* II, 8). This was reported by the Aboisso *chef de poste* in December 1914. However, later in December Swatson was back in the western area of the Gold Coast, under the influence of "angelic visitations".[28] By April 1915 it was being rumoured that Harris had been translated to heaven,[29] and that "the mantle of Elijah has fallen on Swatson's shoulders." In January 1915 the *Gold Coast Leader* reported that John Swatson "who was ordained by Mr. Harris as a prophet has now taken up the work of casting out devils, idols, etc." Gorju reported that he had "had himself consecrated as Bishop of Sanwi, and in a long black robe was also using a long stick with a cross."[30] He was clearly at the time signing his letters as "Bishop Swatson" and within six months was calling the movement "Christ Church, Beyin".[31]

This episode raises a number of questions. If Swatson was already a Methodist, functioning within Methodist structures, why did Harris not simply support and promote his ministry? Why did he need to appoint him as preacher, when he was already so appointed among the Methodists? The case of the clerks in the lagune area is different, since they were not Methodist agents. In this case Harris used his authority to have the man recognised by the colonial authority; his apointee calls himself "Bishop", and his work the "Christ Church Mission."

Was Harris setting up a more inclusive church structure? Or was he setting up a parallel church structure? Certainly this step followed his encounter with opposition from the established missions. In 1916 when asked about the Swatson appointment he told Father Harrington, "Even as Paul did, so do I."[32] Not only did he appoint elders but, like the Apostle Paul, his vocation created an ascendancy over the work of others. Swatson, by June 1916, had been licensed by the Anglican Bishop of Accra, and he worked for several years in the western Gold Coast, with several teachers under his supervision. He

---

[28] *PH*, 218f., citing Gold Coast Archives, Accra: Conf. 7/15, District Commissioner of Sefwi to Commissioner of Western Province, 24 March 1915.

[29] *PH*, 220, citing Gold Coast Archives, Accra: Conf. 9/15, D.C. Sefwi to Commissioner of Western District, 10 April 1915.

[30] J. Gorju, "Un prophète à la Côte d'Ivoire." *Missions Catholiques*, 4 June 1915, 168.

[31] *Cf.* note 29 above.

[32] Father Peter Harrington, "An interview with the 'Black Prophet'". *The African Missionary* 18, March-April 1917, 13–16.

was aging, and by 1919 had "ceased to play any important part in the [Anglican] Mission's work", but up to the end of his life he was convinced that the churches which had developed under his ministry had been stolen from him. His ministry and its relationship to the established churches had the same ambiguity as did that of Harris.

4. At Bingerville, the capital of the colony

Harris saw Governor Angoulvant in late September, and the governor reported that, after baptizing his converts, Harris lavished moral counsel upon them "without pushing them" towards either the Catholic or the Protestant church.[33] Gaston Joseph, administrator at Bingerville, confirmed this. He wrote, ". . . after baptism, [the prophet] left entire liberty to his proselytes to follow the Protestant or Catholic offices."[34] But the governor in authorizing Swatson had left the door open for the formation of a parallel structure.

Father Joseph Hartz was at this time the Roman Catholic Superior in Bingerville. Harris told him that his baptised followers were to let themselves be instructed "by men of God, both Catholics and Protestants." He attended mass at Bingerville, and brought "hundreds of persons" to Hartz for baptism. This Hartz could not do, for they had not been instructed. Yet he recognized an "irresistible attraction of people towards the Catholic Church", and also "a religion of his [Harris's] own kind" taught by "teachers of the new Religion" who had arrived after the prophet.

Father Bedel, also at Bingerville during August, wrote that Harris had pressed the people to be baptized either "by the Catholics or by the Protestants." The Catholics had become more fervent as a result of Harris's passage, and deeply admired his presence at the mass, accompanied by the women and "the black pastor from Grand Bassam"—who must have been Swatson.[35]

After Harris left, tension rose, and there was an active struggle between the Catholics and Protestants, each claiming to enjoy the special sympathy of the prophet. At this time, it was perhaps the Catholic

---

[33] Lt. Gov. Gabriel Angoulvant to Administrators of *Cercles*, 24 Sept. 1914.

[34] Gaston Joseph (*chef de cabinet* to Lt. Gov. Angoulvant), "Une atteinte à l'animisme chez les populations de la Côte d'Ivoire", in *Annuaire et Mémoires du Comité d'Etudes Historiques et Scientifiques de l'Afrique Occidentale Française. Gorée*: Imprimerie du Gouvernement Général, 1916, 344–348.

[35] Rev. Jean-Marie Bedel, "Le prophète Harris. Souvenirs IV. 1908—au 6 avril 1938." Handwritten notebook, in Archives of Archepiscopal Diocese of Abidjan, pp. 27–36.

church which profited most, although Father Hartz recognised that most of the population could not distinguish between the rival churches. But the Protestants were scarcely present, while there were nine churches and sixteen chapels in the Catholic network, with over twenty missionaries, and fifteen catechists.

Father Hartz, however, had never been totally convinced by Harris's presumed pro-Catholic statement, and questioned his line of thinking. But, by the end of October, the Catholics had made a conscious policy decision regarding Harris: they would continue to profit from the movement but would avoid all appearance of agreement or compromise.

In November Father Gorju met with Harris and, according to a report, asked Harris the religion he belonged to. "[Harris] said that he burned the fetishes for the moment, and left to him the responsibility for the believers."[36]

Fear of the fetishes was still a factor; in one section of Bingerville the people reportedly told Harris that when, earlier, they had burned fetishes at the behest of Roman Catholic missionaries, someone had subsequently died. "So the people said to Harris, 'You, perhaps, are sent by God—we want to listen only to you—but don't turn us over to these people.' Then Harris said: 'I will baptize you but other white men will come to teach you about God.'" Harris then sent a Fanti *krak* (clerk) with a Bible to teach them.[37]

This August 1963 statement by five Harris-baptized Methodists indicates a kind of natural fear of the Catholics prior to Harris; a fear not based on ecclesiastical or theological dogma, but arising out of the power dynamics of traditional structures. This fear was overcome, for Harris, by the clerk with a Bible—an instrument of power, and to this extent Harris was favouring the Protestants.

During this period Harris had converted the Abouré village of Bonoua. Reports from the village say that after the baptism he told people to go to either the Protestant or to the Catholic church; also that evangelists would come to encourage and teach the baptized. In fact two catechists, one Catholic and one Protestant, did come. The Roman Catholic missionaries called for the people to come to church and hear the gospel; but they would not accept polygamy.[38]

In this Bingerville period there was in the area almost hysterical

---

[36] *HN.*
[37] *HN.*
[38] *HN*; Bonoua.

enthusiasm, according to Father Gorju, and some exploitation of the situation by unscrupulous clerks. Gorju intervened and informed; there were numerous imprisonments; the government gave to the Catholics "most of the hut-chapels built in the villages by the efforts of the preachers."[39] This was followed by Harris's expulsion, fully approved by Gorju who saw Harris as a "sly fox", and seems to have been later convinced that the whole thing was a "movement created by Protestantism and directed, in short, against us."

Whether Harris knew of Gorju's attitude or of the Catholic supported administrative repression prior to his expulsion we do not know. However the experience in the Ivory Coast with the brutal treatment and ejection enabled him to learn of the collusion between the colonial and ecclesiastical powers. Twelve years later, when talking to Benoît, he classed the commandants and the bishop together as Pharisees: they were united in a crime against Christ.

5. Return along the coast until his expulsion

Before his expulsion Harris was able to retrace his steps west along the coast and visit towns and villages where he had previously preached. He found chapels built, and reportedly preached and told the people that after him various prophets would come. Then the white man would come, and any prophet coming afterwards would be a false prophet.[40] On 10 December he arrived at Grand Lahou, where he found four different groups all owing some allegiance to him. There was a Methodist-oriented group of Fanti and Sierra Leoneans; there was a Catholic-oriented group of Apollonians and Fanti; there was a group of Avikam, and a further, larger, group, which had been split by immoral and dishonest behaviour on the part of some of the Fanti clerks. They asked Harris for a new leader, and he gave them Latta Nandjué, his aide at Grand Lahou and his interpreter at Kraffy.[41]

Harris did not remain in the area long enough to heal the split; thus before the end of 1914 there were already two Harris-oriented churches in addition to the Methodist church and the Catholic nucleus. The differences appear to be ethnic (and linguistic) as much as denominational. Harris recognised the new ecclesiastical reality and

---

[39] J. Gorju, "Un prophète à la Côte d'Ivoire." *Echo*, Sept. Oct. 1915, 116.
[40] *HN.*
[41] *PH*, 51f.

acted in apostolic manner by assuming authority over it and providing it with appropriate leadership.

To summarize: we find Harris, with a Methodist past, but "above all religions, encouraging Methodist clerks in the Ivory Coast to carry on a ministry similar to his own and to provide nurture, until better-trained white missionaries come who would give further Bible teaching. He treated Catholic missionaries in the same way, anticipating that they also would give further teaching, but showing an awareness that the teaching of the Bible was not the usual Catholic pattern. It was only after negative receptions from Methodists and Catholics at Half Assinie and Axim that he seems to have made a temporary resolve to begin his own church, encouraged by Hayford and friends. But he also realised that there was attempted exploitation of his gifts, and he began to distinguish more clearly between his prophetic ministry and the auxiliary role of the churches in teaching. For Assinie, he created a prophetic ministry parallel to the mission churches, and obtained government authorization. Between September and December he seemed to favour neither group, but insisted upon the Bible-oriented teaching which was to follow his own ministry, while aware that this was lacking among Catholics.[42] In Grand Lahou he confirmed the existence of a non-Methodist, non-Catholic ecclesiastical reality and made leadership provision for it. The conditions of his violent expulsion led him to identify official Catholicism with the colonial administration in an anti-Christ opposition to him. His usual pattern was to oppose with his spiritual power those who opposed his ministry.

6. From 1915 to 1926

Harris attempted, during 1915, to return to the Ivory Coast, but was stopped at the border.[43] In 1916, en route to Freetown, he shared his understandings with Father Harrington, missionary at Grand Cess. He recognized that the Catholics "were great teachers" and that the Catholic Church "was the mother of churches", and so he wanted

---

[42] Simon Pierre Ekanza, "Le messianisme en Côte d'Ivoire au début du siècle." *Annales de l'Université d'Abidjan* I, T.3, 1975, 60. Ekanza certainly overstates the case considerably when he sees in Harris's Bible-oriented ministry a "reaction against the Christianity imported by the colonizer", since—in his reasoning—the Bible was still "taboo" within Ivorian Catholicism even into the 1960s. This certainly explains indigenous reluctance to accept Roman Catholicism, but Harris was not fighting it in 1913–14; on the contrary he saw it as auxiliary to his work.
[43] *PH*, 141.

Harrington and his colleagues to attend his public prayers. Harrington guessed that he in fact knew little about the Catholic church. As elsewhere, the prophet went also to the Wesleyan church while in Grand Cess.[44] As in the 1913–14 period, the prophet is preaching "the reign of Christ" as "prophet of the new dispensation of Christ". All the churches—even the "mother of churches"—are his precious auxiliaries but in the end will be transcended by the new dispensation, led by Harris as the greatest of the African prophets. It was in this framework that all the missionary reactions must .be understood, for the missionaries Stauffer and Hartz also knew of the group of prophets. Harris's ways of relating to the various missionary and ecclesiastical structures was not simply as a parallel structure, nor as a specialized prophetic ministry in view of the established churches.[45] It was as future co-leader of a new "universal Christianity" who was preparing the masses for its advent; temporarily the existing churches could contribute their teaching ministry to that programme. This, for Harris, was not just a future vision, but a present reality.

At the time of Harris's death, the Catholic view of him was that "he refused to belong to any church and refused to found a new one . . . [and] bid his converts join any church so long as it was Christian."[46] This appears to be the view of Father Harrington who, although a little cynical about Harris's praise of the Catholic Church, appreciated his work.[47]

When the prophet arrived in Freetown in February 1917 he had an interview with the Bishop of Sierra Leone, and was himself interviewed by the *Sierra Leone Weekly News*. They reported his saying that

> . . . there were twelve prophets set apart to do this reformatory work—eight in the world today Europeans, and four Africans including himself, and that he was the head of all of them.[48]

The editor used the title "reformer" to describe Harris, following Casely

[44] Harrington, *op. cit.*
[45] Sheila S. Walker thus interprets Harris's understanding of his prophetic ministry. *Cf.* "The two mandates", pp. 164–172, in her *Christianity African style*, 1976.
[46] *The African Missionary*, January 1930, 17.
[47] *Ibid.*, 20.
[48] *Sierra Leone Weekly News* 33 (49), 4 August 1917, 17.

Hayford's 1917 pamphlet. Harris did not reject the title, but it did not adequately represent his vision.

In 1918, on his return from Sierra Leone, he visited Father O'Herlihy of the Catholic Mission at the Betu station among the Kroos, and told him that "His mission is not to found any special church but to draw all black men to Christianity, baptize them, and share them out among the different churches."[49] O'Herlihy also reported: "last week he had a special revelation—he is a grand pal of Gabriel's— that Mary, Mother of God was in counsel with the angels to ask God to stop the war." This rare allusion to Mary appears to be almost a new *rapprochement* with Roman Catholic understandings.

Between 1914 and 1926 Harris tried at least eight times to go back into the Ivory Coast to visit and look after the work he had started. He never succeeded.

During those years he frequently visited the Nana Kru Methodist Mission in Liberia, and came into confrontation with the missionary in charge, the Rev. W.B. Williams. Williams became convinced that Harris had done the Methodist work great harm by preaching polygamy and by living in polygamy himself. When Harris in 1925 suffered a paralytic stroke, Williams interpreted it as "God's avenging sword" which had struck him to the ground, paralyzed and dumb. Nevertheless, the missionaries took Harris in and nursed him back to partial health. One day Harris, refusing the boat the missionaries had obtained for him,

> ... rose up very early ... and walked off, dragging his paralyzed leg and able only to utter a word here and there that was intelligible. Since that day, he has visited here, and has partly regained the use of his limbs and his tongue, but he tells us, "I can't preach anymore."[50]

7. The visit of missionary Pierre Benoît, 1926

The prophet Harris probably heard news of the arrival of English Methodist missionaries in the Ivory Coast early in 1926. In June 1926 the mission French language paper *Courrier de l'A.O.F.* records a visit made by a missionary to Harrist believers in Fresco, and communication with Harris as to whether they should join the local Wesleyan Church.[51]

---

[49] Fr. O'Herlihy Diary, 1918–21. S.M.A. Archives, Cork, Ireland.
[50] Rev. Walter B. Williams, *God's avenging sword*. Sino-Kroo Coast, Liberia, December 25, 1928, 6, from *PH*.
[51] *Courrier de l'A.O.F.*, no. 2, June 1926, 3.

And further, at some time between July 1925 and September 1926 Harris had received from a well-wisher in America a published report of the state of the churches in the Ivory Coast when they had been "discovered" by the Methodist missionary administrator in Dahomey, the Rev. William J. Platt. The article, referring to Harris as "the black Elijah", appeared in the 25 June 1925 issue of *The Christian Herald and Signs of our Times*,[52] published in London. It described 150 churches built, Bibles acquired which could not be read, and the people's expectation for "missionaries and teachers". Great tribute was paid to Harris: "Wherever his voice was heard ... the heathen were converted. He established a new and better era in West Africa."

The article went on to make it clear that there was a serious need for further teaching, but that, thanks to Platt's intervention, the Wesleyan Missionary Society was committed to this new work. New workers were being sent; houses for missionaries were being built, and an evangelists' training school was being built in Porto Novo. What Harris read was news that was also available to the English public, for the article was based on another in *The Daily Chronicle* of London.

Harris was understandably touched by this article. Platt was expressing himself in terms which seemed to show that he understood the prophet's own understandings—using expressions like "Elijah", "forerunner", and "great and better era". He was also a Methodist, but how different from Williams in Liberia! The commitment to provide teachers seemed to Harris the fulfilment of his promises and prayers.

Thus, much to the surprise of Pierre Benoît, Wesleyan missionary, the way had been prepared for his visit in September 1926. The article, as well as stating in positive terms the very things Harris wished to hear, did not hint at a number of the Methodist rules and activities which would have distressed him. These included the rebaptizing of thousands of Harris's converts; opposition to polygamy; the new structures for the establishment of a Methodist church. There was nothing to suggest that the role of the missionaries was to be anything but auxiliary, teaching, and temporary. Looking back, it is obvious that Platt in writing and Harris in reading had very different assumptions, but there is no suggestion that these things were concealed by

---

[52] The half-page article contains a photograph of Platt and of Harris with his cross, bowl and gourd. The heading is: **THE AFRICAN "ELIJAH" Missionary Discovers 22,000 Black Christians.**

Benoît in bad faith. The *Christian Herald* article in all innocence gave Harris some wrong impressions.

When Platt arrived in the Ivory Coast in 1924 he had been received very differently by different Harrist churches. Some were enthusiastic; others seemed to hold back with a certain reticence. From his first visit (to Grand Lahou) Platt was conscious of this. He hoped in Grand Lahou to pave the way to a union of the existing Methodist church and the Harrist church, and hoped that the desire for enlightenment would help to bring this about.[53] But the difficulties continued; a successor to Platt, Paul Wood, was encountering them some months later. The older members of the Harrist churches, especially, showed that they would not easily give over authority to young catechists from Dahomey. "The younger generation is happily easier to convince and there we may hope to do good and see fruit."[54] Another problem the Methodists encountered was that of getting churches to make financial contributions to the work; "they have been accustomed to spend their money in feasting and drinking. The financial question is the stumbling block."[55]

The missionaries saw the problem as one of gaining the confidence and the control of the Harrist churches out of high motives of Christian development; however, it was also necessary as a form of validation of their own mission before the colonial administration. Platt encountered a hostile governor, and won him over, after convincing him that the Methodists could give "thorough oversight to our work."[56]. Both Platt and Lethel emphasized their intention to control and teach their converts so that the French administration would find loyal and "French" subjects among the followers of Methodism.[57] Despite this effort in 1924, Platt later reported that

> our success itself increases our difficulty with Government and Romanist alike . . . I am becoming more and more 'unpopular' (!!!) in Government quarters on the Ivory Coast through my constant appeals to government.[58]

Thus the need for mission control to be evident became greater. Another difficulty threatened by August 1926. A French "Baptist fundamentalist"

---

[53] MMS: Platt's 2nd report, April 1924.
[54] MMS: Wood to Thompson, 18 November 1924.
[55] MMS: P. Wood, Report of the Ivory Coast Mission, 1934.
[56] MMS: Platt's 1st Report: "Report on the Work of the Ivory Coast, 1923."
[57] MMS: Platt's 2nd Report, 1924; ICN Archives: Abidjan x–46–?17, Grand Bassam Administrative Report 1924, 2nd Qtr. *Cf. PH*, 176.
[58] MMS: Platt to Thompson, 1 January 1926.

missionary might be sent out to join Rev. Mark Hayford, the brother of Casely Hayford. Hayford, Platt reported, claimed "to be the true successor of Harris", and it was possible that "to annoy us, the Gov't would back him being protected by a white man—a French man, too."[59]

Platt had cause to be concerned. Hayford had first visited the Ivory Coast churches in 1919, and although in 1920 his representative had been refused permission to remain, he had good contacts within the areas where the Methodists were now working, and where some Harrists had already joined the Methodist Church. Here, then, was another possible breach of Platt's hoped-for unity.

Since Hayford could make claim to being the first organisational successor to Harris's work, it became necessary for Platt to acquire from the prophet some kind of accreditation of the Methodist work. This was his reason for Benoît's visit in September 1926.

> I am sending home to you, this mail, news of the interviews between Benoît and Prophet Harris. In view of the possible arrival of Mark Hayford and a dispute arising concerning the succession of Prophet Harris, also in view of the fact that the Harrist Churches which have not joined us continually told us that they still followed Harris, I sent Benoît to Liberia along with the old interpreter used by Harris (who is now one of our catechists) to see Harris.[60]

Benoît himself saw his mission somewhat differently. He wrote of the difficulties caused by the chiefs of the villages evangelised by Harris, who had become used to independence, being their own rulers, allowing polygamy and so on.

> They did not want the Wesleyan mission, although Harris had often said and expressly taught them that one day white missionaries would come to teach them more than he could himself and that at that time all the churches must hear them. ... As soon as our most pressing problems were solved one of us was [sent?] to find again the prophet and ask him for some counsel addressed to the intractable chiefs. It was a matter of getting explicit letters from him bidding the great churches such as that of Lahou ... to return to the fold of the Wesleyan mission, and telling them all to become acquainted with the Bible to enlighten their path.[61]

---

[59] MMS: Platt to Thompson, 20 August 1926, paragraph 137.
[60] MMS: Platt to Thompson, 26 November 1926, paragraph 156.
[61] MMS: *Benoît Report*, translated by Miss Thompson, pp. 2–3.

Benoît, twenty-six years old and fluent in English, had arrived in the Ivory Coast in late 1925 and had been sent almost immediately to Lahou. He had studied religious psychology at the Sorbonne and theology at Union Theological Seminary, New York.

In Cape Palmas, Liberia, Benoît learned what he could before contacting Harris. He heard that the aged man still travelled preaching; that there was a coolness between him and the missions because his baptism was not acknowledged as valid; that he was likely to be mistrustful of any European; that he was a practising polygamist.

When Benoît and his interpreter, Tano, finally went to find Harris, they met him coming out, clothed in his robes, to meet them, for he had been "spiritually" informed of their visit. Benoît tactfully brought him greetings from his followers "and of our churches on the French side." The distinction between "his followers" and "our churches" may not have been clear to Harris, but he was clearly delighted to hear news of those he had baptised.

Before Benoît spoke to Harris again, at his daughter's home, he learned through the interpreter, Tano, that Harris had heard about Platt, and had asked whether the two visitors knew him. He was delighted when he learned that they came in the name of Platt. His first concern was for the mission in the Ivory Coast. It soon became apparent that he desperately wished to return and preach there again. Benoît gave him as much information as possible about the state of the churches and, according to him, Harris "soon decided that all the Christians should be Wesleyans."

Here the confusion begins. "He dictated to me a paper to this effect. Here is a copy of it. [The original document is no longer to be found] Tomorrow I will present him with a translation of this text after improving and correcting it, and he will sign it. He will also dictate to us letters for the leaders of the "Harris" churches of Fresco and Grand Lahou."

After some words of rejoicing that Harris was "now absolutely with us", Benoît reported that Tano "has got him to promise to send messages to N'Drin, the preacher of the Harris church at Lahou, and the leaders of the church bidding them to join themselves again immediately to the Methodist Church, and to enter it with all their children. . . ."

The ease and rapidity with which Harris complied with Benoît's wishes now seems incredible to modern Harrists, and opponents accuse him of exploitation. But Harris had been prepared for the visit by the *Christian Herald* article, and must have learned from Benoît and

Tano the difficulties with the colonial authorities in the Ivory Coast.

The article had written of Harris, his churches, and the Methodist intervention in the most favourable possible light, but the organizational features which presented the most difficulty were not mentioned—membership cards, rebaptism, centralized control of local funds—and these were aspects of Methodism not likely to have been known to Harris from his early contacts in Liberia, and of which he would not have approved. It is surely true to say that Harris did not fully know what he was calling his churches to do; but it is important to note that the original testament [T-1] was authentically from the prophet himself.

We do not know, however, what was in that document. Benoît himself wrote that he intended to improve and correct it; the next day he spent a good deal of time translating it into French [T-2]. This was the document Harris signed, after it had been read to him word by word and "translated [back into English] as literally as possible." This original document found its way into the Ivory Coast archives. The best-known English text we possess [T-3] is a later translation of it into English made by a Miss Thompson in the course of translating the Benoît Report for the London office.

This text reads as follows;

> *I, William Wadé Harris, who have called you to the true gospel and baptism, I have given this message to the Rev. P. Benoît so that he may bring it to you and that you may obey it.*
>
> *All the men, women and children who have been called and baptised by me must enter the Wesleyan Methodist Church, I myself am also a Methodist. No one must enter the Roman Catholic Church if he wishes to be faithful to me. Mr. Platt, the Director of our Methodist Church, is appointed by me as my successor to the Head of the churches which I have founded.*
>
> *All the fetishes, the koubos, and the ju-jus must be destroyed. Burn them all in the fire. [May] Evil befall him who secretly keeps them in his house! May the fire from heaven devour him. All must adore the only true God in Jesus Christ and him alone must you serve.*
>
> *Read the Bible; it is the Word of God. I am sending one to you and I have marked the verses to be read. Search out the light in the Bible. Learn your letters that you may be able to read the Bible; it will be your guide.*
>
> *Be faithful in all things, attaching yourselves firmly to the observation of the ten commandments and to the Word of Jesus Christ our only Saviour.*
>
> *I send you my wishes and my message of joy. May the God of grace bless you abundantly.*
>
> *Cape Palmas   25.9.1926   W. W. Harris*

This is not the document Harris signed, but a later translation into English of the French version, to which he had set his name. Benoît noted in his report, "He altogether approved of it, and considered it even better than the night before." But he added that some additions and deletions had been made.

One important deletion was that of allusions to "the governors and administrators" in the Ivory Coast. An important addition was the name of Mr. Platt. Another addition suggested in conversation with Harris was the order to read the Bible and to learn their letters (i.e. alphabet).

However, this full text was only rarely used in the Ivory Coast. Platt probably felt it had been reworked too much. An abbreviated version was distributed widely in the Ivory Coast with a picture of Harris and Benoît.[62] This text [T-4], translated from the French, reads as follows:

> *I William Wadé Harris, who called you to the Gospel and Baptized you, have dictated this message to Pastor P. Benoît.*
>
> *All the men, women and children who were called and baptized by me must enter the Wesleyan Methodist Church. I am myself a Methodist.*
>
> *You must all worship the only true God in Jesus Christ.*
>
> *Read the Bible, it's the Word of God. Learn the alphabet in order to read it. It will be your guide.*
>
> *May the God of peace bless you abundantly.*
>
> *Cape Palmas   25.9.1926   W. W. Harris*

Finally, this reduced adaptation has again been reduced by the present-day Harrist Church to the last three paragraphs which text [T-5] constitutes for them the authentic words of Harris.[63]

---

[62] The Testament, in French, was headed: **Le PROPHETE WILLIAM WADÉ HARRIS à Cap Palmas, 25 Septembre 1926**. Above the text [T-4] was a photograph of Harris holding his cross and Bible, and wearing the small Huguenot cross. The identical text was also printed with different photographs and headings. One, with a photograph of Harris with Pastor Benoît, his daughter, and three grandchildren, was headed: **Le PROPHETE WILLIAM WADÉ HARRIS avec sa fille et ses petits-enfants et M. le PASTEUR PIERRE BENOÎT à Cap Palmas, 25 Septembre 1926.** The third, with a photograph of Pastor Benoît shaking hands with Harris, is headed: **La Rencontre du PROPHETE WILLIAM WADÉ HARRIS et M. le PASTEUR PIERRE BENOÎT de l'Eglise Méthodiste Wesleyenne, à Cap Palmas, 25 Septembre 1926.**

[63] The text in French can be read inside the Harrist Church at Abobo-Doumé; it was on a banner across the front of the Harrist Church at Anoumabo at its inauguration on 14 October 1979. The text is as follows: *"Message de W.W. Harris*

We thus see that the "Harris testament" was in fact five different texts. T-1, the original English text, dictated by Harris to Benoît, without the latter's important adaptations, is no longer extant.

Our main concern is here is to learn about Harris's attitude to the churches and missions. Was Harris really as positive towards the Methodist Church as the text from Benoît suggests? Was there an anti-Catholic note at this time, as suggested in T-3? The original hand-written "Benoît Notes" are important at this point, since they contain the original messages which Harris dictated for the various churches, after having signed Benoît's T-2.

To Loa, the chief of Grand Lahou, he dictated:

> *Go Methodist—the minister will baptise you—All non-baptised will be baptised by Mr. Platt and his minister only.*
> *The cross the pastor give you you will wear—with Jesus Christ crown of thorns.*

To "my people in Fresno" he dictated:

> *All must do according to the message or they will see things. Join all the Methodist Church.*
> *All go Methodist—no more disobedience.*

To "my people in Tiegba and Yocoboué" he dictated:

> *Join the Methodist Church—I myself am a Methodist. I want you to keep apart.*

Benoît himself was rather surprised by the accent on "Methodist":

> Today he adds this command "Join the Methodists" and in giving it he specifically observes that he himself began as a Methodist and that he entered the Protestant Episcopal Church, not knowing his vocation as a prophet, and urged by a desire to earn a good salary.

It is difficult to know why at this stage Harris's regard for Methodists made him so insistent on joining that church. Only a year earlier he had suffered a paralytic stroke, following a Methodist missionary's word that God would speak to him concerning polygamy. He had

---

aux Eglises qu'il a fondées en Côte d'Ivoire: Tous vous adorez le seul vrai Dieu en Jésus Christ. Lisez la Bible. C'est la parole de Dieu. Apprenez les lettres pour la lire. Elle sera votre guide. Que le Dieu de paix vous bénisse abondamment. Cape Palmas, le 25–9–26. W.W. Harris"

not changed his mind on polygamy, as Benoît found, so his bias against Methodists would still be the expected attitude.

We recall that twelve years earlier Harris had reportedly said that the Methodists did not know Christ because they did not know the cross. Had he changed his mind on this? Benoît had showed Harris the Huguenot cross which French Protestants use, and which missionaries had been distributing for some years against the advice of the Paris and London mission offices. Perhaps after all, the Methodists "knew the cross". But would that change his attitude? In any case he accepted—also for his disciples—the Huguenot cross representing for him the crown of thorns . . . and the Spirit.

When Benoît arrived on the scene, he found Harris troubled about the churches he had left in the Ivory Coast, even though he knew that Platt and his colleagues were working among them. He wanted permission "to finish his work". In response Benoît had "made it clear to him that he must no longer count on crossing the frontier and that the mission will really *take his place and assume his responsibilities.*"[64] It is this latter notion which is made explicit in the improved testament (T-2 and T-3), in stating that "Mr. Platt, the Director of *our* Methodist Church, *is appointed by me as my successor* to the *head* of the churches which I have founded." Benoît wrote that he had discussed the possibility of *recommending Platt* to his churches; the text goes beyond that, but reflects the original concern of Benoît as stated by Platt:[65] that of succession. It is not at all clear that Harris really understood that this is what he was signing. If he did understand, he did not know the full implications, as we have seen. This is the major source of later contention and misunderstanding.

The Kingdom had not come "after seven years"—by 1921—as Harris had originally predicted. Had this caused him to abandon the temporary, auxiliary, teaching role of the missionaries? Was he now ready to turn his succession over to the Methodists? Nothing of what he told Benoît suggests that this was the case. In fact, his apocalyptic language was, if anything, stronger.

---

[64] My underlining. We understand this better because Benoît had discovered Harris to be a practising polygamist; the very day of his arrival at Cape Palmas Benoît wrote that he hoped to be able to use Harris's influence to counteract polygamous tendencies in the recalcitrant churches. If he had returned to the Ivory Coast, Harris would have been a source of trouble for the Methodists, perhaps even among those people who had already joined the Methodist Church.

[65] *Cf.* text referred to in note 59.

Perhaps we can grasp Harris's intention and understanding of the
testamental transaction by looking at the Bible image he used to describe
the relationship between himself and the missionaries. "You missionaries are for me like Aaron for Moses—you are Aaron" [*BN* II, 11f.],
an expression he used twice. In the book of Exodus Moses tried to
avoid God's call by arguing that he was incapable of public speaking,
and he was told to use his brother Aaron as "mouthpiece" (Exodus
4.14–17, 27–31). Benoît took Harris's words to mean that the missionaries were his successors, but for Harris they were neither re-
placements nor successors, but rather, his spokesmen. Through them
he could send his word back to the Ivory Coast. He dictated to Benoît:

> *You are to say to the chief of Grand Lahou that I am here and at the same time*
> *at Lahou. When you speak for me I am there (He points to his cross) This is*
> *my telegraph (BN I, 44)*[66]

Benoît had acquired Harris's total trust, and there was no doubt in
his mind that Benoît would do exactly what he was told to do and
say, under his prophetic authority. We recall his reaction to the Rev.
Elias Butler in Axim.

This perspective must be kept in mind when seeking to understand
Harris's response to Benoît's questions about polygamy. Benoît, in
asking the question, was attempting to discover Harris's point of view;
Harris saw him asking for an authoritative answer. Once he had spoken,
he had every reason to believe that the English Methodists in the
Ivory Coast, unlike the American (Williams) in Liberia, would follow
what he directed. Benoît seemed to Harris to perceive the prophet
as Elijah, the last prophet, as the *Christian Herald* article had indicated.
He told Benoît, "Your questions are a spiritual examination, so you
see I am *the* prophet" (*BN* II, 12). Indeed, Benoît had underlined
the in his notes. This was another text which did not find its way
into the final report.

For Harris, it had become clear that the Methodists were not only
recognising his role, but also putting themselves *under* his authority.
But in the documents T-2 and T-3, prepared by Benoît, Harris

---

[66] We find exactly this same phenomenon in the story of Elisha (II Kings 4.29)
which Aubrey Johnson says is a clear illustration of the biblical phenomenon of the
extension of the power of the individual, and the care not to have it exploited by
misuse. See his *The One and the Many in the Israelite Conception of God*. Cardiff: University
of Wales 1961, *cf.* p. 6.

unwittingly puts himself under Platt's authority, at least legally. Benoît commented

> We ought to see that he is surrounded by attention and some supervision, partly to prevent him from being monopolized by others, partly to assure him an old age. (*BR* I, 22).[67]

But the Methodists could never have entertained the idea of placing themselves under Harris's authority; nor could they be his spokesmen on polygamy. Nor could they ask the Governor of the Ivory Coast for permission for him to return there; Benoît had omitted from the testament "the allusions to the governors and administrators."

In other words, Harris had in no way changed his fundamental stance and understandings; for him it was the Methodists who had changed. So they could be useful to him, and become his spokesmen, "as Aaron was to Moses." As Moses was obedient to God, so they would be to him. As we know, this was not the case, and the inevitable result was misunderstanding between Harrists and Methodists. Today in the Harrist Church in the Ivory Coast Benoît's name has become a byword of infamy, and has created the deepest suspicions concerning the intentions of other churches and especially white missionaries. The Methodist Church continues as recently as 1989 to promote its "missionary version" of the incident, by Amos-Djoro (see bibliography).

What about the prophet's attitude to the Roman Catholic church? "No one must enter the Roman Catholic church if he wishes to be faithful to me," as the text of T-3 states clearly. Benoît's detractors explain this away as Methodist anti-Catholicism shining through Benoît's additions to the text. Rouch[68] and Bureau[69] both contrast this with Harris's "very great tolerance" towards that church. In the period from 1913 to September 1914 they are certainly correct. But Harris's attitudes as they had developed from the period of his mistreatment and expulsion from the Ivory Coast in January 1915 is not taken into account by them.

Before examining further Harris's 1926 attitude, we need to note

---

[67] The obituary of Harris in the English press indicated that the Wesleyan Methodists did precisely that; however, we have discovered no evidence that that was in fact the case.

[68] J, Rouch, "Une Introduction à la communauté de Bregbo", 1963, 161 (my translation).

[69] René Bureau, "Le prophète Harris et le harrisme." *Annales de l'Université d'Abidjan. Ethnosociologie* Série F (3), 1971, 60 (my translation).

the character of the anti-Catholicism of the Methodists. Could it alone
have inspired such a line from Benoît? Platt's administrative concern
in sending Benoît was based on an anti-Hayford position, and for
good reason. Anti-Catholicism does not come into it. His (and Benoît's)
pastoral concern was related to the recalcitrant and polygamous
congregations who were not either Wesleyan or Catholic. This is not
to deny that there was an ongoing Wesleyan preoccupation with
Roman Catholic competition, and this was behind the introduction
of the Huguenot cross.[70] But nowhere in the notes or report coming
from Benoît are Roman Catholics mentioned except in statements
coming from Harris himself.

Harris first mentions Catholicism in telling of being cursed by the
Catholic at Half Assinie. The second mention is in reference to his
stay at Bingerville (*BN* II, 9) where it required the authority of the
governor to stifle opposition from the religious.[71]

However, the patronage of the governor and the Roman Catholic
submission to it did not last very long. In October and November
1914 Catholic opposition to Harris and the movement increased. Harris
knew of this; when he spoke of his expulsion it was in the strongest
terms: "In Abidjan they broke my cross, took my cloth off and the
cloths of the women. That's a crime—they crucify Christ." (*BN* II,
9f.) He clearly associated the Catholic church with the government's
refusal to let him return to the Ivory Coast, and with his maltreatment:
"All the commandants and the bishop live like Pharisees." For Harris,
there had been a conjunction of forces which had him arrested, bound,
beaten with a *chicotte*, stripped naked, imprisoned and expelled; this
resulted ultimately in the death of one of his faithful singers, Helen
Valentine.

The "very great tolerance" noted by Bureau and Rouch must be
seen in this light. Harris had been tolerant, but he had not been
tolerated. He was, what his interpreters have not always been willing
to see, a man of action whose attitudes could change. Thus the anti-
Catholic stance expressed in T-3 was not a "contradiction", but a
hostility which was an expression of realism. But it must not be seen
as a generalized anti-Catholic attitude; he was still positive about the

---

[70] F. Deaville Walker, *The story of the Ivory Coast*, 1926, 42. *Cf.* also pp. 60f., 64f.
[71] Jean-Marie Bedel, "Le prophète Harris. Souvenirs IV. 1908—au 6 avril 1938."
Handwritten notebook, in Archives of Archepiscopal Diocese of Abidjan. pp.
27–36.

Catholic church in Liberia even after his expulsion from the Ivory Coast. However, in his conversations with Tano about the Ivory Coast situation, he must have become informed about the increased Catholic involvement with the regime after 1921, and the persecution of Harrist Christians and churches.[72] And, as always, his opposition was directed to that which opposed his own ministry and its fruit.

The dissension between white churches—Catholic, Methodist, Episcopalian—he saw as confusion, which was rebellion. How could he then align himself with the Methodists, who were part of that confusion? In so far as they submitted to him the situation had changed. The Catholics, even when friendly, had never recognized either his ministry or his churches. The Methodist arrival, however, came as an answer to his prayers. He had dictated to Benoît: "I prayed God to send teacher. He sent you this man. Now you go hear him. All he teach you, you learn." (*BN* II, 15.) He had promised teachers of the Bible and had prayed for their coming. Now they had come, it was important to use them to the fullest.

In an article after Harris's death, W.J. Platt wrote that "in all his work he has remained a 'free-lance', working outside the ordinary activity of the mission in his own country. The one exception to this attitude was when Harris blessed our efforts on the Ivory Coast."[73] It is the exceptional character of that attitude which underlines the Methodist misunderstanding of it. Was he later to be pleased with their work? Would they later on be interested in knowing what he thought?

Before examining his later attitude, what were the responses of the churches in the Ivory Coast to the publication of the re-edited testament, T-4? Many took it as a final word from Harris and were integrated into the Methodist church. Others doubted its authenticity and remained recalcitrant. Others initially joined the Methodists but were disillusioned with what followed.

One of the major nests of opposition was among the Adjukru people, where a prophet, Aké, reputed—falsely—to be the son of Harris,[74] was becoming known. In fact, Aké was responsible for the revival

---

[72] Memories of this abound in the *HN* of 1963–64, e.g. at Audouin, Assaoufoué, Orbaf, Abidjin-Kouté.

[73] *The Methodist Recorder*, 10 October 1929.

[74] He is still occasionally taken by scholars to have been Harris's son, as e.g. T. Christensen, "Karnu", in *Missiology* 5 (2) 1978, 209. A discussion of the Aké conflict with the missionaries will be found in de Billy, *En Côte d'Ivoire* [1931], 41ff., 72ff.

of a number of traditional practices which had disappeared following
Harris's ministry. In the midst of this retrogression, a group of notables
from the Adjukru were reportedly delegated to visit Harris in 1927
or 1928.[75] It is probable they sought Harris's approval of Aké and
rejection of the Methodists. Through them Harris would also have
heard about aspects of the Methodist work which would have disappointed him. But he continued to support the Methodists against
Aké, and the troubles in Adjukru country seem to have died down
by about July 1927, which may give us the date of the delegation's
return. Although he continued to support the Methodists, Harris must
have felt disillusioned and aware of his own continuing responsibility,
and this was surely confirmed when another delegation came to visit
him in December 1928. This group was from the Ebrié village of
Petit Bassam.

8. The consecration of John Ahui, December 1928

The delegation had been sent by Akadja Nanghui, chief of Petit Bassam.
It consisted of his brother, Solomon Dagri, Solomon's son, John Ahui,
then aged about 34, and a Kru translator, John Djibo.

The Harrist congregation at Petit Bassam had been created when
its members were baptized by Harris at Bingerville. For ten years
Chief Akadja was its leader. When the Methodist missionaries arrived,
a split occurred, because of Methodist practices involving "tickets"
for money, and the control of the finances. When Benoît returned
from Cape Palmas in the fall of 1926 with the message from Harris,
numbers of people began to return to the Methodist congregation.
In Petit Bassam and neighbouring Cocody the congregations held back,
although individuals rejoined without their chief. A further difficulty
was polygamy, which Harris had not condemned. But to enter the
Methodist Church as his testament recommended excluded polygamy
as an option.

---

[75] Letter from de Billy to Shank, 8 December 1977 (my translation): "In 1973
during a stay for revisiting the churches where I had worked thirty-one years earlier
Pastor Laurent Lasm told me that he had learned that around 1927 or 1928 a delegation
of notables from the Adjukru tribe around Dabou had been sent secretly by chiefs
who were hostile to the Protestant Methodist Mission, to Cape Palmas in order to
ask the Prophet Harris what he thought of the Protestant Methodist Mission. Harris
is said to have told them all his converts were to join up with it. The whole affair
remained secret because the hostile chiefs did not want to admit their error. But
I recall that about this time the agitation centred around the false prophet Aké was
calmed and that our mission was able to work without opposition."

The disciples at Petit Bassam could not know that the prophet's word to Benoît was that God permitted several wives but condemned adultery. They were thus faced with a grave contradiction. In addition, a serious epidemic among the population was causing them to question whether they were on the right path. As Harris had taught them, their very well-being depended upon their right worship of God; they thus needed to know whether or not they were right in holding back from the Methodist church. So Akadja sent a delegation to Cape Palmas to consult and "to receive orders from the prophet."

Various written accounts give details of the visit. The earliest would appear to be that of Amos-Djoro in 1956,[76] based on contacts with the Harrists and Methodist relatives of John Ahui. In 1961 a short resume of the meeting was published by Dominique Desanti, who wrote of her experience of the conflict in interpretation between the witness, Ahui, and his disciples. They "did not wish to contradict that which they had themselves so often affirmed"[77] when confronted with what Ahui was narrating. This raises serious historical problems about all of the oral tradition of the Harrists concerning the incident.

Several further interviews with Ahui provide additional insight. In 1961 the historian Gordon Haliburton noted his own conversations with John Ahui and his son Paul.[78] The French ethnosociologist René Bureau was able to discuss the event with Ahui in 1966;[79] the Ivorian Methodist theologian Yando was able to do the same for his 1970

---

[76] E. Amos-Djoro, "Les mouvements marginaux du protestantisme africain," 1956, 195–206. It should be noted that the French text of Harris's message to the chief of Petit Bassam was also an interpretation by the translator and is thus deformed. Unfortunately, this was the text which Sheila S. Walker also used, translated back into English. Walker, *op. cit.*, 157–160.

[77] D. Desanti, *L'Atlas des voyages, Côte d'Ivoire*. Lausanne: Rencontre 1962, 70ff.

[78] *HN, cf. PH* 208f.

[79] Typical of the oral tradition within the Harrist Church is that given by Bruno Abéto of Abobo-Doumé in August 1966: "*Jona est allé en 1928. Harris lui a dit: 'J'ai vu le Pasteur Pierre Benoît, mais je crains les questions d'argent: c'est du commerce au nom de Dieu. La Bible est la base. Il faut vite apprendre à lire, faire des écoles pour que les enfants puissent la lire. C'est la base de tout. Je te donne la canne.'*
Ils ont trouvé Harris en train de faire la pénitence (il se préparait et priait Dieu de lui envoyer des hommes; ils les attendait.) Ils sont restés quelques mois [in fact they stayed less than a week.] 'Je vous attendais.' Tous les jours à quatre heures Harris leur montrait le Christ. Ils ne le voyaient pas. 'Je vais tout vous confier. Mais ne faites pas la prière pour le commerce, Dieu ne le veut pas. Il a vu que le Pasteur Pierre Benoît m'aurait corrompu.' Dibo comprenait l'anglais et le Baoulé.
Une nuit brusquement les deux autres ont dormi. Jona a vu Harris tout blanc en Une Vision. Harris lui a pris la main pour qu'il touche son coeur. Jona ne savait pas si c'était Harris. Harris a dit ensuite: 'Tout est fini. On va nous photographier ensemble.' Il lui a donné une procuration

thesis.[80] During 1971–72 the anthropologist Sheila Walker obtained a description of the events from Harrist informants.[81] Perhaps most important of all was the recording of John Ahui's tale by M. Robert Arnaut of Radiotélévision Française in March 1976, with a translation from the Ebrié by Bogui Claver.[82] Finally, in April 1978, we were also permitted to study documents related to the event as well as to discuss the event briefly with John Ahui through the interpretation of his son, Paul. Some correspondence also followed.

In spite of potential erosion and transformation which can overtake any oral narration in the course of time, great authority must be attributed to the 1976 recording by Arnaut. Both the evidence of the son, who testified to the unchanging nature of the story as he had heard it over many tellings, and the evidence of those present at the recording,[83] together with the oath of the narrator, are evidence of this. The account which follows is based on this narrative, supplemented from the other accounts.

The envoys arrived at Cape Palmas on 9 December 1928, to find that Harris was expecting them. They told him of the difficulties their village had encountered: sickness, persecution by the French authorities, the pressure of the Methodist "testament", the Methodist imposition of "tickets" and the non-admission of polygamists. Harris answered that their difficulties were due to their having abandoned the true worship of God before the seven years of promise had been fulfilled. The only remedy for that was to begin all over again and persevere.

During their stay, the prophet was wearing a heavy stone attached to the back of his waist as a kind of penitence which he imposed upon himself for having allowed himself to have been deluded by the pastor Benoît. He was a deceiver and his so-called "testament" a fake; Benoît had also failed to include in the statement Harris's forecast of the end of the French role in the Ivory Coast and of his

---

en anglais. Dans la procuration il est question de Malachie; Harris prenait des Ivoiriens pour des Éthiopiens. 'C'est pour affirmer à l'administration que je te confie le travail.'"

[80] Emmanuel Yando, *L'Évolution du Harrisme en Côte d'Ivoire*. Paris: Faculté Libre de Théologie Protestante: Thesis, 1970, 64–69.

[81] Sheila S. Walker, *op. cit.*, 155–164.

[82] "The meeting with the Prophet Harris", a text transcribed from a recording of 25 March 1976, was made available to me by the courtesy of Robert Arnaut.

[83] Robert Arnaut, *L'Afrique du jour et de la nuit*. Paris: Presses de la Cité 1977, 72f (my translation). The full text of the recording has since been published: Kouassi Boussou Jôh Benoit. *Jonas Ahui, Prédicteur Suprême de la Religion Harriste, Successeur du Prophète William Wadé Harris*. Printed in Abidjan, 1983. The latest "telling" by Ahui is in Paul William Ahui, *Le Prophète William Wade Harris.* . . . Abidjan: NEA 1988.

intent to found an African church. Harris repeated for them the instructions which he had given in 1913–14, which they reportedly had the interpreter write down. They included the clear instruction to have their children taught to read in order to interpret the Bible to them.

Following a test of their sincerity, Harris chose John Ahui to be "his representative on Ivorian territory . . .". He then gave Ahui the instruments of his ministry, both his cross and his Bible.[84] He told Ahui he was giving him his power, indicating it as well with gestures, and finally with the opened and overturned Bible upon Ahui's head, he prayed for a long time.

After a photograph of the group had been taken, he dictated in English a message to be taken back to Chief Akadja Nanghui. The exact text[85] is as follows:

> *The prophet sends greetings to the King and people of Ajah Nangvi, Pettit Bassam, Ivory Coast.*
>
> *The prophet is willing to come, but God is not willing that he should come.*
>
> *France protests against Ethiopian rising. No black man must go to Europe. There will be another Great War in Europe. The French have pronounced the prophet crazy, for this cause their native land "Belle France" will be terribly scourged.*
>
> *The prophet bids you good-bye—He is about to go home. Malachi 4 chapter. You must remember the law Moses the Servant of God.*
>
> *The Peace Conference is War Conference says the prophet.*
>
> *The Liberian Kru Coast is finished.*
>
> *Read Isaiah 4 chapter.*
>
> *Read St. Mark's Gospel 10 Chapter.*
>
> *John Dibo (his mark)*   *William Wadé Harris (his mark)*
>
> *In the house of God, among heathen people who one is trying to bring in the way of God we do not receive tickets to be Baptism nor for confirmation. How do we expect for God to bless us if we are receiving our pay here below. Beware of false prophets . . . those are the ones who receive money on. In the house of God among Heathen people, who one is trying to bring in the house or way of God we do not receive tickets for Baptism nor for confirmation. How do we expect God to bless us, when we are receiving our blessing on earth below?*
>
> *Dear Christians do not let any body deceive you. You must always exercise moral courage like St. Paul of old or Socrates. If you say you are for God you have to suffer many tribulations. Never you give up you God. I shall always remember you to God in my prayers.*

---

[84] Desanti in 1961 saw the Bible in which it was written "in a totally English handwriting: 'to John Ahui . . . William Harris.'" Desanti, *op. cit.*

[85] We have used the original text entrusted to us by John Ahui; it differs from the text of Amos-Djoro and S. Walker as in 76 above.

> *The prophet sends you greeting in the name of one God, the God of Moses,*
> *Isaac, and of Jacob. I feel proud of you to see that you have a strong mind in*
> *God, to send your son and brother here to me in Liberia. May God bless you*
> *for same. I shall always have you in my prayers and all the Christians on the*
> *Ivory Coast. You must always have God before you. It he who will guide you*
> *in all temptation do not forsake you [sic] God to safe your life. I am now old*
> *and sick and God say I must remain home to await my time. It may be soon*
> *or late. We do not pay for our religion here in Liberia. We receive Baptism free,*
> *and confirmation. Hope you will keep Gods' Holy Days and Sundays mostly.*
> *May God bless*
>   *I am yours in Christ*
>   *Marie Agre   William Wade Harris His mark*
> *Again I am telling you in the name of God.*
> *If you are able to marry two women is all left with you if you can do so. God*
> *is not protest against it only thing you must follow your God. Don't let anybody*
> *deceive you. If you can marry 10 women do so only follow God's law.*
>   *William Wade Harris*

With regard to polygamy, Harris is here giving a clear and positive
answer—the answer he thought he had already given to Benoît, but
which was not announced. There is also a very clear denunciation
of the Methodist practice of giving "tickets for money". Harris had
maintained throughout his prophetic ministry a clear testimony on
money, and never ceased to regret that he had run away to the
Episcopalians for money. His openness and refusal to take money
had won him respect from the masses and was a mark of authenticity
for him with the French authorities.

The Methodist missionaries seemed to assume that their collection
of money and use of it would be accepted in good faith by the Ivorians,
despite their known attitude to colonial tax exploitation. But this was
not the case. Even the governor had to advise the mission, in August
1929, to "stop these collections, which . . . make the natives so
discontented, and are in the end more destructive than profitable for
your mission."[86]

Then, too, there is the judgement upon France, apparently reiterated
here since Benoît had been unfaithful in passing on the warning to
the colonial administration. The two complaints—over polygamy and
over the tickets—were the Harrists' major irritants with the Methodists.
They showed Harris clearly that Benoît had acted contrary to his

---

[86] MMS: G. Rodet to W.J. Platt, 3 August 1929, Abidjan.

pattern and counsel. This produced the conclusion that Benoît was a "liar".

There can be no reasonable doubt about the authenticity of the event or the documents brought back by Ahui, since there are in them elements to be found in the Benoît documents. Unfortunately the Methodists have attributed absolute certainty to Benoît's interpretation of his meeting, and then cast doubt and suspicion upon that of the Ebrié delegation. In 1970 the Ivorian Methodist historian and theologian, Yando, wrote

> The testimony of John Ahui and that of Pastor Benoît are not concordant. [Photographs and the testament of Harris written down by Benoît have been published.] But the testament given to John Ahui is not published. There are therefore . . . some serious reservations to be made concerning the authenticity of such a document.[87]

From the Harrist perspective there was solid justification to doubt— as Harris did—the good faith of Benoît and the Methodists who used the prophet's authority to validate and justify their own work which contradicted Harris's own position on money, baptism and polygamy.

Benoît, in addition, did not reveal Harris's predictions about the end of French rule in the Ivory Coast, or Harris's intention to found an African Church—something which in fact he had never heard. To him, Harris's direction to "Go Methodist" meant only one thing. But Harris thought of the Methodists as a temporary, auxiliary agency for teaching. He had already established churches and provided them with structures of continuity. It does not seem to have been the intention of Harris that the Methodists should "take over" the churches he had already founded, but to be the agents of revival and instruction.

So in the Ivory Coast the Catholics had not repented; the Methodists had failed him. There remained only one course: begin again. This was the charge that he is reported to have given John Ahui.

Ahui understood this very clearly, but at first he refused because of fear of the French authorities, and as a result became critically ill. His healing came in 1935 when he took up the charge. The charge

---

[87] Yando, *op. cit.*, 68. As late as 1973, the word from the English missionary Pritchard was that of rejection of Haliburton's report of the Ahui visit, accepting another missionary's report of a one-man delegation who "returned with the wish that all his followers now join the Methodist Mission." But Pritchard did not know of the Benoît notes, the message to Chief Akadja, and the 1928 photo of Ahui and Harris. Pritchard, *op. cit.*, below.

itself was followed shortly by Harris's death, which made him in a very prestigious way the obvious successor to Harris for those who had not followed the Methodist orientation.

However, Ahui was not the only person to whom Harris had given a cross and a Bible. In 1914 he gave them to John Swatson. Several others in Ghana and the Ivory Coast were given them, including Loa, chief of Grand Lahou, in 1926, at the hands of Benoît. So the possession of these symbols, alone, did not give the right of succession. And in fact, since Harris taught that he was "the last prophet" before the imminent return of Christ, it is questionable whether he himself thought in those terms. As the Methodists found, it is not an easy thing for an institution to take over a prophetic succession. The Harrist Church today [1994] is still wrestling with that problem as it looks beyond the present leadership, following Ahui's death in 1992.

The Harrist leadership today apparently understands the question with a sophistication not shared by all their adherents. John Ahui, in 1976, spoke of his position within the church as the end of an historical process:

> It is thus that I have become supreme preacher of the Harrist Church. But Albert Atcho, here present, is the successor of William Harris for the ordering of what is good and for combatting what is evil.

Atcho himself, although called by others a prophet, only claimed to be a lay spiritual healer.[88] And when asked by Arnaut who his own successor would be, his wise and modest answer suggested that the successor, when he came, might not be recognised and might be chased away as happened to Harris and so many other prophets.

The English Methodist missionary, John Pritchard, only partly caught that wisdom when he wrote in 1973:

> Any right the Methodist Church has to consider itself the legitimate heir to Harris should be based not on the 1926 testament but its own watering and reaping where the prophet had sown.[89]

To which one would need to add: "in the spirit of the prophet."

---

[88] David Shank: conversation with Dr. Bruno Claver, Cocody-Abidjan, April 1978.
[89] John Pritchard, "The prophet Harris and the Ivory Coast." *Journal of Religion in Africa* 5 (1), 1973, 30.

The Ivorian Methodist, Amos-Djoro, had sensed the implications better when he commented:

> I approve the attitude of the Harrists [re polygamy] in contrast to the missionaries who brutally imposed monogamy . . . When one refers to the difficulties which the missionaries had, when one seeks to understand why the Catholic and Protestant missionaries failed while the Prophet Harris succeeded, one understands in a certain measure the document that Harris gave to Ahui.[90]

There is nothing to suggest in the documents that Harris excluded whites or their collaboration. Where such a position is held by Harrists it is apparently more a reaction to the subsequent history than derived from anything Harris taught. Yet the notion of an African church[91] had deep roots, if only through the influence of Blyden, and it is hard today to understand why such a vision should have been thought of in years past as incongruous. In that sense Harris was indeed an adherent of "Ethiopianism", as Marty suggested in his report.[92]

Others beside Harris (one being the Episcopalian bishop John Payne) had seen how the Glebo might become the instrument for the spreading of the Gospel in West Africa; others, indeed Blyden had noted the special appropriateness of the African character for the mission of Chist. There is no reason to understand Harris's "Ethiopianism" as any more than "we Africans, too, in our Africa, will obey Christ in our African way, in view of the reign of Christ over the whole world."

---

[90] Dr. Marlin Miller: conversation with Ernest Amos-Djoro, September 1971, Santé-Abidjan. Yet, strangely, and despite the Shank thesis and the publication by Paul W. Ahui (see bibliography) in 1988 of clear evidence to the contrary, Amos-Djoro (Harris et la Chrétienté en Côte d'Ivoire, Abidjan: NEA 1889) still insists on Harris's monogamous practice! (p. 42)

[91] Peter Harrington, "An interview with the 'Black Prophet'." The African Missionary 18 (March-April) 1917, 16. "The Kru tribe . . . was predestined, like the Jews, to play a leading part in some "new dispensation of Christ" and that himself, their prophet, was one of the pillars in the future reconstructed edifice of a universal Christianity."

[92] Paul Marty, "L'impressionabilité religieuse des populations maritimes et lagunaires", chapter one in Etudes sur l'Islam en Côte d'Ivoire. Paris: Editions Ernest Leroux 1922.

CHAPTER TWELVE

PATTERNS OF THOUGHT RELATING TO COLONIAL ADMINISTRATION AND POLITICAL GOVERNMENT

William Wadé Harris became a prophet while in prison for treason and support of the Glebo war against the Liberian Republic in 1910. His action (raising the British "Union Jack" in protest against the American-supported Liberian regime) took place in conjunction with an apparent British-sponsored army mutiny. Harris had used occult powers and threats of death to promote his ends; he was prepared to countenance violence. What, if any, were the differences in his thinking between that time of rebellion and the period of his prophetic ministry? What was his influence upon the embryonic political movement which developed following his mission of evangelism? What were his political understandings?

1. The Ivory Coast and the Gold Coast, 1913–1914

The popular understanding is that Harris "urged the natives to work, and to be obedient towards authority." The source is the *chef de cabinet* of the lieutenant governor of the Ivory Coast.[1] It reflects perfectly the impression Harris gave the governor when they met in September 1914, after which the latter wrote to the *chefs de cercle*:

> he urges them particularly to drink only with moderation and to work six days a week, Sunday being given over to rest.[2]

There is here no mention of "obedience to authority", but it is clear that Harris gave the governor that impression, or he would not have recommended Harris as he did. Bedel insisted that the governor "believed in his [Harris's] mission and became his adept".[3] Only a

---

[1] Gaston Joseph, "Une atteinte à l'animisme...", 1916, 346.
[2] Angoulvant to administrators of the *Cercles*, 24 September 1914 (no. 214 G.P. ICN)
[3] Jean-Marie Bedel (R.P.) "Le prophète Harris". Souvenirs IV, 1908–1938. Handwritten notebook, in archives of Archepiscopal Diocese of Abidjan, 27–36.

week before the letter cited above, Angoulvant had instructed the commandant of the *Cercle des Gouro* "to repress rapidly with severity all acts of rebellion . . ."[4] and shortly before that had instructed vigilance concerning the use of absinth, the possession of which was considered criminal.[5] Despite this usual severity, he encouraged Harris's work, and at a time (September 1914) when no danger to peace and discipline in the colony could be allowed.

Had the governor laid down conditions to which Harris had agreed? Or was Harris's stance obvious? Certainly early reports from *chefs de postes* were positive. He was perceived as advising the natives to live in good relations with the whites,[6] and Jean Ekra, a Harris disciple who was later head of the Bonua Methodist Church remembered the same emphasis.

> He said onl*/* to obey the Word of God. Harris said nothing about obedience tc the French. But he respected them as civil authority, and this was an example to the Abouré who already respected them as the strong authoritative power.[7]

About this time Marc Simon, administrator of the *Cercle des Lagunes*, encountered the movement directly when, out on patrol, his porters refused to march on a Sunday.[8] On 12 November he sent a letter to the governor warning him about the Harris-inspired movement, and in December the governor sent out a memorandum asking the administrators to

> invite the pretended sons of God who have been roaming the villages recently to return to their own country where they will be able to spread the good word easily. The Prophet Harris in particular will find in Liberia, his own country, a sufficiently vast field for activity.[9]

It was this same Simon who ultimately had the Harris team beaten, stripped, jailed, and expelled. His first reaction came about because his porters refused to proceed on a forced march—on a Sunday.

---

[4] ICN Archives: 1 BB 137
[5] ICN Archives: 1 EE 2(4)
[6] ICN Archives: 1 E 119 (2/6), 1 October 1914; and cited in Haliburton, PH, 134.
[7] *HN*: Jean Ekra, Bonoua
[8] Marc Simon, *Souvenirs de brousse*, 1965, 172
[9] Angoulvant to administrators of the *Cercles*, 16 December 1914 (no. 243 G.P.)

We can only conclude that Harris was on the one hand emphasizing respect for the colonial authorities, and yet on the other hand was preaching with a God-given authority that in the end appeared greater than that of the commandant in his own *cercle*.

Harris was not functioning under their authority; under their authorization he preached under the authority of Christ. Governor Angoulvant was reported later to have said to the Catholic fathers, "He went too far, and forbade the populations to obey me, the wharf labourers to work on Sunday."[10]

In his earlier ministry in the Gold Coast a similar situation arose. Hayford was impressed by his fearless preaching—"He is strong against Sabbath-breaking and he makes men realize what he means."[11] He made a personal intervention to the District Commissioner for the abolition of Sunday work on the steamers by the kruboys; his request was refused. *The Gold Coast Leader* from Axim took this as the reason that he left for Seccondee [Sekondi] around 12 August.[12] He saw whites working on Sunday as rebellion just as much as blacks, and prophesied the destruction of the ships.[13] The District Commissioner's version of the story was that he asked Harris to leave Axim because of a threatened shortage of food for the crowds coming to hear him. Father Stauffer endorsed the belief that the conflict arose over Sunday work.

> Prophet Harris was opposed to all work on Sundays and thus stopped the Krooboys from doing their work when even the mailboat called on Sundays. And this brought him into conflict with the authorities. The D.C. called him and strongly reprimanded him for his interference. Being sure of his power, he exclaimed, "Ah, you are not pleased! Well, I leave Axim town and you will see."[14]

Father Stauffer saw Harris as "inciting people to revolt"—although the revolt was nothing more than teaching against laws and practices contrary to God's will and law.

The prophet's position in the Gold Coast might be summarized

---

[10] Rev. Jean-Marie Bedel, as cited above, footnote 3.

[11] Casely Hayford, *William Waddy Harris. The West African reformer. Then man and his message*. London: C.M. Phillips 1915, 8.

[12] *Gold Coast Leader* 13 (727), 15 August 1914.

[13] *HN*

[14] Father Stauffer, 1914, Axim: Notes made in a diary sometime around or after 1926. General Archives, S.M.A., Rome.

as follows: Harris was not against the colonial administration, and in fact had a bias towards the British authority. He was in favour of good administration—but if the government did not obey God's will, the Christian population was expected to obey God's law regardless of the will of the government. God's judgement was pronounced against all who did not obey his law, including political and religious authorities.

Everything in the texts indicates that this was Harris's exact position before he arrived at Bingerville in September 1914. He did not regard himself as under the government's authority or control, but his attitude towards the French colonial regime was no less positive than towards the British. In fact he was predisposed to be favourable, because of the help that Nathaniel Seton had received from French colonial authorities during the 1910 War.

There is no mention in administrative reports of Harris's passage through the western areas of the Ivory Coast. However, reports coming from San Pedro, in October and December of 1913, mention an atmosphere of peace and hard work, and a turning away from "barbaric fetish practices" which could have come out of Harris's influence.[15] He was briefly imprisoned at San Pedro, and at Grand Lahou; arrested at Lozoua and Grand Bassam and again at Assinie where he was threatened with imprisonment unless he left immediately for the Gold Coast (summer 1914).

So when he arrived back in the Ivory Coast in September 1914, and had his interview with Governor Angoulvant, the transformation was from the side of the colony, not from Harris. And since the authorities recognised his ministry, he promoted respect for the authority. But his work was other than, and superior to, theirs. And when in December 1914 the governor turned against him, his work— the work of God—was still to prevail.

Such ascendancy is nowhere better illustrated than at the time of his arrest in the Grand Lahou area by the commandant, Corbière, who openly attacked his authority. When asked with scorn to justify his authority he referred to his Elijah mission, to Jesus Christ, and to Gamaliel's wisdom (Acts 5) that what is of God cannot be destroyed. He went on to give the *chef de cercle* his commission to go even to France and America to carry God's word. He continued until he was reminded by the Angel Gabriel that these "wise" men would never

---

[15] ICN Archives

be convinced by the foolishness of God.[16]

But even in this situation of open scorn and provocation, there is no anti-colonial note in Harris's response. He finds the commandant acting like a "heathen", but there is no anti-French, anti-white note. In Ahui's 1976 recital of his 1928 visit we come closer when Harris spoke of the French regime as "that heavy hand, the white man, that you have today and about which you have implored God because of the *chicottes* and all which you have endured." Even here the word is not anti-colonial; he deplores the rebellion and the breaking of God's laws, but seems to see the colonial regime as an instrument of judgement in God's hand.

His position seems to be close to that of Blyden: the white colonizers were certainly not the ideal, but at the time and in the circumstances the best there was, and necessary because of the African's lack of political expertise in the modern world. At that time Casely Hayford was of the same point of view (though this was later to change.)[17] Harris, looking forward as he was to the reign of Christ, could hardly be expected to think any human regime the ideal, and he had in 1912 predicted the great war in which the European powers would become involved.[18] But before that reign came, the French colonial administration was "the better of the bad" possibilities. And if it would, it could repent and be in fact God's instrument for good. . . . When the kingdom of Christ came, Harris the prophet would become a judge in a reign of peace. This was underlying his orientation throughout his mission through the coasts of the Ivory Coast and the western Gold Coast, and up to Axim, in June 1914.

His emphasis upon Christ's reign of peace, and his prophetic attitude towards violence, was something scarcely emphasised in the early accounts. Jean Rouch commented on it in 1963;[19] his information

---

[16] This is based on *BN* I, 25–26, 29, and has been defended as an interpretation in David A. Shank, "The problem of Christian cross-cultural communication illustrated." *Missiology* 7 (2), 1979, 221–7.

[17] This attitude was to change in the next years due to increased development in African political understandings. Hayford's evolution during this period can be traced in Robert W. July, *The origins of modern African thought. Its development in West Africa during the nineteenth and twentieth centuries.* London: Faber and Faber 1968. See especially chapter 21, "The metamorphosis of Casely Hayford", pp. 433–7.

[18] *Sierra Leone Weekly News*, 4 August 1917, 13.

[19] Jean Rouch, "Introduction à l'étude de la communauté de Bregbo", 1963, note 2, p. 15; also Jean Rouch, "Aspects du harrisme en Côte d'Ivoire. "Résumé by Vittorio Lanternari, in Convegno internazionale di Bouaké sui sincretismi e messianismi dell'Africa Nera. *Revista di antropologia* 50, 1963, 224f.

seems to have come from Harrists, with whom it has remained a tradition. It is taught in Harrist Christian education; the catechism *Premier Livre d'Education Religieuse* (1956) says "The prophet suffered humiliation and violence from the French authorities; never did he return a blow. On every occasion you must show yourself superior to your enemy by the forgiveness which you grant him, even in spite of himself."[20] The same tradition has been preserved among Harrists-become-Methodists, as reported to Haliburton by more than one elderly informant in 1963.[21]

This teaching on peace and non-violence—certainly implicit and, if Rouch is to be followed, explicit—was an additional mark against Harris in the view of a colonial administration whose metropolitan country was entering into a major war. In December 1914 the Ivory Coast administration started to raise its first contingent of 1,000 men for troops to be trained to fight in Europe. A message of non-violence at that moment could have been a threat to the colony's commitment. Ekanza has well demonstrated to what extent the "volunteers" in the Ivory Coast were conscripts who were constrained and forced—as with the "forced labour"—often in spite of their very strong opposition.[22] If Harris's influence in this area was similar to his influence on Sunday work, his presence was not wanted. His ethical stance was clearly undesirable, but his response was rooted in the confidence that God would render justice.

Harris not only did not give any word which would lead to rebellion (as might so easily have been the case), but continued to illustrate his own dignity by respecting those who showed him none. This is well confirmed by the understanding of Pastor Jean Mel at Pass among the Adjukru:

> The administration feared that Harris was spreading ill-feeling, because he spoke in English. Actually he was telling the people to obey the administration; if he had not done so they would have fought for him when he was expelled. There had been war between the French and the Adioukrous before the coming of Harris, and definitely his effect was to bring peace. Even under the wartime conscription, though the

---

[20] P.10 (my translation)
[21] *HN*, 20 July 1963; *HN*, Aizi
[22] In Simon-Pierre Ekanza, *Colonisation et sociétés traditionnelles. Un quart de siècle de dégradation du monde traditionnel ivoirien, 1893–1920.* 2 tomes, Aix-en-Provence, thesis 1972. Cf. T.II: Impérialisme colonial et société traditionnelle, 412–30.

mothers wept to see the finest boys of the village marched off to the army, the Adioukrous remained calm.[23]

One of those drafted in that period was John Ahui, the son of Chief Akadja of Petit Bassam. One suspects that the 1928 message dictated to the latter was bound up with this whole question: "No black man must go to Europe. There will be another great war in Europe."[24]

Liberia and Sierra Leone, 1915–25

After Harris's deportation to Liberia, his attitude towards the French colonial authorities did not change, particularly in view of their refusal to let him return to his churches. Father Harrington recorded his comment, "I cast its [the Ivory Coast's] dust from my feet, and the godless French government will be punished by God Almighty."[25] Following the words of Jesus (Matthew 10.14) Harris had literally turned the French colonial regime over to God's judgement . . . of fire. A political entity, like any other, was doomed and was to be eliminated (unless it repented) in a war that was still raging.

During his stay in the Ivory Coast, Harris was at times reputed to be an agent of German imperialism, particularly since the Germans were especially well installed commercially in Liberia.[26] Father Harrington questioned the prophet about reports on this topic which appeared in the press from Grand Bassam. Harris denied them emphatically. "What could I know about the Germans? What are they to me?" But he did not dismiss them as "god-less", as he did France.

---

[23] HN
[24] The local tradition at Grand Lahou, as reported through John Ahui in 1963, reveals also a kind of "tactic" of non-violence which is illustrative of a basic attitude.

> [The administrator] told him [Harris] he must go to his native village as quickly as possible. The prophet simply asked the Commandant to shoot him. The administrator shook his head and gave him knowledge of a letter unanimously addressed to him by the group opposed to those who wished the prophet not to return to Grand Lahou [HN]

The "power challenge" which he had utilized effectively against traditional practitioners was here applied to the Frenchman. The "power impact" of such an attitude was incommensurable; it is the defiance of one who knows he is absolutely invulnerable ("If they kill me, I go to heaven.")

[25] Peter Harrington, SMA, "An interview with the 'Black Prophet'." *The African Missionary* 18, (March-April) 1917, 13–16.
[26] *L'Indépendant de la Côte d'Ivoire* [Bibliothèque d'IFAN, Dakar] no. 66, 17 janvier 1915: **Départ du Prophète**.

Reports from Sierra Leone in the summer of 1917 make it clear that he was still denouncing the war in Europe as a consequence of transgression against God's law; he was also warning that the same things could happen in Africa, for the Gold Coast, Sierra Leone and Lagos were "blood-red in sin."[27] His prediction of the Great War was recalled, and, later, it was recalled that he had predicted another Great War.[28]

In 1918, when returning from Sierra Leone he told Father O'Herlihy in Kru country:

> when war is coming to end he must go to Europe to give his message there and will be chairman of the Peace Conference. Three minor prophets are to go with him but he is uncertain whether he will let them take part in the conference—and then he will go to see the king and Parliament.

Indeed earlier in the conversation he had described his "new mission as prophet: that he should bring all Africa to Christianity and when that was done he would be king of the whole country."[29] The strong preoccupation with peace, under his authority over the French and others, prevailed.

Cape Palmas, 1926

At the time of Benoît's visit, In September 1926, Harris's view of France remained just as intransigent as it had been in 1916.

> The time is short . . . God will send fire from heaven upon all rebels . . . And the prophet himself will send fire on Abidjan and Bingerville because the French government serves the devil and not the true God. . . . [BR I, 15]
>
> France go call me. Paris go call me, as Pharaon [sic] called Moses. You put big prophet in jail; prophet no man like you he is in transe— Moses and Elijah come to visit me [BN I, 13].
>
> When I say "I", I mean God. Tell Governor, "I" want to make peace with France. Jesus Christ said peace I bring unto you . . . Peace on earth. If they want peace, "I" bring peace. If fire, "I" bring fire. Christ will come . . . Peace on earth [BN II, 12].

---

[27] *Sierra Leone Weekly News*, 4 August 1917, [33 (49)] 13.
[28] *HN*
[29] Father Pat O'Herlihey, Diary 1918–21: Entry for 11 September 1918. SMA Archives, Cork, Ireland.

Here, *only as a result of his expulsion*, we find a new Moses-Pharaoh dialectic, which is suggested by Simon-Pierre Ekanza.[30] But it is the *consequence* of France's "hardening", and not the essential stance that Harris had at the time of his mission in the Ivory Coast. Here too, is a new prediction of the end of French domination over the Ivorian populations. In the *Benoît Notes*:

> The French must look out, otherwise war and fire will destroy them. Let them worship the only true God. The time is short. Let them repent and return to God, for this is the last warning [*BN* III,3].[31]

Our understanding of how Harris understood the situation is as follows: *The French have exercised their authority to pacify the tribes in the Ivory Coast. But their peace is not the peace on earth of Jesus Christ, and in fact, the authorities are in rebellion against that very peace. So they, and their seats of government (Abidjan and Bingerville) will be destroyed, unless they repent. A sign of that repentance would be their willingness to let the prophet continue his work, which is itself a sign of the coming reign of Christ. Their refusal would show that they support the present fetish-worship. The work of the prophet will not be destroyed, but will survive on into the reign of Christ.*

It is not clear that Benoît understood Harris in this respect. The editor of *BR* III appears to have read Harris's talk of peace with France (*BN* II, 12) as a sign that he had forgiven their authorities' earlier treatment of him. But the missionary superintendent understood; Platt wrote beside the "Message to Governor" three exclamation points and then "Not to be used in public! W.J.P."

And indeed this message to the governor was not made public. The Methodist missionaries were working hard to establish a cooperative relationship with the colonial administration; nor did they see France as being under the judgement of God in the same way that Harris did. It is quite likely that at the time of the Petit Bassam delegation in December 1928 Harris believed that the Methodists—like the Catholics before them—had "sold out" to a regime which was under judgement and destined to disappear. The report of John Ahui, which indicated that Harris himself accused the Methodists of "covering up" his predictions, appears to be fully authentic.

It is not possible to know how much of Harris's transformed attitude towards the French had filtered back into the Ivory Coast after 1915,

---

[30] Simon-Pierre Ekanza, *Colonisation et mission catholique en Basse Côte d'Ivoire*, 1895–1919. Aix-en-Provence, thesis 1970.

[31] My translation.

and how much it had influenced developing anti-French attitudes. But a possible connection cannot be excluded.

Cape Palmas, December 1928

There is a clear continuity between the *Benoît Notes* and the message to Chief Akadja Nanghui.

> France protests against Ethiopian rising. No black man must go to Europe. There will be another great war in Europe. The French have pronounced the prophet crazy, for this cause their native land "Belle France" will be terribly scourged.[32]

The continuity is found in the prediction of a war of judgement upon France because of the opposition to the "rising" of the Ivorians (Ethiopians)[33] under the impact of Harris's ministry. For Harris, the French attitude was consistent with their refusal of God's law and way, and of the prophet's ministry. He now saw French colonialism as no better than the Americo-Liberian regime in Liberia.

And of the Liberian Republic he had said, "Liberian Kru coast is finished." By 1928 the situation within Liberia had deteriorated to the extent that a year later a League of Nations Commission was to come to investigate serious charges coming from the Kru Coast, the abuses involved in the labour export "market" out of Sinoe, and the complicities of the Liberian authorities involved in the exploitative practices.

But the prophet still did not call for rebellion against powers in rebellion; the major question seemed to be: what does obedience to Christ call for? If obedience to Christ—as in keeping the Sabbath, the non-use of violence—led to an opposition to a regime in rebellion

---

[32] *Dictated Message to the Chief, Akadja Nanghui* and his people at Petit Bassam, Ivory Coast, via his son John Ahui, December 1928, copied on April 29, 1978, at the home of John Ahui at Petit Bassam. It was hand-written in a copy-page notebook with carbon copies for each page. John Ahui reported that it was written down by the woman Marie Agre on the same day that Harris's photo was taken with Ahui and his uncle, i.e., 13 December 1928.

[33] Sheila S. Walker, *op. cit.*, p. 158, attributes Harris's use of the term "Ethiopians" to his mistaken belief that France had actually invaded Ethiopia. But Harris's use of "Ethiopian" in the *Benoît Notes* is consistent with the universal usage in the 19th century first among American blacks and then African Christians: as a synonym for "African" or "black". It appears to derive from Psalm 68.31 [KJV]: "Ethiopia shall soon stretch out her hands to God." It was so used by Blyden. *Cf.* Maurice Leenhardt, *Le mouvement éthiopien au sud de l'Afrique de 1896–1899.* Cahors, 1902, 42f.

against Christ, that would, of course, result in difficulties. Benoît
questioned him on this very point:

> *Question* Didn't you know the French government would put you in prison
> [on return from the Gold Coast]?
> *Response* Yes, but I couldn't disobey. I had to go. God asked me to
> do so. If God asked me tonight to go again, I will go—and if they
> kill me alright. I won't die. I will raise again. (Here the face of the
> old [man] shines; he laughed quite loud full of joy) . . . raise with Christ
> [*BN* II, 8–9].

The lesson he had learned from his 1909 imprisonment was not, "Don't
revolt; you'll be punished and put in prison."[34] It was rather: "Don't
revolt; it is against Christ the Lord. Obey Christ the Lord even if
others interpret it as revolt."

Hence the report that Harris taught "obedience to authority" must
be seen in the light of this perspective. Balandier is correct when
he says of the Harris impact that "it was the administrative decisions
and missionary opposition which revealed itself as a force of con-
testation."[35] What was contested was the rebellion towards Christ of
those authorities which were intended to be "servants of God for
good."[36]

The French might later have had cause to regret that they expelled
the one man who might in time of crisis have helped them to re-
order the populations into the peace of Christ. But it was not possible;
they were fighting a war, and needed soldiers. The Roman Catholic
missionaries responded admirably to the call,[37] and were therefore
not available when tens of thousands, influenced by Harris, came
knocking on the doors of their churches. The "civilised" churches
were involved in helping to fight a "godless war." The prophetic
perspective was that obedience to Christ was essential, regardless of
the demands of the state.

---

[34] It was thus discerned by John Zarwan in "William Wade Harris: the genesis
of an African religious movement." *Missiology* 3 (4), 1975, 437.

[35] George Balandier, "Nouveaux mouvements religieux en Afrique." *Etudes Sociologiques*
6 (4), 1963–64, 23.

[36] Romans 13.4, in a passage of Scripture which Bishop Ferguson of the Episcopal
Church in Liberia often referred to as the basis of submission to "the powers that
be", meaning the Republic of Liberia, and not the Grebo chiefs!

[37] Bishop Moury himself became a simple corporal at Dakar and set the model
for a large part of the missionary corps who left the "battles of the Lord" in order
to do battle for France.

CHAPTER THIRTEEN

POST-SCRIPTUM

After having observed the messianic dynamics at work in the thought and ministry of the Prophet William Wadé Harris, it is perhaps not inappropriate to point out that his ultimate anti-Christ interpretation of the French colonial administration was to some extent justified. French "liberalism" did not permit direct attack on traditional religion as such, even though it openly attacked its social and judicial expressions. Harris, on the contrary, felt that "fetish worship" should have been denounced. But, in any case, during the period which followed Harris's expulsion, liberalism was not the controlling philosophy. There was an attempt to control religion, even when the "lay" character of the state should have required non-interference, and the French motif of freedom of conscience should have required an equality of respect for different religious traditions. The French Catholic Robert Delavignette, who was former head of the school of colonial administration, was well-placed to comment on this. He wrote:

> Some jurists, deeply set on religious tolerance, were also deeply moved at the idea that Christianity was undergoing strange deviations: Kimbanguism in the Belgian Congo, Harrism in Sierra Leone and the Ivory Coast, to mention only two examples between the two world wars. Thus one could observe the spectacle of a theoretically lay colonialism, imbued with the principle of liberty of conscience and worship, but which becomes the inquisitor for condemning, expelling, imprisoning those people which as such can become the object of a value judgement by a State which separates itself from all religion. In reality, and contrary to a common opinion, which travestied the missionaries as complaisant chaplains and the colonial government as tolerant despot, the relations between State and Church were not facilitated by the colonial system, and if one goes to the bottom of things, they reveal in a clear light, quite to the contrary, the antagonism between God and Caesar.[1]

Compared to Delavignette, Harris's words of judgement are not too harsh. What happened after 1920 demonstrates more clearly the real spirit with which he was confronted.

---

[1] Robert Delavignette, *Christianisme et colonialisme*. Paris: Fayard 1960, 72 [my translation].

In 1920 one of Harris's approved evangelists, the Fanti Goodman, made a complaint to the Bingerville administration. This led the governor, Antonetti, to send an administrator, Bourgine, to make a complete inquiry into the religious situation. Bourgine's two reports, of 28 May and 21 June 1920, were reported to Dakar by Antonetti himself. He made it clear that he did not want to combat religion.

> Much to the contrary, I esteem that a skilful power must know how to use all those who boast of having a celestial police force at their disposal, but I would be able to use them all the better if I were best-armed against them.[2]

This concern was taken up by Dakar in a report from the Governor General of the A.O.F., Merlin, to the Minister of Colonies at Bourdeaux.[3] It was essentially a request for administrative approval to combat—at Antonetti's request—"the principal of a state within a state, of the independence of the spiritual with regard to the temporal, and of the judiciary authority of priests with regard to their believers." He went on to say that these were ". . . principles from which an oral and uncontrolled teaching could draw consequences absolutely contrary to our domination."

> These tendencies, already subversive in themselves, are even more so because they destroy among those whom we administer that conviction—widespread among all primitive milieux—that authority is essentially mystical, and that the head exercises it as the direct representative of the superior Spirit. This idea, which provoked numerous submissions at the time of the French conquest, still maintains the least evolved parts of the population which yet remain quite numerous in an obedience and an acceptance of the *fait accompli*.

---

[2] ICN Archives, no. 629 GP, 4 November 1920.

[3] This document is on microfilm from the National Archives of Senegal (5 G 62: Affaires religieuses). The first three and last pages are missing, obliterating the destination and the sender. It is labelled by the archivist: "Incomplete text, not dated: Prophet Yessu." Haliburton (*PH*, 168) suggests that it represents comments by Lt. Gov. Antonetti on the Bourgine reports. However, Antonetti's own letter is cited in the document, along with Bourgine. The document is clearly from a higher authority than those two, passing on to his hierarchical superior information which had come to his attention along with his own recommendations. We assume it to be the "*rapport spécial et des propositions de réglementation concernant l'enseignement libre, l'établissement et la circulation des missionaires étrangers, européens ou indigènes, dans les colonies du groupe de l'A.O.F.*", which the Governor General, Merlin, referred to in a letter to the Minister of Colonies on 25 January 1921 (copy in SMA Archives, Rome, 10.607: 12/90402, 1921.)

He went on to discuss the implications of this fact: the native populations
would probably see in Harris's power, his use of English, the spread
of Protestantism, and the relationship between Protestantism and the
British Empire, a group of factors which would attribute more authority
to the British than to the French. He concluded, after noting that
the former policy towards missions, of non-intervention, could no longer
be followed:

> The guiding rules which it appears to me must be imposed are reduced
> to a simple proposition: favour the French missions [i.e. Roman Catholic]
> and dam up and control the foreign propaganda [i.e. Protestantism].

Such a proposition clearly betrayed the intention of the Protocol of
St. Germain, of 10 September 1919. Its signatories agreed to support
and encourage in the African colonies all religious propaganda
irrespective of the allied nation from which it came. But the French
administration, by passing strict linguistic laws and very tight educational controls, was able to make it well-nigh impossible for British
or American missionaries to function within the French colonies. At
the same time it felt that it would be "equitable and political" to
reserve favourable treatment for the Catholic missions because they
would "work in the direction of our national interests, and their patriotic
loyalties would oppose any anti-French tendencies of Anglo-Saxon or
American catechists."

Here was stated clearly the policy which was in fact already operative
in 1914, and was responsible for Harris's expulsion, the imprisonment
of the clerks, the destruction or confiscation of the Harrist chapels,
and finally the harassment of many Harris disciples into the Catholic
fold.

Harris perceived this policy for what it was—an antagonism between
Caesar and God. And for him, the French Caesar became anti-Christ.
And as the Governor General wrote six years later, it made a conscious
decision to betray its own traditional secular political philosophy.

One of the Protestant documents from an English mission which
clearly upset the administration was in a catechetical text:[4]

> What obedience for the salvation of Christ is due by the Church and
> all its members to the civil authority of the State?
> Christians are held to obey in civil matters all rules which concern

---

[4] It is highly probable that it was with the documentation which Rev. Mark Hayford

property and taxes; they must present themselves before the courts and submit themselves to the orders laid down, in order to maintain civic order. However, since obedience to Jesus Christ is above all, *every State which disobeys Him receives from Him no authority whatsoever. And no Christian ought to appeal to the civil authority against another Christian as long as all of the means of conciliation indicated by the Church will not have failed.* [Italics as in the original]

This text is not from Harris yet the sentiments are not far distant from his thinking as we have perceived it evolving and the basic position it demonstrates, one adhered to by Harris, was essentially that of the early church in its relationship to the Roman empire. It has been characterized as one of *patientia*,[5] grounded in the knowledge that Christ's authority was definitive and would in fact undo and overcome the sacral authority of the Roman Empire. It therefore required no use of material weapons to combat it. Indeed, the subversive character of this Christian position has been described as one of "revolutionary subordination".[6] These views help to underscore Harris's holistic religio-political position in relation to the governmental authorities of his time. He was definitely not a-political, as suggested by a recent researcher who saw Harris simply "as an evangelist who wanted to save souls for Jesus."[7]

Our own study began with a description of three African Christians from Liberia who

> headed east by foot for the French colony of the Ivory Coast . . . in response to the commission of Jesus Christ . . . : Go and teach all nations, baptising them in the name of the Father, the Son and the Holy Ghost . . .[8]

It would be possible to interpret these lines as meaning, with Zarwan, a mission to "save souls for Jesus." But the intent of Harris was much broader than that. It was involved in bringing all nations under the political, peaceful rule on the earth of the messiah Jesus of Nazareth through his prophet—the last one before the fulfilment of all things in that Kingdom. Perhaps he did not articulate it so clearly; but the

---

had given to the colonial officials to justify his work and position. It is probably also the reason he was refused entry to the Ivory Coast. The text is found in the Merlin report.

[5] Jean-Michel Hornus, *Evangile et labarum*. Geneva: Labor et Fidès, 1960.

[6] John Howard Yoder, *The politics of Jesus*. Grand Rapids: Eerdmans 1972. See chapter 9, *passim*.

[7] Zarwan, article cited.

[8] See chapter I, above, citing Matthew 28.19.

exegesis of his practice makes clear the powerful political dynamics which the text makes explicit for whomever sees Jesus as Messiah, to whom "all power is given ... in heaven and in earth."[9]

In reflecting upon messianism in Central Africa, Roger Bastide has well written:

> Beyond the phenomena of colonisation, indeed, these messianisms are inscribed within a historic movement which was quite earlier and goes infinitely beyond it, that of the propagation of Christianity amidst all the peoples of the earth starting with the little corner of Judea where the Christ was born and launched his message to the world. But in this long itinerary, this message, in order to be understood, must be incarnated in another language than its primitive language and mould itself in new systems of social institutions—those for example of the Greek *cité*, of the Roman empire or of Celtic clans; it must also take into account all of the contingencies of a time which it registers in facts, and accept to change in order to be able to change the world in return. There is then a process of reciprocal adaptation which is well known to us, for the past, thanks to the work of historians, although certain ones have favoured the facts of discontinuity and others have on the contrary favoured the facts of continuity. Let us say, in Gurvitchian terms, that the history of Christianity is that of a discontinued continuity or of a continued discontinuity.[10]

In two decades, Harris the prophet inscribed in the facts of the West Africa of his time such a messianic discontinuity, but as a part of the ongoing Christian continuum; its effects will continue on beyond nations and states, as partial answer to the prayer that he prayed and taught to pray: "Thy kingdom come on earth as it is in heaven." Compared to the fortunes of colonialism during the sixty-five years since his death, the promise of his colorful parable has weathered well:

> When spider spins his web under the eaves of a hut or in the fork of a tree, it sometimes happens that a tornado blows the hut down or uproots the tree; spider dies, but his web remains. The web that I spin, no one will be able to destroy.[11]

---

[9] Matthew 28.18. For comparison, one might well consult Karl Barth, "An exegetical study of Matthew 28. 16–20", in Gerald M. Anderson (ed.), *The Theology of Christian Mission*. Nashville: Abingdon 1961, 55–71.

[10] Roger Bastide, Préface, in Martiàl Sinda, *Les Messianismes congolais*. Paris: Payot 1972, 8 (translation by D. Shank).

[11] Cited by André Roux, Un prophète: Harris, *Le Monde Noir*, special number of *Présence Africaine* 8–9, 1950, p. 137 [my translation].

BIBLIOGRAPHY

The bibliography lists those items dealing specifically with the Prophet Harris and his ministry. Although many of the items also cover related questions the bibliography does not attempt to deal with Harrism or the Harrist Church as a movement. For this one may well consult the bibliography in the work of Sheila Walker, 1983.

African Missionary, The
  1917   No. 20, July, August. [Photo of] Harris the Black 'Prophet' who is stirring up the West Coast of Africa by a vigorous preaching of a Gospel of his own!
  1930   No. 30, January. "'Black Elijah' Dead." 17, 20.
African Spiritual Revival
  1981   "Harris: a prophet for Africans." No. 2, 6–7.
Ahui, W.H. Paul William.
  1988   *La prophète William Wadé Harris: son message d'humilité et progrès*. Abidjan: Les Nouvelles Editions Africaines. 348pp., annexes, plates, bibliography, index.
Allegret, Elie
  1923a   "La situation des peuples de l'A.O.F. et de l'A.E.F. 1822–1922." *Jubilé centenaire de la Société des Missions Evangéliques*. Paris: Société des Missions Evangéliques, 142–177.
  1923b   "The missionary question in the French colonies." *International Review of Missions* 46, 161–181.
Amon d'Aby, F.J.
  1951   *La Côte d'Ivoire dans la cité Africaine*. Paris: Editions Larose.
  1960   *Croyances religieuses et coutumes juridiques des Agni de la Côte d'Ivoire*. Paris: Editions Larose.
Amos-Djoro, Ernest
  1956   *Les mouvements marginaux du protestantisme africain: les Harristes en Côte d'Ivoire*. Paris: Ecole Pratique des Hautes Etudes, Vème Section.
  c.1965   "Prophétisme et nationalisme Africain: les Harristes en Côte d'Ivoire." Unpublished MS.
  1966   "Les églises Harristes et le nationalisme ivoirien." *Le mois en Afrique* 5 (May), 26–47.
  1989   *Harris et la chrétienté en Côte d'Ivoire*. Abidjan: Les Nouvelles Editions Africaines. 60pp., plates.
Armstrong, Charles W. (Rev.)
  1915   "The appeal of Apollonia." Foreign Field 11 (April), 200–211.
  1920   *The winning of West Africa*. London: Wesleyan Methodist Missionary Society.
Arnaut, Robert
  1976   *L'Afrique du jour et de la nuit*. Paris: Presses de la Cité.
Augé, Marc
  1975   *Théorie des pouvoirs et idéologie*. Paris: Hermann.
  1977   *Pouvoirs de vie, pouvoirs de mort*. Paris: Flammarion.
Baëta, C.G.
  1962   *Prophetism in Ghana: a study of some 'spiritual' Churches*. London: SCM Press.

Babi, René
  1969   "L'Eglise Harriste de Côte d'Ivoire. Naissance et Expansion." *Eburnea*,
          September, 2ff.
Balandier, Georges
  1955   *Sociologie actuelle de l'Afrique noire*. Paris: P.U.F.
Bastide, Roger
  1968   "Préface", in Maria Isaura Pereira de Queiroz, *Réforme et révolution dans
          les sociétés traditionelles*. Paris: Anthropos.
Bedel, Jean-Marie (R.P.)
          "'*Le prophète Harris*'. *Souvenirs 1908–38*", in archives of Archiepiscopal
          Diocese of Abidjan.
Bee, Michel
  1970   *Les Missions en Basse Côte d'Ivoire 1895–1939*. Thèse de 3ème cycle,
          Université de Paris (Sorbonne). 2 vols. [See 2nd vol., chapter 2, 255ff.]
Benoît, Pierre
  1926a   *Benoît Notes*. London: Methodist Mission Archives (held at SOAS).[=BN
          I, II. III]
  1926b   *Story of the finding of the prophet William Wadé Harris*. London: MMS Archives
          [=Benoît Report].
Beugré, Alphonse *et al*. (eds.)
  1986   *Alisinya la Afluwa*. Adidjan: Summer Institute of Linguistics.
Beugré, Dja Daniel
  1968   *Les religions didas*. Mémoire presented at E.P.H.E., VIème section, Paris.
Benz, Ernst
  1965   *Messianische Kirchen, Sekten und Bewegungen im Heutigen Afrika*. Leiden: Brill.
Bianquis, Jean
  1924   *Le prophète Harris*. Paris: Société des Missions Evangéliques (Reprint from
          Foi et Vie, 16 Nov. and 1 Dec.
Birkeli, Emil
  1928   *Vekkelsen i Vest-Afrika*. Stavanger: Det Norske Misjonsselskaps Vorlag (see
          37–64).
Bonhomme, [Rev. Père]
  1915   "Lettre du Père Bonhomme . . ." *Echo des Missions Africaines de Lyon* 14
          (2).
Boyé Aké, Alphonse
  1980   *La harriste face à sa religion*. [Anono-Abidjan].
Breidenbach, Paul
  1973   *Sunsum Edwuma, the spiritual work: forms of symbolic action and communication
          in a Ghanaian healing cult*. Ph.D. thesis, Northwestern University.
  1979a   "Madame Harris Grace Tani and Papa Kwesi John Nackbah: Inde-
          pendent Church leaders in the Gold Coast. 1914–1958." *International
          Journal of African Historical Studies* 12 (4), 581–614.
  1979b   "The woman on the beach and the man in the bush: leadership and
          adepthood in the Twelve Apostles Movement of Ghana," in Bennetta
          Jules-Rosette (ed.), *The new religions of Africa*. Norwood, N.J.: Ablex
          Publishing Corporation. 99–115.
Brou, Alexandre (Rev. Père)
  1925   "Afrique—le prophétisme protestant." *Etudes* (Paris) 184 (24), 730–747.
  1931   "Le prophétisme dans les églises protestantes indigènes d'Afrique." *Revue
          d'Histoire des Missions* 8(1), 71–84.
Bruce, Ernest (Rev.)
  1957   "I grew up with history." *Africa Challenge* 7 (4), 6 and 10.
  1961   "Reminiscences of Ghana Methodism." *Foundation Conference Report*, Methodist
          Church of Ghana.
Buell, Raymond Leslie
  1928   *The native problem in Africa*, vol. 2. New York: Macmillan.

Bureau, René
1971 "Le prophète Harris et le harrisme." *Annales de l'université d'Abidjan. Ethnosociologie*, série F. (3), 33–196. [With notes = RB N]
1975 "La religion du prophète Atcho," in Colette Piault a.o., *Prophétisme et thérapeutique*. Paris: Hermann, 87–119.
Campbell, (Mr.)
1924 "Rapport sommaire sur les actes du prophète Wurry Harris pendant un séjour de quelques mois à la Côte d'Ivoire (fin de l'année 1913 au début de l'année 1914)." Appendix I in Bianquis 1924 (above), 33–35.
Cangah, Guy, and Simon-Pierre Ekanza
1978 *La Côte d'Ivoire par les textes*. Abidjan: Les Nouvelles Editions Africaines.
Cason, John Walter
1962 *The growth of Christianity in the Liberian environment*. Columbia University, Ph.D. thesis (University Microfim, 1975).
Ching, Donald S.
[1947] *Old Man Union Jack. The story of Prophet Harris*. London: Cargate Press.
1950 *Ivory Tales*. London: Epworth Press.
1955 "La vie du prophète Harris." *Envol* (Abidjan) May 17–18. (Text based on Ching).
Chirgwin, A.M.
1931 *Yarns on men of Africa*. London: Edinburgh House Press, 46–54.
Christian Herald and Signs of our Times, The
1925 "The African 'Elijah'. Missionary discovers 22,000 Black Christians." 59 (26), 25 June, 326.
Collins, J. (Rev.)
1916 Diary 1913–1919. S.M.A. Archives, Cork, Ireland.
Cooksey, J.J. and Alexander McLeish
1931 *Religion and civilization of West Africa*. London: World Dominion Press.
d'Anna. Andrea
1966 *De Cristo à Kimbangu*. Madrid: Ediciones Combonianas. See El Harrisme, 121–128.
de Billy. Edmond
1931 *En Côte d'Ivoire. Mission Protestante d'A.O.F.* Paris: Société des Missions Evangéliques.
1955 "Le prophète Harris en Côte d'Ivoire." *Envol*, March, 17, 19.
Debrunner, Hans
1959 *Witchcraft in Ghana*. Kumasi: Presbyterian Book Depot.
1967 *A history of Christianity in Ghana*. Accra: Waterville Publishing House.
Decorvet, J.
1977 *Les matins de Dieu*. Nogent-sur-Marne: Mission Biblique en Côte d'Ivoire, rev. 2nd ed.
Delafosse, Maurice
1921 "Sur l'orientation nouvelle de la politique indigène dans l'Afrique noire." *L'Afrique française: Renseignements Coloniaux* 6, 145–152.
1924 "L'Ahmadisme et son action en Afrique Orientale Française." *L'Afrique française: Renseignements Coloniaux* 1, 32–36.
Desroche, Henri
1969 *Dieux d'Hommes*. Paris: Mouton.
1973 *Sociologie de l'espérance*. Paris: Calmann-Levy.
Doji, Robert
1982 "L'histoire du prophète Harris," in [Denis Masson] *A Ca Didà. Apprenons le Dida*. Abidjan: Société Int. Linguistique, 38–44.
Duprey, Pierre
1962 *Histoire des Ivoiriens: naissance d'une nation*. Abidjan: Ministère de l'Education Nationale.

Ekanza, Simon-Pierre
    1970   *Administration coloniale et mission catholique en Côte d'Ivoire (1893–1919)*.
            Université de Provence, mémoire de Maître de l'Histoire, 1969–70.
    1972   *Colonisation et sociétés traditionnelles. Un quart de siècle de dégradation du monde
            traditionnel ivoirien 1893–1920*. Université de Provence, thèse de 3ème
            cycle. 2 vols.
    1975   "Le messianisme en Côte d'Ivoire au début du siècle; une tentative de
            réponse nationaliste à l'état de situation coloniale." *Annales de l'Université
            d'Abidjan*, Série I t.III Histoire, 55–71.
Fenton, Thomas
    [1954] *God's red road*. London: Cargate Press.
    1956   *Black harvest*. London: Cargate Press.
Foley, David Michael
    1963   *British policy in Liberia, 1862–1912*. University of London, Ph.D. thesis.
Fraser, Donald
    1927   "The Prophet Harris. An amazing story of the African coast." *The Scots
            Observer*, 7 May, page 8.
Friesen, J. Stanley
    1973   "The significance of indigenous movements for the study of church
            growth," in Wilbert R. Shenk (ed.) *The challenge of church growth. A symposium*.
            Elkhart, Indiana: Institute of Mennonite Studies, 79–106.
Freligh, Marie
    1930   "The history of the Ivory Coast mass movement toward God." *The Alliance
            Weekly*, 65 (21), May 24.
["Ghanaian"]
    [1981] *Le prophète William Wade Harrisson*. n.p., n.d. Printed by B.C.E.T., Abidjan.
            6p.
Girard, Jean
    1974   "Réfutation du Harrisme comme source de la religion Déïma", Annexe
            1, note, in *Prophètes paysans de l'environnement noir*. T.I. Grenoble: Presses
            Universitaires de Grenoble, 427–432.
Gollock, Georgina
    1928   *Sons of Africa*. London: SCM Press. (German translation, Berlin, 1930)
Gorju, Joseph [Rev.]
    1912   *La Côte d'Ivoire chrétienne*. Lyon: Ve M Paquet.
    1915a   "Un prophète à la Côte d'Ivoire." *Les Missions Catholiques*, 2400, 267–
            268.
    1915b   "Un prophète à la Côte d'Ivoire." *L'Echo des Missions Africaines de Lyon*,
            14 (4), 110–119.
    1917   "La Côte d'Ivoire pendant la guerre." *Missions Catholiques*, 478, 577–
            580.
Goudie, W[illiam]
    1915a   Report of visit to West Africa. London: MMS Archives.
    1915b   "Missions and the changed outlook." *Methodist Recorder* 56 (2998), 6 May,
            5.
Gramberg, Th[eodor] B[erthold] W[illem] G[erhard]
    1935   *Aggrey en het Negervraagstuk in Afrika en Amerika*. The Hague: Algemeene
            Boekhandel voor Inwendige en Uitwendige Zending te den Haag.
Greschat, Hans-Jürgen
    1974   *West Afrikanische Propheten. Morphologie einer religiösen Spezialisierung*. Berlin:
            Dietrich Reimer.
Grivot, R.
    1942   "La cercle de Lahou (Côte d'Ivoire)." *Bulletin de l'Institut Français d'Afrique
            Noire*, IV, Jan-Oct., 1–154.

Guaraglia, Guglielmo
1959   *Prophetismus und Heilserwartungs-Bewegungen als völkkundliches und religions-geschichtliches Problem.* Horn Vienna: Verlag Ferdinand Berger.
Guilcher, René F. (Rev.), S.M.A.
[1937]   *En Côte d'Ivoire avec nos missionnaires.* Lyon: Procure des Missions Africaines.
Haliburton, G[ordon] M[ackay]
1964   "The Anglican Church in Ghana and the Harris Movement in 1914." *Bulletin of the Society for African Church History,* i (3–4), 101–106.
1962   "The Prophet Harris and the Methodist Church." London: unpublished paper.
1966   *The Prophet Harris and his work in Ivory Coast and Western Ghana.* University of London: Ph.D, thesis.
1971a   "The Prophet Harris and the Grebo rising of 1910." *Liberian Studies Journal* 3 (1), 31–39.
1971b   *The Prophet Harris. A study of an African prophet and his mass-movement in the Ivory Coast and the Gold Coast, 1913–1915.* London: Longman.
1973   *The Prophet Harris.* New York: Oxford University Press.
1984   *Le prophète Harris.* Abidjan: NEA (trans. of 1973 above).
Hargreaves, John D.
1969   "Prophet Harris", in John D. Hargreaves (ed.), *France and West Africa.* London: Macmillan, 247–252.
Harrington, Peter
1917a   "An interview with the 'Black Prophet'". *The African Missionary* 18 (March-April), 13–16.
1917b   "Une entrevue avec le Prophète noir." *Echo des Missions Africaines de Lyon* 16 (5), 155–161; 16 (6), 191–195.
1977   "Lettera del padre Harrington." *SMA* 66, 17 (1), 28–32.
Hartz, Joseph (Rev.)
1925   "Ein sonderbarer schwarzer Prophet." *Afrikanisches Missions-Glocklein (St. Pierre, Bas Rhin, France) 3 (3), 56–60. [See French text in von Bulck, and English text in Hargreaves.]*
Hayford, Casely [Ekra-Agyiman]
1915   *William Waddy Harris. The West African reformer. The man and his message.* London: C.M. Phillips.
[Hegba, Meinrad]
1979   "Le Harrisme." *Pirogue* (January-March), 20–21.
Hogan, E.M.
1981   *Catholic missionaries and Liberia.* Cork: University Press.
Holas, Bohumil
1965   *Le séparatisme religieux en Afrique noire.* Paris: P.U.F.
Holden, Edith
1981   *Blyden of Liberia* New York: Vantage Press.
Holt, Dean Arthur
1970   *Change strategies initiated by the Protestant Episcopal Church in Liberia from 1836 to 1958 and their differential effects.* Boston University School of Education, Ed.D. dissertation [University Microfilms 1975].
Hosmer, Rachel (Rev. Sister), A.S.H.
1969   The Prophet Harris. Columbia University Institute of African Studies, typed MS, 42pp. See ftn. 179; and *Historical Magazine of the Protestant Episcopal Church* 48 (3), 1979, 331–356.
Joseph, Gaston
1916   "Une atteinte à l'animisme chez les populations de la Côte d'Ivoire." *Annuaire et Mémoires du Comité d'études historiques et scientifiques de l'Afrique occidentale française.* Gorée (Dakar): imprimerie du Gouvernement Général, 344–348.

1917   *La Côte d'Ivoire. Le Pays, Ses Habitants*. Paris: Emile Larose, 155–160
            [A. Fayard 1944].
Jones, H[annah] A[beodu] B[owen]
1962   *The struggle for political and cultural unification in Liberia 1847–1930*. North-
            western University, Ph.D. thesis.
Kaké, I.B.
1981   "Harris, le prophète des lagunes." *Bingo*, March, 10–11.
Korte, Werner
1971–72   "A note on independent churches in Liberia." *Liberian Studies Journal*,
            4 (1), 81–87.
1976   "Religiöse Dissidenten, Propheten und Kultgründungen im südöstlichen
            Liberia in 19. und 20. Jahrhundert." *Sociologus* 26 (1), 1–28.
Kouadio, André
            Histoire de l'église C.M.A. en Côte d'Ivoire. 10pp. typed MS.
Kouassi Bossou Gôh, Benoît
1983   *Jonas Ahui, Prédicateur Suprême de la Religion Harriste, Successeur de Prophète
            William Wadé Harris*. Printed in Abidjan: 35pp, 17 plates.
Krabill, James R.
1990   "William Wadé Harris (1860–1929): African evangelist and Ethno-
            hymnologist." *Mission Focus* 18 (4), 56–9
Lanternari, Vittorio
1963   *The religions of the oppressed*. London: MacGibbon and Kee.
Leenherdt, R.H. (Rev.)
1949   'Les missions protestantes', in "L'œuvre des missions". *Afrique Occidentale
            Française. Encyclopédie Coloniale de l'Empire Français*.
Légbedji-Aka, Bertin-Charles
1966   Le Protestantisme Méthodiste et les Odjukru de la Côte d'Ivoire. Porto
            Novo: Mémoire de l'Ecole Pastorale Evangélique MMS.
Lehmann, Jean and René Bureau
1977   Le Prophète. Pouvoirs et guérison en Côte d'Ivoire, Unpublished MS.
Liberian Conference Blue Book
1916   The Situation in Africa. Monrovia: College of West Africa Press,
            January.
Lipschutz, Mark R. and R. Kent Rasmussen
1978   *Dictionary of African historical biography*. London: Heinemann.
Livingstone, Thomas W.
1975   *Education and race: a biography of Edward Wilmot Blyden*. London: Frank
            Cass.
Lynch, Hollis R.
1967   *Edward Blyden. Pan-African patriot 1832–1912* London: Oxford University
            Press
1971   *Black spokesman. Selected published writings of Edward Wilmot Blyden*. London:
            Frank Cass.
1978   *Selected letters of Edward Wilmot Blyden*. Millwood, New York: KTO Press.
Maire, Charles-Daniel
1975   *Dynamique sociale des mutations religieuses. Expansions des Protestantismes en Côte
            d'Ivoire*. Paris: EPHE.
Martin, Jane Jackson
1968   *The dual legacy: government authority and mission influence among the Glebo of
            Eastern Liberia, 1834–1910*. Boston University, Ph.D. thesis.
Marty, Paul
1922   *Etudes sur l'Islam en Côte d'Ivoire*. Paris: Leroux
Matthiesen, H.I.F.C.
1928   *Harris et nutidseventyr fra Elfenbenskysten*. Copenhagen: O. Lohse.

M'Bokololo, Elkia
1981 "The prophet Harris." *Balafon* (Air Afrique) 51, 2nd quarter, 30–35.
Moly, L.
1922 "Les Aladians." *Echo des Missions Africaines de Lyon*, 21 (12), 179–180.
Morris, Barry T.
1983 *Some early Protestant responses to the Harrist movement in the Ivory Coast. The work of the "clerks": 1913–1924.* SOAS, University of London, M.A. thesis.
O'Herlihy, Pat (Rev.)
1918 Diary, 1918–21. S.M.A. Archives, Cork.
Oldham, J.H. (ed.)
1915 "A missionary survey of the year 1915." *International Review of Missions*, 4, 3ff., 40–44.
1917 "A missionary survey of the year 1917." *International Review of Missions*, 6, 44ff.
O'Sullivan, John
1972 "The prophets and the tradition." *African Religious Research* (UCLA) 2 (1), 50–55.
Piault, Colette (ed.)
1975 *Prophétisme et thérapeutique.* Paris: Hermann (Collection Savoir).
Pilkington, F.W.
1952 "Old Man 'Union Jack': William Wadé Harris, prophet of West Africa." *West African Review*, 23 293, 122–123, 125.
Platt, W.J. (Rev.)
1934 *An African prophet: the Ivory Coast movement and what came of it.* London: SCM Press.
1935 *From fetish to faith. The growth of the church in West Africa.* London: Edinburgh House Press.
Poivre, N.
1946 *Fils et filles d'Afrique adapté de Sons of Africa and Daughters of Africa de G.A. Gollock.* Paris and Geneva: Société des Missions Evangéliques de Paris.
Premier livret de l'éducation à l'usage de l'Episcopat
1956 Petit Bassam: Programme de l'Episcopat.
Price, F[rederick] A.
1954 *Liberian Odyssey.* New York: Pageant Press.
Price-Mars, Jean
1960 *Silhouettes de Nègres et de Négrophiles.* Paris: Présence Africaine.
Pritchard, John
1973 "Le prophète Harris et le Méthodisme Ivoirien." *Flambeau* (Yaoundé), February, 62–64.
1973 "The prophet Harris and Ivory Coast." *Journal of Religion in Africa*, 5 (1), 23–31.
Ringwald, Walter
1940 "Westafrikanische Propheten." *Evangelische Missions Zeitschrift*, 1 (4), 118–122.
Roseberry, R[obert] S[herman]
1934 *The Niger vision.* Harrisonburg: Christian Publications Inc.
1935 *Black magic. The challenge of an open door.* Chicago: Worldwide Prayer and Missionary Union.
Rouch, J.
1963 "Introduction à l'étude de la communauté de Bregbo." *Journal de la société des africanistes* (Paris), 33 (1), 129–202.
Roux, André
1971a *Un prophète: Harris. Présence Africaine* Nos. 8–9, 133–140. (Special number: *Le Monde Noir*).

1971b   *L'évangile dans la forêt. Naissance d'une église en Afrique Noire.* Paris: Editions
            Cerf.
Schlosser, Katesa
1949   *Propheten in Afrika.* Braunschweig: Albert Limbach.
Schutz, Louis
1942   "William Wadé Harris und seine Massenbewegung." *Evangelisches Missions-
            Magasin* (Basel), 86 (3), 83–92.
Seamands, John T.
1967   *Pioneers of the younger churches.* Nashville, Tennessee: Abingdon Press.
Sedji-Abouya, Solomon
1974   *L'évangile de la forêt à la cité: une approche sociologique de la mission de l'église
            protestante méthodiste en Côte d'Ivoire.* Paris, Faculté de Théologie protestante.
            Mémoire de licence, 53pp.
Shank, David A.
1979   "The problem of Christian cross-cultural communication illustrated:
            research notes on 'The finding of the Prophet Harris by M. Benoît'".
            Missiology 7 (2), 211–231.
1980   *A prophet of modern times. The thought of William Wadé Harris, West African
            precursor of the reign of Christ.* University of Aberdeen, Scotland, Ph.D,
            dissertation, 3 vols.
1983   "Bref résumé de la pensée du Prophète William Wadé Harris." *Perspectives
            Missionnaires* 5 (1983), 34–54.
            The Prophet Harris: a historiographical and bibliographical survey.
            Journal of Religion in Africa xiv, 2, 130–160.
1985   "The Harrist Church in the Ivory Coast" (review article). *Journal of Religion
            in Africa* 15 (1), 67–75.
1986   "The legacy of William Wadé Harris." *International Bulletin of Missionary
            Research* 10 (4), October, 170–176.
Simon, Marc
1965   *Souvenirs de Brousse 1905–1918: Dahomey—Côte d'Ivoire.* Paris: Nouvelles
            Editions Latines.
South African Outlook (Lovedale)
1927   "West African Prophet found." 57 (672), 97–98.
Southon, A.E.
1929   *More King's Servants.* London: Cargate Press.
Stanton, Gregory H.
1975   The Harrist Movement in the Ivory Coast. University of Chicago,
            Department of Anthropology. Unpublished MS.
Tasie, G[odwin] O[nyemeachi] M[gbechi]
1975   "Christian awakening in West Africa, 1914–1918: a study of the
            significance of native agency." *West African Religion* (Nsukka), 16 (2), 45–
            50.
Thompson, E.W.
1928   "The Ivory Coast: a study in modern missionary methods." *International
            Review of Missions* 17 (68), 630–644.
Trichet, (Rev. Père)
1979   "Regard sur le passé du diocèse d'Abidjan." *Nouvelles de l'Eglise d'Abidjan*
            6, 20–27.
Van Bulck, G.
[1961]   "Le prophète Harris vu par lui-même (Côte d'Ivoire, 1914). In Museum
            Messianum, *Devant les sectes non-Chrétiennes.* Louvain: Desclée de Brouwer,
            120 124.
Van Trigt, F.

1948   "De Profeet Harris." *Afrika Ontwaakt* (Oosterbeek, Tafelberg, Netherlands), 19 (4), 59–61.

Walker, F[rank] D[eaville]
[1925]   *The day of harvest in the white fields of West Africa.* London: Cargate Press.
1926a   *The story of the Ivory Coast.* London: Cargate Press (lst ed. June).
1926b   *The story of the Ivory Coast.* (2nd impression with "Addendum" of two pages.
1927a   "The Prophet Harris found at last. The story of M. Benoît's visit to him." *Foreign Field* (London), February, 136–141.
1927b   "More about the Prophet Harris. New information about his personal life." *Foreign Field*, March, 136–141.
1931   *Harris, le prophète Noir: instrument d'un puissant réveil en Côte d'Ivoire.* Privas (Ardêche): ed. par pasteur S. Delattre.

Walker, Sheila S.
1975   [Review of] *The Prophet Harris by Gordon Mackay Haliburton. International Journal of African Studies* 8, Supplement A, 73–79.
1976   *Christianity African style. The Harrist Church of the Ivory Coast.* University of Chicago, Ph.D. thesis.
1979   "The message as the medium. The Harrist Churches of the Ivory Coast and Ghana", in George Bond, Walton Johnson and Sheila Walker (eds.), *African Christianity. Patterns of religious continuity.* New York: Academic Press, 9–64.
1983   *The religious revolution in the Ivory Coast. The Prophet Harris and his church.* Chapel Hill, N.C.: University of North Carolina Press.

Walls, A.F.
1972   "African Church history: some recent studies" (Review article). *Journal of Ecclesiastical History* 23 (2), 161–169.

Weiskel, Timothy
1976   *French colonial rule and the Baule peoples: resistance and collaboration 1889–1911.* London: Oxford University Press.

Welch, A.W.
1979   *Colonial stepchildren: Catholic and Methodist missionaries in the Ivory Coast, 1845–1939.* University of Birmingham, Ph.D. thesis.

Williams, Walter B.
1928   *God's avenging sword....* Sino-Kroo District, Liberia.

Williams, Walter B. and Maude Wigfield Williams
1955   *Adventures with the Krus in West Africa.* New York: Vantage Press.

Wondji, Christopher
1977   *Le prophète Harris. Le Christ noir des lagunes.* Paris: ABC and Dakar/Abidjan: NEA, 96.

Wood, Paul
1924   "Courrier Missionnaire. La Côte d'Ivoire." *L'Evangéliste*, 72 (12), 50f.

Wilson, Bryan
1973   *Magic and the Millennium.* New York: Harper and Row. Cf. p. 174, 152, 35 (note).

Yando, Emmanuel
1970   *L'évolution du Harrisme en Côte d'Ivoire.* Paris: Faculté Libre de Théologie Protestante.

Zarwan, John
1975   "William Wadé Harris: the genesis of an African religious movement." *Missiology* 3 (4), 10. (Resumé of William Wadé Harris, Stanford University 1970: Senior Honours thesis).

Zimmerman, Ada M. and Catherine Leatherman
1936   *Africa calls.* Scottdale, Pa.: Mennonite Publishing House.

INDEX

conversion and baptism 48; 49;
57–61; 170
education 64
work
kruboy 52–4; 148
miner? 54
military duty 66
catechist and teacher 64–8;
78–80
interpreter 3; 77; 80; 82
marriage and family
first wife (Rose Farr) 61–2; 64;
106; 109; 111; 115; 129
children 22; 63–4; 68; 78; 102;
108; 123; 129; 191
later marriages and traditional
wives 11; 20; 21–2; 109;
161–2; 163; 164
grandchildren 22ⁿ; 239
religious history
Methodist upbringing 46; 47–52;
154–5
Episcopalian influences 155; 170
confirmation 62; 63–4
layreader 77; 78
conflict with ecclesiastical
authority 80–2
suspended from church
duties 86–7
rebel
involvement in attempted *coup
d'état* 3; 170
Union Jack incident 3; 10; 89;
92–3; 94–5; 96; 97; 100; 110;
111; 276
trial for treason, 1909 3; 89–91
imprisonments 3; 6–7; 53; 14;
65–6; 96–7; 105–6; 111; 130
prophetic ministry
trance-visitation of 1910 4; 104;
105; 107–30; 154; 174
description of appearance and
symbolic equipment 4; 189;
190–220
public ministry
first evangelistic journey (1913–
14) 3–4; 6–14; 244–52
expulsion from Ivory Coast
13–15;
1915–26 253–5
visit of Pierre Benoît (1926)
255–68
consecration of John Ahui (Dec
1928) 268–75

death (April 1929) and grave 22–3
Harris, Madam Grace Thannie *see
under* Thannie
Harrist Church xii; 16–17; 18; 19;
176; 229; 230ⁿ; 234–5; 268–9
Hartz, Father Joseph 9; 13; 76; 107;
110–1; 113; 114; 115; 120–1; 123;
128; 129; 133; 141; 146; 148; 151;
154–5; 167–8; 176; 185; 186; 196;
201; 202; 218; 225; 228; 230; 237;
250–1; 254
Hayford, Casely J.E. 107; 110; 113;
114; 128; 130; 141; 148; 159–60;
162; 166; 176; 177–8; 185; 187;
191–2; 194–5; 199; 208–9; 212–3;
225; 227; 247; 253; 254–5; 258;
266; 282
Hayford, Rev. Mark 258; 289–90ⁿ
healing 179–80; 187–8
Hemie, Owen E. 40
Hodge, Edwin G. 101; 130; 211
Hoffman, C. 41; 44
Hoffman Station 40; 43; 66; 72; 86
Holt, Dean 37
Houphouet-Boigny, President
Félix 19

Islam 70–1; 85; 93ⁿ; 102; 103; 111;
215
Islamic influences on Harris 117;
192
Ivory Coast (Côte d'Ivoire) 3; 4; 5;
9; 10; 12; 13; 15; 17; 253; 276;
278–9; 280; 287ff

Jacqueville 5; 8; 207; 244–5
Jehovah's Witnesses ("Russellism",
"Russellites") 71–6; 104; 134–5;
151; 153; 156
John the Baptist, Harris compares
himself with 127–8; 145–6; 206
Johnson, Mrs. Hannah 9; 54; 56;
61; 183; 184; 186
Johnston, Sir Harry 50; 51; 191
Joseph, M. Gaston (*chef de Cabinet,*
Ivory Coast) 111; 113; 141; 159;
209; 276
Journal Officiel de la Côte d'Ivoire 17
"juju" 34–5
Julwe, Fr. [Rt. Rev.] Patrick Kla
31–2
Jung, Carl 117

kediba (Glebo age grade) 31

STUDIES OF RELIGION
IN AFRICA

SUPPLEMENTS TO THE JOURNAL OF RELIGION IN AFRICA

1. MOBLEY, H.W. *The Ghanaian's Image of the Missionary*. An Analysis of the Published Critiques of Christian Missionaries by Ghanaians, 1897-1965. 1970. ISBN 90 04 01185 4
2. POBEE, J.S. (ed.). *Religion in a Pluralistic Society*. Essays Presented to Professor C.G. Baëta in Celebration of his Retirement from the Service of the University of Ghana, September 1971, by Friends and Colleagues Scattered over the Globe. 1976. ISBN 90 04 04556 2
3. TASIE, G.O.M. *Christian Missionary Enterprise in the Niger Delta, 1864-1918*. 1978. ISBN 90 04 05243 7
4. REECK,D. *Deep Mende*. Religious Interactions in a Changing African Rural Society. 1978. ISBN 90 04 04769 7
5. BUTSELAAR, J. VAN. *Africains, missionnaires et colonialistes*. Les origines de l'Église Presbytérienne de Mozambique (Mission Suisse), 1880-1896. 1984. ISBN 90 04 07481 3
6. OMENKA, N.I. *The School in the Service of Evangelization*. The Catholic Educational Impact in Eastern Nigeria 1886-1950. 1989. ISBN 90 04 08932 3
7. JĘDREJ, M.C. & SHAW, R. (eds.). *Dreaming, Religion and Society in Africa*. 1992. ISBN 90 04 08936 5
8. GARVEY, B. *Bembaland Church*. Religious and Social Change in South Central Africa, 1891-1964. 1994. ISBN 90 04 09957 3
9. OOSTHUIZEN, G.C., KITSHOFF, M.C. & DUBE, S.W.D. (eds.). *Afro-Christianity at the Grassroots*. Its Dynamics and Strategies. Foreword by Archbishop Desmond Tutu. 1994. ISBN 90 04 10035 0
10.. SHANK, D.A. *Prophet Harris, the 'Black Elijah' of West Africa*. Abridged by Jocelyn Murray. 1994. ISBN 90 04 09980 8
11. HINFELAAR, H.F. *Bemba-speaking Women of Zambia in a Century of Religious Change (1892-1992)*. 1994. ISBN 90 04 10149 7